STILL THE ARMS DEBATE

by Robert A. Levine

A RAND Corporation Research Study

Dartmouth

Published by
Dartmouth Publishing Company Limited
Gower House
Croft Road
Aldershot
Hants GU11 3HR

Gower Publishing Company
Old Post Road
Brookfield
Vermont 05036
USA

Printed in Great Britain by
Billing & Sons Ltd, Worcester

Contents

Foreword

McGeorge Bundy

Debates on arms policy have been a part of national and international life throughout the nuclear age. The first such debates were secret, fragmentary, and unbalanced; there is a great distance between the thoughts of nuclear scientists and the choices of Harry Truman. In later years there has been much more interconnection; NATO, as a primary center of both action and debate, exhibits these interconnections in case after case. When missiles are deployed and when they are bargained away, when alliance doctrines are accepted and when they are amended, when there is new hope or new fear in one place or another—in all these cases, whether as cause, accompaniment, or effect—we have debates. And most of the time, for most of us, these debates are things we take part in. Whether we write the arguments or listen to them, we are essentially participants. So is Robert Levine, and some of the best paragraphs in this book are lucid and temperate statements of his own conviction. But the book as a whole is something much more unusual: It is an account, historical and analytical, of the major and minor schools of thought that have dominated public discussion of arms policy on both sides of the Atlantic in the last thirty years.

Levine brings two great advantages to his work. First, he has done it before, and very well too, *The Arms Debate* in 1963. Second, he then worked for more than twenty years on other subjects, so that when he came back in the 1980s to assess the debate afresh, he was extraordinarily well equipped to notice what had changed and what had remained the same. It is the combination of familiarity and freshness that gives unusual dimensional strength to every chapter of his book.

Levine knows where he himself stands on the major issues of the debate, and the reader should know that in broad terms—though not on every issue—he and I are now of the same school. But as far as I can judge he is exceptionally careful to keep his thumb off the scales. It is inescapable, as he repeatedly reminds the reader, that when you assign a large number of people to one general school or another, and when you define their views with a few short quotations, you run the risk of oversimplification. Perhaps most of those quoted in this book, no matter what school they are assigned to, will think of arguments of their own that Levine has left out. I felt that way once or twice, so the reader who wants a full understanding of the thought of anyone quoted herein will want to read that individual's writing. But incompleteness is not at all the same as unfairness, and the reader can be sure that what is quoted here is genuinely representative of the main argument of the writer *at that time;* I add the last three words partly because I believe it is not a sign of weakness to have had different views in different decades.

Nonetheless, Mr. Levine's object is not the analysis of single minds, but the assessment of broad schools of thought. He believes, I think correctly, that in the taxonomy of strategic thought the general counts for more than the individual. So when he tells us about the four general views of American strategy toward the third world, he is giving us a panorama of thought that is more important than any one analyst's opinion. The same thing happens when he tells us about the different but cognate majorities in American and European views of NATO—the American "Maintainers" and European "Couplers."

Most of all, when Levine divides the central majority of strategic nuclear thinkers into "Extenders" and "Limiters" he is correctly defining the basic dividing line between those who expect more of nuclear deterrence and those who expect less. He recognizes, sometimes better than debating analysts, that both schools vastly prefer deterrence to war, and that neither claims it is cheap or easy; but he also understands that the dividing line is clear both in logic and in behavior. They—the Extenders—believe there is usually a need for more and more sophisticated systems, offensive and defensive, to meet old threats and new ones. We—the Limiters—believe there is usually a case for moderation—unilateral or bilateral or both—that "good" new capabilities are likely to bring "bad" new responses, and that the mere existence of survivable nuclear strength is much more important than its exact size and shape. But unlike Levine, I am prone to argument, so I leave the analysis of the two classes to him; all I mean to say is that he is right about their existence and knows them both well.

Although this is not a book about Soviet thought as such, the government of Mikhail Gorbachev nonetheless plays a major part in the analysis. Levine has recognized, along with the steadily growing majority of strategic analysts, that the recent change in Soviet policy and behavior is the largest new reality since the Cold War began, and he has worked hard to test theories of all schools by assessing their views of this new reality. The subject is not static, and not even Levine can keep up to the minute with Gorbachev's surprise-of-the-month diplomacy. Nonetheless, the assessment is acute. It is especially relevant to the evolving shape of debates about NATO, which Levine perceptively describes as the "subjective" alliance—an enterprise whose strength and effectiveness depend largely on what its members think about its strengths and effectiveness. What happens to a subjective alliance when the objective danger changes shape? Can the good news about Gorbachev be bad news in disguise? Levine does not think so, and he takes care to say why.

This book is mainly about beliefs and theories, and only secondarily about choices in action. Much of strategic theory, as Levine repeatedly reminds us, has never been put to the test in real life. My own belief is that historical events do shed light even on untested theories, and I indeed think Levine makes good use of such events in his own assessments. Nonetheless, his central interest is in assessing strategic thought to help us all think better: In his words, "analysis of . . . ideas and arguments can improve understanding; by improving understanding can improve the debate; and by improving the debate can improve arms policy." I agree, and I believe his book can help in exactly this way.

He does one thing more. Correctly observing that debate in recent decades has often been shrill and harsh, he calls for a return to civility, and he has given us a thoroughly civil book to show just what he means. In the process he has shown us persuasively that civility itself is a part of understanding.

—McGeorge Bundy
New York
May 1989

Preface

On New Year's Day of 1957, I came to the state of California for the third time in my life, the first two having been brief visits in transit while in the United States Navy during the Korean War. On January 2, 1957, I became an employee of The RAND Corporation, a "think tank" then working almost 100 percent for the U.S. Air Force.

The intellectual baggage I brought with me was represented by a soon-to-be-formalized Ph.D. in economics, the political baggage was that of a conventional liberal Democrat in the Roosevelt/Truman/Stevenson tradition. Since the pre-World War II conflicts with the isolationists of the right and left, that tradition had included military as well as political, social, and economic activism in international affairs—the Truman Doctrine as well as the Marshall Plan. This was, in fact, conventional among liberals in the East where I had grown up and been educated; that there might be a conflict between active pursuit of my political beliefs and employment by an Air Force think tank had never occurred to me.

It had also never occurred to RAND or the Air Force. Where the conflict did arise, however, was with the conventional liberals of California. Their tradition had taken the Henry Wallace rather than the Truman direction after the war; although brought back into the Democratic fold by Stevenson, they continued to reflect a philosophy that was strongly anti-military, strongly anti-Cold War. The conflict in my mind came to a head when a local Democratic candidate suggested that I must be mentally ill because I worked for RAND. I voted for a Republican for the first time in my life; since the district was at that time heavily Republican, my accuser returned to his law practice and has never been heard of (by me) since.

The whole matter also induced substantial introspection on my part. One immediate result was a journal article, "Facts and Morals in the Arms Debate,"[1] in which I contended that even though RAND viewpoints seemed to be based on "hard facts" and Californian liberal views on "humanitarian morals," each had to have both a factual (analytical) and a moral (value judgment) base and that to understand the differences over policy, one had to examine both sets of facts and morals. I then spent the academic year 1961–62 at the Harvard Center for International Affairs, where I wrote *The Arms Debate,*[2] a more thoroughgoing analysis of the range of differing views on national and international security policy. The book attempted to answer two questions: *What* are the issues over which those who debated arms policy differed? *Why*—logically, not psychologically or politically—did they differ?

Two years later, in 1965, Arthur Herzog, then and now an excellent professional writer, produced a somewhat similar book;[3] so far as I know, no other analysis of the debate itself has appeared subsequently. Shortly after my own book came out, I began a series of moves between RAND and the U.S. government in pursuit of a career in public policy analysis, concentrating on the government's domestic programs.

In 1985, however, I became interested in returning to parallel analysis of national security policy, and at that time, Enid C. B. Schoettle of the Ford Foundation and Johan Jorgen Holst, then Director of the Norwegian Institute for International Affairs and now Defense Minister of Norway (and a fellow research associate at the Harvard Center for International Affairs when I wrote *The Arms Debate*), suggested that I consider doing a late 1980s version of my 1963 book. Labelling me the "Rip van Winkle of national security analysis," Dr. Schoettle was able to provide support through her Ford program, and subsequently the Carnegie Corporation of New York and RAND supplied additional assistance. This highly appreciated team effort was rounded out by the Atlantic Institute for International Affairs, which provided office facilities in Paris and knowledgeable colleagues for the research on the NATO portion of the project. The effort

---

[1] *World Politics*, January 1962.
[2] Robert A. Levine, *The Arms Debate*, Harvard University Press, Cambridge, 1963.
[3] Arthur Herzog, *The War-Peace Establishment*, Harper and Row, New York, 1965.

produced an initial paper on the SDI debate,[4] and then three RAND reports[5] on the key issues of the debate of the 1980s, which have been incorporated into this book.

I hope that the title of the book, *Still the Arms Debate*, can be considered a mild pun at worst. It is, in fact, *still* the same arms debate. The constancy is more obvious on the questions near the frightening nuclear end of the debate than it is on the less open-ended issues in which evidence from Vietnam and elsewhere has changed the debate. Across the board, the similarities over 25 years dominate the differences, but the Soviet Union under Gorbachev and the United States after Reagan may bring the debate to a new phase.

And, taken in the imperative voice, to "*Still* the arms debate!" is one intended objective of this study: not to turn it off—debate of this nature is essential to the making of policy in a democracy—but to calm it down. That may help restore the civility in debate that had continued to produce reasoned national security policy through the time of my first book.

In addition to the three institutions that have supported this study—the Ford Foundation, the Carnegie Corporation, and The RAND Corporation—and to the personal support and critique of Dr. Schoettle, many others have provided criticism and other assistance. At RAND, they have included Arthur Alexander, Charles Cooper, Keith Crane, Stephen Drezner, Nanette Gantz, James Hodges, Arnold Kanter, Conrad Kellen, Leslie Lewis, David Lyon, Richard Neu, Jack Stockfisch, James Thomson, Alan Vick, Kenneth Watman, Barbara Williams—and Helen Turin, who edited it. Others who provided important critical assistance are Richard Brody of Panheuristics, Andrew Pierre of the Atlantic Institute, Gregory Flynn of the Carnegie Endowment for International Peace, John Chipman of the International Institute for Strategic Studies, McGeorge Bundy of New York University, and my wife Carol who read every last word at least once. In addition, numerous American and European officials and scholars provided both current and philosophical off the record insights. Many of them are represented here by quotations from their published works; I thank all of them for their essential assistance.

---

[4]Robert A. Levine, "The SDI Debate as a Continuation of History," CISA Working Paper No. 55, Center for Strategic and International Affairs, University of California, Los Angeles, March 1986.

[5]Robert A. Levine, *The Arms Debate and the Third World: Have We Learned from Vietnam?* The RAND Corporation, R-3523-FF/CC/RC, May 1987; Robert A. Levine, *The Strategic Nuclear Debate*, The RAND Corporation, R-3565-FF/CC/RC, November 1987; Robert A. Levine, *NATO, the Subjective Alliance: The Debate Over the Future*, The RAND Corporation, R-3607-FF/CC/RC, April 1988.

1. Introduction

> In a way arms policy *is* an intellectual problem. Certain value objectives exist, determined by the electorate and the President; how do we best go about fulfilling them? . . . But consistency in any national policy should not be expected and probably should not be desired. What should be desired, and perhaps may be expected, is that the intellectual portion of the political process by which arms policy is made, be thoroughly understood by those who participate in the debate.
>
> —*The Arms Debate*[1]

The Arms Debate, written in the early 1960s, analyzed conflicting ideas about the arms policies of the United States: policies concerning military postures, political uses for these postures, and arms controls to constrain the postures and uses. The analysis examined the ideas as they were expressed in public arguments intended to convince voters, legislators, officials, and sometimes other nations.

I was under no illusion then, nor am I now, that ideas and debates determine policies. They do play a role in the complex process that also includes political and economic interests and personal and organizational routines; and in a modern democracy that process ultimately produces plans, stated policies, and implementing actions. The whole is brought together by intricate political and bureaucratic mechanisms.[2]

Nor are an individual's policy positions determined entirely by the logic of his own ideas; interests and routines play equivalent roles here. This is clearly true for politicians: That political interests play a role in political thinking is a truism. The stronger version of this assertion, however—that

---

[1]Robert A. Levine, *The Arms Debate*, Harvard University Press, Cambridge, Mass., 1963, pp. 331–333.

[2]The classical case study of how all these influences were brought together in a national security crisis is Allison, 1971. Allison's three alternative models of decisionmaking—the "Rational Actor" (which includes the analysis here), "Organizational Process," and "Governmental Politics"—can be applied, albeit somewhat differently, to noncrisis and nonsecurity decisionmaking.

ideas, arguments, and national interests play *no* important role in political decisionmaking—is far too cynical. In a 1963 review of *The Arms Debate*, Marcus Raskin, then organizing the anti-Establishment Institute for Policy Studies, contended that the book was meaningless because it excluded discussion of the backgrounds and interests of the debaters.[3] Albert Wohlstetter, then and now a pillar of the defense-intellectual Establishment, provided a stirring defense of my book and of ideas as such.[4] Obviously I agreed with Wohlstetter, and I still do on this issue. The informing belief of *The Arms Debate*, and of this book, is that ideas and arguments do play a crucial role, and that analysis of the premises and logic of ideas and arguments can improve understanding; by improving understanding, can improve the debate, and by improving the debate can improve arms policy.

Improving arms policy, both the process of making the policy and its substance, is the objective of this study. Although it is conventional to call the current period—*any* current period—a turning point,[5] the onset of a changing Soviet Union under Mikhail Gorbachev, together with the departure from office of Ronald Reagan after having made substantial changes in many aspects of defense policy,[6] may mean that this really *is* a turning point. If so, the potential for improvement in American arms policy and in world security is much greater now than it has been for a long time. President George Bush's administration has entered office with a distinctly different tone from Reagan's. It is less ideological than its predecessor. It is staffed by conservatives in the sense of that term connoting steadiness; compare Secretary of State James Baker, National Security Advisor Brent Scowcroft, and Secretary of Defense Dick Cheney with Reagan's entering team of Alexander Haig, Richard Allen, and Caspar Weinberger. The Bush administration seems less likely to be prone to the kind of erraticism over time (from the "Evil Empire" to yearly summits with friend Mikhail) and geography (simultaneous Red Square promenades and Contra threats) that characterized Reagan's.

All this leads to substantial potential for improvement in arms policy. But if this *is* in fact a "turning point," we cannot ignore the parallel potential for deterioration. If we continue merely to debate the old issues in the old ways, we may miss opportunities for change; more dangerous, we may miss new issues presenting new threats to security.

As in the earlier book, the arms policy analyzed in here is primarily the arms policy of the United States. In the 1960s, however, that debate was

---

[3]Raskin, 1963, p. 6.
[4]Wohlstetter, 1963, p. 18.
[5]This is particularly true for NATO. See Part III.
[6]See in particular Part I on the Third World.

carried on almost exclusively by Americans, plus a few British experts: *The Arms Debate* mentioned only one author who was neither American nor British (French General Pierre Gallois). No American or other reader thought this Anglo-Saxon exclusivity worthy of comment; but since then the debate itself has broadened greatly, which is crucial in particular to the NATO portion of the analysis.

The remainder of this chapter takes up the "Better Red than Dead" issue, which was central to *The Arms Debate* but is less so to *Still the Arms Debate*; it introduces the three substantive sections of this study, mentions several constructs used to analyze the past and the present debates, and frames the current debate historically, projecting some of the history into the future as well. The next three parts contain the substantive analysis of the three segments of the current arms debate (on the Third World, Strategic Nuclear Policy, and NATO). They are followed by a chapter summarizing the debate and a final one examining the future of arms policy and the arms debate after another 25 years.

RED AND DEAD

The central theme of *The Arms Debate* was the controversy over the "Better Red than Dead" slogan, which may or may not have been coined by Bertrand Russell. Although a good part of the book was devoted to demonstrating that things weren't that simple, more complex versions of Red and Dead did provide the major guidelines for the debate. Pervading the discussion was the clash between the fear that military manipulations could lead to nuclear war and potential world annihilation and the fear that without sophisticated use of military means, including nuclear weapons, the Free World could succumb to the inexorable Communist drive against its values. The dichotomy underlay both the philosophical dialog (whether it was more important to avoid Red or Dead) and the analytical debate (what were the actual risks and benefits of alternative policies.)

Few debaters, of course, made an absolute choice between the two poles; they searched rather for balances of risk. And most debaters on the various sides strove for the dominant Pareto optimum, a set of policies that would run less chance of Red while not increasing the chances of Dead, or vice versa. Frequently, whether or not such optima actually existed, the debaters argued as if they did; that is a standard debating technique. Proponents of "strong" arms policies contended not only that they prevented Communist advance but that by improving nuclear deterrence they made nuclear war less likely; opponents argued that disarmament would not only protect the world but also free it. In spite of such contentions of logical dominance, however, it was ordinarily possible to grade the explicit or implicit weights put on Redness and Deadness by debaters across the spectrum.

This is less true today. The world is recognized as being more intricate than it seemed to be 25 years ago, and the "Red or Dead" language has disappeared from the debate. On the Red side, Communism is hardly the monolithic threat that it once seemed to be: Starting with China's split from the Soviet Union it has become a set of factions and fractions; the USSR itself has seemed in recent years to be less threatening militarily than in the earlier period, although most American debaters still perceive it to be opportunistic. One central question raised in the most recent debate is whether Gorbachev may really be bringing the Soviet Union beyond hostility toward the stability-seeking model that a few optimistic members of the peace movement thought they perceived a quarter of a century ago.

As for the threat of nuclear death, the weapons themselves seem no less dangerous than at the earlier time, but the world seems more stable. Less talk is heard of C. P. Snow's "statistical fact"[7] that nuclear weapons would go off and cause holocaust within ten years (from 1960); the last potentially nuclear confrontation between the superpowers, the Cuban missile crisis, took place soon after Snow's statement—many years, presidencies, and Soviet Communist chairmanships ago.

Dead as well as Red has thus changed substantially. Neither peril is obsolete, but they may be drifting apart over time. The Red danger appears mainly in settings of internal turmoil where nuclear weapons seem irrelevant; the nuclear danger may grow fastest in areas of concern to the superpowers but out of the control of either (and mostly outside the current arms debate), particularly in the sweep of south Asia from Israel to India.

THE STRUCTURE OF THE STUDY

The Three Segments of the Debate

The analytical body of this book consists of three essays, each adapted from a RAND Corporation report. They are:

---

[7]Snow, 1960, p. 14.

4

- *Have We Learned From Vietnam?* Two characteristics distinguish the Third World portion of the debate. First, whether or not we have learned anything (the essay suggests that we have), we certainly gained an overwhelming quantity of real experience from Vietnam and subsequent events there and in other parts of the Third World. Second, although pre-Vietnam theory may have suggested that nuclear threats or use might have been appropriate in Third World conflicts, in the event, no serious consideration was given to such escalation in the American war in Vietnam or thereafter.[8] The debate utilizes real evidence about the consequences of American activities in this type of conflict. As a result of the nonescalation, Third-World strategies of militant American anti-Communists are untrammeled by nuclear fears and play a greater role in that portion of the arms debate of the 1980s than in the strategic nuclear or the NATO segments. *Red or Dead* still lives in the Third World.
- *The Strategic Nuclear Debate.* This is the most lacking in military or political evidence—zero since Nagasaki—and for that reason resembles theological as much as policy discourse. The debate has changed remarkably little since the early 1960s; theological controversy is ordinarily measured in demi-millenia, not quarter-centuries. In spite of changes in technology such as the Multiple Independently Targeted Reentry Vehicle (MIRV) and the Anti-Ballistic Missile (ABM), political changes exemplified by the Sino-Soviet split and the subsequent growth of multicentric Communism, and even major military changes such as the development of effective strategic parity between the United States and the Soviet Union, most of the sides and contentions in the strategic nuclear portion of the debate are faithful reproductions of those of 25 years ago.
- *NATO, the Subjective Alliance.* The NATO debate is based on almost as little evidence as the strategic nuclear debate. During the Soviet repressions of the Hungarian uprising of 1956 and the Prague spring of 1968, and particularly during the recurrent Berlin crises of the late 1950s and the early 1960s, NATO nations at least examined the possibility of combat, but war between the Alliance and the Warsaw Pact never came close. The consequent lack of experience has produced theological strains similar to those of the strategic debate, but much of the creative imagination called forth has taken a different direction; it has been devoted to debating the internal military and political structure of

---

[8]This is the strong contention of McGeorge Bundy in *Danger and Survival: Choices About the Bomb in the First Fifty Years*, Random House, New York, 1988.

NATO itself; hence the title "the Subjective Alliance." One necessary condition for this introspection has been a view of the Soviet threat, the *raison d'être* of the Alliance, as being unchanging in its essentials. The growing belief that Gorbachev really is different from his predecessors is causing NATO to look outside itself.

These three essays cover the arms debate as it has been in the 1980s and as it was in the 1960s. Questions to be raised toward the end of this introductory chapter and in the concluding chapters are whether new categories may become necessary as new areas of the world and new fields of competition become more central to American arms policy and how new debates may develop out of those now taking place.

Analytical Constructs

Three analytical artifacts of *The Arms Debate* have been continued, sometimes in changed form, in *Still the Arms Debate*.

The Logical Structure of a Policy Argument. *The Arms Debate* defined the outcome of any meaningful policy contention as a *Recommendation*, "a statement suggesting that some action be taken by an individual or corporate actor whom the maker of the statement believes capable of taking that action."[9] Without such a recommendation, the contention is a piece of philosophy, not policy. The recommendation is based in turn on two other logical categories. One consists of *Value Judgments*, "matters of personal preference which are considered by the individual holding them not to be dependent upon other value judgments."[10] The other is made up of *Analyses*: "Analyses provide the connecting links which show the interactions between what should be (values) and what is, and which transform the present world of what is into the future world of what can be and what will be if."[11]

Use of Direct Quotations. In the Preface to *The Arms Debate* I wrote that "By summarizing viewpoints in the words of their holders rather than in my own words, I hope to avoid at least the extremes of misinterpretation. . . . [On] rereading the written material produced by the individual or individuals, I found that they did not say precisely what I had believed up until then . . . and that what they really did say made more sense than what

---

[9]Levine, *The Arms Debate*, p. 27.
[10]Ibid., p. 15.
[11]Ibid., p. 22.

I had thought."[12] This study continues the same method so that both the readers and I can check my interpretations.

Schools of Thought. The third construct in *The Arms Debate* was the use of "Schools of Thought," groupings of debaters created by the study, not by themselves. Although opinion exists along a continuous spectrum and the boundaries between such groupings are thus admittedly and recognizably arbitrary, it is possible to organize what would otherwise be a very diffuse analysis of a very large number of individual viewpoints.

The debaters of the early 1960s were categorized into five schools, covering all topics of the debate. These schools were arranged not along a conventional straight line but on a horseshoe, indicating that those at the two extremes were in many way closer to one another than they were to the adjoining more moderate schools with which they shared some policy views. Members of the militant "peace movement," for example, were in some ways closer to militant anti-Communists than they were to moderate arms controllers.

This study continues the schools concept, but in a different way. To avoid the confusion that would be caused by tying the diverse parts of the much more complex current debate into a single elaborate structure, each of the three parts (Third World, strategic nuclear, NATO) utilizes its own set of schools regarding the issues central to that specific analysis. Ultimately, however, meaningful broad groupings crossing the range of specific issues are useful for understanding the full arms debate of the 1980s. The next-to-last chapter summarizes the debate by tying the specific schools of the three sections into one set of overall schools, still horseshoe-shaped, and connects this historically to the horseshoe of the early 1960s. Putting this full construction off until after the basic substantive analysis of the three sections is necessary to avoid overcomplicating some already very intricate material, but the ancient and curious reader who was bemused by the horseshoe of the 1960s is invited to peek ahead at Tables 1 and 3 in Chapter 22.

In fact, it is mainly the ancient and curious reader—and his successor, the latter-day specialist or student in national security policy—who will be interested in analytical structures and artifacts. Broader interests in public policy can be satisfied by skipping Chapter 22 and concentrating on the three substantive essays on the Third World, the strategic nuclear debate, and NATO; and on Chapter 23, which ties together the three segments of the debate.

---

[12]Ibid., pp. v–vi.

7

A BRIEF HISTORY OF THE PLAYS AND PLAYERS

Informing all the segments of the study is history. Each of the three major sections contains a historical treatment appropriate to that segment: For the Third World, the development of current views out of the Vietnam experience is taken up integrally in the discussion of each school; the analysis of the strategic nuclear debate is preceded by an intellectual history of this most intellectual of debates, beginning with its self-conscious origin in the late 1950s; the NATO debate is put into the context of the development of the Alliance itself beginning in the late 1940s. This introductory section discusses some changes in the debate that cut across the three segments. In addition to what did change, it suggests potential changes that might have been expected to take place but did not and changes that did not take place historically but may take place in the future, beginning now.

Actual Changes in the Debate

The major changes in the American debate stem from the major American trauma of the last quarter century, the war in Vietnam and the ultimate American defeat. One obvious set of changes in the debate concerned wars in the Third World, of which Vietnam was the exemplar. These are detailed in Part I. Chief among them are:

- The reinterpretation of American interests in the Third World: away from the stress on the "containment" of Communism everywhere in the world because the fall of one "domino" even in an obscure area could lead to the collapse of other interests throughout the world; and toward a debate centered around the specific defense of specific U.S. interests. The opposing schools interpret these specific interests differently, and these differences remain at the core of the Third World debate.
- A shift toward civil and away from military action in response to Third World events, with different debaters weighting the civil-military balance differently.
- A belief, shared by all schools, that action in the Third World must never again be as predominantly American as in Vietnam.
- A new appreciation by all schools that American public opinion matters a lot.

Less obvious than the conceptual changes, but more pervasive, have been shifts in the positions of some key individuals, and a consequent rebalancing of the weight of the schools, not only in regard to the Third

World, but across the debate. The individuals here include many of those who directed the U.S. defense effort, including the Vietnam War, in the Kennedy and Johnson administrations of the 1960s; the most outstanding and most voluble examples are the "two Macs," Defense Secretary Robert McNamara and National Security Advisor McGeorge Bundy. Others include Bundy's brother, Assistant Secretary of Defense William Bundy, and Defense Department and National Security Council staffer Morton Halperin.

In and after the 1960s, the positions of these officials and analysts shifted not only on Third World arms policy but notably also in regard to strategic nuclear policy. The connection between the two shifts, if it exists, has never been made clear by the participants. It is easy to speculate that the shock of overwhelming failure in Vietnam led to rethinking of nuclear positions too, but that is not necessarily the case; the nuclear shift has its own purely logical trail, discussed in Part II. In any case, this study examines the logical basis of the arms debate, not the psychological basis, and no attempt is made to delve into this aspect of the connection. What is important here is that the double shift led to major changes in the strategic nuclear debate as well as the Third World debate in the late 1960s and early 1970s. The changes in the nuclear debate were not in the arguments presented, which stayed remarkably constant, but in the positions of the players making the different arguments and consequently in the policy influence of the opposing sides in that segment of the debate.

In the Third World debate itself, the start of the Kennedy administration saw only a few radicals in clear opposition to intervention in Southeast Asia. More accepting of the need for containment but highly dubious of its application was a mixed group of liberals exemplified within the administration by UN Ambassador Adlai Stevenson and by Undersecretary of State Chester Bowles, who had expressed the need in the underdeveloped world "to shape the minds of men" rather than to act militarily. Kennedy's inclusion of this group in his administration was a grudging political concession to the liberal wing of the Democratic Party; the president and the hardheads around him considered them "soft."

The power of the administration was concentrated in the hands of John and Robert Kennedy, McNamara, Secretary of State Dean Rusk, and the Bundys, all of whom believed that a retreat in Southeast Asia could lead to a collapse of the dominoes everywhere; who thought initially that Ngo Dinh Diem was the best we had around and when they changed their minds tacitly agreed to his overthrow; who thought that military action, including escalation, must precede and if necessary dominate civic action; and who moved into an American war with few second thoughts. *The Pentagon Papers*[13] and other materials document the change in the minds of many of them, as the major intervention of 1965 began to call forth an immense investment of American lives and materiel and bring about unprecedented domestic dissension, without nearing the elusive "light at the end of the tunnel." By the second half of the 1960s, the documents show many of the earlier enthusiasts starting to believe that they had been sucked into a quagmire. Whether or not the domino theory was relevant initially, it had been made so by the prestige that had been committed earlier; and they were overwhelmed by the prospect of a downward path with no clear alternative. Their public and private positions in the years after they left office up to and including the late 1980s grew closer to those that Stevenson and Bowles had expressed in the early 1960s. The school they joined gained both intellectual tone and political weight; it dominated the Carter administration. Other former officials, particularly those who had continued to pursue the Vietnam war in the Nixon administration, were less changed by the Vietnam experience. They remained in favor of active intervention in the Third World (e.g., Central America) and played an important role in the Reagan years.

The changes in the strategic nuclear debate are detailed in Part III. The logical process was different from the one that changed the Third World debate, but the cast of characters and the political process were similar. The strategic debate began in the late 1950s; although nuclear weapons had certainly been debated intensively before that, the discussion had been more philosophical than it was strategic in the sense of considering alternative utilization and potential response. By the late 1950s, intensive systematic discussion and analysis of the use and control of nuclear weapons had begun in a Harvard-MIT seminar in Cambridge, Massachusetts and at the RAND Corporation in Santa Monica, California. With the beginning of the Kennedy administration in 1961, many of the people involved and most of the ideas migrated to Washington. McNamara was most recently from Detroit, but many of his assistants in the Department of Defense (and Bundy in the White House) were from one or the other of the two coastal centers.

The strategic ideas, which entered early on into McNamara's policies, centered on:

- The planned controlled use of nuclear weapons in a graduated strategy featuring "counterforce" targeting against Soviet military power. The

[13]The version used by this study is *The Pentagon Papers as published by the New York Times*, Bantam Books, Toronto, New York, London, 1971.

object was prevention of nuclear war by deterring it, and control if deterrence were to fail. This strategy substituted for John Foster Dulles's "Massive Retaliation" against serious aggression, by use of nuclear weapons against the enemy's economic and social structure.

- The creation of the "arms control" concept, by which nuclear weapons were to be controlled unilaterally or by multilateral agreement in ways that would enhance stability through deterrence. In the late 1950s and early 1960s, the emphasis was on avoiding "preemptive" attack, defined as an attempt to preclude an enemy's first-strike advantage by striking first oneself. Disarmament—arms reduction—was a lesser included case of arms control, if the disarmament was conducive to stability. If not, it was a bad idea.

These concepts were central to the school of thought that included the Establishment in and out of the administration—McNamara and the others who were simultaneously applying the containment theory to Vietnam. Such opposition as there was consisted of a largely academic group, mostly not from Cambridge, who thought that counterforce deterrence was unlikely to work, and stressed instead careful steps to nuclear disarmament. As in the case of Bowles and Stevenson on Vietnam, most of these academics were not considered serious people by the hardheads of the Establishment.

Although in the Third World debate the Vietnam war had simultaneously changed both the terms of reference and the positions of the players, the terms of reference for the strategic nuclear case never changed. The theology is in fact still pretty much the same as it was 30 years ago. But the positions of individual players changed; they were the same players as in the Third World debate and the change was in the same direction, but with a different (although not inconsistent) logic. The key here was McNamara.

Coming into office in 1961, the new Defense Secretary was appalled by the indiscriminate nature of Massive Retaliation and its inappropriateness for most conflict situations. The needed changes had been made clear by studies from the Harvard-MIT and RAND centers, from an elite commission headed by Ford Foundation president H. Rowen Gaither, and from within the Defense Department itself. These all called for creation of a series of more discriminating options centered on counterforce. McNamara moved rapidly in this direction, going public with the new strategy in a series of statements in 1962. By 1967, however, he had changed his emphasis. Without abandoning either discrimination or counterforce, he made clear his doubts that these careful strategies could work once a nuclear war had begun, and he stressed the need for "assured destruction" of the enemy's assets—the society as well as the military forces—as the ultimate deterrent. Assured destruction bore some resemblance to Massive Retaliation, although unlike Dulles's earlier doctrine, it was a last and not a first resort.

Over the years after leaving office, McNamara's public doubts about the utility of carefully designed nuclear strategies increased. He never abandoned counterforce targeting as preferable to counterpopulation targeting, but he put no faith in it and stressed instead the need for strategic arms control agreements, with an emphasis on disarmament. Others who had worked in the Kennedy and Johnson administrations moved in the same direction. McGeorge Bundy also emphasized the uncertainties of nuclear warfare and coined the phrase "Existential Deterrence" to describe the ways in which these uncertainties contributed to prevent the outbreak of nuclear war and of nonnuclear hostilities between the great powers that might lead toward escalation. McNamara, Bundy, and others proposed serious consideration of "No First Use" of nuclear weapons by the West.

As in the case of the Third World debate, these moves away from nuclear discrimination and toward arms control and disarmament meant that much of the weight of the Establishment had left the earlier strategic consensus and joined the doubters, adding major political strength to a group that had been centered in academe. Also paralleling the changes in the Third World debate, a strong group, exemplified in the nuclear case by Albert Wohlstetter, remained with the old ideas. Unlike the Third World case, however, the new division was a very bitter one, with the Old Believers accusing the Heretics of espousing "Mutual Assured Destruction" (MAD) in which populations were deliberately put at risk even though they might be protected by damage-limiting controlled use of nuclear weapons. McNamara, Bundy, and company replied that the likelihood of high mutual destruction if a nuclear war broke out was an inevitable state of the world, not a deliberate strategy.

These disputes are detailed in Part II. Although the substance of the strategic debate has changed much less over the quarter century than that of the Third World debate, the political balance (or at least the balance of the experts, which may not be the same thing) has shifted in parallel in both segments, with both moving toward a greater recognition of limits on the use of American military power.

The third segment of the debate, on NATO, is the only one that did not manifest a similar rebalancing of participants. The American Establishment of the 1960s considered the North Atlantic Alliance to be the keystone of our vital interests; the American Establishment of the 1980s still gives much the same weight to the Alliance. In the earlier period, the only major dissent from the pro-NATO consensus was concerned with the rearming of West Germany in the light of its Nazi past. That worry has long since dissipated, so in that sense the consensus is even stronger. Although a small group on the right has more recently given up on NATO, the pro-Alliance link remains strong between most of those Americans who disagree over the Third World and who divide bitterly over strategic nuclear policy. Those who advocate planning for controlled use of nuclear weapons and those who have moved to Existential Deterrence evaluate their proposals in terms of effects on the Alliance and on deterrence and defense in Europe.

Why has the NATO debate not manifested the same division of the Establishment and rebalancing of forces as the other two? The major reason is that it is a different kind of debate. The same values-versus-risks (Red or Dead) considerations as in the other segments underlie the NATO debate, but they lie far under. At least since the Berlin crises of the early 1960s, the likelihood of direct Soviet military aggression in Europe has been perceived as being very low mainly because of the continued existence and vigor of the western Alliance. This view has caused NATO to turn in upon itself, becoming the "subjective alliance" of the title of Part III. Although the debate is expressed in military terms over defense issues, it has in reality been a political one centered on NATO members' perceptions of one another: how to keep the Soviets at bay by keeping the Alliance strong by keeping the members' perceived needs satisfied. This has raised issues quite different from those that caused the restructuring of the schools in the other two segments of the arms debate. The American Establishment has held together and, instead of debating with itself, debates with the Establishment of officials and analysts in the nations of Western Europe.

Potential Changes That Did Not Take Place

The first example of these changes that might have been expected but did not take place is that just discussed: The schools that divided and reassembled in the Third World and strategic nuclear debates did not do so in the NATO debate.

The NATO Debate. NATO and the NATO debate did undergo one major change, but it was at the very beginning of the interval covered in this history. Three sets of events in the early to mid-1960s combined to bring about the change. One was the backing off from the simple Massive

13

Retaliation doctrine and the consequent building of complex conceptual links among NATO's conventional force posture, nuclear weapons in Europe, and new American strategic theories à la McNamara, all culminating in the "Flexible Response" doctrine of 1967. Related to this was the increase of French doubts about the reliability of the American commitment to Europe, which together with de Gaulle's beliefs about national independence led to France's independent nuclear deterrent and her 1966 withdrawal from the NATO military structure. And third, suspicions of Germany by other Alliance members were laid to rest by a combination of specific events (e.g., the political rise of Willy Brandt, with his impeccable anti-Nazi credentials, to the West German chancellorship) and the simple erosion of time. In 1960 the Alliance had been as much a device intended to control German arms as to check Soviet ones; by the end of the decade, it considered Germany a full partner.

These three factors *did* change the NATO debate in the 1960s, but from the late 1960s through the late 1980s, it settled down and remained fairly constant. This constancy has remained despite a major change that might have been expected to restructure the NATO debate and the strategic nuclear debate as well—the perceived decline of American strategic power. The Third World debate has changed since the early 1960s, in large measure because of the demonstrated decline (or weakness relative to previous expectations) of U.S. capabilities to manipulate events in underdeveloped nations. But the more evanescent decline of America's strategic nuclear power, the onset of "strategic parity" in the 1970s, has had much less of an effect on the NATO or strategic nuclear segments.

One reason for the insensitivity of the debate to the change in the strategic balance may be that the *real* effect of strategic parity on the "correlation of forces" between the United States and the Soviet Union has been rather less than had been perceived or feared. In the 1970s the Soviets certainly brought their strategic nuclear capabilities up to and in some ways beyond those of the United States in terms of warheads, megatons, and destructive capabilities. But for some years before the 1970s, the Soviets could threaten high enough retaliatory damage with high enough probability to make American initiation of nuclear war too risky a matter to be of much use as a political or military threat. And what is quite clear in retrospect is that American presidents since Truman have believed and acted as if the nuclear dangers to the United States now blamed on strategic parity have existed at least since the first Soviet nuclear explosion.

Nonetheless, some participants in the NATO debate have blamed a perceived weakening of the Alliance in the 1970s on the onset of strategic parity and the consequent European perceptions of the weakening of the American commitment to the defense of Western Europe. These phenomena or perceptions played an immediate role in the creation of the Intermediate-Range Nuclear Force as an attempt to strengthen the Alliance in that period. Historically, however:

- Strategic parity is blamed for a weakened U.S. nuclear commitment to the defense of Europe, *but* the same perception of a weak commitment was a major factor leading De Gaulle to build his independent deterrent 30 years ago.
- Strategic parity is used as a reason for the urgent need to rebuild NATO's conventional capabilities, *but* such an urgent need has been adduced since NATO's Lisbon conference of 1953.
- *And* since soon after the Lisbon conference, NATO members have made clear that neither the strategic situation nor anything else was going to lead them to cough up the funds needed to build up the Alliance's conventional capabilities in any substantial way. That remains true today.

In fact, the strategic balance has had little effect on the NATO debate, and if changes in the balance have actually occurred, they have had just as little effect.

The Strategic Nuclear debate. The same is true for the strategic nuclear debate itself. As has been noted, the shift in that debate has been in the positions of the players, not in the ideas expressed. In the 1960s, one school of thought stressed the possibility that nuclear war, once started, would get out of hand, and the need for arms controls to prevent this; the other school emphasized control of the use of nuclear weapons in a complicated skein of deterrence. In the 1980s, after the onset of strategic parity, very little of the debate has changed. Table 2, on the strategic debate, reproduced from *The Arms Debate,* shows a remarkable likeness to the positions of the schools today.

This constancy of the strategic nuclear debate is even more remarkable because much more concrete changes than those in the not easily definable strategic balance have occurred over the period. Some of these were technological. In the early 1960s, the Cambridge and Santa Monica theorists and the Washington practitioners of deterrence and arms control aimed for strategic stability based on the principle that because it took more than one first-strike warhead to kill one protected warhead reserved for retaliation, only gross imbalances between the nuclear forces of the two superpowers would encourage an attempt to disarm the enemy by going first. But later in the decade, the advent of the Multiple Independently Targeted Reentry

Vehicle (MIRV) reversed the ratio by allowing the many warheads of a single launched missile to target many unlaunched enemy missiles. The advantage shifted, to going first to kill more enemy missiles than were expended by the killers. Yet this profound shift has changed the debate very little. Another technological change, related to MIRV, has been the onset of the Anti-Ballistic Missile (ABM), mentioned as a possibility in the early 1960s but entering the debate hardly at all. ABM has now become a central topic of debate, but the arguments made on both sides about the effects on deterrence of these conjectural defensive weapons are close replicas of the old arguments about varieties of offensive weapons.

It takes much more evidence than is likely to be forthcoming to change a theological belief. Certainly the new technological possibilities of MIRV and ABM provide evidence of a sort. But lacking their ultimate military test in nuclear combat and a test of the possibilities of terminating that combat on "favorable terms" the strategic Talmudists on both sides need not change their basic contentions.

The debate is also insensitive to political change. Both the NATO and the strategic nuclear debates have remained unchanged in the quarter century since *The Arms Debate* despite fundamental change in the nature of the enemy. What was believed to be monolithic Communism in the 1950s (with only the Yugoslavs as heretics) was beginning to be perceived in the 1960s as two-headed with the appearance of the Sino-Soviet split. In the 1980s, the possibility is discussed of bridging the wide and bitter chasm that has opened in the interim; in any case, Communism has become far more multifaceted than in the earlier period. In Eastern Europe, a much greater degree of autonomy from Moscow has appeared than seemed possible earlier; even the last expression of ultimate Soviet control, in Poland in the early 1980s, had a substantially more ambiguous outcome than in Czechoslovakia in 1968. In Western Europe, the strength of Communist parties has eroded greatly, and many of the parties themselves have become "Eurocommunist," somewhat independent of the Kremlin.

These changes have affected the debates very little. But the next moves in the same direction are likely to make a major difference.

Changes That May Take Place in the Future

The Soviet Union. The first and most important relates to Communism, the Soviet Union, and Gorbachev. Gorbachev is very different from his predecessors; that much has been established. He is making a difference within the Soviet Union, although whether he can make economic *perestroika* work well enough to support the design of whatever political *perestroika* he wants is not so sure.

Less certainty also attaches to the meaning of the rapid changes in Soviet foreign and military policy. These policies themselves are changing much faster and more radically than in the past. That is clear from the opening of the USSR to arms control inspection and verification, the acceptance of asymmetrical force reductions in the INF treaty and in the conventional negotiations in Europe, the retreat from Afghanistan, and various unilateral force reductions announced by the Soviets. Whether these represent "fundamental" or "irreversible" changes—or how those terms might be defined—is an open question. The changes themselves are unarguably major compared with previous Soviet policies and activities. And these changes are changing the arms debate. Even if they were abruptly terminated tomorrow, termination is unlikely to return the *status quo ante*, and many aspects of the debate are going to be very different from the years before 1985.

The segment of the debate most disturbed thus far by Gorbachev's changes, and the one most likely to change in the future, is that related to NATO. In 1986, a French defense analyst suggested that "the Soviet Union has appeared, without doubt, as the only constant"[14] in the previous three decades of the Franco-German dialog and, by extension, in the overall NATO debate. This constancy remained through changes in Soviet leadership and in internal political controls, through Cold War and détente. The West could count on the Soviet's wanting to separate the United States from Europe and thereby dominating the continent at least politically; it could count on Soviet policies that varied between open threats (e.g., in Berlin in the early 1960s) and tempered opportunism; it could count on Soviet unwillingness to make the real concessions necessary to the preservation of Western security under arms control agreements. The sudden change of the Soviet Union from a constant to an uncertain variable has been profoundly unsettling for NATO. The NATO debate, for many years based largely on internal Alliance relationships, has been forced to reexamine the opponent who remains the underlying *raison d'être* for NATO.

Should the Soviet Union under or after Gorbachev snap back to something like the old suspicious and suspicion-raising colossus, the debate might return to the old verities, but probably the Soviet changes have already been substantial enough to change the debate and perhaps the Alliance. These changes are unlikely to destroy the Alliance; it will be a long time before the West can treat with the Soviet Union as, for example,

---

[14]Gnessoto, 1986, p. 11.

France and Germany now treat with one another despite their millenium of hostility. What is to be guarded against, then, is that the debate itself might weaken NATO.

Whatever changes are taking place in the USSR probably will not change the strategic nuclear debate. Almost nobody in the United States believes that nuclear weapons can be done away with; the exceptions are the very small school of Disarmers, and possibly also former President Reagan. Even though major arms controls seem to be on the way, including substantial reductions in numbers of nuclear warheads, the old issues will continue: how the remaining weapons can deter their own use, whether and how damage may be limited if they are used, how they affect political balances, and so forth. They will continue in much the current form so long as two superpowers are each able to mightily injure each other and the world. When another nation (China?) enters the super category, new theology will be needed. But so long as the weapons are not used, the debate will continue to be theological.

The Third World (Old). Paradoxically, the segment of the debate in which Redness remains a real issue, that concerning the Third World, is also least likely to be affected by changes in Communism-Marxism-Leninism. True, one of the changes in the Third World debate that has occurred since (and in part because of) Vietnam has been the reinterpretation of the "domino" theory. Going into Vietnam, the feeling was that the fall of the South Vietnamese domino would inevitably end up with the fall of countries on one side or the other of the Arabian Sea, if not the English Channel. One reason for this was the belief in the monolithic nature of Communism; the relaxation of the domino assumption came with the realization that the opponent resembled a pile of rocks more than a monolithic slab of granite.

What remains in the Third World, at least in the minds of the more strongly anti-Communist debaters, is a set of Marxist-Leninist threats to American interests. If the Soviet Union is not behind the Third World radicals—and those on that side of the debate believe that the Soviets remain the main prop for these groups—then Cuba or Vietnam or some other Soviet proxy is. Unless and until the USSR moves much further away from support of Third World radicalism there will be some basis for American fears and there will be some inevitable conflict between our interests in that world and Soviet interests, Gorbachev or no. And changing the views of the most confrontation-minded Americans may take reconstitution of the Soviet Union as an English-speaking Quaker republic. The Third World debate is thus likely to be the least affected by Gorbachev or post-Gorbachev changes. The Bush administration, however, will undoubtedly be substantially less confrontation-minded in the Third World than President Reagan and his zealots, and the American debate may at least calm down.

Other prospective changes in the debate are unrelated to what may happen with the Soviet Union or with Marxism-Leninism. Visible on the horizon are at least two new categories, outside of the three that provide the main analysis of this book.

The Third World (New). One new category may be carved out of what so far has been termed the Third World. The analysis and the debate up until now have covered strategic nuclear issues and Europe, and by then defining the Third World as "the less wealthy world outside of North America, Europe, northern Asia, and parts of Oceana," the set becomes logically complete.

The Third World essay concentrates on insurgency, counterinsurgency, and counter-counterinsurgency, from Vietnam to Nicaragua. But the realities are moving and the debate is likely to catch up. One burgeoning set of problems beyond the insurgency issues and thus outside of the Third World essay, that of the Middle East, has already been mentioned; that is only the initial example of a prospective set of new security problems and new categories for the arms debate. These contain issues not related to strategic nuclear exchange between the superpowers, not directly related to Europe, and yet not related to insurgency. Their locale is (or will be) in nations that are either not poor (e.g., Japan, Israel) or so large as to be different in kind from Vietnam or Nicaragua (China, Mexico). Their revolutions are also different from those in Vietnam and Central America (Iran).

Perhaps most germane to the arms debate as such, the military issues within these new categories will in many ways resemble those of Europe more than those of Southeast Asia or Africa. Israeli-Arab wars have already involved tank and air warfare far more sophisticated than any that has ever taken place in Europe; the Iran-Iraq conflict has utilized tactics and massed troops akin to the situation in World War I. Should future combat occur in these areas, or in China, Japan, Korea, the Indian subcontinent, South Africa, Mexico, or Brazil, it is likely to call for combining the military skills of an Ariel Sharon with the political skills of an Ayatollah Khomeini. (Our preparation for wars of the future has ordinarily been such that we may instead combine the political skills of a Sharon with the military skills of a Khomeini.)

A related set of prospective changes may either create another new segment or radically restructure the existing strategic nuclear debate. That debate until now has covered nuclear warfare, whether strategic or "tactical" (in Europe), as being a matter almost completely under the control of the two superpowers. Although the British and French nuclear forces are independent, and the French in particular stress their independence, their prospective use has been closely connected, politically and doctrinally, to that of American nuclear forces. Snow's 1960 assertion of the "statistical fact" that nuclear war would occur within ten years will soon be disproved for the third time, and it is entirely possible that the feared holocaust can be averted indefinitely. Should the world continue to develop in current directions, the use of nuclear weapons will probably *not* be by the superpowers and *not* in Europe: A besieged Israel or perhaps South Africa or a preemption-minded India or Pakistan suggest themselves. This is not to say that "lesser" nuclear wars have now become a statistical certainty. However, the more powerful and more experienced possessors of nuclear weapons may be called upon to design new policies to avoid such wars becoming likely and to insulate themselves and the rest of the world if they do occur. Consideration of such policies will call forth a very new kind of nuclear debate.

Economics. The other new category covers the entire globe including the Third World. For forty years, international security policy and international economic policy have been considered different topics, albeit clearly related. Neither in 1963 nor in 1987 did the economic context require more than a mention, except in regard to national budget constraints on defense spending. Now, however, the United States is no longer *the* undisputed economic power of the world.

The most obvious consequence concerns the issue of "burden-sharing." Japan spends a far smaller portion of her GNP for defense than does the United States, yet the United States shares major responsibility for the defense of Japan. Why? How will or should U.S. defense policy for the Pacific change because of this disproportion, increasingly perceived in the United States? The same issue has long been joined for Western Europe, where most of the NATO allies spend a smaller share of their resources for defense than does the United States; there, the disagreement has been somewhat muted by other Alliance concerns but it is being raised again. And the "Year of Europe" of the European Economic Community (the Common Market) will not only accentuate the burden-sharing issue for NATO, it will raise the possibility of a transatlantic trade war that could endanger the political/military Alliance more than any dispute stemming from the security sphere itself.

Burden-sharing issues are West/West. Other issues in which economics may come to affect security much more than in the past are in the East/West realm. One latent stream in Western thought has long held that what we really had to do was to tie the East to us economically, so that a war would be unthinkable. It has never been tested, but under Gorbachev and *perestroika* it is likely to be. The economic ties concept is by no means unchallengeable; it will be debated, vigorously and perhaps centrally to the arms debate itself. Any economic effects on political/military issues will be some time in coming for an economy as massive as that of the Soviet Union; the debate can proceed alongside of the effects. For some of the other nations in the East Bloc, Hungary for example, the economic ties to the West and the potential benefits or costs are very nearly upon us. The issues here revolve not around *tying* anybody to the West, but *untying* them from the East; the military/political effects could be profound.

The final economic category is West/Third World; the possibilities here relate to the potential changes in that world discussed above. One possibility has to do with power, the other with U.S. national interests. That military power more often than not proceeds from economic power is a truism. That the next quarter-century will see major new economic powers in the world is obvious; if one includes Japan, it too is a truism. It follows that the United States may well have new and major military threats or allies in this period. And on the economic interest side, the coupled traditional interests of resources and markets may well reassert themselves in the future as objectives for U.S. military policy and debate. For the past forty years, the ideological and potential military conflict with the Soviet Union has so dominated arms policy that we have forgotten that ideology is a late comer (World War II or perhaps World War I) to the pantheon of interests for which the United States would do battle; "Red or Dead" dominated the debate for a while but not forever. With the potential waning of the struggle with Communism as a *casus belli,* arms policy and the arms debate may well become far more diffuse.

All of these issues will be raised again in the concluding chapter, as the logic of the three-segmented current arms debate is projected into the future. That chapter and the preceding one suggest that the major participants in the American arms debate can for the most part be divided into two overarching schools of thought: an "active" one that advocated the use of U.S. military power to achieve tactical or political gains in the central struggle against Communism, and a "reactive" one that considered weapons as defensive hedges against attack and uncertainty. The question for the future is to what extent will these divisions, derived from the East/West conflict, apply to the new set of threats and interests that may be upon us?

In any case, the tranquil linearity of even the theological debates of the last quarter of a century may be about to go around some sharp corners.

PART ONE

HAVE WE LEARNED
FROM VIETNAM?

2. The Structure

Plus ça change, plus ça change.

—*Exception to an old cliché*

Somewhat surprising to those who, like me, tend toward cynicism, the answer to the question asked in the title of Part I is a conditional "Yes: We have learned a few things." We have learned more than to merely counterbalance an oversimplified "Vietnam" analogy against the oversimplified "Munich" analogy that helped lead us into Southeast Asia. For most of the current participants in the debate on American arms policy in and toward the Third World, empirical evidence counts. The evidence, particularly the overwhelming evidence stemming from the American failure in Vietnam, has led them to reexamine their views in detail and adjust to a newly recognized reality.

The debate over Third World arms policy thus differs from the other two major components of the Great American Arms Debate, strategic nuclear policy and European/NATO policy. In neither of these cases has arms policy been tested by the use of the arms, and lacking evidence from such tests, the *plus ça change, plus c'est la même chose* theme remains dominant.

Two major changes in American views on Third World policy are attributable to the Vietnam experience:

- Nobody now advocates American military intervention in the Third World on a scale approaching that in Vietnam. We learned from Vietnam that such intervention is far more difficult than we had thought

25

and the American people will not automatically support the long and costly commitment that such difficulties imply.

- Among those who do contemplate a possible need for some intervention somewhere, sometime in the future, nobody believes that military force alone will do the job without major economic, political, and social action. We learned that we know a lot less than we think we do about structures and situations in countries we are not very familiar with.

The adaptation of policy views to Third World evidence is not, however, uniform across the entire range of viewpoints. Policy views consist logically of value judgments about desirable states of the world, analyses of possible states, and recommendations about actions policymakers should take to move toward desirable outcomes within the realm of the possible. For Third World arms policy, the debaters at the ends of the range tend to base their views primarily on strong value judgments that cannot be (and should not be) changed by changed evidence and analysis. Thus, those who believe that the United States *must* oppose Marxist-Leninist expansion wherever it threatens want to continue to confront such threats in spite of our failure in Vietnam; they just want to do it better the next time. Those who believe that the United States should *never* intervene in opposition to Third World insurgencies, even Marxist-Leninist insurgencies, want to stay out as they wanted to before Vietnam.

The majority of the participants in the debate lie between the two extremes. Their recommendations are based on analyses as well as value judgments, and the value judgments themselves are mixed and conflicting. One can oppose both Marxist-Leninist threats *and* some of the distasteful regimes that line up with us against such challenges. Given such internalized conflict, changed analysis based on changed evidence can also change the weights put on values, and the Vietnam experience has done this. For most of these centrist debaters, the evidence of Vietnam and subsequent events has allowed them to remain in the center, but the center itself has shifted. American interests can still be engaged in the Third World, but much less automatically, universally, or ideologically than the centrists believed in 1961; there is a much greater appreciation for the difficulties of U.S. intervention, particularly military intervention, in the Third World. U.S. interests are interpreted more broadly than being based on anti-Communism alone.

Indeed, the evidence of Vietnam and of post-Vietnam events has led some important debaters to shift toward the middle from previous positions at either end of the spectrum. Richard Nixon in 1985 recorded as unchanged the belief he held when he became President in 1969, that:

A Communist victory would be a human tragedy for the people of Vietnam. It would imperil the survival of other free nations in Southeast Asia and would strike a damaging blow to the strategic interests of the United States. It would lead to further Communist aggression, not only in Southeast Asia, but in other parts of the free world as well.[1]

Nonetheless, in the same 1985 book, he uses words that could have come from the anti-Vietnam opposition during his presidency, to advocate a more discriminating course for the future:

There is too much of a tendency to see all Third World conflicts as part of the larger conflict between East and West. While the Soviet Union profits from most of them, it is not responsible for all the conflicts in the world.[2]

Although Nixon still advocates strong anti-Communist international policies, these are words not likely to have come from him before or during Vietnam. And in a more explicit rethinking from the opposite extreme, Tom Hayden, a leader of the radical anti-Vietnam opposition in the 1960s and 1970s, writes from his vantage point as a liberal Democratic California legislator in the 1980s:

I certainly have regrets of my own that I will always live with. I regret that Hanoi has an imperial design on Cambodia and has largely done away with pluralism in the south. I regret that I was not more critical of the cynical motives of the Soviet Union. . . . I will always believe that the Vietnam war was wrong; I will never again believe that I was always right. . . . It remains true . . . that we cannot be the policeman of the world, but it is also true that we cannot simply withdraw from the world and believe that all conflicts can be peacefully negotiated.[3]

The center has shifted and some individuals have shifted toward the center. The Reagan administration, however, remained to the right of the center, at least rhetorically. President Reagan himself, and the more voluble members of his staff and administration, spoke in terms reminiscent of the 1960s about continual confrontation with the Communists. This did not move national policy far off the center, however; even before the Democratic legislative victories of 1986, the majorities of both the House of

---

[1]Nixon, 1985, p. 100.
[2]Ibid., p. 216.
[3]Hayden, 1986.

Representatives and the Senate stymied a variety of administration Third World efforts, particularly in Central America. The tug-of-war along Pennsylvania Avenue, reflecting the controversy within the nation, led to a U.S. policy somewhere in the middle, but much less well-defined than before Vietnam. This may now be changing under the attempts by the Bush administration to find viable compromises with the Congress as well as the Communists.

Clear policy definition is seldom possible, and if possible would not necessarily be desirable. Ambiguity has its uses, particularly in creating or maintaining a degree of consensus by tacitly agreeing to leave some difficult issues unresolved. But to reach such a partial consensus, it is important to understand what these issues are and why reasonable people disagree over them.

3. Structure of the Analysis

To analyze both the current debate and its roots required creation of two sets of categories: the schools of thought into which the debaters are divided, and the key issues over which they differ. The examination covers several time periods beginning with the pre-Vietnam era. Each of the four schools of thought is discussed in narrative form, covering the key issues and using the time periods as guides.

SCHOOLS OF THOUGHT

At either end of the spectrum, there are:

- The *Confronters*, who believed in the early 1960s and still believe that the worldwide struggle with Communism (now limited, in the concerns of most of the Confronters, to Soviet-sponsored Communism) remains a zero-sum game. This school was well represented in the Reagan administration, including the president himself, at least rhetorically.
- The *Disengagers*, who believe that Third World revolutions are justified, and that although Communism may well play a role in such revolutions, it is neither a threat to the United States nor a relevant consideration for American policy. Typical of the Disengagers are a variety of regular writers for *The Nation* magazine.

Between the two ends:

- The *Interventionist Middle* school, those who believe that we are engaged in and must continue to be engaged in a conflict with the Soviet Union in various areas of the world. The conflict is military as well as political and economic, with military security frequently being a necessary initial condition for progress in the other fields. Typical here are most of the writers of the Kissinger Commission report on Central America,[1] including, both here and in his other writings, Henry Kissinger himself. Not all the signers of the Commission report agreed with all the findings, however; some set forth partial dissents that place them in the other Middle grouping. President Bush and Secretary of State Baker seem to fit comfortably in the Interventionist Middle.
- The *Noninterventionist Middle* school, the group that agrees that we are in competition (a term preferred to "conflict") with the Soviets, but who stress that this competition in the Third World should be waged in the main economically, socially, and diplomatically. Military power is necessary, at least as a potential last resort, but its use is ordinarily self-defeating, American military power almost inevitably so. The human rights emphasis of former President Jimmy Carter puts him in this school.

(To be explicit at the outset, I am inclined to place myself in the Noninterventionist Middle, although frequently pulled intellectually toward the more pessimistic realism of the Interventionist Middle. In any case, the line between the Middle schools is far less important than the boundaries between both these schools and those on the ends.)

The boundaries between the schools of thought are, in fact, necessarily blurred; policy statements are complex, and debaters who are close on some points may disagree on others. The line dividing the Interventionist Middle from the Noninterventionist Middle is particularly fuzzy because it depends upon an arbitrary assessment of how much emphasis should be put on the military factors as against how much should be put on the political and economic. Frontiers between other schools are sometimes crossed also: Nixon's defense of his Vietnam policies falls under the Confronter rubric, but his fairly moderate recommendations for the future tend to fit into the Interventionist Middle school.

---

[1] *Report of the National Bipartisan Commission on Central America*, hereafter called the Kissinger Commission report.

ISSUES

The issues over which the schools divide fall into three major categories: the national interests of the United States, judgmental views about what is important to us; the nature of insurgency, analytical statements about causes and responses; and the role of the United States, recommendations about what we should be doing about it. In more detail, the categories are:

- The delineation of U.S. worldwide *interests*. In the recent Third World arms debate, these have taken on a more restricted definition than is implied by the historic sweep of the term "national interests." Such interests have traditionally been thought of in terms of the economics of resources and markets, geopolitics, and protection of American citizens, as well as ideology. From 1945 (or perhaps 1939) until recently, however, ideological and moral considerations became almost the only criteria for determining the objectives of U.S. foreign policy. In World War II the ideology was anti-Nazism; since then it has been anti-Communism. In recent years, the scope of interests for which military power might be considered relevant has been broadening again: economics (the Persian Gulf); citizen protection (terrorism, drugs); and ideology other than anti-Communism (the Philippines). The debate has not yet caught up, however. Particularly in terms of the Third World, this ideological "game" with the Soviet Union continues to dominate the discussion, raising such questions as: How important is it to maintain or advance our position in this conflict/competition? Is it necessary to pursue the struggle everywhere in the world, or can our interests be differentiated geographically? In particular, does a loss in one country substantially increase the chances of a loss in others and, if so, does this "domino" theory operate on the basis of geographical proximity or is it worldwide? In addition to being more ideological than economic, such interests are for the most part defensive. This is traditionally true of "have" nations, satisfied with their own economic and political conditions; as a result, Americans tend to think of national interests in terms of avoiding threats rather than advancing causes. In the conflict with Soviet Communism, however, some Confronters believe that a good offense is necessary for a winning defense and aim to rescue as well as preserve nations from Communism.
- The *causes* of insurgency and other turmoil in the Third World, and the effectiveness of various *responses*. To what extent are insurgencies brought about by Soviet/Cuban/Vietnamese/etc. covert or overt interventions, to what extent do they develop from internal economic and

political problems? The appropriate role of military force in combating such insurgency and turmoil, compared with economic and social measures designed to meliorate or cure the basic conditions, depends in large measure on the causes attributed for the problems.

- The *role of the United States* in general and the U.S. military in particular in combating insurgency. This is the central "should" issue to which recommendations are addressed, and the schools' answers here proceed from their view of both the previous issues—what are the U.S. interests to be pursued, and how is it possible to pursue them? To what extent should or can we intervene in the Third World, how and with what instruments? What is the role of public opinion in determining intervention or nonintervention? And, as a subcase of particular importance, when, if ever, should we participate in (or not oppose) the changing of a leader (Diem, the Shah, Somoza, Marcos) who we believe to be incapable of bringing victory to "our side"?

TIME PERIODS

The analysis examines these issues over four time periods:

- *Pre-Vietnam*, primarily the early 1960s, before the major American intervention. Some of the material on this era is taken from my 1963 book, *The Arms Debate*,[2] which also provides the structure for this essay.
- *During Vietnam*. Much of the material here—the unclassified and declassified writings of participants and critics during the war—became available in 1971 with the publication of *The Pentagon Papers*.[3] Also used for materials, but even more for structure of the debate at that time, is an unpublished paper that I wrote with Harvey Averch in 1971, before the release of *The Pentagon Papers*.
- *Vietnam retrospectively*, analyses published after the final victory of the Communists, of what went wrong. After 1975, nobody argued that things had gone right, although Nixon and Kissinger do contend that they would have gone right except for politics in the United States.
- *Now*, policy writings in the current arms debate about the Third World. The most recent of these have focused on Central America.

---

[2]Levine, 1963.
[3]The materials used here are quoted from *The Pentagon Papers*, 1971.

THEMES

From the crossing of the categories, four themes will emerge. They lead to a normative policy conclusion based on the analysis and my own value judgments about what is important to the United States.

1. The major issue dividing the two central schools of thought, the Interventionist and Noninterventionist Middles, from the two end schools, the Confronters and the Disengagers, is their view of the Soviet threat to U.S. interests in the Third World. The central schools, which see the threat as variable over both time and geography, differ from both those who perceive Soviet Communist expansionism as a continuing and universal threat to our interests as they define them, and those who deny the legitimacy of American interests other than those of universal morality.

2. The Interventionist Middle and the Noninterventionist Middle are divided over several issues. The major one, as befits their names, is the weight put on the need for the United States to intervene in Third World situations. Neither school opposes any and all intervention, but the Noninterventionists are much more skeptical, particularly when the emphasis of the pro-intervention argument is on a global "domino theory," a need for the United States to intervene in a particular spot to maintain "credibility" elsewhere in the Third (or any other) World, rather than on a specific local American political, economic, or military interest. In addition, the Middle schools differ over the relevance of military force compared with political, economic, and social factors. Each school considers both sets of factors important, but with different weights. As a consequence of these value and analytical differences, they come out differently on the roles in the Third World they perceive as possible and desirable for the United States.

3. For the Middle schools in particular, the view of what is achievable and how it can be achieved has changed substantially as a result of Vietnam. Virtually nobody in any of the schools favors intervention of the scale and type of 1965–1972. For some of the Confronters, this is primarily because of the recognition that a repeat of Vietnam would be completely unacceptable to the American people and that any attempt would be so constrained as to again make victory impossible. For the Middle schools, particularly the Interventionist Middle, however, Vietnam has led to a substantial reinterpretation of the U.S. national interest and how it can be furthered. Our initial major military steps into Vietnam were almost unanimously assumed to be appropriate (only two senators voted against the Tonkin Gulf Resolution), following the automatic response traditions set by the Korean War and the Truman Doctrine; in the 1980s,

33

intervention, whether in Central America, Asia, or Africa, is a subject of substantial and searching debate.

4. Because, for the first time in recent history, most of the key policy-makers in the Reagan administration (including the president) were in the Confronter school, one major locus of the Third World arms debate has been the frontier between that school and the adjacent one, the Interventionist Middle; more frequently in the past the most important disagreements have been those between the Interventionist and Noninterventionist Middle schools. Again, however, the centers of gravity of both Houses of the Congress during the Reagan administration remained near the Middle, and national policy as it came out of Washington was not very far to the right of center. This centrist policy was not the result of any national consensus; it was the political summation of several substantially different viewpoints. As a result it was frequently both fuzzy and inconsistent, made up in large measure of tentative and mainly symbolic steps in differing directions. One factor that has kept Third World policy from veering off in one direction or another has been the understanding, common to all schools, that American public opinion, largely ignored as a foreign policy factor from the end of World War II to the beginning of Vietnam, is a crucial consideration. Public opinion, if nothing else, keeps substantial U.S. military intervention from being a serious option anywhere in the Third World.

We have—all of us—learned from the evidence of Vietnam. Ironically, however, our new education has destroyed our old consensus on U.S. arms policy toward the Third World. Before Vietnam, the Truman, Eisenhower, and Kennedy administrations extended to the Third World the containment-of-Communism policies that had begun with the Truman Doctrine applied to Greece and Turkey in the 1940s. Vietnam showed that such containment was not possible at all times and places, and perhaps it was not always desirable. The consensus was thus destroyed, and so far no new one has formed.

Once called a "bipartisan foreign policy," such consensus can be very important for both the effectiveness of foreign policy and the stability of the American body politic. It might be regained in one of two ways. One would be the adoption, by a substantial majority, of the Confronter value judgments espoused by the Reagan administration. This could produce consensus by overriding differences among analytical views of how to go about defeating Communism throughout the Third World. Such a consensus seems unlikely. Alternatively, were political change to move the debate back to its more traditional locus in the center, rather than between the center and the Confronters, consensus could proceed on the basis not of unanimity but of common assumptions about where we want to go, together with known but debatable disagreements about how to get there. There seem some grounds for hope that that is where President Bush is heading.

4. The Confronters

U.S. INTERESTS

In 1961, Robert Strausz-Hupé, William Kintner, and Stefan Possony wrote in *A Forward Strategy for America*, the book that set forth the theme of "Protracted Conflict" between the United States and the Soviet Union:

> Guerrilla or revolutionary war has become the principal communist military technique for the reduction, by installments so to speak, of Western influence in the underdeveloped regions of the world.[1]

This has remained the Confronter view of U.S. interests in the Third World. Rather than resource-rich regions or strategic locations, the focus has been on "the underdeveloped regions of the world" as a whole. The central interest of the United States in these regions has been ideological— to win the battle against Communism politically and economically and, as necessary, militarily.

Two decades after the publication of *A Forward Strategy*, Jean-François Revel, the French prophet adopted by the American Confronters, put it even more sharply, in terms of a zero-sum struggle:

---

[1]Strausz-Hupé, Kintner, and Possony, 1961, p. 156.

It is natural for communism to try with all its might to eliminate democracy, since the two systems are incompatible and communism's survival depends on its rival's annihilation.[2]

This stark statement does not differentiate between nations moving from our "camp" to East-West neutralism (e.g., Sudan) and those going all the way to what the Confronters see as Soviet control (Nicaragua). In fact, today's Confronters ordinarily do make the distinction, stressing the latter cases, although back in the days of John Foster Dulles, they saw little difference.

To the zero-sum game, a speech by Reagan administration Secretary of State George Shultz added another element, the ratchet effect:

For many years we saw our adversaries act without restraint to back insurgencies around the world to spread communist dictatorships. The Soviet Union and its proxies, like Cuba and Vietnam, have consistently supplied money, arms, and training in efforts to destabilize or overthrow noncommunist governments. . . . At the same time, any victory of communism was held to be irreversible. This is the infamous Brezhnev doctrine. . . . Its meaning is simple and chilling: once you're in the so-called "socialist camp," you're not allowed to leave. Thus the Soviets say to the rest of the world, "What's mine is mine. What's yours is up for grabs."[3]

The zero-sum game and the ratchet effect—What's mine is mine; what's yours is up for grabs—were at the root of the Confronter interpretation of U.S. interests in the Third World long before Brezhnev formalized his ratchet doctrine. Under Reagan, however, the Confronters gained power in Washington for the first time. Administration support of those they call the "Freedom Fighters" in Nicaragua, as well as the Afghan rebels and the Savimbi movement in Angola, were attempts to move ahead in the game by breaking the catch on the ratchet. The Confronters believed previous administrations had been gradually losing the game by tacit acceptance of the Brezhnev doctrine and its Stalinist predecessors.

The third major basis of the Confronter interpretation of U.S. interests is a strong interpretation of the domino theory. The theory itself is shared in greater or lesser measure by the Middle schools, but not as strongly as put by former President Nixon in his review of Vietnam:

---

[2]Revel, 1983, p. 7.
[3]Shultz, April 1985a, p. 17.

Saigon's fall ten years ago was the Soviet Union's greatest victory in one of the key battles of the Third World war. . . . After we failed to prevent Communist conquest in Vietnam, it became accepted dogma that we would fail everywhere. For six years after Vietnam, the new isolationists chanted "No more Vietnams" as the dominoes fell one by one: Laos, Cambodia, and Mozambique in 1975; Angola in 1976; Ethiopia in 1977; South Yemen in 1978; Nicaragua in 1979.[4]

This view was brought into Central American policy by Reagan Undersecretary of Defense Fred Iklé:

We want to prevent the expansion of totalitarian regimes—particularly Leninist ones. . . . Leninist regimes are particularly dangerous: Once entrenched they tend to become irreversible, and they seek to export their totalitarianism to other nations. . . . If we signal that we are afraid of victory over the forces of violence, if we signal that we have opted for protracted failure, we will only encourage the Soviets to redouble their efforts.[5]

The domino theory provides an additional support for the Confronters' ideological/moral definition of U.S. interests in the Third World—if we don't stop them in Managua, they'll be at the gates of Harlingen, Texas. The need to counter these three mutually supporting aspects of the Communist threat to non-Communist nations—the zero-sum game, the ratchet, and the dominoes—is the major theme underlying the Confronters' view of U.S. Third World interests and was the main motivation of the Reagan administration's Third World policies.

INSURGENCY: CAUSES AND RESPONSES

Before, during, and after Vietnam, the Confronters have maintained a consistent position on insurgencies: Certainly they are based on indigenous grievances, but for the United States the more important point is that these grievances are exploited by international Communism. To attack the insurgencies by attacking the grievances is to miss the point; the Communists can perpetuate the grievances by continued disruption, and therefore military response to defeat the Communists is central.

---

[4]Nixon, 1985, p. 212.
[5]Iklé, 1983.

Strausz-Hupé, Kintner, and Possony wrote in 1961 that:

> [W]ars of national liberation appear to stand highest on the agenda of communist strategy. . . . The poverty and discontent of under-developed peoples provide the fertile soil for "national liberation" warfare. However, if we wish to deal with economic issues on the basis of economics, we must restore respect for American military power and our capability to handle the guerrilla warfare.[6]

This was the policy applied to Vietnam by the Kennedy and Johnson administrations. The Confronters would have moved faster, and they differed over such major details as U.S. participation in the overthrow of Vietnamese President Ngo Dinh Diem, whom they favored, but their thrust was the same as that of the two administrations. Whether the basic cause of the conflict in South Vietnam was the poverty and discontent of the people or Communist subversion within the South coupled with invasion from the North, U.S. policy before the large-scale intervention of 1965 stressed military advice and training for the Army of Vietnam, together with such economic, social, and military programs as the gathering of rural Vietnamese into "strategic hamlets" where they would be somewhat protected from Communist attack or subversion. In 1965, the Johnson administration escalated to large-scale direct military intervention. The rationale for such intervention, stated in retrospect by Nixon perhaps more clearly than was seen at the time, was that:

> North Vietnam . . . shrewdly camouflaged its invasion to look like a civil war. But in fact the Vietnam War was the Korean War with jungles.[7]

That is the way the Kennedy and Johnson administrations treated it initially. It was the Korean War, calling for a conventional military effort, first by indigenous forces and then when they proved insufficient, by American troops; the jungles meant that we had to pay attention to guerrilla attacks, too. The principal instrument chosen for U.S. intervention—advisory at first and then directly and ultimately massively military—was the Army. It is unfair to pin the Confronter label or any other on the U.S. military services; they used the techniques they were trained in to reach the objectives laid on by the political government that commanded them. Nonetheless, the language of the soldiers conveys the military-first flavor

---

[6]Strausz-Hupé, Kintner, and Possony, 1961, pp. 156–157.
[7]Nixon, 1985, p. 47.

with which the United States approached the Third World in Vietnam. In his public report of June 1968, General William Westmoreland, the U.S. commander in Vietnam, laid out his overall strategy up until that point and into the future:

> The first phase involved arresting the losing trend, stifling the enemy initiative, protecting the deployment of our forces, and providing security to populated areas to the extent possible. I estimated that this phase would carry through to the end of 1965. In the second phase, U.S. and allied forces would mount major offensive actions in order to destroy both the guerrilla and organized enemy forces, thus improving the security of the population. This phase concluded when the enemy had been worn down, thrown on the defensive, and driven well back from the major populated areas. The third phase would involve the final destruction of the enemy's guerrilla structure and main force units remaining in remote base areas.[8]

This was the famous "search and destroy" strategy embodying the military-first viewpoint. The strategy was complemented by the escalatory bombing of North Vietnam, which, even many years later, some airpower enthusiasts feel could have won the war in Vietnam:

> Once they had engaged America in the war, United States political leaders owed to their people and to the men they committed to battle an opportunity to achieve the country's limited objectives in Vietnam. This could have been done through the use of airpower, the "major unplayed trump card." The difficulty was not a quantitative restriction on the use of American air forces. . . . The key . . . was striking North Vietnam's heart and major logistic arteries and not squandering precious assets as the United States did on the capillaries in southern North Vietnam, South Vietnam, and elsewhere.[9]

As the Vietnam war was entering its final convulsions in 1970, by which time many of the early backers of Vietnam intervention had either moved to less military interpretations of that conflict or fallen off the bandwagon completely, Nathan Leites and Charles Wolf continued to pursue a harder line. Using evidence from a variety of events, including but not limited to Vietnam, they argued against what they considered the prevailing "hearts and minds" theory, which they believed had engulfed much of the earlier

---

[8]Westmoreland, 1968, p. 100.

[9]Gropman, n.d. The manuscript is undated, but the bibliography contains references as late as 1985.

40

consensus. The hearts and minds theory as they describe it (using "R" to designate "Rebellion" and "A" to designate "Authority") contends that:

the primary activating force behind R lies in popular likes and dislikes; the erosion of public sympathy and support for established institutions; and the acquisition of such sympathy and support by R. In the same manner, the theory contends that for counterinsurgency to be successful, support must be recaptured by A.[10]

Instead, Leites and Wolf suggest a tough four-part program exemplified by:

— control [by] the police establishment . . . and . . . border surveillance by the military.
— measures that cause R's forces to be on the move at times and places of A's choosing [or] target R's production mechanism directly—for example by destroying crops that are relied upon to provide food for R's forces.
— counterforce [in which] R's forces are targeted directly. This is the traditional military task.
— "passive defense" [such as] relocating the population and fortifying the new living areas against attack by R.[11]

These are Confronter measures designed both for direct military victory and for political victory through the use of coercion.

Although in the mid-1980s the Confronters, like the centrist schools, advocate a mixture of measures, they still stressed that, whatever the source of Third World problems, military forces must be a major part of current solutions. According to S. E. Finer:

Armed force is the single most important political actor in the Third World. . . . A very high proportion of the Third World states are in latent but chronic crisis. . . . Precisely because of this, all such states require a strong executive . . . [and therefore] all such states are those with governments that are abnormally dependent on their armed forces. . . . The outlook for a majority of the states is the gloomy one of a first military regime to be succeeded by a second, with the interval filled by alternative bouts of indirect rule, monopartism, or feebly functioning party competitive systems backed up by martial law or states of siege.[12]

---

[10]Leites and Wolf, 1970, p. 6.
[11]Ibid, pp. 76–82.
[12]Finer, 1983, pp. 75–114.

This analysis would not necessarily be antithetical to the Interventionist Middle school, and today's Confronters are not steely eyed, military-minded zealots. (Such zealots exist but they are out of the scope of this analysis.) Vietnam *has* moved the Confronters toward more complex explanations of Third World turmoil than those of the 1960s. They continue to admit the role of poverty and discontent in creating insurgencies, and, more than they did before Vietnam, they concede the importance of attacking poverty and discontent in opposing insurgencies.

Nonetheless, the stress now as it was 25 years ago is on the Communist role in exploiting the poverty and discontent, and the military role in containing the manifestations of discontent. In El Salvador, for example, the stated Reagan administration policy was to defend Jose Napoleon Duarte, the elected President, against the extremists of the Salvadoran right wing as well as against the Communist guerrillas. (Some American zealots explicitly embrace the far right within the military and the civilian elite.) The administration did in fact take substantial steps in this direction, but they included neither threats to lessen military support until Salvador curtailed the right-wing "death squads," nor strong pressures to revive moribund land reform measures. U.S. policy favored justice and land reform, but military resistance to the insurgency came first.

And in another Central American nation, Reuters reported in regard to a Contadora Treaty draft opposed by the United States:

In Guatemala, where President Vinicio Cerezo has vowed to follow an independent policy in the region, U.S. officials also spoke with military officers and members of the powerful rightist oligarchy, cautioning them of the dangers of signing a resolution which would imply too close ties with co-signer Nicaragua, officials said.[13]

If the Third World government declines to confront Communism, we will. When the chips are down, it is the Communist threat and the military defense against that threat that dominate both social economic issues and the rights of an elected client government.

THE ROLE OF THE UNITED STATES

The Confronters still advocate a forward strategy for the United States. They continue to believe that opposition to Communist advances anywhere in the world is vital. That is why for the first time on an open basis, U.S.

---

[13]Reuters newswire, May 29, 1986.

support is being provided for military attacks on Marxist/Leninist regimes. And the Confronters believe that these policies need not wait for public support; they should lead public opinion.

Before Vietnam, American intervention to oppose Communist aggression anywhere in the world was an automatic assumption. It was not Richard Nixon but John Kennedy who proclaimed in his 1961 Inaugural Address:

> Let every nation know, whether it wishes us well or ill, that we shall pay any price, bear any burden, meet any hardship, support any friend, oppose any foe, in order to assure the survival and the success of liberty.

This was a dramatic restatement of existing policy, not a new direction. Through the early years of American involvement in Vietnam, all but the Disengagers (88 out of 90 senators, for example) supported the application of the automatic assumption to Southeast Asia. It was only in the later years of the 1960s that many of those whom we now characterize as the Noninterventionist Middle broke out of the automatic consensus; toward the very end and after the Vietnam experience, many of those in the Interventionist Middle began to question it. For the Confronters, however, even in retrospect, we went into Vietnam appropriately and we won the war *in* Vietnam politically as well as militarily. As put by Nixon, "In the end, Vietnam was lost on the political front in the United States, not on the battlefront in Southeast Asia."[14] Because of the Watergate distraction and other events, we failed to provide South Vietnam with promised backing when the North invaded massively in 1975—so, to our shame, our allies lost.

Ten years later, the Confronters remained loyal to the old belief that the United States must meet Soviet Communism, militarily if necessary, wherever it manifests itself. Secretary Shultz made the case for the potential or actual utilization of military power to oppose Communism in the Third World:

> How do we protect the peace without being willing to resort to the ultimate sanction of military power against those who seek to destroy the peace? Americans have sometimes tended to think that power and diplomacy are two distinct alternatives. This reflects a fundamental misunderstanding. The truth is, power and diplomacy must go together. . . . The need to combine strength and diplomacy in our

---

[14]Nixon, 1985, p. 15.

foreign policies is only one part of the answer. . . . But we do not have to look hard to find examples where the use of power has been both moral and necessary. . . . Grenada is a tiny country. Although there were some tough actions, as military campaigns go, it was quickly done. But the *moral* issue it posed was of enormous importance for the United States. . . . We have to accept the fact that often the moral choices will be much less clearly defined than they were in Grenada. Our morality, however, must not paralyze us.[15]

Less officially, a few Confronters make the point in more aggressive terms, reminiscent of the 1960s version of the forward strategy and going beyond the general consensus which now includes most Confronters, that military intervention à la Vietnam cannot be repeated. According to Dr. Neil Livingstone, the United States should:

Support any force around the globe that is resisting the Soviet Union, its allies, and ideological fellow travellers. . . . Incrementalism is a formula for disaster. Congress and an impatient American public are unlikely to support a long and drawn-out conflict. While it runs many risks, we should seek a "quick kill," escalating the conflict as rapidly as feasible.[16]

For Col. Rod Paschall, this implies direct ground attack against enemy "sanctuaries":

Our future doctrine must not continue to ignore essential, effective operations against those nations that sponsor insurgency. The United States has subjected its soldiers to two wars since World War II wherein the enemy was afforded contiguous sanctuary. . . . The regular and regional forces that [the] insurgent must create will be harbored, nurtured, and poised in the sanctuary awaiting the opportune moment. For the counterinsurgent to win, these forces must be defeated. For the counterinsurgent to survive, these forces must, at a minimum, be engaged.[17]

Whether Col. Paschall's attack on sanctuaries would be supported by Dr. Livingstone's "Congress and an impatient American public"—or would have to be—is a very open question. This is the great pragmatic issue of

---

[15]Shultz, 1985b, pp. 2–3.
[16]Livingstone, 1984, pp. 11–15.
[17]Paschall, 1985, p. 43.

American politics left by Vietnam: the extent to which intervention requires public support. Secretary Shultz shared Nixon's belief that "Vietnam was lost on the political front in the United States." He was wary of repetition but nonetheless contended that we cannot afford to lose international position because of domestic public opinion.

[O]n such occasions we will be able to count on the full support of the American people. There is no such thing as guaranteed public support in advance. Grenada shows that a president who has the courage to lead will *win* public support if he acts wisely and effectively. And Vietnam shows that public support can be frittered away if we do not act wisely and effectively.[18]

Shultz was frank about the ambiguities inherent in defining "moral choices." Although such doubts are difficult to resolve philosophically, the Confronters are willing to act on the maxim that anti-Communist immorality is easier to change later on, and is less antithetical to U.S. interests, than is Communist immorality. Jeane Kirkpatrick is known for her expression of this thesis:

Only intellectual fashion and the tyranny of Right/Left thinking prevent intelligent men of goodwill from perceiving the *facts* that traditional authoritarian governments are less oppressive than revolutionary autocracies, that they are more susceptible of liberalization, and that they are more compatible with U.S. interests. . . . [T]he history of this century provides no grounds for expecting that radical totalitarian regimes will transform themselves. At the moment there is a far greater likelihood of progressive liberalization and democratization in the governments of Brazil, Argentina and Chile than in the government of Cuba; in Taiwan than in the People's Republic of China; in South Korea than in North Korea; in Zaire than in Angola; and so forth. Since many traditional autocracies permit limited contestation and participation, it is not impossible that U.S. policy could effectively encourage this process of liberalization and democratization, provided that the effort is not made at a time when the incumbent government is fighting for its life against violent adversaries, and that proposed reforms are aimed at producing gradual change rather than perfect democracy overnight.[19]

---

[18]Shultz, 1985, p. 3.
[19]Kirkpatrick, 1982, pp. 49–51.

Ambassador Kirkpatrick is not a bad prophet: Brazil, Argentina, Chile, Taiwan, and South Korea *have* liberalized to various degrees; on the other side, however, so have Angola and Mozambique. In any case, her philosophy leads Kirkpatrick to another of the strong policy views for which she is noted: We should not overthrow our friends no matter how distasteful they may be in some ways:

> [I]n one year, 1979, the United States suffered two . . . major blows—in Iran and Nicaragua—of large and strategic significance. In each country, the Carter administration not only failed to prevent the undesired outcome, but actively collaborated in the replacement of moderate autocrats friendly to American interests with less friendly autocrats of extremist persuasion. . . . [B]oth Somoza and the Shah were, in central ways, traditional rulers of semitraditional societies. . . . Though each of the rulers was from time to time criticized by American officials for violating civil and human rights, [this] did not prevent successive administrations from granting—with the necessary approval of successive Congresses—both military and economic aid. . . . But once an attack was launched by opponents bent on destruction, everything changed. The rise of opposition in Iran and Nicaragua set in motion a succession of events which bore a suggestive resemblance to one another and a suggestive similarity to our behavior in China before the fall of Chiang Kai-shek, in Cuba before the triumph of Castro, in certain crucial periods of the Vietnam War, and more recently, in Angola. . . . [If this pattern repeats] the United States will have been led by its own misunderstanding of the situation to assist actively in deposing an erstwhile friend and ally and installing a government hostile to American interests and policies in the world. At best we will have lost access to friendly territory. At worst the Soviets will have gained a new base.[20]

All this changed in the Reagan administration: Shultz was Secretary of State; Kirkpatrick was Ambassador to the United Nations. The United States adopted a forward strategy that, although prudent in terms of direct military intervention, was otherwise worthy of Strausz-Hupé, Kintner, and Possony.

In 1987, this strategy focused on Nicaragua, and in Nicaragua the conscious effort was being made to use U.S. power to reverse the fall of the dominoes by either overthrowing the Sandinista regime or changing it so drastically as to amount to a doctrinal overthrow. Some non-Confronters hoped to use Contra

---

[20]Ibid., pp. 23–28.

military pressure to force the regime into a negotiated agreement which would at a minimum limit Soviet and Cuban presence in Nicaragua and prevent the Sandinistas from assisting insurgencies in neighboring Central American countries. The Confronters, however, wanted either to oust the Sandinistas or force changes that would transform the regime into a mildly social democratic one. Defense Under Secretary Iklé put it quite frankly:

> Let me make this clear to you: We do not seek a military defeat for our friends. We do not seek a military stalemate. We seek victory for the forces of democracy. And that victory has two components: *One*: Defeating militarily those organized forces of violence that refuse to accept the democratic will of the people. *Two*: establishing an adequate internal system for justice and personal security.[21]

Or, put more simply by President Reagan in a *Time* magazine interview (the italicized paragraph introductions are the *Time* headings):

> *On the U.S. goal.* The cancer that has to be excised is Nicaragua. We can try and help those people who want freedom to bring it about themselves. We have a right to help the people of Nicaragua who are demanding what we think are any people's rights—the right to determine their own government. . . .

> *On what the* Contras *could accomplish.* The Sandinistas have to look at one of two choices: the possibility of a military defeat and being totally overthrown, or a choice of having a political settlement in which, while they would have to give up this monopoly on power they have, at least they could be in a position to run for office if they could get the people's approval.[22]

Indeed a forward strategy for Confronters.

---

[21]Iklé, 1983, pp. 4–7.
[22]"Reagan: 'We Have a Right to Help'," *Time*, March 31, 1986, p. 16.

5. The Disengagers

U.S. INTERESTS

If the Confronters have consistently defined U.S. interests ideologically, in terms of resistance to the worldwide Communist threat, the Disengagers have equally consistently opposed this ideology and attacked the concept of the Communist threat as a red herring. Sometimes they have suggested that the herring was dragged across the trail to distract attention from policies to promote and protect American business interests in the Third World. This contention was difficult to apply to Vietnam, however. Even in debates over Central America, the Disengagers' accusation has more frequently been that policy has been misled, rather than that it is deliberately misleading. The Disengagers' own view of U.S. interests is also ideological, but the ideology is very different from that of the Confronters: The interests worth supporting are those of universal morality; the United States is a rich nation that needs no other interests.

In 1961, Erich Fromm attacked not only the zero-sum game concept of U.S. interests in the Third World (and the rest of the world), but decried the game itself on both sides as being artificial and misleading:

To sum up: the cliché of the Soviet offensive against the United States in Berlin, Laos, the Congo, and Cuba is not based on reality but is rather a convenient formula to support further armament and the continuation of the cold war. It corresponds to the Chinese cliché that pictures the United States as seeking world domination by support of Chiang Kai-shek, by the domination of Southern Korea and Okinawa, by the SEATO pact, etc. All these mutual accusations can not stand up to sober and realistic analysis.[1]

More radically, C. Wright Mills, best known for his belief that American foreign and domestic policies were manipulated by and for the benefit of a "power elite," wrote:

> [T]he appeal of Soviet communism to strategic agents of change in underdeveloped countries is attested to by the historical fact that, with one or possibly two exceptions, only in such countries has communism been successfully installed as a political and economic way of life. . . . Most of these contain colored races—and Russia is free of color prejudice. They are illiterate and impoverished—as was Russia only two generations ago. They inherit much ill will toward capitalist behavior of a colonial sort. . . . Moreover the underdeveloped countries are in a hurry and the Soviet way is fast. . . . The intellectuals of the underdeveloped world, as well as the people generally, know how far from reality capitalist notions of industrialization now seem for them. . . . Accordingly many of these people, quite understandably, look to Russia as a model of their own future.[2]

Mills's expression is notable for the straightforward connection made by a non-Communist radical between Third World revolution and Soviet Communism. By the time the writings of the Disengagers began to proliferate a few years later in the mid-1960s, not only was substantial experience from Vietnam beginning to come in, but Communism was beginning to subdivide into many varieties; and it was possible for these writers to dissociate Third World revolution—even in Vietnam, but more so elsewhere—from the strictly Soviet model. By 1965, Norman Thomas, a quintessential anti-Communist radical, argued that our intervention in Vietnam played directly into Communist hands:

---

[1]Fromm, 1961, pp. 116–117.
[2]Mills, 1958, pp. 68–69.

[T]he final justification [of the Vietnam war] is that it is necessary immorality to stop Communism. On the contrary we could hardly do more to help Communism in the world and divert attention from its own failure and weaknesses. Our whole policy in Vietnam makes us appear as the imperialists, and white imperialists at that.[3]

Thomas's long-time history of opposing Communist influence in American socialism led him to agree at least that stopping Communism was a plausible American interest; not all Disengagers did. According to Noam Chomsky:

[T]he core principle of United States foreign policy [is] that somehow we must "stop communism." This belief is not questioned or examined; it has become a matter of faith. It does not come from a rational study of communism in its complexities and contradictions.[4]

Whatever their views on stopping Communism, the Disengagers agreed that morality as such was an interest worth promoting, one that was being badly violated by American policy and actions in Vietnam. W. H. Harris wrote, in a liberal religious journal:

We have no right to intervene in the affairs of other nations to give them what *we* conceive as good government. We do have a responsibility as great as our enormous capacity for mischief: to refrain from . . . strengthening bad governments. We certainly have no right to keep another people from getting rid of an oppressive government or of traditional patterns of exploitations.[5]

Finally, the Disengagers worried about the effect of the Vietnam war on life within the United States. Norman Mailer conveyed the passion of the times as well as the core fear:

For no one can know, not even Johnson himself, if escalation is our best defense against Communism, a burning of orphans to save future orphans, or if the war is the first open expression of a totalitarian Leviathan which will yet dominate everything not yet nailed down in American life: art, civil rights, student rebellions, public criticism in mass media. We may be living in the shadow of the biggest hype of them all, our last con game: red-neck dynamics; liberal rhetoric. There is the ineradicable suspicion that liberal rhetoric was conceived

---

[3]Thomas, 1965, pp. 7–8.
[4]Chomsky, 1969, p. 353.
[5]Harris, 1965, pp. 1156–1157.

by Satan to kiss the behind of something unspeakable. The editors ask for a counter-policy. I offer it. It is to get out of Asia.[6]

Not much has changed in the ensuing years. Perhaps the Disengagers have less to explain away about Vietnam than any of the other schools; not that they were necessarily more *correct*, but since their solution—get out unilaterally—was not tried, they are less demonstrably *incorrect* than the others. (Nixon and Kissinger contend that the Disengagers' pressure led to U.S. abandonment and defeat of our allies in Vietnam.)

The emphasis has shifted to Latin America in general, and Central America more specifically. The Disengagers contended that at worst, U.S. policy there was based on support of American business interests, a theme not much seen in the Vietnam controversies. The United States had had few such business interests in Indochina before the entry of private contractors in support of the major American military intervention beginning in 1965.

In Latin America, however, U.S. business interests have been substantial. Criticizing American pressure on Chilean President Salvador Allende before his overthrow (allegedly with our assistance) in 1973, James Petras and Robert LaPorte wrote:

Despite the appearance of a pluralistic decision-making structure with competing viewpoints, the overall thrust of U.S. foreign policy is largely in the direction of supporting U.S. business interests abroad. Policy tends to follow the line favored by a single interest—the U.S. investor community. U.S. economic interests appear to be the only concrete, specific, and visible reference point to which policy-makers refer. U.S. corporation images of political reality have become the point from which policy-makers begin to define their positions.[7]

With the more recent spotlight on Central America, particularly El Salvador and Nicaragua, the Disengagers have stressed that as in Vietnam our interests there are self-created and unnecessary. U.S. business interests, and past political and military interventions in support of such interests, must take substantial blame for the current sad economic and social state of Central America, but current policies are based less on disingenuousness covering U.S. business interests with idealistic rhetoric than they are on simple-minded anti-Communist ingenuousness. William LeoGrande stressed the administration's anti-Communist motivations:

[6]Mailer, 1965, p. 642.
[7]Petras and LaPorte, 1972, p. 135.

When Secretary of State Alexander Haig declared in 1981 that in El Salvador the new administration was "drawing the line" against communism, he expected to win the war within a few months. A success in Central America would be Reagan's first foreign-policy victory, and its ramifications would be global. It would send a message to Cuba and the Soviet Union that the United States would no longer tolerate their international adventurism; it would send a message to Western Europe that the United States was once again committed to firm and aggressive world leadership; and most important, it would demonstrate to the American people that the United States could project military power in the Third World without becoming entangled in another Vietnam. . . . For the past three years, the Administration has defined Central America as vital to the security of the United States, and President Reagan has said more than once that he is not going to lose another country to communism on "his watch."[8]

After Secretary Haig was followed by Secretary Shultz, Michael Klare took up the cudgels against Shultz's use and interpretation of the domino theory:

It is not possible in an article of this length to discuss the numerous inconsistencies and contradictions in Shultz's thesis, but it should be obvious to anyone with even the barest grasp of history that many of the regimes that have fallen to leftist insurgencies, including those in Vietnam, Nicaragua, Angola and Mozambique, were colonial artifacts or military dictatorships lacking even the slightest pretense to democratic rule.[9]

And Noam Chomsky, as strong in his beliefs on Central America as he was on Vietnam twenty years earlier, suggested that if anything *we* had been tipping the dominoes, in an antidemocratic direction:

The brutal and corrupt Somoza dictatorship had long been a reliable U.S. ally and a base for the projection of U.S. power: to terminate Guatemalan democracy in 1954, to attack Cuba in 1961, to avert the threat of democracy in the Dominican Republic in 1965 and in El Salvador in 1972.[10]

---

[8]LeoGrande, 1984, pp. 72–75.
[9]Klare, 1986, p. 715.
[10]Chomsky, 1985, p. 5.

As in Vietnam, morality should lead us in the other direction. One interesting difference from the 1960s is that not only have some segments of the Roman Catholic church advocated this revolutionary morality—which began in the 1960s when many religious Catholics joined the Disengagers on Vietnam—but because Latin America is overwhelmingly Catholic, revolutionary Catholics have taken the moral lead:

> Liberation theology rejects capitalism as a viable means to the development of Latin American society and accepts Marxism as one tool of socio-economic analysis. At the same time, it rejects atheistic communism, which it finds as dehumanizing as capitalism because it denies that there is a spiritual dimension to life.[11]

And the Confronters' policies again threaten our internal political well-being. Klare put it less colorfully than Mailer, in a less extreme situation:

> The ascendancy of the Shultz doctrine will also pollute the domestic political atmosphere. If U.S. intervention in the Third World is defined as a necessary defense of freedom and democracy, those who oppose it are perforce enemies of democracy and, by extension, legitimate targets of government repression. . . . If that distortion is allowed to continue unchallenged, we could face a serious threat to our *own* rights and liberties.[12]

INSURGENCY: CAUSES AND RESPONSES

The Disengagers of course still believe that, as in Vietnam, the sources of insurgency are poverty, misery, and the desire of "another people" to get "rid of an oppressive government or of traditional patterns of exploitation." The 1980s differ little from the 1960s. As in Vietnam, revolution in Central America is caused primarily by poverty and oppression—in the newer case more directly attributable to intervention by the United States:

> [T]he revolutionary movements in Central America are historically logical responses to centuries of domestic and foreign oppression, in which the United States has played a dominant role. . . . In one country after another, the revolutionary remedy has appeared as the only path to popular democracy and national independence. The

[11]Montgomery, 1983, p. 77.
[12]Klare, 1986, p. 716.

course of human events does not now admit of more moderate solutions at a leisurely pace.[13]

The revolution succeeded in Nicaragua because of the particularly heavy hand of the Somozas and the ability of the Sandinistas to organize, but for the Disengagers, each of the other countries is at a different stage, all on the road to some variety of revolution. The article headlines in *The Nation*'s special 1984 issue on Central America tell the story: "Terminal El Salvador: Death Squads, D'Aubuisson & 'Democracy'"; "Fortress Honduras: Delivering a Country to the Military"; "Guatemala Under Siege: Chaos in the Scorched Earth"; and "'Model' Costa Rica: Class War in the Latin Switzerland."[14]

The unifying theme across all these countries is the heavy role of the United States:

> U.S. politicians may worry about torture and death squads when the press accounts grow lurid, but the oligarchies whose work the murderers are doing are solidly integrated in the U.S. economic system. The bananas of all the Central American republics have always been fruits in the North American corporate compote.[15]

All of which has been abetted by Central American military establishments under the tutelage of the American armed services.

> The process of [military] professionalization accomplished under the ideological hegemony of the United States thus *catalyzed* the heterogeneous ideological elements and allowed them to be ordered and ranked. The military established an identity and unity *apparently* independent from internal political struggles. . . . The armed forces acquired a new profile that included a higher degree of professionalism and a definite ideology. What the Latin American propertied factions had not been capable of attaining was at last achieved by U.S. instructors.[16]

Just as the Confronters contend that the Communists cause the kind of Third World turmoil against which the United States must defend and the military provide the defense, now as in the 1960s, 180 degrees away, the

---

[13]*The Nation*, "Contra Kissinger" (an editorial), January 28, 1984, p. 67.
[14]Ibid., pp. 88–96.
[15]Ibid., p. 68.
[16]Varas, 1985, p. 12.

Disengagers believe that the United States and the military are the causes, and the Third World must defend itself against us, now as then.

THE ROLE OF THE UNITED STATES

The key word in prescribing a role for the United States is *Out!* Mailer's bottom line on Vietnam was "Get out of Asia." Now in the Third World, the admonition is "Stay out."

On Vietnam, Howard Zinn argued in fairly pragmatic terms, directly confronting the American fear of falling dominoes, to reach out for support beyond the moral consensus of the Disengagers themselves:

> History does not show that a nation which liquidates a bad venture suffers a serious loss of prestige where it can compensate in other ways. Proud, powerful England surrendered to the ragtag thirteen American colonies, removed her armed forces ignominiously, and did not suffer for it. More recently and more pertinently, France moved out voluntarily from Algeria and from Indochina. . . . There is a kind of prestige this nation should not worry about losing—that which is attached to sheer power, to victory by force of arms, devoid of moral content. Which is more terrible: to have people in the world say that the United States withdrew from an untenable situation, or to have it said, as it is now being said everywhere, that the United States is acting foolishly and immorally in Vietnam?[17]

In the 1980s, "Get out" is of course applied by the Disengagers to U.S. support of the Contras in Nicaragua, but beyond that, Klare worries about the overall implications of what he sees as:

> [T]he Reagan Administration's aggressive doctrine of low-intensity conflict, or L.I.C., as it is rapidly becoming known. . . . Unless vigorously opposed by Congress, a prospect that appears increasingly unlikely at this time, the doctrine will lead us into another round of Third World interventions just as surely as counterinsurgency led us into Vietnam. . . . The growing popularity of L.I.C. doctrine stems from interrelated phenomena: the armed services' desire to develop a publicly acceptable formula for the use of force in regional conflicts, and the Reagan Administration's desire to build public support for its

---

[17]Zinn, 1967, p. 108.

military campaign against pro-Soviet forces and regimes in the Third World.[18]

And finally, the Disengagers' concerns over getting in when we should be staying out, and the Vietnam analogy on which the emotional content of this feeling is based, lead them back to the political methods by which they helped hasten the end of American participation in Vietnam—by helping to move public opinion:

> If disaster in Central America is to be averted, the wars of the region must be brought home and the political basis for U.S. policy must be changed. This is a staggering task, but it is not impossible. Already there is activity on many fronts. Church groups have organized a variety of anti-interventionist projects.... Solidarity organizations... support the popular struggles in the region. Labor groups... are beginning to mobilize against Reagan's policy. Women's and peace groups... are now projecting a... campaign... that includes Central American issues. Artists and professionals are involving themselves.[19]

The Nation and Nixon are *correct* in their agreement that American public opinion was a major element in forcing withdrawal from Vietnam; which one is *right* is another issue.

The middle groups maintain that truth is somewhere in between.

---

[18]Klare, 1986, pp. 697–710.
[19]*The Nation*, January 28, 1984, pp. 67–68.

6. The Interventionist Middle

U.S. INTERESTS

Typically and traditionally in the United States, the policymaking "establishment" responsible for national security has been within the Interventionist Middle. In the years following World War II, their fundamental—not too closely examined—premise was that maintaining the U.S. position against Communist expansion was both in our own national interest and in the interest of preserving world stability. We could not avoid being a rich and powerful nation, thus we could not retreat again into an isolationist shell. The policy establishment was not of a bent to delve deeply into the moral philosophy underlying this premise; they were too busy implementing it. For Henry Kissinger, who went deeper than most, the requirement to pay attention to the demands of stability was among the natural responsibilities of a great power, and had been at least since 1815.

Proceeding from this premise, the Interventionist Middle entered the 1960s with a view of U.S. interests similar to that of the Confronters: The need to contain Communism, as laid out by the Truman Doctrine, was as relevant to the Third World as it had been to Greece and Turkey, as applicable to Vietnam as to Korea. But, unlike the Confronters, President Johnson's advisers were chastened by the course of the Vietnam War. They believed it necessary to stay in Vietnam because the commitment had been made, but by the second half of the 1960s they wished it had not been made. This questioning lasted long beyond Vietnam and continues with regard to current policy. The Interventionist Middle still considers defense against the Soviet threat the central U.S. interest in the Third World, but such a defense is no longer universal and automatic. Communism today is anything but monolithic, Soviet interests in the Third World are opportunistic and variable, and, indeed, our own interests are not uniform. It is not a vital interest of the United States that the anti-Communist forces prevail in every confrontation from Angola to Nicaragua.

In the innocent year of 1961, when the Kennedy restatement of America's containment policy—"We shall pay any price . . . to assure the survival and the success of liberty"—still rang through Washington, and when the domino theory was applied automatically and universally, Secretary of State Dean Rusk and Secretary of Defense Robert McNamara wrote in a memorandum to the President:

> The loss of South Viet-Nam to Communism would involve the transfer of a nation of 20 million people from the free world to the Communist bloc. The loss of South Viet-Nam would make pointless any further discussion about the importance of Southeast Asia to the free world; we would have to face the near certainty that the remainder of Southeast Asia and Indonesia would move to a complete accommodation with Communism, if not formal incorporation within the Communist bloc. . . . The loss of South Viet-Nam to Communism would not only destroy SEATO but would undermine the credibility of American commitments elsewhere.[1]

Not only dominoes in the Far East were involved but, because of the loss of U.S. credibility, dominoes worldwide. By 1964, still before the major U.S. military intervention, McNamara sounded somewhat more defensive in tone:

> Unless we can [maintain an independent] South Vietnam, all of Southeast Asia will probably fall under Communist dominance (all of Vietnam, Laos, and Cambodia), accommodate to Communism so as to remove effective U.S. and anti-Communist influence (Burma), or fall under the domination of forces not now explicitly Communist but likely then to become so (Indonesia taking over Malaysia). Thailand might hold for a period with our help, but would be under grave pressure. Even the Philippines would become shaky, and the threat to

---

[1]Dean Rusk and Robert McNamara, memorandum to President Kennedy, November 11, 1961, in *The Pentagon Papers*, 1971, p. 150.

India to the west, Australia and New Zealand to the south, and Taiwan, Korea, and Japan to the north and east would be greatly increased. All these consequences would probably have been true even if the U.S. had not since 1954, and especially since 1961, become so heavily engaged in South Vietnam. However, that fact accentuates the impact of a Communist South Vietnam not only in Asia, but in the rest of the world where the South Vietnam conflict is regarded as a test case of U.S. capacity to help a nation meet a Communist "war of liberation."[2]

In other words, maybe we shouldn't have committed as deeply as we did, but we did, and now we *are* committed.

Less than two years later, after we had intervened massively and as the enormity of the situation became clear, Assistant Secretary of Defense John McNaughton was quite explicit that the issue was much more our commitment than it was our military position:

The present U.S. objective in Vietnam is to avoid humiliation. The reasons why we *went into* Vietnam to the present depth are varied; but they are now largely academic. Why we have *not withdrawn* from Vietnam is, by all odds, *one* reason: (1) to preserve our reputation as a guarantor, and thus to preserve our effectiveness in the rest of the world. We have not hung on (2) to save a friend, or (3) to deny the Communists the added acres and heads (because the dominoes don't fall for that reason in this case).[3]

Nixon came into office with a view of Vietnam that, according to Henry Kissinger, was based on an "optimistic estimate of our endurance," and he maintained the high level of the stakes bet on American/South Vietnamese victory. Kissinger quotes him as saying, in July of 1969:

I am utterly convinced that how we end this war will determine the future of the U.S. in the world. We can maintain the American position in Europe and Asia if we come out well.[4]

But Kissinger himself in retrospect described the goals of 1969 in fairly modest terms, akin to McNaughton's a few years earlier:

---

[2]Robert McNamara, memorandum to President Johnson, March 16, 1964, in *The Pentagon Papers*, 1971, p. 278.

[3]John McNaughton, memorandum of January 19, 1966, in *The Pentagon Papers*, 1971, p. 492.

[4]Kissinger, 1979, p. 969.

The basic challenge to the new Nixon Administration was similar to de Gaulle's in Algeria: to withdraw as an expression of policy and not as a collapse. . . . [The] momentum of American politics was in the direction of unilateral concessions. For the Nixon Administration to have kept these turbulent forces in harness as we designed a self-confident policy of orderly disengagement was no small feat.[5]

Also in retrospect, however, General Bruce Palmer, who had commanded the Army's forces in Vietnam before becoming Vice Chief of Staff of the Army during the final years of direct American involvement in Vietnam, has come to a more negative conclusion:

From the beginning our leaders realized that South Vietnam was not vital to U.S. interests. Yet for other reasons the nation became committed to the war. As hostilities dragged on interminably, with no clearly discernible end in sight . . . legitimate questions were raised as to whether our goals in Southeast Asia were worth the high costs. Was the war in our national interest?[6]

Palmer thus implicitly rejects the Confronter interpretation of U.S. interests being engaged anywhere it is necessary to stop Communism. The vital interests he does not believe were at stake in Vietnam are the more traditional ones exemplified by economic relevance and strategic location.

A similar view of U.S. interests was taken by the BDM Corporation, a by-no-means-dovish consulting group to the Pentagon. In a recently declassified study quoted by Larry Berman, they put the point less questioningly than Palmer:

Early on, American leadership mistakenly believed Vietnam to be vital not only for itself, but for what they thought its "loss" would mean internationally and domestically. Once the commitment was made, each subsequent president reaffirmed the commitment rather than reassessing the basic rationale as to whether vital U.S. interests were involved or not. . . . There was a time when monolithic communism may have justified the anticommunist approach of the U.S. in the 1950s. Equally, it seems possible that the U.S. might have tailored its policy toward Vietnam more closely to observable changes in the Sino-Soviet relationship earlier than it did (during the Nixon presidency). Unfortunately, the problem arose that the investment of

[5]Ibid., p. 298.
[6]Palmer, 1984, p. 189.

U.S. political, economic and military prestige, not to mention U.S. casualties, came to override the intrinsic importance of Vietnam to the U.S.[7]

Berman's own conclusion is that "[President] Johnson was the cause of his ultimate undoing." Even after many of his advisers had begun to look for ways out, Johnson believed that were we to abandon our commitment,

Hanoi's propaganda would focus on the United States as a paper tiger; China and the Soviet Union would laugh in the face of U.S. integrity, and there was always the spectre of China's "picking up the pieces at the fringe." Allies would never trust the seal on the treaty with the United States.[8]

The major lesson learned from Vietnam is the realization that not every containment is a vital interest. Vietnam probably had not been vital in 1961, but by the mid-1960s it was perceived that the U.S. commitment must be honored to avoid "humiliation." The Interventionist Middle, the school that until the Reagan administration was at the core of the decision-making center, had gone into the 1960s with an interpretation of U.S. interests that automatically necessitated a defense against Sino-Soviet Communism wherever a potential Communist expansion might occur—or else the dominoes would start falling. *Retrospectively, for this school as well as those to its "left," the application of this interpretation to Vietnam was perhaps the greatest mistake in American history, at least since those that led to the Civil War.*

This rethinking demands specific definition of vital interests—examination of the potential gains and losses in maintaining any strategic position. It governs the "U.S. interest" views of the Interventionist Middle today, and falls between the Munich metaphor, which made "appeasement" of Communism the most dangerous sin, and a Vietnam metaphor forbidding any kind of intervention in pursuit of any kind of American interest.

The Interventionists now believe, in a way they did not when it was simply a test of wills between Kennedy and Khrushchev (or Johnson and Kosygin or Nixon and Brezhnev), that Communist objectives and strategies are mixed and mutable. Even before Gorbachev, Interventionist Sovietologists in the early 1980s, while far from suggesting that the U.S.-USSR conflict was in any way ending, did suggest that Soviet approaches were chang-

---

[7]BDM Corporation, *The Strategic Lessons Learned in Vietnam*, Vol. 3, quoted in Berman, 1982, p. 131.
[8]Ibid., pp. 145–146.

ing and that it was in our interest to change with them. Stephen Hosmer and Thomas Wolfe wrote that:

> Our listing of Soviet objectives begins with the U.S.S.R's overwhelming aim to assure its own security. . . . Considerations of state security have . . . led Moscow to regulate its Third World activities so as to avoid situations that pose a high risk of direct Soviet-U.S. military conflict. . . . A set of related long-standing objectives has been evident in Soviet Third World policy since the mid-1950s. The first has been to weaken Western control and influence in the formerly colonial areas. . . . A parallel objective has been to shape the sociopolitical and economic development of the newly independent countries and to bring the so-called nonaligned movement of the Third World into accord with Soviet goals and interests. Where feasible, the Soviets have sought also to foster the establishment of pro-Soviet Marxist governments. . . . From the mid-1960s on [the Soviets have been] securing access and basing arrangements in Third World areas . . . accompanied by parallel Soviet efforts to erode existing U.S. overseas base structures. . . . Finally, the U.S.S.R has sought over a long period to improve Soviet-bloc access to primary resources in the Third World and . . . ultimately to control or deny the West access to such resources. . . . [As a result, the] Soviets have intervened cautiously in the Third World, taking full advantages of the opportunities open to them but supporting intervention mainly in conflicts to which they had reason to assume that the United States would not respond militarily. . . . In contrast to observers who argue that Soviet military involvements derive directly from an overall master plan . . . we believe that such interventions have come largely in response to indigenous developments not of Moscow's making or to the action or inaction of other outside powers.[9]

This is different from the Confronters' concept of malevolently directed Soviet operations in the Third World. In 1988, Harry Gelman updated the situation to the Gorbachev era.

> Gorbachev evidently does indeed desire to minimize costly or dangerous new commitments, and also to reduce expenditures that have grown onerous in places like Angola, Vietnam, and Cuba. His most radical step to reduce commitments, of course, has been the withdrawal from Afghanistan. . . . This much is quite new and

---

[9]Hosmer and Wolfe, 1983, pp. 127–135.

encouraging in Soviet policy. Nevertheless, his Third World policy remains intensely competitive, and the Gorbachev Politburo seems to me by no means ready to accept a general retreat from the geopolitical bridgeheads in the Third World inherited from clients.[10]

In other words, real operational change has taken place, but hardly full Soviet retreat.

Leslie Lewis applied the concept of variable Soviet interests more specifically to Latin America and added the reminder that Soviet interests and other Communist interests in the Third World can no longer be equated:

> The Soviets view Latin America as a tertiary region. . . . A major difference between Soviet activities in Africa and Latin America is that Africa is judged by the Soviets to be strategically important to the survival of the Soviet Empire. . . . Cuba's foreign policy in Less Developed Countries (LDCs) is different from that of the Soviet Union. Castro sees nationalistic revolutions in the Third World as a national priority. Castro wants Cuba to be recognized as the leader of the non-alignment movement.[11]

She applied the same sort of variability to American interests in Latin America:

> The United States must clarify which Latin American nations are strategically important. For example, strategically Mexico is much more important to the United States than are El Salvador and Nicaragua.[12]

Reagan Defense Secretary Weinberger made the point more abstractly but more forcefully:

> We should engage our troops only if we must do so as a matter of our own vital national interest. We cannot assume for other sovereign nations the responsibility to defend their territory—without their strong invitation—when our own freedom is not threatened.[13]

Hedged as this remark is, it still marks a clear departure from the Confronter view of the need to oppose Communist expansion wherever it appears. This is particularly true in the context of the well-noted Shultz-

---

[10]Gelman, 1988, pp. 13–14.
[11]Leslie Lewis, 1985, pp. 25–31.
[12]Ibid., p. 39.
[13]Weinberger, 1985, p. 8.

Weinberger debate over the uses and limits of U.S. military forces. Secretary Shultz's contribution has been quoted above.

In any case, whether because of Gorbachev or Castro—or Reagan—Central America was the arena of the mid-1980s. The report of the Kissinger Commission on Central America did not make a clearcut distinction between Soviet and Cuban activities; like most reports of presidential commissions, it was somewhat hazy in several aspects. Otherwise, however, the report reflected a view of an opportunistic Communist strategy similar to that expressed by the Sovietologists of the Interventionist Middle, and it drew implications of that view for U.S. interests:

> Soviet policy in this hemisphere has followed the pattern of Soviet policy elsewhere in the world: Moscow has exploited opportunities for the advancement of Soviet influence. . . . To the extent that a further Marxist-Leninist advance in Central America leading to progressive deterioration and a further projection of Soviet and Cuban power in the region required us to defend against security threats near our borders, we would face a difficult choice between unpalatable alternatives. . . . From the standpoint of the Soviet Union, it would be a major strategic coup to impose on the United States the burden of defending our Southern approaches.[14]

Such a Soviet coup would violate a central principle laid down by the Commission, the wording of which echoes the title of one of the books that started Henry Kissinger on his career, *The Necessity for Choice*:[15]

> [A] great power can choose what challenges to respond to, but it cannot choose where those challenges come—or when. Nor can it avoid the necessity of deliberate choice. . . . No agony of indecision will make that challenge go away. No wishing it were easier will make it easier.[16]

The Soviet Union continues to challenge us; we have more choices than we thought we had in the 1960s; but we still must respond. In a briefing presented to the Kissinger Commission, four social scientists presented a slightly less sweeping view, but still came out in about the same place:

---

[14]Kissinger Commission, pp. 89–92.
[15]Kissinger, 1960.
[16]Kissinger Commission, p. 2.

Just how important are U.S. security interests in Central America? Viewed in isolation they seem to be modest. From a strategic viewpoint, however, they assume importance because Central America is part of our strategic rear area, the Caribbean Basin, and because the Soviet Union is seeking targets of opportunity there. . . . Security is not the only issue. . . . The United States has a *moral obligation* to protect and support those moderate forces that share this basic commitment to human rights and other democratic values. . . . The United States has important interests and values at stake . . . and these merit U.S. involvement in, not disengagement from, Central America.[17]

Going into Vietnam, the Interventionist Middle represented a substantial majority consensus—a consensus that began with the Containment theory and the Truman Doctrine of the late 1940s, received strong negative reinforcement from the "loss" of China, and continued, although under strain for a while, through the Korean War. In the 1980s, Communism became fractionated. The key word in discussion of Soviet strategy in the Third World became "opportunism"—and yet we must continue to oppose Communism, at least in "our own backyard." For the moderates of the Interventionist Middle, Soviet actions and our interests have changed— moderately. So have the ways in which these Soviet actions interact with indigenous Third World movements for change, and the ways in which we must oppose them when we do oppose them.

INSURGENCY: CAUSES AND RESPONSES

For the Interventionist Middle, the causes of insurgency have included a well-stirred mixture of economic and political grievances deliberately exacerbated by Communist insurgency. Responses to insurgency must include measures of all sorts, but military responses take precedence so that economic and political remedies can be pursued in security. In the early days of Vietnam, the military measures were fairly conventional, but as these steps, mounted first by the Army of Vietnam and then by massive U.S. forces, failed to gain victory, the emphasis began to shift to "pacification"—economic and social action backed by localized applications of military force. Since Vietnam, civic action and pacification have dominated Interventionist Middle thinking—and the counterinsurgency doctrine

[17]Gonzalez et al., 1984, p. v.

65

of the U.S. military. How well these doctrines have been implemented, or can be implemented by current force structures, is a matter of controversy.

In the early 1960s, the mindset of the Interventionist Middle with regard to U.S. actions in the Third World was exemplified by quotations from two analysts who were by no means rabid anti-Communist militarists:

> If the United States military are without a peer in any one technique of warfare, it is in putting forces ashore across a hostile beach. For the Bay of Pigs, all the necessary means were at Kennedy's hand. . . . Only after the disaster was upon them did he and his men realize that the venture which was essentially a military one had been fatally compromised in order to satisfy political considerations.[18]

> High Policy may still have been right when, under the leadership of Ambassador Averell Harriman, the decision was taken to gamble that a neutralist coalition might gradually tranquilize Laos. . . . There is no reason why, in such dealings, Harriman should be expected to think like a soldier. But someone should be doing so.[19]

Fighting Communist insurgency in the Third World was primarily a military matter. To be sure, the successful counterinsurgencies in Malaya and the Philippines were recognized as being political (and economic and social) as well as military, but the nonmilitary factors were evaluated for their contribution to the military suppression of the guerrillas. In Malaya, the British moved the peasants into separate settlements to isolate them from the guerrillas, and it worked. This was the root of the "strategic hamlets" program in Vietnam in the early 1960s, which failed signally; no note had been taken of the fact that the Malayan peasants and the guerrillas were ethnically different; the Vietnamese were not.

These were the attitudes with which U.S. civilian as well as military leadership entered Vietnam. At the very beginning of the Kennedy administration in 1961 there was a tendency to view the Vietnam situation as an internal political/military problem in which we could help with military and other advice. As we became more deeply engaged, and with our participation in the overthrow of President Diem, however, our attitudes became increasingly military. From that time until the years after 1965 when the enormity of the task began to be recognized, four basic assump-

---

[18]Murphy, 1961, p. 96.
[19]Marshall, 1962, p. 5.

tions governed American thinking about the types of actions to be pursued in Vietnam.

- The war was primarily military—the Korean War in the jungles two thousand miles to the southwest, to pick up Nixon's terminology. Guerrilla warfare was a lesser included case.
- The military war, both conventional and guerrilla, was mostly within South Vietnam, but it was substantially and materially supported by North Vietnam (the Democratic Republic of Vietnam, or DRV), and by the Soviet Union and Red China. The DRV was a sanctuary for the Communist forces in the south.
- In addition to fighting the military war on the ground, escalatory violence against the DRV—from the air only, in order to avoid Chinese and perhaps Soviet counterescalation—would show the enemy our resolve and convince him to withdraw.
- Within this context existed the Viet Cong (VC) revolutionary insurgency within South Vietnam, which would have to be kept under control and eventually overcome.

The overall military emphasis is apparent in a 1965 memorandum from Defense Secretary McNamara to President Johnson:

Our objective is to create conditions for a favorable settlement by demonstrating to the VC/DRV that the odds are against their winning. [To this end, we should] expand substantially the military pressure against the Viet Cong in the South and the North Vietnamese in the North and at the same time launch a vigorous effort on the [worldwide] political side to get negotiations started.[20]

The weight given to conventional military measures as compared with anti-guerrilla efforts is shown by the fact that McNamara recommended 13 concrete conventional military steps—four in South Vietnam, seven against North Vietnam, and two steps to strengthen forces within the United States—eight worldwide political initiatives, and only two counterguerrilla efforts. The last two consisted of one sentence each in a memorandum of many pages.

Such counterinsurgency effort as was attempted in the days when the United States was still acting in an advisory capacity tended to miss the point anyhow. Writing recently, General William Depuy contended that:

---

[20]Robert McNamara, memorandum for the President, quoted in Berman, 1982, pp. 179–186.

We now know that profound and subtle political issues lie at the heart of counterinsurgency. But in 1962 the program was more grossly defined as a combination of functions and activities in which we excelled—building roads, setting up medical clinics, distributing surplus farm commodities, broadcasting anticommunist arguments and training local armies in the use of U.S. weapons. The political issues were simply assigned to the State Department on a functional basis.[21]

In any case, so long as the war in the South was being abetted—perhaps directed—from the North, no effort within South Vietnam, conventional or counterinsurgent, could suffice. In a 1965 memorandum to the President, National Security Advisor McGeorge Bundy wrote:

We believe that the best available way of increasing our success in Vietnam is the development and execution of a policy of *sustained reprisal* against North Vietnam—a policy in which air and naval action against the North is justified by and related to the whole Viet Cong campaign of violence and terror in the South.[22]

Nor would the air war suffice to call off the North Vietnamese, never mind to win the direct war against the Viet Cong in the South. A few months later, Ambassador Maxwell Taylor cabled Secretary of State Rusk from Saigon:

The air campaign in the North must be supplemented by signal successes against the VC in the South before we can hope to create that frame of mind in Hanoi which will lead to the decisions we seek.[23]

Back and forth. In any case, by 1965, the military issues of conventional war—on the ground in the South and in the air over the North—clearly dominated, and political and counterguerrilla activities had become secondary.

It took little more than a year for the emphasis to begin shifting back to the much stickier counterinsurgency war, the still primarily military effort with major political and economic overtones that had come to be known as "pacification." In a memorandum to the President in October 1966, Secretary McNamara reported:

---

[21]Depuy, 1986, p. 25.

[22]McGeorge Bundy, memorandum to President Johnson, quoted in *The Pentagon Papers*, 1971, p. 423.

[23]Maxwell Taylor, cablegram to Secretary of State Rusk, quoted in *The Pentagon Papers*, 1971, p. 445.

We have done somewhat better militarily than I anticipated. . . . Yet there is no sign of an impending break in enemy morale and it appears that he can more than replace his losses by infiltration from North Vietnam and recruitment in South Vietnam. . . . Pacification has if anything gone backward. As compared with two, or four, years ago, enemy full-time regional forces and part-time guerrilla forces are larger; attacks, terrorism and sabotage have increased in scope and intensity; more railroads are closed and highways cut; the rice crop expected to come to market is smaller; we control little, if any, more of the population; the VC infrastructure thrives in most of the country. . . . [B]ecause the 1967 trend of pacification will, I believe, be the main talisman of ultimate U.S. success or failure in Vietnam, extraordinary imagination and effort should go into changing the stripes of that problem.[24]

In retrospect, the initial overemphasis on the conventional military as compared with the political, economic, and social counterinsurgency effort is even clearer, particularly to those participants at the time who were generating such doubts and stressing pacification and related programs. Kissinger wrote of his observations in 1965:

It seemed to me that regular North Vietnamese units, which were the chief target of our military operations, played the role of the matador's cape: they tempted our forces to lunge into politically insignificant areas while the Viet Cong infrastructure undermined the South Vietnamese government in the populated countryside.[25]

Robert Komer, who spent the early Vietnam years on McGeorge Bundy's National Security Council staff lobbying a new pacification program through the bureaucracy, and then went to Vietnam to administer it, retrospectively repeated his contemporary criticism of the overall U.S. thrust:

What has been termed the "overmilitarization" of the war can be traced partly to such institutional factors as the dominant role of the military in the U.S. aid and advisory structure and, over time, in the GVN [Government of Vietnam]. . . . When, moreover, the military controlled the vast bulk of the resources going into the war effort, it is hardly surprising that military considerations became predominant. . . . [This led to] the

[24]Robert McNamara, memorandum for President Johnson, October 14, 1966, quoted in *The Pentagon Papers*, 1971, pp. 542–549.
[25]Kissinger, 1979, p. 233.

adverse side effects of primary focus on the big-unit war; increased civilian casualties, economic damage, creation of refugees and the like. In their concentration on defeating the enemy in battle, the U.S. and GVN military gave wholly inadequate weight to the alienating impact of these side effects on the population whose control, if not support, was presumably the ultimate objective of the counterinsurgency effort.[26]

Neither the Kissinger nor the Komer view is mere hindsight. The pacification program started by Komer in Vietnam in the last years of the Johnson administration was taken over by the Nixon administration (with Henry Kissinger as National Security Council Director) and, according to a more disinterested analyst than either Komer or Kissinger, it worked:

By the end of 1968, the government was sufficiently recovered [from the Viet Cong Tet offensive] to plan and launch a systematic pacification offensive to recover lost ground and exploit the Tet-generated enemy weakness in the countryside. The drive called the Accelerated Pacification Campaign was Komer's final initiative. . . . [B]asic structural change in the government's rural policies [led to] steady improvement in levels of economic activity, reflecting better security as well as the payoff from many years of increasing development inputs. . . . These results were an outstanding success.[27]

Some think, in fact, that counterinsurgency was overemphasized in the later years of Vietnam. General DePuy, who himself has an extensive background in counterinsurgency, believes that toward the end of American participation in the Vietnam War:

Emphasis on the military dimensions of the war ran counter to the newly conventional wisdom. The pendulum had been given a mighty push. If you were "for" counterinsurgency, you were "against" conventional military thinking. Military operational plans were regarded at best as unnecessary and at worst reactionary, unenlightened and stupid.[28]

The differences are on the margin. In any case, to the extent that the new counterinsurgency doctrine worked, it was too late for Vietnam. But the evidence of Vietnam had changed the Interventionist Middle, and their viewpoints on current policy reflect the changes.

---

[26]Komer, 1986, pp. 42–60.
[27]Blaufarb, 1977, pp. 264–267.
[28]Depuy, 1986. p. 28.

Nobody in the Interventionist Middle school today believes that insurgency in the 1980s *begins* with externally inspired Communist disruption (none of today's arenas of guerrilla conflict is adjacent to a "sanctuary" equivalent to North Vietnam). Rather, insurgency in the 1980s is based on a complex mix of indigenous political, economic, and social factors. After insurgency begins, Communists may exploit it, and counterinsurgency must be similarly complex. For the Interventionists, military power is still an unfortunately necessary requirement, perhaps a central requirement, but to be applied successfully it must be appropriate to the insurgency at hand. Such an application is not easy.

Over the last decade, various writers starting from similar analytical bases have suggested somewhat different mixes of military and political, economic, and social causes for insurgency and measures for counterinsurgency. Gérard Chaliand, whose earlier writings were considered quite radical—the Foreword to his 1976 book stated that it was "the work of someone engaged in the struggle for revolution," written "without malice, and without apologetics"[29]—has more recently mounted his analyses from the standpoint of the counterinsurgents, still without malice and without apologetics. His 1985 book assumes, without detailed discussion, all of the justifiable causes for revolution, and then goes on to discuss the primary reason that the Communists gain control of indigenous revolutions and the outcome when they do:

> The necessities of the hard and prolonged struggle oblige the party to be strong, disciplined and rigid—in a word, militarized. A party of the Marxist-Leninist type is an admirable war machine, maintaining secrecy, organization and control. It is a remarkable instrument of battle which in its most difficult moments can stay afloat, but reveals itself after the victory not as a lever of development, but as an instrument dominated by bureaucrats and police.[30]

Realism about the insurgency leads to realism about the counterinsurgency:

> It is wrong to believe that the state must necessarily have the support of the population to win. So long as the guerrillas do not have the support and control of a very large part of the population—and that is rare—the state needs, in order to guide the counterinsurgency intelligently and energetically, only the support of a relatively small social base, and military predominance. Nonetheless, the state has a general

---

[29]Immanuel Wallerstein, "Foreword" to Chaliand, 1978, p. ix.
[30]Chaliand, 1985, p. 72.

interest in bringing concrete if limited benefits to the social sectors it wants to win over (clinics, schools, feeding programs, etc.). Other tasks are more urgent, however. . . . The state should try to take the initiative against the insurgents, harassing them with mobile forces and forcing them to employ their energies to defend themselves and survive, attacking the guerrillas in the zones where they are established, tracking them, setting up night ambushes with hunter-killer squads. Above all, the state must menace and destroy—after a long period of reconnaissance—their logistics (lines of communication and supplies).[31]

Chaliand is no Confronter, and he has a full understanding, from the inside, of guerrilla strategies, tactics, and ideologies, yet his prescription sounds remarkably close to the Vietnam search and destroy strategy. Douglas Blaufarb adds somewhat more political, economic, and social flavoring into the mix—but still as an additional seasoning rather than a primary ingredient. He emphasizes the military while apologizing for it:

We have seen that competent, professional police and military services are essential, and they must proceed in accordance with the principle of "making the people the target." Small, lightly armed units . . . should be the main reliance of the military side of the effort. The police . . . should play a major role in . . . programs requiring frequent contact with the public. Both soldiers and police must be brought to recognize the overriding importance of good relations with the population and make consistent programmatic efforts in pursuit of that goal, which will probably include small-scale civic action. Part-time popular militia . . . will also be essential. . . . This somewhat prolonged discussion of military aspects may give the impression that we see them as the major factor. In fact, they should be fully complemented by a program confronting the economic, social, and political problems of the affected regions, which, in the long run, is of equal importance. *Military aspects have a priority in time*, since other factors cannot progress far unless some measure of security exists. In the longer run, however, military and police operations, while they can greatly reduce and limit the insurgent movement, cannot be relied upon to eliminate it permanently. To do this, the regime must be shown to be deeply concerned about major popular

---

[31]Ibid., pp. 96–97.

needs and aspirations and also as able to do something effective to begin to meet them.[32]

In 1981, concepts of this sort were formalized by the United States Army in a Field Manual entitled *Low Intensity Conflict*[33] (the document decried by Disengager Michael Klare). The Manual, intended more for indigenous armed forces trained by the United States than for direct American intervention, is remarkable both for the emphasis put on nonmilitary activity (more than seems implied by Chaliand or Blaufarb) and the detail provided on both military and civil matters. The Manual's introduction to its basic concept, internal defense and development (IDAD), shows the broad civil/military sweep of the effort but lays down as a premise a military "priority in time" like that of Blaufarb.

> IDAD strategy involves the art and science of using political, economic, psychological and military powers of a government, including all police and internal security forces, to prevent or defeat insurgency. The U.S. concept is based on the strategy of simultaneous internal defense and internal development programs. The primary objective under this strategy normally will be a level of internal security which will permit economic, political, and social growth through balanced development programs. It is directed both toward the populace and insurgent.[34]

The scope and the major emphasis given to civil activities is shown by the fact that of the roughly 250 text pages, only about 100 are concerned with strictly military matters. One area not covered in the 1981 Manual, however, is U.S.-sponsored offensive guerrilla warfare against existing governments; the debate on the Nicaraguan Contras has raged over *whether* we should assist them, but very little has been written about *how* such operations can best be mounted and carried out.

In any case, the Army's Manual shows major learning since and because of Vietnam, learning facilitated by such civilian writers as Blaufarb, Komer, and Chaliand, not to mention dozens of less widely published military officers. How well it all works, however, is still an open question. The only place it has been tried (or may have been tried) since its publication in 1981 is El Salvador, where British military correspondent Tammy Arbuckle contends that it has not worked very well:

---

[32]Ibid., pp. 308–309. Italics added.
[33]Department of the Army, 1981.
[34]Ibid., p. 46.

[T]he American-sponsored, Vietnam-style military counterinsurgency strategy in El Salvador is not a success. . . . [This does not] stem solely from Salvadoran misapplication of U.S. counterinsurgency strategy. It is traceable to serious flaws in American military counter-insurgency strategy itself—mistaken strategic priorities; "top-down" offensive planning; static, unconcealed defenses; and inappropriate military aid. . . . These weaknesses in America's military counterin-surgency strategy, exemplified in El Salvador, were first apparent in Vietnam, where they caused thousands of unnecessary American casualties through ambushes, communist shellfire on unconcealed positions, and other avoidable battlefield situations. Washington, however, has failed to understand that these military defects contri-bute almost as much as political mistakes toward its poor performance against insurgents. . . . [There] has been no post-Vietnam reform of the American military's counter-guerrilla methods.[35]

The Arbuckle article brought a sharp rejoinder from a U.S. Marine Corps adviser to the Salvadoran military:

Throughout his article, Arbuckle betrays an ignorance of guerrilla doc-trine and current U.S. counterinsurgency strategy that can only be attributed to intellectual laziness. . . . It's only too obvious to me that Arbuckle lacks an appreciation for the tremendous strategic, tactical, and material improvements in Salvadoran military capabilities during the last year. . . . During the last year and a half, the Salvadoran guerrillas have been forced to backpedal. . . . [Even when they have won a battle, it is a] Pyrrhic victory that makes them consistent losers in the day-to-day grind of small-unit contacts. The most pervasive myth in Arbuckle's article is an alleged Vietnam similarity. The many *differences* between El Salvador and Vietnam are too numerous to cover here. Let me make one distinction, however. In Vietnam, 500,000 American servicemen were directly involved. . . . In El Sal-vador, the Salvadoran armed forces [have] the limited assistance of 55 American trainers and technical specialists.[36]

Military and civil concepts have changed substantially since and because of Vietnam; practices may be lagging. The 55-troop limitation in Salvador was due more to the conflict between the Noninterventionist Middle forces in the Congress and the Confronter administration than it was to the

---

[35]Arbuckle, 1985, pp. 46–56.
[36]Cole, May 1986, p. 72.

prescriptions of the Interventionist Middle. Nonetheless, that might be where many of the members of the Interventionist Middle would come out in considering the key "should" questions of the appropriate U.S. role in Third World conflicts; there is no magic in the number 55, but a lifting of the ceiling would raise fears of an open-ended approach to a new Vietnam in Central America.

THE ROLE OF THE UNITED STATES

Since 1969, the first year of the Nixon administration, one major constant in the Interventionist Middle's view of the U.S. role has been: Never again should we take over a counterinsurgency effort and run it by ourselves. Within this constraint, however, lies a vast area of ambiguity. The Interventionist label implies a willingness to intervene in some circumstances, but they have debated what circumstances, how large an intervention, which civil and military functions must remain indigenous and which may be appropriate for U.S. action, what kinds of forces should be used for these actions, and what we should do when our indigenous allies march off in directions we see as unpalatable or ineffective (or disastrous) without reaching any firm answers.

In July 1969 President Nixon told the correspondents covering him at a Guam stopover on the way to the Philippines that:

I believe the time has come that the United States, in our relations with all our Asian friends, [should] be quite emphatic on two points: One, that we will keep our treaty commitments, for example, with Thailand under SEATO; but, two, that as far as the problems of internal security are concerned, as far as the problems of military defense, except for the threat of a major power involving nuclear weapons, that the United States is going to encourage and has a right to expect that this problem will be increasingly handled by, and the responsibility for it will be taken by, the Asian nations themselves.[37]

This was the Nixon Doctrine. In his own review of Vietnam, Nixon gives as its background:

Since 1965, the United States had furnished most of the money, most of the arms, and a substantial portion of the men to help the South Vietnamese defend their freedom. . . . But as a result of this policy,

---
[37]Quoted in Kissinger, 1979, p. 224.

75

the South Vietnamese military had developed an unhealthy, and unsustainable, dependence on the United States. Now we decided to train and equip South Vietnam's army so that it would have the capability of defending the country itself. . . . Secretary of Defense Melvin Laird carried out this plan and dubbed it, appropriately, "Vietnamization." Our whole strategy depended on whether this program succeeded.[38]

The accuracy of Nixon's first statement about the initial predominant U.S. contribution (and, unstated, control) of the war is clear from the material quoted above from McNamara, Bundy, and Westmoreland. Whether Vietnamization was a sharp change of direction in 1969 or the formalization of a trend that had already begun in the Johnson administration is more conjectural. In any case, one lesson learned from the Vietnam War was that countries being defended by the United States must play the major role in their own defense.

The problem is that, once the principle had been established, its specific applications did not spring forth as a usable set of guidelines. Nixon and Kissinger claimed that the principle worked in Vietnam, but that the South Vietnamese Army could not defend itself against major invasion from the North without promised American aid, which was not forthcoming because of the Democratic Congress. For El Salvador, the Kissinger Commission report underlined the proposed U.S. role:

> The Commission recommends that the United States provide to El Salvador—subject to the conditions we specify later in this chapter—significantly increased levels of military aid as quickly as possible, so that the Salvadoran authorities can act on the assurance that needed aid will be forthcoming.[39]

The needs of the Salvadoran military, most of which had to be supplied or financed by the United States, included "Increased air and ground mobility, increased training, higher force levels, greater stocks of equipment and supplies, improved conditions for the troops, particularly medical evacuation helicopters."[40] And the major attached conditions were:

> demonstrated progress toward free elections; freedom of association; the establishment of the rule of law and an effective judicial system;

---

[38]Nixon, 1985, pp. 104–105.
[39]Kissinger Commission, p. 102.
[40]Ibid., p. 101.

and the termination of the activities of the so-called death squads, as well as vigorous action against those guilty.[41]

The recommendations for El Salvador, addressing the specific crisis conditions in that nation, were primarily military with a set of political conditions that the majority of the commission (but not three key members including Chairman Kissinger)[42] insisted should be required because they were necessary for political/military success in the country.

The military recommendations are expressions of the military-security-first view of the Interventionist Middle school. For Central America as a whole, however, given the luxury of time, the Commission stressed the basic need of the region, economic stabilization: "The crisis in Central America has no single, simple cause, but the troubled performance of the region's economies has been a major factor."[43] As the American role in the program to approach this (called by the press "a Marshall Plan for Central America"), the Commission proposed for the immediate emergency:

> new initiatives to deal with Central America's serious external debt problems . . . that the United States provide an immediate increase in bilateral economic assistance . . . that new official trade guarantees be made available . . . that the United States provide an emergency credit to the Central American Common Market Fund . . . that the United States join the Central American Bank for Economic Integration.[44]

For the medium and long term, the Commission recommended "that economic assistance over the five-year period beginning in 1985 total $8 billion."[45] Such economic assistance did not begin in 1985, and under Gramm-Rudman budget constraints, it is not likely to in the near future, which illustrates a major problem with the Interventionist Middle view of appropriate U.S. roles in preventing turmoil in the Third World.

Funding is and will continue to be a problem. At least as fundamental is the issue of the degree of U.S. control that goes with U.S. participation, in particular, what we do when indigenous leadership is acting so inappropriately (in our view) that they/we cannot win. The issue first arose, and in its most acute form, in 1963, as the Kennedy administration and its representatives in Vietnam came to believe that President Ngo Dinh Diem, under the malign influence of his brother, Ngo Dinh Nhu, and Madam Nhu, was

[41]Ibid., p. 104.
[42]Ibid., p. 130.
[43]Ibid., p. 40.
[44]Ibid., pp. 37–50.
[45]Ibid., p. 53.

becoming so unpopular as to make impossible a plausible defense against the Viet Cong. The *Pentagon Papers* show an agonized ambivalence within the U.S. administration as "Diem will lose it all" confronted "But we cannot contemplate the overthrow of a friendly and legitimate government."[46] On November 1, 1961, Vietnamese military commanders overthrew the regime, and Diem and Nhu were assassinated. Although the United States did not plan the coup, toward the end it was certainly not discouraged; the assassinations were undesired add-ons. The change of government led to a long period of instability in Saigon. It might be argued that without the U.S.-tolerated coup, defeat in Vietnam would have come 13 years earlier than it did; it might also be argued in the light of history that that would have been a good thing. Without taking that viewpoint, Kissinger records his views at the time:

I was appalled by the direct role the United States had played in the overthrow of South Vietnam's President Ngo Dinh Diem, which led to his assassination. This folly committed us to a course we could not foresee while undermining the political base for it.[47]

Kissinger has been accused of supporting, when Secretary of State, the 1973 overthrow of the left-wing President of Chile, Salvador Allende Gossens, but he denies it strongly:

[C]ontrary to anti-American propaganda around the world and revisionist history in the United States, our government had nothing to do with planning his overthrow and no involvement with the plotters. Allende was brought down by his own incompetence and inflexibility.[48]

In any case, Allende was not classed as a friend of the United States, and Kissinger has remained true to his doubts about overthrow of "friendly" governments and, indeed, about strong interference short of overthrow. He was appalled by the much more passive U.S. role in the overthrow of the Shah of Iran in 1978 (but not, with Ambassador Kirkpatrick, Somoza); as noted above, he dissented from the report of his own Commission on the degree of pressure to be put on El Salvador. Even in the case of the highly popular U.S. action in tolerating or encouraging the overthrow of President Ferdinand Marcos of the Philippines, he expresses specific and general doubts:

---

[46]*The Pentagon Papers*, 1971, pp. 194–231.
[47]Ibid., p. 231.
[48]Kissinger, 1982, p. 374.

[W]hatever else may be said about the Marcos regime, it contributed substantially to American security and had been extolled by American Presidents for nearly two decades. . . . My misgivings about the prevailing self-righteousness include no doubt about the impeccable democratic credentials of President Aquino. [But] I have grave concerns about the implications of these actions for the future, especially if this special case emerges as a general strategy. . . . Should America be the global arbiter of democratic elections? Are there no other overriding national interests? . . . [T]he U.S. government can only deal with a finite number of problems at one time. Finding the right moment will always be difficult. . . . Choosing the right means can prove even more complex. Knowing what in fact constitutes democratic reform is something the West has clearly not thought through.[49]

Komer seems to favor more active intervention when necessary, although more abstractly than Kissinger, and without specific reference to U.S. activity to change regimes:

When the U.S. is supporting local programs, it should not hesitate where necessary to use the leverage provided by this support to ensure that it is optimally utilized. . . . Should the local government prove so weak and ineffective that the U.S. decides on direct intervention, some form of combined command is probably indispensable.[50]

He is not explicit about what he would do if the local government were not only "weak and ineffective," but also uncooperative, or what action to take if that occurred at the highest levels. For Komer, as for most of the Interventionist Middle (even including Kissinger, at least as regards Marcos), such delicate issues must be decided case by case.

The Interventionist Middle sees the United States role as exerting *some* control and providing some economic and military assistance. The military assistance certainly includes finances, weapons, and training. How much more of a direct role for U.S. armed forces is called for, and how able they are to perform this role, are questions with no clearcut answers. In testimony before the Senate Armed Services Committee in 1984, General Paul Gorman, then Commander in Chief of the U.S. Southern Command, used a joint U.S./Honduran training exercise to illustrate his view as to the appropriate role for the American military:

---

[49]Kissinger, 1986g, pp. 1–3.
[50]Komer, 1986a, pp. 171–172.

Proper Role for U.S. Forces: The United States has a clear and consistent national strategy on the proper use of U.S. forces in a counterinsurgency role in low intensity conflicts. This has been called in turn the Truman, Eisenhower, Counterinsurgency (under Kennedy) and Nixon Doctrine. We assist and train; they fight. The United States is applying this same division of labor now in Latin America. AHUAS TARA II, the most recent U.S. and Honduran exercise, was designed to execute this strategy by assisting Honduras to deter and defend itself from external threats. AHUAS TARA II emphasized the use of [American] medical, intelligence, and engineer units—not combat forces.[51]

Were U.S. medical and engineer units to be involved in an actual war, they would very likely come under fire; whether this would lead to further American involvement is an open question. In any case, the U.S. Army has planned for further contingencies. The 250 pages of the Army's Field Manual on Low Intensity Conflict include a 46-page chapter on "U.S. Foreign and Internal Defense Operations" up to and including "Brigade-Size Backup Forces." As noted earlier, however, the Manual's stress is on indigenous forces trained by the United States in counterinsurgency techniques.

The capacity of U.S. forces to carry out counterinsurgency operations is not clear. In 1981, Richard Gabriel wrote:

The truth is that American forces today lack the doctrines, tactics, experience and even the manpower to fight a successful unconventional war in El Salvador or anywhere else. . . . Allowing the unconventional warfare capability of the United States to fall into disrepair is dangerous, given that they are the most likely type of forces to be required in the years ahead. The danger is increased by President Reagan's belief, and that of his advisers, that the Army does have the ability to engage in unconventional operations in Latin America if necessary.[52]

Gabriel wrote before the issuance of the 1981 version of the Field Manual on Low Intensity Conflict, which for better or worse substantially updated doctrine and tactics. In 1983, however, Edward Luttwak, a critic of the Pentagon respected by many in the building, wrote that the problem is:

---

[51]Gorman, 1984, p. 1126.
[52]Gabriel, 1981, pp. 4–8.

the defense establishment as a whole still operates under the implicit assumption that "low-intensity" warfare is merely a lesser included case of "real" war. . . . Let the United States go to war, virtually any war, and we would again see the Air Force's Tactical Air Command bombing away, and the Strategic Air Command too, most probably; if there is a coastline anywhere near, the Navy will claim two shares, one for its own tactical air and another for the big guns of its gloriously reactivated battleships; none would dare to deny the Marine Corps its own slice of territory. . . . Nor can the Army be expected to harm its own internal conviviality by failing to provide fair shares for all, armor even in the jungle, artillery even if the enemy hardly gathers, and so on. . . . [I]t is not merely specialized units that are needed but rather a separate branch so autonomous that it begins to resemble a separate service.[53]

No changes of this sort have been made, and in 1985 Deputy Assistant Secretary of Defense Noel Koch still admitted that "our national defense strategy is . . . woefully deficient at the low-intensity end of the spectrum."[54]

It is not completely clear what actual forces the United States would apply to any intervention requiring many more than 55 soldiers. Substantial controversy surrounds the Special Operations Forces (SOFs), direct descendants of President Kennedy's Green Berets.[55] The SOFs' role in counterinsurgency would be similar to the pacification approach in Vietnam (which raises the question of whether this can or should be attempted by other than indigenous forces). Other suggestions have been made to consider the Army's Light Infantry Divisions as a counterinsurgency force, which would imply more of a traditional conventional warfare approach to counterinsurgency. So long as troop limits remain at the two-digit level, the issue is moot, but it illustrates how far we are from a real capability to intervene with more than training and supplies, should we want to.

General Gorman discussed an additional U.S. role, somewhat akin to the deterrent function of our nuclear forces, and subject to the same question: What if the deterrent were to fail and we were called upon to use the forces? Gorman suggests:

---

[53]Luttwak, 1983, pp. 12–15.
[54]Meyer and Schemmer, 1985, p. 42.
[55]See, for example, Cohen, 1986; Bounds and McMichael, 1985.

the presence of U.S. military forces which [will] make evident both a willingness and a capacity to employ conventional fire and maneuver should our interests so require. And so long as these forces remain "over the horizon," in international waters or aerospace, and outside the interdicts of the War Powers Resolution, such deployments seem to be readily accepted by both Congress and the public.[56]

General Gorman's last sentence implies a constraint on expansion of counterinsurgency capabilities may be even more binding than budgets—public opinion. To some extent, opinion is still resonating to Vietnam. Difficult as it may be to remember in the 1980s, the assumption going into the 1960s that "of course the United States will respond to attempted Communist advances" did not allow for concern whether public or political opinion would endorse such response. An earlier search through the "limited-war" literature of the early 1960s and before turned up only two pages in one book that discussed domestic politics.[57]

When it turned out, in events culminating in the retirement of President Johnson and the traumatic political polarization of the late 1960s and early 1970s, that politics and public opinion had a lot to do with Vietnam, the lesson was well-learned, and it remains central today. Former Defense Secretary James Schlesinger, however, put the current issue into an even longer historical context:

Americans historically have embraced crusades (such as World War II) as well as glorious little wars. The difficulty is that the most likely conflicts of the future fall between crusades and such brief encounters as Grenada. Yet these in-between conflicts have weak public support. . . . The role of the U.S. in the future is that it must be prepared for, be prepared to threaten, and even be prepared to fight those intermediate conflicts that are likely to fare poorly on television. Whether this nation, the leader of the free world, can measure up to such challenges will to a large extent define the future shape of international politics.[58]

The dilemma of the Interventionist Middle is that they would like to believe, with Secretary Shultz, that "on such occasions we will be able to count on the full support of the American people. . . . Grenada shows that a president who has the courage to lead will *win* public support," but they

---

[56]Gorman, 1985b.

[57]The book was Morton Halperin's *Limited War for the Nuclear Age*, Wiley, New York, 1963. See Levine, 1972, p. 125.

[58]Schlesinger, 1985, p. 24.

have some difficulty in reading the polls, the tea leaves, or the politics that way. Edward Gonzalez thinks that perhaps sweet reason will do the trick:

> Unless there emerges a broader national consensus on Nicaragua that encompasses conservatives, moderates, and liberals, the President's options are likely to remain restricted in scope and ultimately ineffective, perhaps leading U.S. policy into a cul-de-sac. He can help build that policy consensus by addressing the more legitimate concerns of his critics, but his liberal opponents in particular will also need to meet the Administration half way if U.S. national interests are to prevail.[59]

Secretary of Defense Weinberger, however, was less sanguine. In what was widely taken as a challenge to Shultz's view that we must not overstress public opinion as a limitation on the use of power, Weinberger argued that:

> The single most critical element of a successful democracy is a strong consensus of support and agreement for its basic purposes. Policies formed without a clear understanding of what we hope to achieve will never work.[60]

Reflecting what has become the conventional wisdom among Confronters and some members of the Interventionist Middle—that politics and public opinion undermined the U.S. armed forces in Vietnam by forcing limitations and ultimately a withdrawal that turned victory into defeat, and that we cannot let this happen again—Weinberger also contended that:

> If we decide it is necessary to put combat troops into a given situation, we should do so wholeheartedly and with the clear intention of winning. . . . Before the United States commits combat forces abroad, there must be some reasonable assurance that we will have the support of the American people and their elected representatives in Congress.[61]

Where the Shultz-Weinberger debate comes out is not clear. What is quite clear, however, is that Confronters as well as the Interventionist Middle accept the constraint—based on public opinion or prudence—that the United States is not going to send substantial numbers of troops into combat in the Third World except (perhaps) to meet the direst threats to the national interest. *This is a major change wrought by Vietnam.*

---

[59]Gonzalez, 1986, p. 2.
[60]Weinberger, 1985, p. 2.
[61]Ibid., p. 10.

U.S. public opinion continues to limit actions in Central America. Aware of the constraints imposed by opinion, the Interventionist Middle generally endorsed U.S. support for the Nicaraguan Contras but, unlike the Confronters, did so with the clear objective of forcing the Sandinistas into accommodation with other Central American nations and with us, not treating them as a "cancer that has to be excised," in Reagan's words. In 1985, General Gorman told the Senate Armed Services Committee:

> I am one soldier who strongly approves of efforts to find a negotiated settlement of the conflicts in Latin America. . . . But I would emphasize to this committee that there would be no dialog, no negotiations, no practicable diplomacy with the Nicaraguans were it not for those freedom fighters, and were it not for the U.S. military presence in Central America. . . .[62]

The Kissinger Commission endorsed negotiations with more conditioning detail, and endorsed the Contras more tentatively:

> [W]e recommend, first, an effort to arrange a comprehensive regional settlement. . . . The original peace initiatives of Nicaragua have given little cause for optimism [but] more recently [as of January 1984], after the U.S. actions in Grenada, Managua has hinted at some accommodations in its external and internal policies. . . . The Commission believes, however, that whatever the prospects seem to be for productive negotiations, the United States must spare no effort to pursue the diplomatic route. . . . [T]he majority of the members of the Commission, in their respective individual judgments, believe that the efforts of the Nicaraguan insurgents represent one of the incentives working in favor of a negotiated settlement and that the future role of the United States in those efforts must therefore be considered in the context of the negotiating process. The Commission has not, however, attempted to come to a collective judgment on whether, and how, the United States should provide support for these insurgent forces.[63]

The chairman of the Commission, however, speaking for himself two years later, was much more explicit about the mutually supporting roles of negotiations and Contra pressure:

---

[62]Gorman, 1985a, pp. 1206–1207.
[63]Kissinger Commission, pp. 115–116.

The debate over aid to the Nicaraguan *Contras* is at last coming to an end. It is likely that the Reagan Administration will receive much of what it requested for military aid. . . . [T]he United States [has] three broad policy choices: a) It can let existing trends in Nicaragua continue and then seek to contain the resulting military, intelligence and political machine. The National Bipartisan Commission on Central America, of which I was chairman, rejected this approach unanimously. . . . b) It can seek to overthrow the Sandinista regime. This is impossible without direct military intervention. . . . c) It is therefore time to bring rhetoric in line with operating policy. The most realistic course is a combination of negotiation and pressure designed to deprive the Sandinista regime of the capability to subvert or undermine its neighbors. A joint strategy should seek to separate Nicaragua's internal arrangements from its ability to project purposes across its frontiers. . . . The immediate goal must be for Nicaragua to reduce its Cuban and Soviet connections to traditional state-to-state relations.[64]

Kissinger's program illustrates the major division over Central American policy between the Confronters and the Interventionist Middle. The Confronters, in constant pursuit of gains in the zero-sum game against the Communists, wanted to use the Contras to overthrow the Sandinista government in Nicaragua, or to change the Bolsheviks to Mensheviks, which amounts to the same thing. The Interventionist Middle exemplified by Kissinger did not eschew the Contras, but it saw them as a pressure tool to achieve stability in Central America by forcing the Nicaraguan regime, not necessarily changed internally, into acceptance of an idiosyncratic role, isolating it from its Communist sponsors and insulating its neighbors from Sandinista threats.

Until 1981 or perhaps 1977, the Interventionist Middle was the dominant school—the "Establishment" school. (In the making of American arms policy, one could argue that with the Carter administration the weight shifted toward the Noninterventionist Middle, which had traditionally been the loyal opposition within the Establishment.) In any case, with the election of Reagan, the Confronters gained control over Third World arms policy for the first time in recent history. The shift may be permanent and the crucial debates of the future may be those between the Confronters and the Interventionist Middle; but political "regression to the mean" could return the policymaking power to a position near the border between the two Middle

---

[64]Kissinger, 1986, pp. 1–6.

schools. President Bush and Secretary of State Baker seem to be moving in that direction. At any rate, the Noninterventionist Middle will continue to exert substantial influence on these policies as indeed it has, using the Congress and the media to force the Reagan administration to implement Third World policies considerably milder than their Confronter rhetoric would imply.

7. The Noninterventionist Middle

U.S. INTERESTS

Opposition to foreign interventions has roots in American history going back to the Mexican War of 1846. For the next 100 years, this opposition was generally ignored or overcome by decisionmakers, and we won the ensuing wars. Korea was ambiguous; Vietnam provided the first clear instance in which the Noninterventionists could truly argue that we had lost. The loss caused a national rethinking of the automatic every-Communist-expansion-is-a-threat concept of U.S. interests; for the Noninterventionist Middle, the consensus movement toward the limited concept of national interests that they had espoused all along required a more serious and perhaps less rhetorical approach than had previously been necessary. The Carter administration tried such approaches, exposing themselves to attacks like Kirkpatrick's on the substitution of left-wing for right-wing dictatorships.

In any case, with the election of Reagan the Noninterventionist Middle returned to the more comfortable position of critical opposition, expressing national interests mainly in terms of the current policies they opposed rather than the principles they favored. Because the Reagan administration was predominantly Confronter in philosophy and (perhaps slightly less) in policy, the Noninterventionist quarrel was with the Confronter administration, and their shots usually passed harmlessly over the heads of the Interventionist Middle.

At the beginning of the Vietnam war, the Noninterventionist Middle was the loyal opposition to a substantial consensus accepting the automatic assumption that the United States should intervene almost anywhere in the Third World to prevent the collapse of dominoes.

The assumption was accepted by the Eisenhower administration, and was not an issue between Kennedy and Nixon in the 1960 election. The Noninterventionists were within the Kennedy camp, but as a minority, under suspicion because many of them had favored Adlai Stevenson for the nomination. In 1958, their theme had been expressed in a classic phrase of Chester Bowles: "the decisive advantage would be held by those who understood the political, economic and ideological forces which increasingly would shape the minds of men."[1]

About the same time—several years before Vietnam became a salient American issue—Walter Lippmann attacked the military aid on which the Noninterventionist Middle believed the Eisenhower administration had predicated its Third World strategy:

[T]he most pressing issue is the Russian and Chinese challenge for the leadership of Asia and of Africa. If we are to meet it with success, we must, I am sure, abandon the notion that the Russian and Chinese revolutions can be reversed or that the spread of communism in the surrounding countries can be contained by giving armaments to the local military commanders and by establishing our own bases.[2]

And as Vietnam came to the fore at the beginning of the Kennedy administration, *The New Republic* set forth what with hindsight appears to be some pretty good prophecy about the slippery slope they saw the administration starting down. In May 1961, the magazine editorialized:

The decision on May 14 to send in nearly 100 of the specialists in irregular warfare who have been trained at Fort Bragg may prove a most fateful one. For if these Americans are ever under fire . . . once there have been even a few well-publicized casualties, the prestige of the U.S. will have been . . . committed. . . . The choice will then be humiliating withdrawal as the size of the challenge grows clear or progressively deeper involvement in a stalemate which may not admit of

[1]Bowles, 1968, p. 6.
[2]Lippman, 1959, p. 41.

a conclusive "victory" in anything less than a decade—some experts say longer.[3]

Within the administration, John McNaughton would not refer to "humiliation" until five years later. In November 1961, another *New Republic* editorial attacked the interventionists in language that mimicked nearly perfectly the highly classified memos Rusk, McNamara, and others were writing at the time. The people advocating deeper U.S. involvement in Vietnam were:

> those who insisted that either we stand up and fight now or fall later, that the U.S. cannot tolerate a defeat here because it would accelerate the flight into the Communist orbit of all Southeast Asia—Indonesia, the new Malay State, Cambodia, Laos, Thailand, Burma, Singapore. The line can be held, however, if there is a prompt infusion of U.S. fighting men. Such intervention—so say the "hardboiled"—would show Asians that we really mean business and are prepared to take grave risks.[4]

In 1965, Hans Morgenthau continued the line of argument against the dominoes:

> If one probes beneath the rationalizations for our military presence in South Vietnam, one finds as the dominant motivation the fear that if South Vietnam were to go Communist, no nation threatened by Communism would entrust its protection to us. . . . We have even dignified this historic determinism with the name of a theory, the so-called "Domino Theory." . . . This theory is . . . but a replica of a vulgar Marxism which also believes in the inevitable spread of Communism from one country to the rest of the world.[5]

In the meantime, within the administration and presumably unknown to the editorialists and writers for *The New Republic*, George Ball, President Johnson's loyal dove, was making similar arguments. In 1965, Ball urged the President to get out instead of getting in, and argued the weakness of the domino theory. Again, "humiliation" was a key word:

> Once we suffer large casualties, we will have started a well-nigh irreversible process. Our involvement will be so great that we cannot—without national humiliation—stop short of achieving our complete objectives. *Of the two possibilities I think humiliation would*

[3]"Commitment in Saigon," *The New Republic*, May 22, 1961, pp. 3–4.
[4]"Going But Not Gone," *The New Republic*, November 6, 1961, p. 5.
[5]Morgenthau, 1965, p. 13.

be more likely than the achievement of our objectives—even after we have paid terrible costs. . . . In my judgment, if we act before we commit substantial U.S. troops to combat in South Vietnam we can, by accepting some short-term costs, avoid what may well be a long-term catastrophe. . . . We have tended to exaggerate the losses involved in a complete settlement in South Vietnam. . . . On balance, I believe we would more seriously undermine the effectiveness of our world leadership by continuing the war and deepening our involvement than by pursuing a carefully plotted course toward a compromise solution.[6]

As befits a middle school, however, the Noninterventionists did not all go all the way. Running for President in 1968, Senator Robert Kennedy, a fairly recent convert to nonintervention from his super-"hardboiled" stance in the early days of his brother's administration, wrote (repeating a 1967 speech), that:

Without doubt, the so-called "domino theory" is a vast oversimplification of international politics [but if] the domino theory is an unsatisfactory metaphor, still it contains a grain of truth. World politics is composed of power and interest; it is also spirit and momentum. A great power does not cease to be that because it suffers a defeat peripheral to its central interests.[7]

After the war, the Noninterventionist Middle did not accept the Nixon/Kissinger contention that they (and the Disengagers) had forced the United States to renege on a commitment to South Vietnam, which in turn led to the fall of the South and a decade of falling dominoes throughout the 1970s. They were distressed when it turned out, in the words quoted earlier from Tom Hayden, "that Hanoi has an imperial design on Cambodia and has largely done away with pluralism in the south," but they challenged even the assertion that dominoes had fallen the wrong way since and because of Vietnam. In 1986, Carter administraton Assistant Secretary of State Richard Holbrooke looked within Asia itself:

After a period of widespread concern over the political stability of East Asia in the wake of America's Indochina debacle, the region's dramatic economic achievements were "discovered" by the West. At the same time there was a realization, and a sense of relief, that the "dominoes" of Southeast Asia did not fall, and that the United States,

---

[6]George Ball, memorandum to the President, in *The Pentagon Papers*, pp. 450–454.
[7]Kennedy, 1968, pp. 186–187.

contrary to widely voiced fears, did not abandon its historical interest and involvement in the region. . . . Most important is the virtual absence, with the single notable exception of the Philippines, of communist insurgencies that threaten national stability. For this situation, Asia owes a considerable debt of gratitude to the Vietnamese, who have so successfully discredited the attractiveness of Soviet-style revolutionary government.[8]

Holbrooke went on from there to generalize from Asia and history to the entire globe and policy:

The attitude recently in vogue in some influential American political circles was to deny that such transitions in the developing world ever work to the advantage of the West. Indeed, some commentators have gone so far as to suggest that all transitions from right-wing authoritarian regimes end up benefiting only equally or more repressive extremist, and perhaps pro-Soviet, leftists. But this fatalistic attitude is both pointless and short on historical substantiation. It ignores Portugal's peaceful "revolution of flowers"; it overlooks the successful restoration of democracy in Spain by Generalissimo Francisco Franco's handpicked successor; and it shortchanges the most dramatic political developments in this hemisphere in the past decade: the revival of democracy in Brazil, Uruguay and Argentina. And now, most dramatically, it cannot account for developments in the Philippines.[9]

The clear object of Holbrooke's attack is Ambassador Kirkpatrick, who has claimed some of these democratic restorations as evidence for her contention that we should hold to "authoritarianism" because it is reversible. Holbrooke's contention is that Kirkpatrick's protective measures for authoritarian regimes would prevent the reversions to democracy.

The Noninterventionists differ too from the Confronters on the objectives and strategy of the Soviet Union, but differences between the two Middle schools are small. The central theme of the Interventionist Middle Sovietologists was fairly cautious Soviet opportunism. The Noninterventionists tend to agree. The editors of one survey of Third World policy used their summary to criticize the Reagan administration viewpoint for ignoring the constraints imposed by reality on Soviet activities. They questioned the administration's:

---

[8]Holbrooke, 1986, pp. 733–741.
[9]Ibid, p. 748.

vision of Marxism as a hostile, aggressive ideology whose adherents in the Third World were inherently and irretrievably anti-American and typically pro-Soviet. . . . The Administration . . . tended to ignore the deep rifts that had arisen among Third World radicals and between them and the Soviet Union.[10]

More generally, Stephen Rosenfeld, an editor of *The Washington Post* specializing in foreign affairs, attacked the Reagan administration's Third World premises and policies in what might be taken as a manifesto setting forth the Noninterventionist Middle's concept of the national interest in the 1980s:

As practiced by Presidents Truman, Eisenhower, Nixon and Carter . . . containment is a defensive theory referring to efforts to limit the further spread of Soviet power. The Reagan Doctrine goes over to the offensive. It upholds liberation, the goal of trying to recover communist-controlled turf for freedom. . . . It was not . . . a sense of history that produced the Reagan Doctrine. It was an event in history, the appearance during the 1970s of a third wave of newly-declared or alleged Marxist states, following the earlier waves launched by the two world wars. . . . On the [American] right . . . they were immediately received as the integrated and consequential reflection of a new global imbalance brought on by a default of American will—the "Vietnam syndrome"—and by the Kremlin's sure-handed orchestration of Soviet troops, arms and surrogates. . . . It was precisely here that the Brezhnev Doctrine of 1968 assumed a new life in the American mind. . . . Still, the Reagan Administration's inclinations on this score needed to be jolted into life. The opportunity came suddenly in the fall of 1983 in Grenada. . . . [F]or the first time, communism—if you apply the label to the elements deposed in Grenada—had been shown to be reversible . . . [Grenada] gave the Reagan team new courage to deal with its considerable frustrations in Nicaragua. . . . What is the record in Nicaragua and Afghanistan and the other places where the Reagan Doctrine is being tested? The President's defenders say he is performing a moral duty and fulfilling a strategic purpose and doing so prudently, without undue cost or risk to the United States. But this is too simple. The President, without conveying a clear sense of purpose, has pointed the country more deeply into open-ended conflicts with major geopolitical implications on three continents. In each of these places he states an intent to produce a

---

[10]Sewell, Feinberg, and Kallab, 1985, p. 6.

negotiation leading to reconciliation, democracy and civil peace. No such result has yet come about. . . . So far the President has not raised the level of American commitment in any of these insurgencies to any degree that truly threatens the Soviet position [but] the possibility exists that Washington, in a heady mood, could push too hard for Soviet tolerance in the 1980s. . . . The issue finally facing us is not simply the measure of devotion to our ideals. It is the wisdom and value of American involvement in foggy conditions and the question of how best to preserve American interest in the long run.[11]

Rosenfeld suggested that the administration is impelled by a "moral duty" as well as a "strategic purpose." If Ronald Reagan was the first Confronter president in recent history, however, Jimmy Carter may have been the first Noninterventionist president since Hoover; and Carter put his own typically Noninterventionist moral imperatives into his "human rights" view of U.S. interests. He writes in his *Memoirs*:

Our country has been strongest and most effective when morality and a commitment to freedom and democracy have been most clearly emphasized in our foreign policy. . . . However, since Truman's days in the White House, persistent support of such a foreign policy has often been lacking. . . . Because of the heavy emphasis that was placed on Soviet-American competition, a dominant factor in our dealings with foreign countries became whether they espoused an anti-communist line. . . . When I announced my candidacy in December 1974, I expressed a dream: "That this country set a standard within the community of nations of courage, compassion, integrity, and dedication to basic human rights and freedoms."[12]

The extent to which this ideal was actually implemented in the Carter years is open to some question, but it has remained an important influence on the thinking of the Noninterventionist Middle. Congressman Stephen Solarz (D-NY), in a column headlined "It's Time for the Democrats to Be Tough-Minded," set as his central theme, "The beginning of wisdom here would be for the Democrats to recognize that it is the Soviet Union that poses the most serious threat to our values and interests," but he embraced human rights morality as a major mode of combating that threat:

---

[11]Rosenfeld, 1986, pp. 699–714.
[12]J. Carter, 1982, pp. 142–143.

In the third world, we must distinguish between wars of national liberation—as in Afghanistan and Cambodia where it is appropriate for us to aid indigenous resistance forces—and civil wars—as in Nicaragua, where it is inappropriate for us to engage in efforts to overthrow internationally recognized governments. The Democrats ... differ from the Administration on human rights. We must make clear our opposition to tyranny on the left but also continue to oppose repression on the right. ... Indeed, in many third world countries, such as the Philippines and South Africa, ... the best way for us to contain Communism is not to embrace authoritarianism but to promote democracy.[13]

Alan Tonelson, Associate Editor of *Foreign Policy* magazine, argued, however, that any "universal" standard for foreign policy going beyond a narrow definition of national interest fails to budget our limited means against our highest priority objectives; and on this basis, he attacked *all* American foreign policy from Nixon through Reagan (and also Solarz):

More than 10 years after the end of the Vietnam War, American foreign policy still suffers from delusions of universalism. ... Much less attention has been paid to anchoring policy to a concrete idea of national interest—a finite set of intrinsicially important goals either essential or beneficial to the country's survival, its prosperity, the psychological well-being of its population, or any combination of these. ... Where Nixon and Kissinger looked to détente with the Soviets as a way of preventing challenges to U.S. interests too serious for American allies and clients to handle, Carter looked to new varieties of national behavior, and to certain alleged characteristics of Third World upheaval, that defined these challenges out of existence. ... Because the Nixon-Kissinger and Carter foreign policies fundamentally agreed that America's interests were universal, the foreign policy controversies of the 1970s [did not] focus ... on clashing sets of U.S. priorities. ... The need to show American resolve for its own sake is sometimes explicitly cited in Reagan administration rhetoric. ... Yet there is less to this form of international image making than meets the eye. Those who emphasize credibility tend vastly to overestimate even a superpower's ability to project an impression of power and capability regardless of whether that power or capability truly exists. Representative Stephen Solarz ... implicitly equated the national-interests standard in importance [for U.S. aid to resistance struggles] with considerations such as whether a rebellion is

---

[13]Solarz, 1985, p. A27.

a genuine national liberation struggle and whether a satisfactory negotiated settlement seems possible.[14]

Everyone agrees, of course, that the "national interest" should be the primary (or, properly interpreted, the sole) criterion for U.S. policy in the
Third World or anywhere else. Since everyone defines it his own way,
however—and within the Middle schools the definitions get rather
complex—the national-interest standard does little to end controversy.

Examining American policy in Central America against various interpretations of the national interest, the Noninterventionist Middle does not
dismiss the importance of the area to the United States. In addition to
such issues as economics, immigration, and drugs, potential military threats
are taken seriously. Joseph Cirincione and Leslie Hunter argue that:

> The real problem is not leftist regimes per se but that Soviet military
> facilities might be established in the wake of Soviet-aligned guerrilla
> victories. . . . The United States must prevent the introduction of
> powerful offensive weapons such as MiG-23s into Central America. It
> must also be vigilant against incremental steps . . . which could
> transform Nicaragua's ports and other military facilities into bases
> from which the U.S.S.R. could operate. . . . The United States can
> live with the Sandinistas as long as they refrain from acting as instru-
> ments of Soviet foreign policy.[15]

Where the Noninterventionist Middle did attack the Reagan administration, and disagreed also to a substantial extent with the Interventionist Middle, was on Central America as a test of U.S. credibility, and on the resulting effect on Latin American and other dominoes. Echoing the chastened
view that all the schools except perhaps the Disengagers brought out of
Vietnam, the Noninterventionists believe that credibility issues in Central
America are largely self-created. One writer (at the American Enterprise
Institute, which was generally counted as a conservative institution before
Reagan) suggests that, "The Reagan Administration chose to make the Sal-
vadoran civil war the central test of its foreign policy toward the Soviet
Union during its initial weeks in power because it wanted a test, not
because it was justified."[16]

More generally, Viron Vaky, former Assistant Secretary of State for
Interamerican Affairs and Ambassador to several Central American countries, contends that:

---

[14]Tonelson, 1985/1986, pp. 49–72.
[15]Cirincione and Hunter, 1984, pp. 173–189.
[16]Dominguez, 1982, p. 33.

It is not hard to be at best confused and at worst alarmed over the thrust and likely outcome of the administration's policies in the region. . . . Terms such as "vital interest" and "security threat" have been freely used without precision, almost as code words. . . . The administration's affirmation that Central America is vital to U.S. security is defended basically on three grounds: (1) credibility; (2) dominoes; and (3) protecting America's rear. . . . It is not that the credibility argument never has substance, but [its] preoccupation with global images diverts attention from local realities, and fosters simplistic approaches to complex situations. . . . The flaw in the domino argument is that is it presented as if it functioned automatically. What happens in one country obviously influences what happens in another, but how much, in what form and with what result depends upon circumstances. . . . The "ripple effect" within the confines of the relatively similar nations of Central America is one thing; its extension to Mexico, Colombia, Venezuela, and the United States is something else. What is implicit in [the strategic rear] argument is the assumed requirement for hegemony, i.e., for the United States to be the dominant and uncontested external influence in the region. . . . The implication of these arguments, moreover, is that a negotiated political settlement will not do if it perpetuates a "leftist" foothold in the region. . . . The point here is that the Reagan administration's security premises are cast in a Manichaean absoluteness straight out of the 1950s.[17]

Of course, it was fairly easy for the Noninterventionist Middle to attack the extremes of Reagan administration policy, but they exhibited the same doubts about the more moderate Kissinger Commission report, stressing the portions of this somewhat fuzzy consensus document with which they most disagree. To Latin Americanist James Chace, "The most grievous flaw of the report . . . is its insistence on staking the 'credibility' of the U.S. itself on a desirable outcome in two small, weak, and poor countries in Central America," and he contrasted the Commission report to the Cirincione/Hunter piece quoted above, recommending that we focus on precluding any Soviet military threat rather than worrying about leftist regimes as such. Chace said that "This suggests a negotiation that would be well worth considering. It is not brought up in the Kissinger report."[18]

In sum, the Noninterventionist Middle agrees with the Interventionists on the cautious and opportunistic nature of Soviet activities in the Third

[17]Vaky, 1984, pp. 235–241.
[18]Chace, 1984, pp. 45–46.

World, and on this they both differ from the Confronters and their zero-sum game; neither Middle school would return to the automatic responses of the 1960s. Interventionists, however, continue to stress the need for the United States to play the nonzero-sum game against the Soviets, maintaining the credibility of our willingness to defend our worldwide interests. The Noninterventionists are more inclined to say, as they did before and during Vietnam, "So what, unless the particular area of play or issue impinges on a very specific American security concern."

The events since the fall of Saigon in 1975—the weight of Soviet-supported Hanoi on the rest of the Indochinese peninsula, the Soviet invasion of Afghanistan, and some of the more blatant antidemocratic activities of the Sandinistas—keep the Noninterventionists from returning all the way to the innocent 1950s "minds of men" interpretation of insurgency.

INSURGENCY: CAUSES AND RESPONSES

From before Vietnam to the present, the Noninterventionist Middle has remained consistent in its views of the causes of insurgency and the appropriate responses. The causes are economic and political, exacerbated by Communist exploitation—a statement with which even many Confronters would agree. Agreement ends here, however: the Noninterventionists believe that the economic and political causes of insurgency should lead to responses in kind, reforms, and an end to repressions. While the Interventionist Middle might agree in principle with the need for reforms, they would still put military security first, at least in time and probably in importance also. An additional emphasis of the Noninterventionist Middle—their belief that a repressive regime will ultimately engender an insurgency to overthrow it—differs substantially from the position of the Interventionist Middle

As the United States prepared to take its first steps into Vietnam, the Noninterventionist Middle disagreed not only about "whether," but about "how." To Chester Bowles, the struggle for the minds of men meant that the issues between democracy and Communism, particularly in the Third World, were other than military:

In many countries our efforts should put less emphasis on the maintenance of outsize ånd out-of-date military machines and more emphasis on people—on effort to raise the level of literacy, to provide equitable distribution of land, to foster community development projects, to stimulate the growth of free institutions such as labor unions, to establish public health programs, and to train public administrators in modern techniques.[19]

The Noninterventionist Middle did not join the Disengagers in dismissing military force as irrelevant on both sides or irrelevant on ours, but they suggested that the direct use of such force was both secondary:

> In South Vietnam ... the United States seeks to win the struggle by mechanical means (helicopters and weed-killers) forgetting all over again that a revolutionary war can be won only if the little people in the villages and the hills can be persuaded that they have a stake in fighting on our side.[20]

and damnably difficult to apply:

> For in Vietnam, U.S. troops would face three kinds of enemies: first, the real "farmer-by-day fighter-by-night" types. ... Then there are the guerrillas who are trained and infiltrated from the north and the west [with] support and guidance from professional leaders who are infiltrated with them. Third, there are the specially trained troops who may or may not be indigenous to South Vietnam and who are infiltrated across the border to reassemble near their selected points of action. ... They operate as regular military units.[21]

This analysis, in the *New Republic* showed no illusions about the war being simply a rebellion by grievance-laden indigenous backwoodsmen; it was, in fact, quite prescient for 1961. By 1965—after four years of war against the Viet Cong by the American-advised South Vietnamese government, and at the beginning of the major U.S. military intervention—the same magazine was in something of an "I-told-you-so" posture:

> [T]he Viet Cong still exercise effective political control over a third to a half of the population of the South, manage to levy taxes of sorts in 41 of the South's 44 provinces, and do so with a military strength that the U.S. officially estimates at 140,000 or 165,000 men who are pitted against 600,000 South Vietnamese soldiers and 150,000 American ones. The "interference" of Hanoi does not explain this. ... Oppressed subjects of despotic or corrupt Asian governments may seek relief from their woes by turning to some kind of Marxist-led movement ... but our armed forces cannot save governments from

[19]Bowles, 1960, p. 35.
[20]"Z," 1962, p. 5.
[21]*The New Republic*, November 6, 1961, pp. 4–5.

their own people, or prohibit others from making "unwise" political choices.[22]

And in a 1968 debate with Senator Eugene McCarthy, his Disengager rival for the Democratic presidential nomination, Senator Robert Kennedy did not abandon the need for military pressures to help force the Communists to serious negotiations preserving an independent South Vietnam. Rather, he argued that the Viet Cong are:

> not going to turn over their arms [and] live in peace if the Government is going to be run by General Ky and General Thieu. . . . I would demand privately and publicly an end of public corruption . . . a land reform program that's meaningful so that they can gain the support of the people themselves.[23]

Robert Kennedy's program for Vietnam was not tried; Richard Nixon's was. It did not save South Vietnam, but Nixon and Kissinger claim that the fault lay in American politics.

Charles Maechling bridges the gap between Vietnam and Central America, apologizing for his 1960s within-government contribution to oversimplifying the issues of counterinsurgency and suggesting that there has been little improvement in the intervening 25 years. Decrying the lack of an applied strategic theory of counterinsurgency then and now, he writes:

> [W]hen the Kennedy White House called on the National Security Council for a counterinsurgency policy embracing military, economic, social, and psychological factors, this was translated by agency heads into a request for an operational directive that would carve out agency missions, provide the basis for military "doctrine," and set guidelines for furnishing equipment and training to foreign security forces. The result was a 30-page document, drafted by an interdepartmental committee which I chaired. [It] was a somewhat simplistic document. . . . [Today, in] Central America, "free elections" without a guarantee of drastic social and economic reform is a cop-out. . . . Political change without redistribution of land and wealth, and an end to autonomy of armies and security forces, is a meaningless charade. . . . An effective counterinsurgency strategy should be part of a foreign policy that is

---

[22]"Dare We Negotiate?" *The New Republic*, November 6, 1965, p. 6.
[23]"Highlights of Kennedy-McCarthy Television Debate," *The New York Times*, June 3, 1968.

both detached and flexible toward revolutionary change in other countries.[24]

The difficulties of the military priority for El Salvador are made quite explict by another analyst who attacks

the Reagan administration's pursuit of that hoary policy . . . of "building democracy" by backing up right-wing military establishments. Nowhere is it more dangerous than in El Salvador. . . . The great setback for the guerrillas in 1980 came not in their rural strongholds but in the cities, not as a result of the [land] reforms but precisely because of the ruthless repression that killed almost 10,000 people in a year, among them many key members of the rebel organizations. Washington repeatedly condemned the abuses as both morally wrong and politically counterproductive. U.S. Ambassador Robert White and his successors in the U.S. mission argued that right-wing death squads and the military's semi-clandestine slaughter ultimately benefitted the rebels. . . . Yet this rather abstract reasoning . . . was difficult for many officers to understand.[25]

Robert Leiken generalizes the Noninterventionist view of the causes of revolutionary turmoil to Central America as a whole, and then relates it to specifics in a number of countries, damning all sides:

Thus economic, social, and ideological transformations [of the early 1970s] were not followed by adjustments in the political apparatus. . . . Instead, democratic political channels were blocked. Agrarian reform was stymied or paralyzed. Labor unions encompass only a small minority of the working population. . . . Instead in El Salvador, Guatemala and Nicaragua, left-led popular organization and guerrilla movements, often with powerful Soviet and Cuban influence, have incorporated and directed popular discontent. . . . [T]he Nicaraguan revolution seems to contradict its own rhetoric. Nor has it provided the "pluralistic, democratic, non-aligned model" that the revolutionary leadership promised the Nicaraguan people and their international supporters. . . . The credibility gap in Sandinista rhetoric is surpassed by the difference between image and reality in "reformist," "democratic" Honduras. . . . Honduran leaders seem to have democracy on their lips, but war on their minds. If the democracy of Honduras is America's standard, U.S. avowed support for democratization will appear to Central Americans as

[24]Maechling, 1984, pp. 34–40.
[25]Dickey, 1984, pp. 36–39.

100

one more example of U.S. hypocrisy masking U.S. hegemonism. Central America is at an impasse.... Honduras and Nicaragua presented as alternatives, sometimes appear rather as mirror images: Honduras of reform with repression, inequality and dependence; Nicaragua of revolution with repression, scarcity and dependence.[26]

After a quarter-century, the Noninterventionists still find the problems and seek the solutions—economic and social change—in the "minds of men."

THE ROLE OF THE UNITED STATES

The Noninterventionist Middle view of the proper U.S. role in the Third World can be summarized as: Select, Reform, Negotiate. Select those cases most important to the United States. As quoted above, Congressman Solarz selects Afghanistan and Cambodia but not Nicaragua, a judgment with which not all Noninterventionists would agree, but what is important is the concept of selectivity. Reform or change those regimes where repression will inevitably engender revolution. Negotiate solutions with nations like Nicaragua and factions like the Salvadoran insurgents. For the most part, the Noninterventionists believe that such negotiations can be carried out on the basis of reasoned discourse, although some ultimately have come to the belief that Contra pressure on Nicaragua might provide a useful incentive to get the Sandinistas to negotiate.

Although his functions in the Kennedy administration did not have directly to do with policy in Southeast Asia, Arthur Schlesinger, Jr. marched with the band into Vietnam, writing in retrospect in 1965, after he had left the government: "Whether the domino theory was valid in 1954, it had acquired validity seven years later, after neighboring governments had staked their own security on the ability of the United States to live up to its pledges to Saigon."[27] By 1967, however, he was agonizing:

I think a middle course is still possible if there were the will to pursue it. And this course must begin with a decision to stop widening and Americanizing the war—to limit our forces, actions, goals and rhetoric. Instead of bombing more places, sending in more troops, proclaiming even more ardently that the fate of civilization will be settled in Vietnam, let us recover our cool and try to see the situation as it is:

---

[26]Leiken, 1984, pp. 7–13.
[27]A. Schlesinger, 1965, p. 538.

a horrid civil war in which communist guerrillas, enthusiastically aided and now substantially directed from Hanoi, are trying to establish a communist despotism in South Vietnam, not for the Chinese but for themselves. . . . Obviously, military action plays an indispensable role in the search for a political solution. Hanoi and the Viet Cong will not negotiate so long as they think they can win. . . . They must have no illusion about the prospect of an American withdrawal. The serious opposition to the escalation policy in the United States seeks not an American defeat but a negotiated settlement.[28]

None of the schools today contemplates an American military entry into any Third World situation at a level that would ever raise the question of "an American withdrawal." Beyond this, the Noninterventionist Middle, like the other schools except the Disengagers, recognizes the existence of American interests leading to potential American involvement. Like Schlesinger, they believe that military power is sometimes a necessary but limited part of that involvement, and they want to keep it limited by stressing negotiations.

Chace's critique of the Kissinger Commission report attacked its committee-spawned inconsistencies as throwing doubts on the parts that Noninterventionists might otherwise favor:

What is most striking about the report is its deep contradictions. On the one hand, the commission sets forth a brief and simplistic geopolitical analysis that sees Nicaragua as the implacably dangerous arm of Soviet and Cuban power and El Salvador as mainly threatened by outside forces. From this one may conclude that negotiations with the Nicaraguan government or the Salvadoran opposition are doomed from the start and that only military pressure can work to advance American interests. On the other hand, the report recommends a series of negotiations with the Sandinistas that, if seriously pursued, might help bring peace to the region.[29]

Two years later, at the beginning of 1986, Abraham Lowenthal reviewed Latin America as a whole:

Latin America's leaders in the early 1980s had to deal with a U.S. administration they found disconcertingly ideological. Instead of obtaining the help of the U.S. government to face the hemisphere's economic problems, these leaders perceived that—with rare excep-

---

[28]A. Schlesinger, 1967, pp 105–106.
[29]Chace, 1984, p. 45.

tions—the few officials in Washington who concern themselves with Latin America at all were obsessed with Central America. The possibility that the United States would escalate the militarization of Central America particularly concerned the leaders of the Contadora nations rimming the isthmus: Mexico, Panama, Colombia and Venezuela. . . . These democratic leaders believe that the most overwhelming threats in the hemisphere are debt, poverty and unemployment—not guerrillas, Soviet influence, terrorists or drugs. . . . [A] new U.S. policy adequate for the late 1980s . . . should include provisions to stretch out Latin America's debt for a generation, . . . provide orderly write-downs of debt for those small countries that are hopelessly over-indebted, . . . further increase the resources that are available for lending by the international financial institutions, and expand trade credits to facilitate Latin American imports. . . . Furthermore, the United States needs to adopt trade policies that will reverse protectionist pressures.[30]

This is not very different from the Kissinger Commission economic aid program. But one economist questions whether the military recommendations of the Commission report would drive out the economic recommendations— and not only on budgetary grounds:

The cost of the carrot rises with the application of the stick. Military and social expenditures are interdependent. The priority given to military, rather than negotiated, solutions, which is implicit in much of the report, would add to the destruction of the region and raise the economic and social costs of recovery.[31]

The difficulties of actually implementing the military priority are illustrated graphically for the cases of El Salvador:

Not surprisingly, the Salvadorans are remaining Salvadorans. The U.S.-trained second lieutenants and cadets are carefully watched by their superiors to make sure they conform to the traditions of the Salvadoran, not the United States army. . . . Washington has retreated from virtually every demand it has made on the Salvadoran government regarding these cases [of the murder of American citizens]. After four churchwomen were killed on December 2, 1980, the Carter administration suspended all economic and military aid to the country. But the economic assistance was renewed after a few days, and

---

[30]A. Lowenthal, 1986, pp. 540–560.
[31]Reynolds, 1984, p. 5.

after the guerrillas' offensive six weeks later military aid was not only renewed but greatly increased by the new Reagan administration.[32]

These words were written in 1983. They are quoted here to exemplify a point of view in the arms debate; to discover whether the situation in El Salvador has changed since then would require a different sort of analysis.

Other than questioning the overall role of the United States in general and the U.S. military in particular in combating modern counterinsurgency, the Noninterventionist Middle has had little to say about the specific ways in which U.S. forces might participate. The quotation "the traditions of the Salvadoran, not the United States army" suggests that U.S. Army influence over the Salvadoran military is less than meets the eye. Another occasional concern is that even in the United States, elite forces, such as the Special Operations Forces discussed above, may carry with them antidemocratic tendencies:

> Beyond the temptations of easy solution, elite forces are colorful and distinctive, and elite force leaders—in the West at least—are often found at the extremes of the political spectrum or seen as symbols thereof. In the way of yet another more subtle dimension of the problem relative to the political realm, it is not wholly reassuring that in the riots that swept the United States in the mid 60s, some citizens found Regular Army officers who temporarily assumed the reins of power more sophisticated and more visibly competent than the political leaders and local civil servants with whom they usually dealt. The role of the *paras* in bringing de Gaulle to power and the dependency of Lyndon Johnson and Richard Nixon on symbols of military power in their hours of travail suggest the elements of a pattern as yet only partially glimpsed.[33]

What may be more reassuring is that these words of caution appeared not in any radical publication, but in *Parameters*, the Journal of the U.S. Army War College.

The Noninterventionists are, in fact, quite different from the radical Disengagers, and this makes it as difficult for them as for the Interventionist Middle to come up with a compelling answer to the question of what we should do about perverse or ineffective "friends" in the Third World. (The Disengagers do not consider them friends; at the opposite extreme, the Confronters consider such friendship a superordinate political and moral principle.)

---

[32]Dickey, 1984, pp. 41–47.
[33]Beaumont, 1979, p. 23.

During the early days in Vietnam, the Noninterventionist Middle led the public criticism of Diem:

Remembering their own earlier commitments [American policymakers] cannot abandon Ngo Dinh Diem. Instead they now tell us that although he is not very good, he is "the only man we've got," and that, in any case, "one doesn't change horses in midstream." At the same time, they begin to point subtly toward the Communist guerrilla wars in Malaya and the Philippines . . . forgetting to tell the American people that the wars in the Philippines and Malaya were won . . . precisely because the Philippines and Malaya had the courage to change political horses in midstream. Magsaysay and Tungku Rahman became the leaders of reform administrations in the midst of a bitter guerrilla war and led their people to victory.[34]

In fact, the Interventionist Middle policymakers of the Kennedy administration were saying much the same things privately. When Diem was overthrown, however, and was followed not by a Magsaysay or a Tungku Rahman but by a series of somewhat slippery Vietnamese generals, the Noninterventionist critics had little to contribute about what to do next.

Since Vietnam, the Noninterventionists have consistently taken the opposite side from Jeane Kirkpatrick and Henry Kissinger, opposing Somoza, the Shah, and Marcos (but not Duarte), and always looking for the magic Menshevik. Joseph Nye criticizes Ambassador Kirkpatrick in terms parallel to her own, on the morality and the practical effects of choosing the "authoritarian" over the "totalitarian": "When it becomes known that integrity plays no role and we will always choose the lesser of evils in terms of immediate consequences, we open ourselves to blackmail by those who play dirty games."[35]

In El Salvador, for example, President Duarte was less than the hero the Noninterventionist Middle would like, at least in his shaky control over the right-wing forces in the country. To the extent that he did well and did good, then fine, but the Noninterventionists were willing to have the United States put his regime at risk. Tom Farer laid out the basic problem:

The fundamental dilemma for U.S. policy remains: How to reform a system of power which seems responsive only to the threat of its destruction, when we begin by guaranteeing its survival? To exit from this dilemma, we must change and condition the guarantee. We must

<hr>

[34]"Z," 1962.
[35]Nye, 1985, p. 17.

change it because democracy cannot sustain itself alongside a standing army led by a self-perpetuating officer corps hostile to the very idea of civilian control. . . . And it must be clear that, if the conditions are not satisfied by a stated time, Washington will forthwith suspend all military and economic aid, withdraw its advisers and discourage any other states from continuing to assist the Salvadoran armed forces.[36]

In another article, Farer put his view of American policy toward our "friends" more succinctly: "An administration which seeks pleasant relations with every right-wing thug in the hemisphere is simply unconvincing when it claims to be struggling for democracy in Central America."[37]

A *Los Angeles Times* editorial suggests that not only is the administration policy "unconvincing," but is self-defeating in a massive way:

Che Guevara wanted to ignite the fires of revolution throughout Latin America. He failed. But the United States is acting as if it wanted to do the job for him. . . . Blind to the history of U.S intervention in Nicaragua and in Latin America, the Reagan Administration does not see the bitter irony of its actions: the United States is providing a basic tenet of the revolutionary left—that the transformation of Latin American society can be defined only in terms of the United States as the Archenemy.[38]

What the *Los Angeles Times* contends is repellent to the Latin Americans may also be becoming unpalatable to American public opinion. By 1980, survey data led to

two tentative conclusions. . . . First, the Vietnam War experience seriously tarnished the "communist threat" rationale as a legitimizing symbol for American military interventions in the Third World. Second, the public may be beginning to discern a difference between the ideological issues associated with the "communist threat" and the military dangers of the "Soviet threat." . . . For the Vietnam generation, intervention will need moral justification, but not solely in terms of anti-communism.[39]

This had a substantial effect in constraining the Reagan administration approach to the Third World. I. M. Destler suggests the way in which these constraints have operated:

[36]Farer, 1984a, p. 293.
[37]Farer, 1984b, p. 105.
[38]"Che Lives," *Los Angeles Times*, July 20, 1986, Part V, p. 4.
[39]Tarr, 1980, pp. 56–59.

As of November [1983], the domestically popular Grenada invasion had generated a political swing in the President's favor [but] Grenada could not alter the deeper forces that have rendered domestic support of Reagan's Central America policies so shaky. If broader consensus is the goal, a less ambitious approach to the region might have better prospects of achieving it. . . . We do not wish to "lose" countries to communism, but neither do we want to lose American lives in obscure, intractable civil wars. Right-wing oppressors are politically unattractive, but so are anti-Yankee Marxists. . . . Will getting in deeper bring Americans together? It is hard to see how it can do anything but drive us further apart. A more intrusive U.S. engagement in Central America might make sense in regional policy terms, although this observer is skeptical. But it is almost certainly *not* the route to a durable American consensus.[40]

More generally, at the height of the Reagan administration, Destler, together with Leslie Gelb and Anthony Lake, mourned the loss of the centrist policy consensus that once facilitated coherence in U.S. foreign policy:

By neither cracking down hard on abuses by the Salvadoran right nor making an all-out effort at a negotiated settlement, the Reagan Administration may well be pursuing the path of losing slowly and painfully for all. Alternatively, the United States might step back from the quagmire of internal Central American politics, and declare that we could live with whatever regimes came to power in the region, so long as they did not align themselves with the Soviet Union (or Cuba). A strong center provides the fulcrum for being able to move forward toward more decisive action when necessary. . . . This leadership stratum is out there, in communities across the nation, waiting to be energized by national political leaders and would-be Presidents who are prepared to talk sense. . . . These community leaders can be the core of a new and very broad American center, a new political culture that will demand and allow Presidents, working with the Congress, to formulate and conduct a serious foreign policy. There are no ready miracles and recipes for doing this. It requires an alteration of attitudes, a new civility, and a return to some old principles.[41]

For the Noninterventionist Middle, the Destler, Gelb, Lake "all-out effort at a negotiated settlement" is the appropriate prescription for Central

[40]Destler, 1984, pp.320–334.
[41]Destler, 1984. pp. 273–286.

America, including both areas of actual conflict, El Salvador and Nicaragua, although the Noninterventionists do not accept the simple equation of the two:

> Administration spokespersons have argued that there is "symmetry" between the situations in El Salvador and Nicaragua. . . . In fact, the cases of El Salvador and Nicaragua are not symmetrical, though they are analogous. Both countries are polarized, but they are polarized in different ways. In El Salvador the polarization is vertical—poor versus rich. In Nicaragua it is horizontal, with pro- and anti-Sandinista workers, businessmen, peasants and clergy.[42]

This lack of symmetry leads Tom Farer to advocate a set of related but asymmetrical negotiations:

> I am confident that the Cubans and Nicaraguans and the Salvadoran Left, including most or all of the guerrilla groups, would enter a linked set of negotiations to be conducted under the auspices of the Contadora group. I am confident that most of the Salvadoran left would settle for temporary power-sharing followed by elections. . . . I am equally confident that the United States can negotiate the neutralization of Nicaragua. . . . While we would agree to end military harassment, we would continue to treat the country as a pariah, denying it . . . economic assistance and access to U.S. markets . . . until the leadership began moving toward the democratic objective announced in the neutralization agreements.[43]

Most Noninterventionists eschewed the Contras even as an instrument for exerting pressure to bring Nicaragua to realistic negotiations. In a dissent to the report of the Kissinger Commission, of which he was a member, San Antonio Mayor Henry Cisneros contended that:

> The United States should suspend "covert" aid to the anti-Sandinista rebels. The period for aid suspension should be through the year 1985 so that the Sandinista government can demonstrate its capacity to move toward pluralism and fulfill its promise to hold free and fair elections in 1985.[44]

The Reagan administration did not adopt Cisneros's minority recommendation to suspend aid to the Contras, the 1985 election in Nicaragua

---

[42]Leiken, 1984, p. 18.
[43]Farer, 1984b, p. 113.
[44]Cisneros, 1984, p. 129.

was arguably not "free and fair," and Cisneros may well have changed his mind since. Some Noninterventionists did. In 1984, Leiken wrote that:

> The biggest incentive for negotiations in Nicaragua is not the use of force against the Nicaraguan regime from bases in Honduras, but the promise of negotiations in El Salvador. That carrot will be far more effective, far safer and more humane, and far less costly, than the stick of intervention.[45]

By 1986, however, he had shifted to advocating the use of a reformed Contra movement to provide needed pressure to bring the Sandinistas to realistic negotiations

> if the Sandinista government accepts the February 6 proposal of six Nicaraguan political parties. . . . These offers—along with Salvadoran president Jose Napoleon Duarte's March 4 proposal to Daniel Ortega for parallel government-guerrilla negotiations in the two countries— provide a framework for a viable regional peace settlement. . . . But for any of this to happen, the United States must reform its policy. It must support the creation of a broad internal and external united front against the Sandinistas. . . . [It] should support efforts to create a coalition of the resistance forces . . . which would then receive U.S. military aid.[46]

Leiken's shift created immense controversy in some circles, particularly those New York circles that thrive on controversy. The Disengagers blamed the change on his selling out; Leiken and his partisans attributed it to his close observation of developments in Nicaragua in the last two years, particularly the election of 1985, which he considered manifestly rigged.[47]

The roots of Leiken's—or other—views are not central here. What is crucial is the permeability of the border that separates the Noninterventionist Middle from the Interventionist Middle. The central tendencies of each of the two schools remain distinctly different. But changing evidence, from Vietnam and since Vietnam, has moved people from one to the other; even more important, it has moved the schools themselves to new positions based on new facts and analyses.

One political litmus test that might compel members of the Middle to choose one side or the other would be a significant Communist threat to a

---

[45]Leiken, 1984, p. 23.
[46]Leiken, 1986, pp. 19–20.
[47]See Garber and Leiken, 1986, pp. 43–44; and Alexander Cockburn's regular column, "Beat the Devil," *The Nation*, December 18, 1985, January 4, 1986, and March 15, 1986.

regime that passes the Noninterventionists' tests of palatability—the Aquino government of the Philippines suggests itself. It is hoped such an occasion will not come about. In the meantime, lacking such a traumatic test, the differences between the two Middle schools are of the sort in which it is possible to find a middle ground for policy, rather than forcing policy to depend on the acceptance of strong value premises about U.S. interests in opposing Communism wherever it appears in the Third World.

8. Conclusions

The four themes set out at the beginning of this Part were:

1. The major issue dividing the end schools from the two Middle ones is their value-judgment-driven view of U.S. interests in the Third World.
2. The major issue dividing the Interventionist Middle from the Noninterventionist Middle is the weight put on the need for U.S. intervention in Third World situations, particularly as that weight is related to the "global credibility" version of the domino theory.
3. All the schools have learned from Vietnam that massive American military intervention in the Third World is a doubtful proposition. The Middle schools have reinterpreted their view of U.S. interests on the basis of the Vietnam experience.
4. Because the Reagan administration was made up largely of Confronters, the major locus of the recent Third World arms debate has been the frontier between the Confronters and the Interventionist Middle. In the past it was the boundary between the two Middle schools, and public opinion continues to push it that way to some extent.

These themes can be traced through Table 1. The table summarizes—and necessarily oversimplifies—the views of the four schools across the major issues discussed in this analysis. The table shows several overlaps among the schools, particularly between the two middle ones; nonetheless, the four are in fact different and distinct.

Table 1

SCHOOLS AND ISSUES IN THE THIRD WORLD DEBATE

Issue	Confronters	Interventionist Middle	Noninterventionist Middle	Disengagers
U.S. interests (value judgments)	Win 0-sum game	Discourage Soviet opportunism	Discourage Soviet opportunism, encourage democracy	Morality, encourage revolutionary change
Nature of insurgency (analytical views)	Communist exploitation of indigenous grievances	Indigenous grievances, sometimes exploited by Soviet opportunism	Primarily indigenous grievances	Legitimate grievances
Nature of counterinsurgency (analytical views)	Military	Military security is first necessity but social programming is fundamental	Social programming is most important, military as needed	Counterinsurgency is illegitimate, correct grievances
U.S. role (policy recommendations)	Intervene always	Intervene for any legitimate interest	Intervene seldom but assist with social programming	Get out and stay out
Military role	Crucial	Subtle	Backup	Never
Role with friends	Any anti-Communist deserves support	Do not betray friends	Corrupt friends betray us	Third World friends of the U.S. are suspect
Role of public opinion	Break constraints by leading it	Must observe constraint	Important and useful constraint, sometimes too strong	Mobilize it as in 1960s and 1970s
Role in Central America	Support El Salvador, use Contras to oust Sandinistas	Military training, etc. to establish security for social programs, use Contras to press for negotiations	Use social programs/ pressures to achieve democracy and negotiations, mostly eschew Contras	Get out and stay out

The two end schools, the Confronters and Disengagers, have such strong views, primarily about the nature of the worldwide interests of the United States, that each differs substantially from all of the other three. The two Middle schools by no means agree with one another, but they have essentially the same values about the way the world should be, and similar analyses about the way it is. The values and analyses are weighted very differently, however, leading to substantially different recommendations for Third World policy.

American foreign policy consensus—Destler, Gelb, and Lake's "new political culture that will demand and allow presidents, working with Congress, to formulate a serious foreign policy"—is not really all that new. The civil agreement that used to be called a "bipartisan foreign policy" disappeared into Vietnam and has never been revived. This does not mean it is not revivable. Vietnam was followed by two weak presidents and then a strong but extreme chief executive; neither weakness nor extremity is necessarily a natural and permanent condition in the White House. The President of the United States is not likely to return to the status of sole maker of American foreign policy, but a nonweak, nonextreme incumbent may well be able to lead a Congress that would prefer not to carry dissent beyond the water's edge. Revival of the consensus need not begin with Third World policy, but the controversies over the Third World are so sharp that revival must include Third World policy at an early stage. The consensus did disappear in Vietnam; and to a great extent it is the fears, in all schools, of a replay of Vietnam that prevent easy agreement.

Yet, we *have* learned from Vietnam, and that learning should make a renewed consensus easier. We all—every school—have learned that massive military intervention in a Third World nation is either à last resort or no resort at all, a major lesson that should preclude a repeat of Vietnam. Perhaps, as the passions of Vietnam continue to fade, other subtler lessons will spread more widely, as they have in some of the thoughtful statements quoted here.

There are two ways to restore a consensus. For a Confronter leadership like the Reagan administration to do it, it would have had to be the consensus of a crusade. The fairly extreme Confronter views would have had to be adopted not merely by a majority—constitutionally, President Reagan had that, although the opposing Congressional majority indicated the qualified nature of the President's mandate on these issues—but by most of those who are now in the Middle schools. This was always extremely unlikely. For me it would also have been extremely unpalatable; my prejudices were set forth at the start.

President Bush, however, seems to fall into one of the Middle schools, probably and presumably the Interventionist Middle. Given this reversion to the middle ground occupied by all post-World War II presidents from Truman to Carter, perhaps the real debate over the differences between the Middle schools and among their members will resume and will lead to the long-desired consensus. Consensus will not be unanimity, but it will encompass civility, and it will be based on the willingness of serious debaters to make their points, and if they lose them to understand why and continue to debate. It will not make possible a focused and sophisticated foreign policy à la Metternich or Palmerston; both the internal and external political conditions for foreign policy have become far too complex. But if we cannot go back 150 years, perhaps we can go back 25 and recapture the "serious foreign policy" we have lacked since Vietnam. Whatever else is included in one's concept of American interests, that must be a major component.

PART TWO
THE STRATEGIC NUCLEAR DEBATE

9. The Debate

> In the American View, [the 1972 ABM Treaty] was meant to seal a Faustian bargain with the devil of nuclear destructiveness. By the terms of this bargain, both sides had to guarantee their own devastation on a possible Judgment Day, when one side, having been attacked by the other, would want to avenge this attack. Thus, Judgment Day would never dawn.
>
> —Fred Charles Iklé[1]

> Today—as often in history—the scientist is lured from his laboratory into the outer world by the attraction of power and influence. . . . In a sense, like Faust, he has sold his soul to the devil. . . . But never before have scientists dealt with . . . weapons whose use could mean the end of civilization as we know it—if not of mankind itself.
>
> —Sidney D. Drell[2]

The potential inferno of nuclear war frequently evokes the Faustian metaphor, but the image of hell can be seen through many lenses. From one side of the debate over nuclear policy, Reagan administration Undersecretary of Defense Fred Iklé interpreted the ABM Treaty as a dreadful bargain enabling us to turn our heads away from nuclear damnation at the price of making it even more damnable if we ever arrive there; from the other side, arms controller Sidney Drell invoked Goethe to describe the birth and very existence of nuclear weapons.

Theology comes naturally to the nuclear debate. This discussion suggests why.

The policy debate in the untested realm of strategic arms control and other aspects of strategic nuclear policy has shown remarkable continuity. One major reason for this is precisely *because* policy in this area is untested, indeed essentially untestable. Unlike the debate over western arms policy toward the Third World, in which the traumatic experience of Vietnam produced evidence enough to change virtually all views

[1]Iklé, 1985, pp. 814–815.
[2]Drell, 1983, pp. 58–60.

117

substantially, the lack of implemented nuclear strategy since 1945 has allowed free play among premises and logical structure, all of which have been based at best on partial analogies to very different circumstances.[3]

The debaters must fall back ultimately on some kind of faith; and the resulting discussion *is* theological, sometimes even Manichaean, because of the depth of the issues exemplified by the use of the Faustian image. Thirty years is a short period in theological discourse, and although the world has changed technologically and politically, the major schools of thought on strategic nuclear policy are still saying the same things about different things. Perceived shifts in the weight of evidence stemming from current events have caused some debaters to cross boundaries, moving from one school to another. Even when they do move, however, they pick up lines of argument already in existence, sometimes bringing new life to these arguments by the weight of their authority as well as their reasoning.

The two major U.S. schools of thought on strategic arms policy—defined as major because they are closest to the decisionmaking center and thus have the greatest effect on the actual making of policy—divide primarily over two sets of recommendations:

- Whether (and in what circumstances and how) nuclear weapons should be used or threatened for any purpose other than to deter or defeat use of such weapons against American territory.
- How hard to strive for explicit agreements with the Soviet Union to control such weapons.

One school, called here the *Extenders* (for the importance they place on the extension of the role of nuclear weapons beyond the simple deterrence of their own use) stresses the need to maintain nuclear deterrence of such Soviet actions as nuclear or nonnuclear aggression against Western Europe and perhaps other "vital" areas. The Extenders believe in "thinking about the unthinkable,"[4] planning for the potential use of nuclear weapons, perhaps to fight such drastic Soviet actions, but certainly to limit damage in a nuclear war should it start, and to prevent its escalation to doomsday levels. This school does not eschew explicit arms control agreements with the Soviet Union, but its members are very suspicious of such agreements, believing that the Soviets use them primarily to gain unilateral military advantage.

---

[3]True, on various occasions, particularly earlier in the period, use of nuclear weapons was contemplated—the Chinese crossing of the Yalu, Dien Bien Phu, the Berlin crises of the early 1960s, the Cuban missile crisis, for example. But they were never used; Bundy (1988) contends that their use was never seriously considered at the presidential level. In any case, no test was mounted of the hypotheses of either the nuclear or the antinuclear strategists.

[4]The title of an influential 1982 book by Herman Kahn.

The other major school, called the *Limiters* (for their belief in limiting the use of nuclear weapons to primary deterrence of nuclear attack) believes that the *only* reasonable function for nuclear weapons is to deter their own use in a world in which they cannot be uninvented and thus might go off in some circumstances. Not every member of this school brings this single-function reasoning to the point of a policy of "no first use" of nuclear weapons. This school stresses the design and negotiation of explicit agreements with the Soviet Union, not for their own sake but for their role in reinforcing stability.

A third school of thought, the *Disarmers*, is unwilling to accept any use, first or otherwise, of nuclear weapons. Whereas the Limiters accept some degree of deterrence as necessary in the world as it is and is likely to be, and want to strengthen deterrence, the Disarmers stress moving away from deterrence as fast as is feasible. Because they are further from the decision-making center, the Disarmers are less important to the main debate than are the two major schools, indeed less than they were 30 years ago. A fourth school, willing to take substantial risks of nuclear war to wipe out Communism, did exist 30 years ago; it no longer does, at least not in any form worth discussing.

The Extenders and the Limiters divide *over* their recommendations in these two central areas of nuclear use and importance of agreement *because of* the different weights they put on key value judgments and, more important, because of different world views on two overarching analytical issues.

The value judgments go back to the "Better Red or Dead?" debates of the 1950s and the 1960s, although as noted in Ch. 1, that phraseology has disappeared because the either/or starkness led nowhere. The current debate is over the subtler issue of relative weights. Both schools agree to the unprecedented potential destructiveness of nuclear weapons. In the United States at least, neither school has the "they're just like us" view of the Soviet Union that informed some of the earlier debate; Prague and Afghanistan took care of that. Nonetheless, the preferences revealed by the Extenders' willingness to contemplate use of nuclear weapons as part of a strategy to resist Soviet threats to vital American interests and the Limiters' doubts about such uses do indicate real differences in the weighting of values. These values sometimes become explicit, as in Drell's reference to "weapons whose use could mean the end of civilization as we know it—if not of mankind itself," or President Reagan's language about the Soviets' "evil empire."

Such value differences are closely related to analytical views of the character and extent of each of the evils—nuclear war and Soviet world dominance. To some degree, in fact, the values may depend on the analyses, although there is some question as to which is the chicken and which the egg. Two detailed issues form the frontiers dividing the analytical views of the nuclear and Soviet dangers held by the two major schools.

- The key dividing question on views of nuclear war is whether and to what extent the use of nuclear weapons, once begun, can be controlled; and, specifically, the extent to which such use can be confined to "counterforce," avoiding both deliberate and "collateral" damage to civilian populations and other targets. Insofar as the weapons can be controlled, they can be used, including for lesser purposes than deterring enemy use of nuclears.
- The corresponding issue with regard to the Soviet Union is based on the debaters' perceptions as to the balance between aggressive ideological Soviet motivations pushing always toward imperial expansionism on the one hand, and on the other fear parallel to our own of nuclear conflict, which leads them toward substantial prudence. The question of the balance of Soviet motivations has always been a central one; Gorbachev's recent changes are leading to examination of the extent to which they may be changing that balance, even in its nuclear manifestations.

In addition to these two primary sets of analytical issues, three other categories are germane but, for various reasons, of lesser fundamental importance in understanding the differences between the two major schools of thought:

- Views of the "arms race" are at the cutting edge of the differences between the schools, but analyses of the nature of the race are derived largely from views of the Soviet Union. The Extenders see Soviet aggressiveness as implying that they will increase their nuclear power regardless of what we do; the Limiters interpret the arms race as mutual reaction, one side to the other, in which they would cease or slow down if we did.
- All schools have some concern with the possibility of a nuclear accident leading to "unintended" war, and all favor steps to minimize the likelihood of both the accident and subsequent escalation. Some on the Limiters' side believe that more nuclear weapons lead to a greater probability of such an accident; most of the Extenders (and some Limiters as well) believe that the details of nuclear control minimize the likelihood of both accident and escalation, even though they may call for more various weapons. The issue is less important as a divider between the schools than it was 25 years ago.

- One set of analyses of unquestionable importance includes those having to do with technology. The specific recommendations made at any given time are based largely on the technology of the time and what is foreseen. In terms of the debate, however, forecasts of advanced weapon technology are always highly conjectural; and even among technologists, the debaters tend to choose their technological outlooks on the basis of their other views, rather than vice versa.[5]

To summarize the two major schools' views in terms of the two major paradigms—the controllability of nuclear weapons and war, and the tractability of the Soviet Union—the Extenders believe that with careful planning, nuclear (and nonnuclear) weapons can be used in a limited counterforce strategy that can limit the damage to both sides and stop the escalation spiral far short of ultimate holocaust, if war does begin between the United States and the Soviet Union. This makes plausible the extension of deterrence to other vital interests beyond simple prevention of nuclear attack upon ourselves, and such plausibility in turn makes nuclear war less likely by discouraging the initial steps. Nuclear control is thus feasible; but because the Soviets are prudent, realistic deterrence is possible.

The Limiters do not refuse to think about the unthinkable. They strongly favor steps to increase the invulnerability of our nuclear retaliatory forces, and they prefer counterforce targeting of enemy military forces to targeting of populations. But they do not believe that such steps are likely to control death, damage, or escalation if nuclear war does begin. It is not careful attention to detailed control that is the key to deterrence of nuclear or nonnuclear Soviet attack on U.S. vital interests, it is the uncertainties inherent in nuclear war *in spite of* all that control may (or may not) promise. These uncertainties deter both nuclear attack and initial adventurism. It is because of the uncertainties that the Soviets will continue, as they have for a quarter-century, to stay far from any overt military threat to Western Europe. This Soviet conservatism, plus the desire to divert resources from military to civil uses, increasing rapidly in recent years, makes possible arms control agreements based on mutual rational self-interest.

Disagreement is by no means complete, however. Members of the two major schools, and in some cases the Disarmers as well, generally agree upon many issues germane to nuclear strategy and arms control. These issues therefore do not enter the debate as such, and they are not dwelt upon in this analysis. Some of these issues have been more divisive at other times or remain as dividing lines in other areas of the current arms debate:

---

[5]See, for example, Levine, 1986, pp. 25–28.

- None of the debaters treats nuclear weapons as "normal" or in any way less than frightful and unprecedentedly dangerous. Iklé and Drell, in the quotations introducing this report, use the Faustian metaphor to very different policy ends, but the equation of nuclear war and classical hell is appropriate for each. In the early 1960s, some debaters—a few in the Air Force and several outside—insisted that nuclear weapons were merely a different kind of munitions, frequently more cost-effective than nonnuclear ones, but this viewpoint has long been obsolete; and the importance of the "firebreak" between nonnuclear and nuclear weapons is universally recognized.
- As noted, none of the debaters treats the Soviet Union as very much like us in a value sense. In addition, analytically, no important partipants in the debate believe either that the Soviets are likely to take any great risk of nuclear war except perhaps under extreme provocation (perhaps not even then); or that they will refuse to pick up political opportunities handed to them with no risks. This too has changed over time: In the 1960s some serious and strongly anti-Communist debaters believed that the Soviet ideological drive might even lead them to risk nuclear war.
- Nuclear arms control is an integral part of overall nuclear strategy, and it should not be confined to explicit agreements. All schools espouse various unilateral actions they believe will increase nuclear stability and bring us closer to other objectives they adduce for control.
- There is general agreement on the desirability and importance of avoiding further proliferation of nuclear weapons to nations not now having them. The debate analyzed here is largely an American one, and Americans find it easy to agree that we want as few *other* people as possible to possess nuclear capabilities. Anti-proliferation measures form part of the discussion over arms control, but not of the debate as such, except insofar as some Disarmers point out that if there were no nuclear weapons, they could not proliferate.

For all of the theological reasons suggested above, less has changed over the long run in this segment of the debate than in the other two. The same is true of the short run. Changes in American administrations have led to marginal shifts in the balance between Extenders and Limiters, but weapons and strategies have been largely channeled by budgets and by real-world constraints, not by the kind of doctrinal differences represented by the debate. Neither President Carter nor President Reagan could figure out how to base the MX missile; Bush National Security Advisor Brent Scowcroft was Ford National Security Advisor and is approaching the same issues in the same way. And whatever else Gorbachev's Soviet changes are doing, they are not going so far as to allow either of the two major American schools to consider dropping deterrence; although new Soviet attitudes have been affecting the debates over the details, these shifts too have been marginal.

10. The Background

Over the 30 years covered by this study, strategic developments and the strategic debate have moved in tandem, although by no means in lockstep. Until the late 1950s, the debate was embryonic at best, and many strategic developments went largely unrecognized, at least compared with the intense scrutiny such developments received in the 1960s and subsequently. Certainly the advent of the nuclear age in 1945 impelled a deluge of writings, but these ranged from the scientific to the high philosophical; and few bore on the strategic issues of procuring, deploying, and planning to use (or not use) nuclear weapons. Writings about arms control were largely confined to disarmament as such—reducing the numbers of nuclear weapons or getting rid of them completely—rather than the intricate discussions of the later years that emphasized prevention or control.

The postwar era began with an American monopoly of nuclear weapons. Although the Soviets broke this before long and both sides developed hydrogen weapons in the early 1950s, the unexamined American assumptions behind John Foster Dulles's "Massive Retaliation" policy were that nuclear weapons provided a very cost-effective way of containing inherent Soviet aggressiveness throughout the world; we had a lot more weapons than they did; and nuclear war would consist of U.S. attacks on Soviet cities, à la Hiroshima and Nagasaki, with our air defenses hindering their retaliation (or first strike). Massive Retaliation was highly controversial, but most of those who challenged it publicly did so on moral and philosophical grounds rather than strategic ones, which questioned feasibility or examined potential Soviet response or initiation. One major exception among early analysts was Bernard Brodie, but by himself Brodie hardly constituted a debate.[1]

By the late 1950s, the modern ballistic missile, based on German V-2 technology at the end of World War II and dramatized by the launching of the Soviet *sputnik* in 1957, forced public questioning of the earlier, unexamined premises. It was believed in the United States, far too pessimistically as it later turned out, that the Soviets were about to outrace us in means of intercontinental delivery of nuclear warheads (the "missile gap").

In fact, private reexamination of strategic premises had already been underway for several years; it began to enter the public debate by the late 1950s. Threaded throughout the discussion from then until now are the names of five analysts whose writings and actions have been seminal in the debate over the entire period: Albert Wohlstetter, Thomas Schelling, Robert McNamara, McGeorge Bundy, and Henry Kissinger.[2] The earliest major contributions came from Wohlstetter and Schelling. Through the 1950s, Wohlstetter headed a RAND Corporation team that started out to optimize the U.S. strategic basing system and ended by questioning the premises on which the system was based.[3] In 1959 he went public with an article, the crucial point of which was that nuclear deterrence, far from being automatic, required care to make sure that the enemy did not wipe out our entire retaliatory capability in a first strike, thus leaving us naked.[4]

The problems raised by Wohlstetter's article were considered crucial by a group of analysts that could be considered then and through the early 1960s as a single school of thought.[5] This school has since divided over the central issue of the extension of the use of nuclear weapons beyond simple deterrence or defeat of a Soviet nuclear attack. Wohlstetter has become a leading Extender, stressing the importance of careful planning for a variety

---

[1]The first several chapters of Fred Kaplan's *Wizards of Armageddon*, 1983, present an excellent picture of Brodie's early thinking and writing.

[2]Evaluation of individual contributions is not a purpose of this report. The five people listed are not only seminal contributors, they represent different aspects of the strategic arms debate on crucial issues at crucial times throughout the period. A fuller list of still-active major participants over a long period of time would have to include, at a minimum, Morton Halperin, George Kennan, Paul Nitze, and Henry Rowen.

[3]The two other major members of the team, Henry Rowen and Fred Hoffman, have also continued to be active in the debate throughout the entire period, with Hoffman being one of the developers of the strategic implications of President Reagan's Strategic Defense Initiative (SDI).

[4]Wohlstetter, 1959.

[5]Called the "Middle Marginalists" in Levine, 1963.

of deterrent uses and, if absolutely necessary, actual uses for nuclear weapons.

Schelling, then and still a Harvard professor of economics, can now be counted among the Limiters; but his most important initial and continuing contribution has been to set the terms of reference used by almost all of the debaters in the major schools, before and after they divided. His 1960 book, *The Strategy of Conflict*, laid out in a fairly abstract manner a set of propositions derived from economics and game theory concerning the ways opponents do and can deal with each other, and the conditions for stability in such conflicts.[6] In 1961, he and Morton Halperin published a book that applied the propositions, still somewhat abstractly, to possible rules for nuclear stabilization. They stressed the then-novel idea that many arms control steps could be unilateral (e.g., protection of Side A's retaliatory forces so that A is not tempted to a first strike, particularly a *preemptive* first strike, mounted out of fear that Side B was going to go first and wipe out A's retaliatory capability), as well as multilateral in the classic treaty form.[7]

The use of nuclear weapons in both national and international patterns to strike at enemy forces rather than populations, to deter and to signal, to control and to stabilize, and to work politically without being used militarily has been the basis not only of 30 years of arms debate but of 30 years of U.S. nuclear arms policy. (One question frequently raised is whether such considerations also form the basis of Soviet policy, and if not, what the implications of the asymmetry may be.) The continuing importance of this book is indicated by Schelling and Halperin's preface to a reissued 1985 edition: "We wrote this book twenty-five years ago and are reprinting it now without any changes. . . . This study presents basic ideas that are as valid as they were twenty-five years ago."[8] Few strategic debaters would disagree.

Although Wohlstetter and Schelling were not in substantial disagreement with one another in the late 1950s and early 1960s, they did represent a geographic division in the strategic arms debate of that time. Through 1960, the centers of the American debate were Santa Monica, where RAND is located, and Cambridge, where Schelling and others had organized the Joint Harvard-MIT Faculty Seminar on Arms Control. With the election of John Kennedy as President, many of those who had been involved in the early discussions joined the Defense Department in the new

[6]Schelling, 1960.

[7]Schelling and Halperin, 1961. Halperin has also remained in the debate throughout the period, in recent years as one of the intellectual leaders of the Limiters.

[8]Schelling and Halperin, 1985, p. xi.

administration. From RAND came Rowen, Charles Hitch, Alain Enthoven (a junior analyst on the basing study), and later Daniel Ellsberg; from the Cambridge seminar, Bundy moved in as Kennedy's National Security Advisor, Harvard Law School Professor John McNaughton took a key Assistant Secretaryship, and Halperin later joined in a junior role. Those who remained in Santa Monica and Cambridge, including Wohlstetter and Schelling, consulted with their colleagues and others, and many of the ideas that had been incubated in academe and the "think tanks" entered directly into national policy.

It is a commonplace among sophisticated observers of interaction between academe and policymakers that ideas generated on the campus enter actual policy only through the strong distorting filter of politics, if at all. Although the general rule applied to this case as to all others, the never-never abstract and theological nature of nuclear strategy combined with the Kennedy administration's suspicions of the uniformed military establishment meant that more of the raw unrefined product than usual seeped through and entered national strategy. The movie *Dr. Strangelove* satirized the strategic consultants, among others; the material was gathered largely at cocktail parties thrown for director Stanley Kubrick and author Peter George by the consultants in Cambridge and Santa Monica. The strategic views of the consultants were substantially distorted by the caricature, but the extent of their influence was not.

Robert McNamara, the third seminal contributor to the strategic arms debate, was appointed Secretary of Defense as a manager, not a strategist. He learned quickly from his new staff, notably from William Kaufmann, a consultant with deep roots in both Cambridge and Santa Monica. One thing they all soon learned was that the missile gap existed in reverse; the United States was still far ahead of the Soviet Union in delivery systems as well as warheads. This, plus the fact that we were taking steps to protect our nuclear forces—through emphasis on the sea-based portion, hardening of land-missile sites, and airborne alert for bombers—meant that it would take many first-strike missiles to kill a single retaliatory missile. Since the Soviets had many fewer, they could not strike first; and in most foreseeable circumstances, we would not. Putting a discount rather than a premium on a first strike meant the preemption fears that had preoccupied many of the academic arms controllers were ill-founded, and stability based on unilateral measures was at hand.

Another lesson was that the plans set forth in the early 1950s for a massive conventional defense of Western Europe to be mounted by the NATO nations were seen by the nations at risk as far too costly to put into place;

American nuclear deterrence of Soviet invasion of Western Europe, nuclear or nonnuclear, was still considered basic.[9] The political road to nuclear war remained dangerously open, and the Berlin crises of the first year of the Kennedy administration led Kennedy, McNamara, and the Defense Department to think very seriously about the use of nuclear weapons. In October of 1962, the Cuban missile crisis again stimulated serious consideration of "what if" we had to use the weapons, and many (but not all) analysts believed that our ability to do so made an important contribution to the successful resolution of the crisis. The two years of crises in 1961 and 1962 confirmed the belief in the need for containing the aggressive hostility of the Soviet Union. By 1963, however, the resolution of the missile crisis made possible the first significant arms control agreement between the United States and the Soviet Union, the Atmospheric Test Ban Treaty. The treaty had little to do with stability as such, however, and few analysts thought that it implied more than a tactical change in the relations between the two superpowers.

All these events led to very concrete planning as well as thinking about the uses of nuclear weapons. McNamara was the swing man. Initially, he adopted the ideas of the nuclear strategists with whom he surrounded himself. In a still-famous 1962 speech made in Ann Arbor, Michigan, he contended that our "principal military objectives, in the event of a nuclear war stemming from a major attack on the [NATO] Alliance, should be the destruction of the enemy's military forces, not of his civilian population."[10] In other speeches and statements made earlier in the year he espoused the "city-avoidance" counterforce theory of nuclear targeting, both as a common-sense humanitarian philosophy and as a strategy for using the threat of nuclear attack (or additional echelons of attack after the first exchange) as a bargaining device, particularly in a NATO context.[11]

The Ann Arbor speech was the high water mark of "declaratory" counterforce policy in the 1960s. Five years later, toward the end of his tenure as Secretary of Defense, McNamara stressed not the details of bargaining, but the pure deterrent functions of nuclear weapons used as a threat of near-total devastation to the enemy: "Now it is imperative to understand that assured destruction is the very essence of the whole deterrence concept. . . . It means the certainty of suicide to the aggressor—not merely to

---

[9]See Ch. 16.

[10]McNamara, 1962, p. 67.

[11]See the many quotes from McNamara in 1962, in Kaufmann, 1964, Ch. 2, "The Search for Options." Kaufmann had drafted the Ann Arbor speech and many of the others.

his military forces but to his society as a whole."[12] This was not the "*Mutual* Assured Destruction" ("MAD") that the Extenders contend deliberately puts our population at risk to Soviet attack—the Faustian bargain decried by Iklé—but it is a major move away from the details of counterforce and nuclear bargaining. It moved McNamara toward the Limiters' school, signalling a crucial change in the strategic arms debate, the development of the Limiters as more than a tolerated loyal opposition considered to be lightweights within the policy establishment. And it earned the strong and continuing opposition of Wohlstetter and others who remained steadfast Extenders.

The change was, in fact, primarily in *declaratory* policy—what was *said* about nuclear weapons and plans. The actual nuclear strategy of the United States, once McNamara achieved control of it early in his tenure, emphasized the targeting of enemy military forces, not populations. This shifted only marginally back and forth as McNamara revised his views and, indeed, has remained quite constant through various changes in declaratory emphasis from then until now. McNamara has not written of the events that led him to shift his emphasis; others have speculated. Perhaps the demonstration in Vietnam that detailed calculations do not always work out precisely as planned had something to do with it. Within the strategic nuclear realm itself, events had moved away from the comfortable stability of "it takes more than one to kill one" of the theorists of a few years earlier. The Soviets had begun to build very large warheads, and many of them, which put even well-protected hard sites at additional risk. Perhaps more important, however, the advent of the Multiple Independently Targetable Reentry Vehicle (MIRV), meant that one missile with a lot of warheads could kill more than one enemy missile in a silo, and the equation was reversed toward a new premium on a first strike.

It is not clear to what extent MIRV was a reaction to the then developing Anti-Ballistic-Missile (ABM) capability, to what extent ABM was a reaction to MIRV, or whether perhaps both were results of the inexorable advance of military technology. McNamara was dubious about ABM, going along with the concept of its development on the questionable rationale of the need for a defense against Chinese missiles. What is clearer from his 1967 speech, however, is that the action-reaction arms race typified by MIRV and ABM had been one factor leading him to shift away

---

[12]McNamara, 1967, pp. 443–444. The speech was drafted by Morton Halperin, then in the Defense Department. Halperin, by then on his way to becoming a strong Limiter, shifted to the National Security Council staff in the first year of the Nixon administration, where he was such an anomaly that his phone was tapped by his superiors before he quit.

from the stress on detailed counterforce. He had begun to believe that such details could lead to no conclusion.

The ABM itself became a major—perhaps the major—factor in the debate in the late 1960s. The Soviets had been working on the system throughout most of the 1960s. Some Americans believed this to be a part of the general Soviet attempt to achieve a strategic advantage, but others suggested a strong Soviet bias toward defense because of the traumas of World War II, as illustrated by the massive Soviet investment in air defense. In any case, knowledge of the Soviet efforts led to pressure for similar U.S. systems.

In a debate with many similarities to the more recent one over SDI (but lacking any discussion of the possibility of an absolute hard-shell protection of the United States set forth in President Reagan's more recent dream), the Extenders favored ABM as one more tool to sophisticate the American nuclear arsenal and strategy. Most of the Limiters opposed it, primarily on the basis that an effective ABM would be destabilizing because it could be taken as an effort to allow a U.S. first strike by protecting targets in this country from ragged Soviet retaliation against such a strike.

Then as now, the Extenders accused ABM opponents of espousing the "MAD" strategy of deliberately putting the U.S. population at risk.[13] And a sharp controversy over the use and misuse of data arose between Wohlstetter and three Limiters—George Rathjens, Steven Weinberg, and Jerome Wiesner. Wohlstetter brought the matter before the Operations Research Society of America (ORSA), and after due investigation an ORSA committee and the organization's council decided in his favor. The Limiters contended that any analytical errors they had made were based on irregular release of relevant data by the Defense Department. More important for understanding the differences between the Extenders and the Limiters as they persist today, however, Wohlstetter believed strongly that precise calculations relating to nuclear exchange were crucial to the design of offensive and defensive postures; Rathjens, Weinberg, and Wiesner argued that: "The scope of the inquiry outlined by Mr. Wohlstetter is far too narrow. Any even-handed inquiry ought to look in considerable detail into the arguments and analyses offered by members of the Administration. . . . It should examine not only the technical details of these statements."[14] Their

---

[13]For example, in a 1973 article in *Foreign Affairs*, Fred Iklé, then Nixon administration Director of the U.S. Arms Control and Disarmament Agency, opened the line of argument for which he later used the Faustian metaphor. See Iklé, 1973.

[14]Letter to T. E. Caywood of ORSA from George W. Rathjens, Steven Weinberg, and Jerome B. Wiesner, reproduced in U.S. Senate Subcommittee on National Security and International Operations, Senate Committee on Government Operations, *Planning-Programming-*

point was that the role of ABM in deterrence and stability depended much more on broad strategic and political considerations than on precision of quantitative detail. This difference between the schools remains crucial today in the arguments over counterforce and the appropriate uses of nuclear weapons.

For a variety of reasons, rather than becoming another stride in the arms race, ABM development in the late 1960s and early 1970s provided an opportunity for the first U.S.-Soviet arms control agreement. Unlike the Atmospheric Test Ban Treaty, it potentially affected the stability of the nuclear arms balance. The arguments of the Limiters undoubtedly had some effect in encouraging U.S. acceptance of the ABM Treaty signed in 1972. Perhaps more important, however, were President Nixon's political imperatives (and perhaps similar pressures on Brezhnev). And a major permissive factor was that useful deployment of the ABM proved difficult enough that, even after the Treaty was signed permitting one ABM complex each to the United States and the Soviet Union, we soon abandoned our efforts as being insufficiently cost-effective given the technology of the times, and strategically meaningless.

Together with the ABM limitations, the Strategic Arms Limitation Treaty (SALT) of 1972 put the first limitations on offensive missiles.[15] Lawrence Freedman characterizes the basic bargain of SALT: "Implicit in the agreement was a trade of Soviet numerical superiority in missiles for U.S. superiority in technology and bombers."[16] The Extenders detested this tradeoff, the more so because it allowed the Soviets to multiply their advantage by putting more MIRVed warheads on their heavier missiles. In any case, SALT, signed in 1972, became SALT I, as an interim SALT II imposing further limits on bomber delivery systems in addition to missiles was negotiated, again over the strong opposition of the Extenders.

Deterioration of U.S.-Soviet relations, largely because of Soviet aggression in Afghanistan, meant that President Carter never presented SALT II to the Senate for ratification. It was then disowned by President Reagan but its limitations were observed through Thanksgiving of 1986. Although such atmospherics of U.S.-Soviet relations had an important positive effect on making the ABM Treaty and SALT I possible in 1972, and a major negative effect in making ratification of SALT II impossible in 1979, they bore little relationship to longer-run and more fundamental U.S. views of the Soviet Union. Most Americans' views remained in the range bounded

---

Budgeting—Defense Analysis: Two Examples, Washington, D.C., 1969, pp. 1250–1251. The Senate Committee print includes all of the documents in the controversy.

[15]The ABM Treaty is sometimes considered part of SALT, sometimes a separate entity.
[16]Freedman, 1981, p. 357.

131

at one end by the belief that the Soviets would remain highly aggressive and attempt to increase their military power no matter what we did (the Extenders' view) and at the other end by the belief that Soviet aggressiveness was tempered by prudence and a desire to shift resources away from the arms race, with their military posture designed in substantial measure in reaction to our own (the Limiters).

To a great extent, the "détente" of the early 1970s had been the handiwork of Henry Kissinger, the fifth of the major voices in the arms debate. Kissinger differed from the others less in viewpoint than in frame of reference. In the late 1950s and early 1960s, his policy recommendations as a member of the Cambridge branch of the consulting debaters put him well within the establishment consensus that included Schelling, Wohlstetter, McNamara, and everyone else who aspired to have a real effect on real policy. When McNamara and others veered off toward the Limiter school, Kissinger remained an Extender and, in spite of his détente/SALT aberration—which later brought him into a sharp confrontation over history with Henry Rowen,[17] a confrontation so esoteric as to be very difficult for an outsider to follow—he remains an Extender.

Unlike the other three, and, indeed, unlike most of the contributors to the strategic nuclear portion of the overall arms debate (Brodie is another exception), Kissinger took a primarily *political* view of the issues. From the 1950s, he concentrated more on the effects of potential or actual use of nuclear weapons on world power structures than on the logic and arithmetic of nuclear exchange. In 1957, he espoused a "limited" nuclear war strategy in Europe, contrasting it to Dulles's Massive Retaliation as a better instrument to protect our real interests in Western Europe.[18] A few years later, he changed this view toward conventional defense, not Massive Retaliation, but he continued to promote the concept that nuclear and other weapons were instruments in an essentially political conflict between the superpowers.[19] Political conflict might lead to nuclear war, and it was to the political sphere that we must look to prevent such war as well as to promote our own interests. Kissinger's Ph.D. dissertation had been about the post-Napoleonic balance-of-power stability created in Europe by Metternich and Castlereagh, and his objective, as writer and later as public official, was to reproduce that kind of stability in the world, without sacrificing U.S. interests. His early writings, his activities in office, and his current columns and comments have added an important real-world political dimension to the strategic debate.

---

[17]See Rowen, 1984; and Kissinger and Scowcroft, 1984.
[18]Kissinger, 1957.
[19]Kissinger, 1960.

Because of his different way of thinking, Kissinger had become something of an outsider in Washington and among the academic debaters after the first year or two of the Kennedy administration. When Nixon made him National Security Advisor and then Secretary of State, he directed much of his early effort toward such nonnuclear issues as Vietnam, the Middle East, and China; but he was central in creating the atmosphere of détente with the Soviet Union that made the ABM Treaty and SALT I possible. He was a key negotiator on the treaties, but preparation of U.S. positions on the precise numbers and definitions was more within the realm of the Department of Defense.

SALT I and the ABM Treaty were consistent with the stress on assured destruction as the central deterrent to strategic nuclear war between the United States and the Soviet Union that McNamara had begun in the previous administration. In 1974, however, James Schlesinger, a RAND alumnus and Extender analyst in good standing (and a Harvard College classmate of Kissinger), became Secretary of Defense. Schlesinger moved declaratory policy back toward the emphasis on selectivity, counterforce, and potential bargaining, and away from the sole objective of deterrence of attack upon ourselves. His aim, he told the House Armed Services Committee, was

> that the President of the United States, under conditions in which there is a major assault against the interests of the United States or its allies, will have strategic options other than the destruction of the society and the urban industrial base of the society attacking us.[20]

At the same time, however, SALT II, which the Extenders believed put additional limits on U.S. capabilities to actually implement such a selective strategy, was agreed to in principle by President Ford and Chairman Brezhnev; it took several more years to negotiate the details, and by the time it was ready to present to the Senate for ratification, President Carter decided not to do so because of Afghanistan. The Extenders believed that SALT I and the ABM Treaty, abetted by the defense budget cutbacks of the first Carter years, had allowed the Soviets to take a giant step toward catching up to us in strategic capabilities and laying the groundwork to surpass us dangerously. The Limiters too agreed that effective "parity" was the condition coming out of the 1970s, but the Extenders' attribution of causation to U.S. carelessness and political error is far more controversial. To the Limiters, the American strategic dominance that lasted at least through the early 1960s was inherently transitory and convergence between the

---

[20]J. Schlesinger, 1974, p. 46.

superpowers inevitable. Their belief all along has been that "strategic superiority" is militarily meaningless in the nuclear age and is therefore politically useless.

Nobody interested in nuclear arms control and stability was very happy with the years after 1972. The two major schools attributed the slowing of progress and the decline of hopes to rather different causes, however. Two thoughtful analysts, one from each school, have summed up their own discontent. Paul Nitze, an Extender who has been in the thick of arms control negotiations and debates since the Kennedy administration, laid the blame on continuing Soviet efforts to squeeze out the last drop of advantage:

> From 1972, when the Soviets passed the United States in number, size, and throwweight of offensive missile systems, they proceeded to develop and deploy one generation after another of more modern systems. . . . Once the Soviets judged the military correlation of forces had become favorable, they were adamant in refusing to consider any agreement which would result in rough equality or which would improve crisis stability.[21]

Thomas Schelling presented a Limiters' view of the same years and events. In addition to criticizing U.S. and Soviet arms control positions that he believed substituted mindless numerical limitations on weapons for consideration of their stabilizing or destabilizing characteristics, Schelling attacked the counterforce doctrine that he saw as the central U.S. strategic concept of those years:

> Since 1972, the control of strategic weapons has made little or no progress, and the effort on our side has not seemed to be informed by any coherent theory of what arms control is supposed to accomplish. . . . Ten years ago, late in the Nixon administration, secretaries of defense began to pronounce a new doctrine for the selection of nuclear weapons. This doctrine entailed a more comprehensive target system than anything compatible with the McNamara doctrine. . . . What has happened is that a capacity to maintain *control* over the course of war has come to be identified with a vigorous and extended *counterforce* campaign, while *retaliatory targeting* has been identified with what Herman Kahn used to call "spasm."[22]

In the 1980s the Reagan administration moved strategic concepts firmly into the hands of the Extenders. From 1981 to 1983, the dominant theme was simply the procurement of *more* strategic weapons—B-1 bombers and

---

[21]Nitze, 1985a, p. 5.
[22]Schelling, 1985/86, pp. 224–230.

large MIRVed MX missiles in silos. The Limiters' proposal for the small, single-warhead Midgetman missile, with mobility intended to preserve the retaliatory capabilities of the land-based leg of the triad, has been opposed by some in the administration because a single warhead is not cost-effective: It provides less bang for a buck. Multiple warheads, however, would make more difficult the mobility that is central to the Limiters' retaliatory objective; and that plus the multiplicity itself would imply to them a first-strike stress.

In any case, President Reagan's speech of March 23, 1983, introducing the Strategic Defense Initiative, changed the subject matter of the debate substantially. Even though the President's firm and continuing espousal of a concept almost nobody else believed feasible—a near-perfect defense of U.S. population against all enemy missiles—added a great deal of confusion to the debate,[23] most of the lines between Extenders and Limiters held.

The proposals made or not made by both sides at the 1986 Reykjavik pseudo-summit meeting added more confusion. Both Reagan and Gorbachev made proposals beyond the previous positions of their nations. Both drew back. But at least in the case of the United States, the President's apparent leapfrogging of not only some of his Extender advisors but even some Limiter positions led to both a few tentative shifts in the details of the debate and doubts about whether the Presidential position was real. In fact, the 1987 treaty abolishing Intermediate Range Nuclear Forces (INF) in Europe (discussed in Part Three) and the 1988 negotiations over the START treaty on strategic nuclear weapons made clear that American policy had changed. This happened in part as a result of changes in President Reagan's views; perhaps in larger part because of radical Soviet reversals in regard to such central issues as verification.

Nonetheless, the main thrust of the American debate at the start of the Bush administration remains constant, as it has since the 1950s, with the major schools adapting old theologies to new issues.

---

[23]See Levine, 1986, pp. 1–6.

11. The Extenders

> Everyone sensible in the West assigns primacy to deterring nuclear war.... The questions are how best to deter, whether that can be done without using apocalyptic threats, and whether we have to surrender freedom if deterrence fails. Nor should there be any issue about the West's need to rely less on nuclear weapons to deter a *non*nuclear attack.... Are we more likely to deter an attack by improving our ability to answer with the destruction of military targets rather than innocent bystanders, and by keeping the conflict under gross control? Or by making any nuclear war in which the West takes part as horrible as possible even if it means ending civilization and possibly the species? I have for many years advocated the first course. But that by no means implies that I think a war, even a non-nuclear war, is likely to be fought neatly [and] cleanly.... The *live* issue is whether we should be trying to increase or to decrease our ability to discriminate between military and civilian targets and to confine destruction to the military.
>
> —Albert Wohlstetter[1]

The "ability to discriminate" among targets, to "confine destruction to the military" insofar as possible, and to avoid having "to surrender freedom if deterrence fails" are at the center of the Extenders' thinking about nuclear weapons and war and have been for many years. The Extenders see nuclear war as conceivable in spite of all best efforts, and they want to keep it as limited as possible if it does come; their value system suggests that it may be necessary to risk it or even to use nuclear weapons first in case of an extreme threat to freedom, but their analytical system implies that a willingness to take such risks reduces the risks themselves. All this contributes to world nuclear stability; therefore it is arms control. Arms control agreements as such are evaluated skeptically, for their contribution to this discriminating posture.

---

[1]Wohlstetter, 1985, pp. 989–990.

ANALYSES

The Extenders pride themselves on cool analysis; the reasoning behind their conclusions starts with their analyses of what can be done, rather than their value judgments about where we want to go. The two main analytical roots are:

- We can limit damage in nuclear war, both by care in mounting our own nuclear strikes and defending against the enemy's, and by deterring escalation to larger strikes.
- Politically and strategically, the Soviet Union uses and will continue to use actual or potential military force to achieve its objectives, but it does so in a prudent pattern that we can deal with realistically if we examine it without illusions.

Damage limitation depends on defense and "intrawar deterrence." Since March 1983 when President Reagan introduced his plans for SDI, much of the discussion of limiting damage in nuclear war has revolved around the contribution of ABM defenses. The concept of defensive damage limitation, however, does not depend solely upon shooting down incoming missiles. Even lacking such a capability, other defensive measures are feasible and, in the view of the Extenders, desirable. According to Samuel Huntington, who had been on the staff of the National Security Council during the Carter administration:

> The United States needs to expand its ability to protect its leadership and population. . . . [In] 1978 . . . President Carter approved PD-41 authorizing planning for the evacuation of U.S. cities in the event of a nuclear (or other comparable) emergency. . . . In addition, it would be wise for the administration to launch a serious study of the possibility of providing hardened shelters for a portion of the urban population. . . . [The] Carter administration also directed that measures be taken to enhance the survivability of U.S. leadership, provide for the continuity of government, and protect U.S. command, control, and communications facilities.[2]

More important than defense as such (with the possible exception of SDI), however, is the ability to use offensive nuclear weapons in a discriminating manner ourselves, to limit damage to the enemy and induce him to respond in kind—through graduated deterrence, carried out once a war has

---

[2]Huntington, 1982, p. 39.

started and implemented by careful control of our actions even in the midst of a nuclear exchange. Wohlstetter contends:

> We should be prepared to use discriminating offense, strategies, tactics and precise weapons with reduced yields and deliberately confined effects—such as weapons that penetrate and explode deep beneath rather than at the surface of the earth close to an underground military target; and to direct our weapons at the military rather than at bystanders—to select targets of a sort, number and location that will accomplish an important military purpose and yet contain the destruction. . . . Among the most revolutionary changes in precision that are in process, some will permit one or a few non-nuclear warheads effectively to destroy a variety of military targets which previously had been thought of as susceptible only to nuclear attack or to huge non-nuclear raids.[3]

Neither Wohlstetter nor any of the other Extenders, however, contends that precision by itself will suffice to limit damage once war between the United States and the Soviet Union has begun. Rather, the key is to use the precision and discrimination to control escalation, and thus confine even a nuclear conflict to levels far below the megaton holocaust feared by everyone. According to Richard Burt, who shortly after writing this became Assistant Secretary of State in the Reagan administration, and later Ambassador to Germany then nuclear negotiator for the Bush administration:

> The threat of escalation will continue to provide both sides with incentives for exercising restraint in local conflicts. But the degree of Soviet restraint will depend, in large part, on American possession of nonsuicidal options for escalation. Accordingly, a new emphasis must be placed on generating nuclear responses that are militarily meaningful—that is, nuclear responses that can effectively deny, as well as deter, the Soviet Union from achieving both limited and expansive military objectives.[4]

None of this comes with a guarantee, but it has a good chance and must be tried. As put by Colin Gray: "Counterforce/damage limitation theorists do not exclude the possibility that catastrophe might occur. . . . They argue that [a lesser strategy] guarantees unlimited catastrophe, while their prefer-

---

[3]Wohlstetter, 1985, pp. 990–992.
[4]Burt, 1981, p. 170.

ence at least holds open the hope of containing the scale of potential damage."[5]

Most of the Extenders argue that such sophisticated planning for nuclear exchange at all levels actually makes nuclear war less likely because it leaves the Soviets with no illusions about taking risk-free action against us. Wohlstetter criticizes Father Brian Hehir, staff director of the committee that drafted the American Catholic bishops' statement on nuclear deterrence,[6] for turning deterrence into a dangerously obvious illusion that might lead to war. Wohlstetter's interpretation of Father Hehir's view is that "to deter nuclear attack, we must *convince* other nations that our 'determination to use nuclear weapons is beyond question' [but] we should never intend to use nuclear weapons." Wohlstetter's comment is that: "Precisely how this volubly revealed deception is to fool allies and adversaries 'beyond question' has not itself been revealed."[7]

Rather than permitting such illusions, Nitze argues for:

The objectives of assuring parity, or at least rough equivalence between the capabilities of the two sides, and of assuring crisis stability. . . . [Our] military forces as a whole must have the necessary characteristics of effectiveness, flexibility, survivability, and diversity to dissuade the Soviet Union from contemplating reckless action.[8]

Not all Extenders would agree. Gray criticizes both stability and parity as being too weak:

The principal intellectual culprit in our pantheon of false strategic gods is the concept of stability. . . . If it is true, or at least probable, that central war could be won or lost, then it has to follow that the concept of strategic superiority should be revived in popularity in the West.[9]

Most Extenders would agree with Nitze, however: accepting parity and stability as the best that we can obtain under existing political and other constraints, but fearing that Western carelessness can lead to instability if we fall into inferiority.

This first premise of the Extenders—that the technology and other conditions for control of nuclear warfare make stability possible through precise

---

[5]Gray, 1984, p. 62.
[6]National Conference of Catholic Bishops, 1983. The bishops' statement itself does not express the deter-yes/use-never view Wohlstetter attributes to Father Hehir.
[7]Wohlstetter, 1963, p. 16.
[8]Nitze, 1985a, p. 2.
[9]Gray, 1979, pp. 82–86.

discrimination and escalation control—comes together with their second premise—that the objectives and strategy of the Soviet Union make such measures necessary—to form the analytical basis for their strategic views.

The Limiters as well as the Extenders have assumed that the Soviets continue to seek opportunities for expansion of their power and their ideology. The two analytical questions for strategic nuclear policy are: How strong an expansive push? How will they pursue it? The Extenders answer the questions: still too strong, and too military, for us to risk anything based on any assumption about changed Soviet ways; even such reversals as the Gorbachev acceptance of verification procedures long rejected by the Soviets are discounted as indicators of change substantial enough for us to act on.

Wohlstetter describes the balance between Soviet prudence and Soviet aggressiveness: "We and the Soviets share an interest in avoiding mutual suicide. . . . But the Soviets also have interests in expanding their influence and control and, in the process, destabilizing the West, if necessary by the use of external force rather than simply by manipulating internal dissension."[10] And, concluding a comprehensive analysis of Soviet strategy written shortly before he joined the Reagan administration State Department, John Van Oudenaren summarized the Soviet attitude as he saw it, a year after the start of the Gorbachev era:

> It is disturbing that, for whatever reasons, the top leadership of the past 15 years has identified the general interests of the Soviet state with continued high levels of military expenditure, and that, even in retrospect, it seems reasonably satisfied with the return on its investment. Soviet military power is credited with "sobering" the U.S. and compelling it to accept détente, with accelerating the rise of "progressive" forces in the Third World, and generally with preserving world peace and hence permitting the continuation of Communist construction.[11]

Soviet nuclear and other military strategy does not consist of a clear and agreed set of "if . . . then" steps, however. Different Extenders have interpreted Soviet nuclear strategy in substantially different ways. Richard Pipes, a Harvard Sovietologist and alumnus of the Reagan National Security Council, contends that the Soviet General Staff's "strategy for the contingency of war [for the last thirty years] has called for massive preemptive strikes against the U.S. deterrents, accompanied by defensive measures to

---

[10]Wohlstetter, 1983, p. 34.
[11]Van Oudenaren, 1986, p. 41.

protect Soviet forces and civilians from U.S. retaliation."[12] Such a Soviet strategy might lead to a U.S. emphasis on defenses of our own, but it would not be conducive toward Wohlstetter's discriminate American strategy. Wohlstetter, in fact, argues that the Soviets want us to believe in their massive-attack strategy, but only in the interests of misleading us; their real strategy is much like that he recommends for the United States:

> When the Soviets talk primarily for Western ears, they indicate that if they ever attack they will do so massively and indiscriminately, even if it means the end of the world—either to frighten us into believing that it is futile to prepare to use nuclear weapons even in reponse to their use of nuclear weapons, or to lull us into believing they would never use them. Or both. Such Soviet statements are in good part disinformation. . . .

> When Soviet military planners write primarily to inform each other, they may demonstrate an interest both in using force "massively," that is "decisively," to accomplish a key military purpose, and in using force selectively so as not to defeat that or any wider purpose. . . . The development of their military forces confirms this double interest. They are increasingly capable of selecting some targets to be immobilized or destroyed with important military effect while leaving others essentially untouched. They have been moving toward more precise, lower-yield weapons. . . . Moreover . . . their force development shows a strong interest in keeping the battle under *their* control.[13]

Wohlstetter reinforces his arguments for a discriminating U.S. strategy by contending that the value system of the Soviet leadership makes a counter-force threat to their power a stronger deterrent than any massive threat to Soviet populations:

> One need not assume that Soviet values are the same as our own; nor that the Soviets are simply monsters who don't care or even like to see civilians killed. We need only observe that the Soviets value military power and the means of domination at least as much and possibly more than the lives of Russian civilians. This is surely evidenced by a long history . . . in which the Soviets have sacrificed civilian lives for the sake of Soviet power. Their collectivization program in the 1920s gained control over the peasants at the expense of slaughtering some 12–15 million of them. . . . The Soviet government sharply increased

---

[12]Pipes, 1986a, p.5.
[13]Wohlstetter, 1985, pp. 981–982.

grain exports during the famine year of 1933, when 5 million Ukrainian peasants were dying. If Robert Conquest is right, the Great Purge of the late 1930s killed several million more Soviet citizens. If Nikolai Tolstoy is right, Stalin and the NKVD were responsible for more than half of the 20–30 million deaths suffered by the Soviets during World War II. . . .

Whatever else one may say of these actions, they do not suggest that Soviet leaders value the life of Russian citizens above political and military power.[14]

This harsh picture of the Soviets' military objectives carries over to the ways in which they utilize negotiations. Nitze and other Extenders frequently quote Carter administration Secretary of Defense Harold Brown (in terms of his current recommendations and other views, a Limiter) "When we build, they build. When we don't build, they build."[15] Indeed, the Extenders contend that the Soviets have continued to build even in violation of existing treaties.

These views of Soviet objectives and strategic and negotiating postures extend to another analytical issue, albeit one considered much more important by the Limiters than the Extenders—the arms race. Brown's quotation summarizes much of what the Extenders think about the arms race: The one thing worse than a two-sided arms race would be a one-sided race—the Russians only. Nitze has been quoted above as contending that the Soviets raced unilaterally in building delivery systems in the 1970s; a Defense Department study group on SDI, headed by Fred Hoffman, who had been one of Wohlstetter's associates in the 1950s RAND studies, adds another dimension:

The public in the United States and other Western countries is increasingly anxious about the danger of nuclear war and the prospects for a supposedly unending nuclear arms race. Those expressing this anxiety, however, frequently ignore the fact that the U.S. nuclear stockpile has been declining, both in numbers and in megatons, while Soviet forces have increased massively in both.[16]

Beyond this, however, the Extenders look very skeptically at arms reduction agreements. Still within the framework created by Schelling and Halperin in 1961, "Whether the most promising areas of arms control

---

[14]Wohlstetter, 1983, p. 27. p. 27.
[15]Nitze, 1985a, p. 5.
[16]Hoffman, 1983, p. 5–6.

involve reductions in certain kinds of military force [or] increases in certain kinds of military force . . . we prefer to treat as an open question,"[17] Nitze carefully introduces a crucial adjective into a paragraph endorsing arms reductions: "Significant reductions in *destabilizing* systems can be crucially important to enhancing stability."[18] Stability, not an increase or decrease in the number of weapons, is the key. And in regard to one of the "tentative accords" reached between Reagan and Gorbachev in Reykjavik, Kissinger argues, "Grotesque as it may sound to the layman, a 50 percent cut of strategic forces would not ease the growing vulnerability of land-based missiles. It would increase the vulnerability of sea-based forces."[19] Kissinger saw no need to change this belief in the next year, as Reykjavik led to the START negotiations.

Because of fears of not racing and thereby losing, and ambiguities associated with the reduction of arms, although the Extenders do not endorse arms races, they consider the issue much less important than do the Limiters. Another similar issue—important to many Limiters, much less so to Extenders—is the possibility of nuclear accident. Extenders have endorsed or, when in power, sometimes initiated many devices designed to lessen the risk of accidents or the risk of escalatory response if accidents occur; the Permissive Action Link for strong central control over nuclear weapons and the Washington-Moscow "hot line" are two examples. And, as has been noted, one of the Extenders' central considerations is control over escalation, including escalation of a conflict beginning with unintentional launch or other nuclear accident. The possibility of the initial accident is not considered very important to the design of nuclear strategy or the desirability of arms control, however, and is not written about.

VALUE JUDGMENTS

The emphasis on control over escalation in case of accident or any other first step in nuclear exchange is consistent with the Extenders' overall analytical emphasis on detailed steps for control at all levels; it is also consistent with their value emphases. The Extenders of course want to avoid nuclear war. But their two key value judgments match their two key analytical premises. One relates to control, the other to the Soviets:

---

[17]Schelling and Halperin, 1961, p. 2.
[18]Nitze, 1985b, p. 71. Italics added.
[19]Kissinger, 1986b, Part V, p. 1.

- Limiting damage in a nuclear exchange, should one occur, is an important thing to do. Their analyses indicate that it is *possible* to reduce the number of deaths in a nuclear war—e.g., from 200 million to 20 million. Their value judgments stress that on grounds of morality planning to do so *should* be a major policy consideration.
- It is worthwhile to defend the Western world against Communism. Were the "Better Red than Dead" distinction at all meaningful, the truth would be somewhere in the middle. (In the current debate over nuclear strategy, the Limiters would also agree to the same statement. This was not always true in the past, however,[20] and it is not true now in areas of the arms debate other than the realm of nuclear strategy.)

The worth of defending the United States and Western Europe against Communism is, in fact, seldom singled out for mention by the Extenders precisely because it is so uncontroversial as to make any discussion gratuitous. Wohlstetter's piece, "Between an Unfree World and None," mentions the "Unfree World" only in the title, not in the body of the article.[21] His litany, quoted above, of Soviet leadership sins against their own people, certainly indicates a strong distaste for their mode of governance, but he presents the list to argue about the Soviet value system he believes we should target, not as a moral indictment.

It was not always thus. In the early 1960s a major debate was mounted between such Disarmers as Bertrand Russell, who was reputed to have coined the "Better Red than Dead" slogan, and opposing philosophers such as Sidney Hook, who found it necessary to argue passionately that: "Intelligent fear is aware that not only is there a danger of nuclear holocaust, *there is also as great a danger of Communist takeover and destruction of free society.*"[22] Such views today might come from an Extender or a Limiter; even most Disarmers have been wise enough to join the consensus that the idea is to avoid both disasters rather than choosing between them. In areas of the arms debate more removed from nuclear fears, however, the old passions still exist. Indeed, in the debate over U.S. arms policy in the Third World, compared with the situation of 30 years ago, the memory of Vietnam has intensified the emotional content. And because the stakes are less than in the strategic nuclear area—little fear of holocaust on the one side and little danger of Communist hegemony over civilized people like us and the West Europeans and the Japanese on the other—it is possible for the debaters to indulge these passions.

---

[20]See Levine, 1963, particularly Ch. 5.
[21]Wohlstetter, 1985.
[22]Hook, 1961, p. 12.

In the strategic realm, however, the passions of the Extenders are reserved for the other of their two major values, the importance of damage limitation. The weight they put on the absolute morality of preventing the worst, should nuclear war occur, can be measured by the opprobrium they heap on those Limiters who they believe want to maintain a high level of potential damage because they think it will help deter the initiation of such war. The Limiters' own views are discussed below, but the Extenders' views of those views are indicated by Iklé's Faustian metaphor, which began this Part, and by continued assault on the "MAD" image:

Wohlstetter:

John Newhouse succinctly stated . . . the "frosty apothegm": "Offense is defense, defense is offense. Killing people is good, killing weapons is bad." The late Donald Brennan . . . was not sympathetic. He noted that the acronym for Mutual Assured Destruction—MAD—described that Orwellian dogma.[23]

Hoffman:

[T]he MAD doctrine . . . holds that to deter nuclear attack we must threaten deliberately to kill innocent Soviet civilians; consequently deterrence depends only on the destructiveness of offensive forces used in retaliation for Soviet attack.[24]

Reagan Defense Secretary Caspar Weinberger:

True believers in the disproven MAD concept hold that the prime, if not the only, objective of the strategic nuclear forces of both the U.S. and the Soviet Union is the ability to destroy each other's cities.[25]

Not all Extenders feel comfortable using the MAD image. Gray suggests that "The politically effective acronym MAD . . . is not helpful for constructive debate,"[26] but this is a matter of taste and debating style.

What the hard arguments over damage limitation come to logically is a balancing off of hypothetical quantitative estimates of death and damage avoided against equally hypothetical estimates of increased willingness to dare war because damage can be limited. But such estimates are of course impossible; the point, even for the highly numerical Extenders, is not the provision of a Cartesian proof of the need for damage limitation; it is the

---

[23]Wohlstetter, 1983, p. 16.
[24]Hoffman, 1985, p. 26.
[25]Weinberger, 1986.
[26]Gray, 1984, p. 61.

value judgment—the moral imperative of trying—together with the analytical belief that it can be done, without increasing the likelihood of nuclear war at all.

POLICY RECOMMENDATIONS

The Extender viewpoint leads to myriad policy recommendations in many directions, concerning the details of weapons procurement and posture, for example. Three groups of recommendations are central to the Extender strategy and distinguish the Extenders from the Limiters.

- *Nuclear Strategy and Planning.* Plan and be prepared for the use of nuclear weapons in many situations for several purposes going beyond deterrence of attack upon ourselves, particularly to deter Soviet aggression in Europe.
- *Arms Control.* Be serious about explicit arms control agreements if, and only if, they enhance our overall deterrent and political strategies.
- *The Strategic Defense Initiative.* Use SDI as a potentially important component of a discriminating counterforce strategy, important enough to bend or break out of the existing ABM treaty. SDI provides one example—a major one—of the weapon implications of the Extender strategy and some of the arms control implications as well.

Although in common with the other schools the Extenders put the highest priority on avoiding nuclear war, the central recommendations that differentiate them from the others concentrate on being prepared to use nuclear weapons for purposes other than deterrence of attack on ourselves. Their analyses say we can, their values say it is desirable; to this end, their recommendations endorse the kind of detailed nuclear strategy and weaponry laid out by Wohlstetter and others. Gray puts it generally and succinctly: "[T]here is everything to be said in favor of planning for controlled and limited employment of nuclear weapons in support of foreign policy objectives."[27]

The most important of these objectives and the one for which the potential use of nuclear force is most integral is, of course, the defense of Western Europe. American nuclear deterrence of Soviet aggression in Europe is the central issue in the NATO debate analyzed in Part Three. Indeed, that NATO Europe must remain tied to the United States under the American nuclear umbrella is a proposition agreed to by many of the

[27]Ibid., p. xix.

146

Limiters, although they would not agree that the detailed plans and weaponry of the Extenders are necessary or desirable for this purpose.[28] What other geography beyond Europe should be covered is a more open question. Huntington extends the concept of deterrence, although not necessarily nuclear deterrence, well beyond NATO:

> Initially . . . the United States was primarily concerned with deterring a Soviet attack on Western Europe. In the 1950s, largely as a consequence of the Korean War, Japan and Korea were brought within the deterrence perimeter. . . . [The 1970s] saw the emergence of three major new deterrent needs. First, the increasing dependence of the United States, as well as its allies, on Persian Gulf oil plus the enhanced capabilities of the Soviet Union to threaten that oil militarily inevitably directed American attention to the security of the Gulf region. . . . Second . . . [as] relations between China and the United States gradually improved in the 1970s, the extent of the American interest in deterring or defeating a Soviet attack on China correspondingly increased. . . . Third . . . [was] Poland in 1980–81. Top officials of both the Carter and Reagan administrations repeatedly warned of the serious consequences that would follow if the Soviets interfered in "the Soviet sphere of influence."[29]

For Poland at least, it seems likely that the sanctions behind deterrence were more economic than military, let alone nuclear. Nonetheless, any confrontation between the United States and the Soviet Union runs some risk of involving military action, and any military confrontation between the two superpowers involves nuclear risks, which, it is generally agreed, is why the two have avoided such military confrontations. Where the outer limit lies for U.S. interests so vital as to invoke the nuclear threat directly has not been defined either officially or by any unofficial Extender consensus, but it is for this variety of possibilities that the Extenders want to design our nuclear capabilities.

If the major positive recommendations of the Extenders involve nuclear war-fighting capabilities, their chief cautionary recommendations have to do with explicit arms control agreements with the Soviets. For most of the Extenders, however, "cautionary" is the right term, not "negative." Paul Nitze expressed the Reagan administration view. (His references to "arms control" here mean specific agreements with the Soviet Union; the debaters,

---

[28]Nor, to be clear, do the Extenders want to depend solely or even mainly on nuclear weapons in Europe. Like the Limiters, they favor stronger conventional defenses for NATO and a policy of no *early* use of nuclear weapons.

[29]Huntington, 1982, pp. 6–9.

including the Extenders, sometimes use the term to cover unilateral restraints as well.)

> The primary security objective of the United States and, I believe, of the Western alliance in general is to reduce the risk of war while maintaining our right to live in freedom. Consistent with this objective, we have long based our security policy on deterrence. . . . In this context, arms control should be viewed as one element of our security policy. . . . Arms control is not a substitute or replacement for adequate defenses. Indeed, experience indicates that while arms control hopefully can play an important role in enhancing our security and bringing about a more stable strategic relationship, what we are able and willing to do for ourselves is more important.[30]

Wohlstetter agrees: "A serious effort to negotiate agreements with the Soviets might enable us to achieve our objectives at lower levels of armaments than might otherwise be possible. . . . Being serious about arms agreements, however, is not the same as being desperate."[31] And together with Brian Chow, he has proposed a detailed arms control agreement on anti-satellite weapons that they believe would enhance the carefully stabilized deterrence they favor. They contrast this approach with a more emotional one:

> The pious insincerities of Capitol Hill suggest the issue is to avoid militarizing the untouched heavens. But the U.S. and the U.S.S.R. will use and have used space for 25 years to further their rival political and military ends. . . . [The real aim should be] to encourage an agreement with the Soviets that would protect the many satellites that supply reconnaissance, warning, communications, navigation and guidance, and other critical information for the defense of the two superpowers and their allies.
>
> Can an agreement do that? Some agreement with the Soviet Union conceivably could help the U.S. protect the functioning of key military satellites. But it would take a fresh approach. The standard sort of ASAT ban that is supposed to be a way of defending satellites would very likely end by preventing the U.S. from protecting them. Then many (not all) proponents of the treaty would ignore its disas-

---

[30]Nitze, "1985a, pp. 1–2.
[31]Wohlstetter, 1983, p. 34.

trous failure to accomplish its purpose of helping satellites survive. Instead, they would celebrate the survival of the treaty.[32]

Pipes, however, having left the government, moved outside of the official consensus, which remains open to at least some forms of arms control as a part of the overall strategy for stable deterrence:

Even a good deal would be a mistake, for the root of the problem is not nuclear weapons. . . .

It is undeniable that the Soviet Union faces a crisis and that if its economy is not reformed it risks forfeiting the status of a great political and military power. But it is equally true that the Soviet elite wishes to carry out these reforms in the manner that least upsets the existing Stalinist system and the advantages it gives them. . . .

Arms control thus helps Moscow preserve the Stalinist system intact and continue its expansion while giving the appearance of good will.[33]

In spite of substantial doubts about the way we go about negotiating arms control agreements, Kissinger dismisses as impractical and undesirable the abandonment of arms control efforts. In a series of 1986 newspaper commentaries, he painted a picture of arms control as he sees it and would like to see it in the political worlds of Washington, Brussels, Reykjavik, and Geneva:

The "defense unilateralists" have refused to face the fact that arms control is now an essential element of both domestic and allied politics, that their choice may be between a negotiated agreement and a legislated unilateral one. . . . The unresolved U.S. debate tempts the Soviets to choose among a flood of schemes from contending elements of the U.S. bureaucracy. America is perilously close to negotiating with itself.[34]

There is considerable risk that over the next decade some conflict or other will slide out of control in a strategic environment made increasingly intractable by arms control diplomacy. . . . Moreover the present negotiating method leaves too big a gap between the numbers crunchers at Geneva and the secretary of state or the President. . . . There can be no real progress by endlessly modifying numbers. It is

[32]Wohlstetter and Chow, 1985.
[33]Pipes, 1986b.
[34]Kissinger, 1986b, Part V, p. 1.

necessary to begin with a vision of a more secure world and develop negotiating positions and strategies in relation to it.[35]

Once the "vision" has led to "positions and strategies," then the details begin to fall into place, and there are no absolutes among such details. Although some Extenders will accept only fully verifiable agreements, for example, and the Reagan administration put great weight on alleged Soviet violations of SALT, Kissinger places verification and compliance within the overall political/strategic context:

> Verification is another slogan in search of a program. It is not a substitute for meaningful agreements. It depends on three factors: the intrinsic importance of an agreement; the margin within which it is estimated violations are possible; the strategic importance of the violations and the degree to which countermeasures have been prepared.[36]

In any case, with a few exceptions the Extenders agree that although arms control agreements are not centrally important to nuclear strategy or world stability, the proper sorts of agreements, negotiated in the proper way—with our eyes open—can provide a useful adjunct to unilateral plans and postures.

The Strategic Defense Initiative provided a central operational example of the Extenders' view of the interrelationships among strategy, weapons choices and, to some extent, arms control agreements. Iklé brings these elements together, seeing a role for new arms agreements in spite of his Faustian view of the last ones:

> We need to accomplish a long-term transformation of our nuclear strategy, the armaments serving it, and our arms control policy. . . .

> The key now for the needed transformation is technological development to make effective defensive systems possible for the United States and our allies. . . . As strategic defenses make it increasingly unlikely that Soviet offensive forces can accomplish their mission, the incentive for new Soviet investment in them is reduced. We thus enhance Soviet willingness to join us in deep reductions of offensive forces.

> To this end we ought to take two complementary approaches. We should energetically seek Soviet cooperation, since it would greatly ease and speed the transformation. But we must also be prepared to

---
[35]Kissinger, 1986a.
[36]Ibid.

persist on the harder road, where the Soviet Union would try as long as possible to overcome our defenses and would resist meaningful reductions in offensive forces. The better prepared we are and the more capable of prevailing on the hard road, the more likely it is that the Soviet Union will join us on the easy road.[37]

The issue of ABM defense provides a good microcosm of the debate between the Extenders and the Limiters, and has for 20 years; however, the SDI version comes with a major twist that must be straightened out before specific views can be fitted into overall strategic concepts. The twist is the vision with which President Reagan launched SDI, the vision of a near-perfect "hard-shell" system that would defend our entire population and our allies against almost all incoming ballistic missiles—thus a substitute of defense for deterrence. Virtually none of the Extenders, who back SDI (and none of the Limiters), believe in the feasibility of the presidential system. They handle it by largely ignoring it and then going on to debate their own more modest versions, which fit within known strategic concepts as well as technological ones.[38]

What is left is ABM defense of missile and other military sites as a part of the Extenders' overall discriminating counterforce strategy. Even so, some division remains among the Extenders, depending largely on the stress they put upon the contribution of our unilateral military posture to deterrent stability, compared with the possible integration of arms agreements into a stable deterrent system. Hoffman stresses the military. Describing the views of the group in which he counts himself, he writes that it

> sees possible territorial defenses of the U.S. and of potential theaters of operation such as Europe as a means of increasing the stability of deterrence by denying the achievement of Soviet attack objectives. This group believes that Soviet peacetime nuclear strategy emphasizes the erosion of Western resolve to resist Soviet aggression and Soviet plans for the use of nuclear weapons aim at the destruction of Western military power to resist Soviet attack rather than the destruction of U.S. cities. They believe defenses effective enough to frustrate a Soviet attack on critical Western military target sets could help to counter this strategy long before reaching the higher level of effectiveness sufficient to preclude catastrophic damage in a massive Soviet attack intended to destroy cities. Such transitional defenses would,

---

[37]Iklé, 1985, pp. 824–825.
[38]See Levine, 1986, pp. 1–6.

however, protect population against collateral damage in *likely* kinds of Soviet attack.[39]

The word "transitional" in the last sentence is a slight bow toward the objective of full population protection, but Hoffman's stress on the near-term military defense is clear. He explicitly favors "an evolutionary approach to SDI seeking early opportunities to achieve useful levels of defense effectiveness rather than a program that delays any employment until an essentially impenetrable defense becomes feasible."[40]

Kissinger would not necessarily disagree with this. His political experience leads him to a fuller understanding of Reagan's dream (or at least a more explicit endorsement of it), but he too strays, not in military terms but in the diplomatic ones of wanting to negotiate about SDI, in contrast to Reagan's refusal to use it as a "bargaining chip." To Kissinger, SDI is the key to:

a policy on defense and arms control that reflects the revolutionary changes in weapons technology, reduces the reliance on nuclear weapons and responds to the global yearning to banish nuclear apocalypse. . . . The administration has an opportunity to bring about a historic change in strategic relationships and vastly reduce the threat of a nuclear apocalypse. To safeguard the opportunity the administration must do more than simply reject Gorbachev's proposals, it needs an alternative. It must state explicitly that it will not accept a ban on missile defenses but that it will negotiate the scope and nature of strategic defense simultaneously and in relation to agreed levels of offensive forces.[41]

The difference between Hoffman and Kissinger is not primarily one of viewpoint. It is the difference in frame of reference and style between the Extender/strategists such as Hoffman and Wohlstetter, and the Extender/diplomats such as Kissinger and Richard Burt. In spite of engendering occasional heated exchanges, however, the two styles are largely complementary. The beliefs that unite the Extenders and make it appropriate to call them a "school of thought" are that:

- The adversary is tough and sophisticated.
- Careless deterrence will fail to deter him and could lead to war through miscalculation.

---

[39]Fred S. Hoffman, letter to the author, dated June 27, 1985.
[40]Ibid.
[41]Kissinger, 1985, Part V, p. 1.

- A detailed counterforce strategy is technically feasible, strategically desirable, moral, and more conducive to stable deterrence than a strategy that depends on city-busting.
- If a nuclear exchange does take place, such a strategy is more likely than the alternative to limit escalation and damage.
- Arms control agreements are useful precisely insofar as they fit such a strategy, militarily and diplomatically.

12. The Limiters

Is it realistic to expect that a nuclear war could be limited to the detonation of tens or even hundreds of nuclear weapons even though each side would have tens of thousands of weapons available for use? The answer is clearly no. . . . Under such circumstances it is highly likely that rather than surrender, each side would launch a larger attack, hoping that this step would bring the action to a halt by causing the opponent to capitulate. . . .

Thus, "mutual assured destruction" is not, as some have alleged, an immoral policy. Mutual assured destruction—the vulnerability of each superpower to the awesome destructive power of nuclear weapons—is not a policy at all. It is a grim fact of life. . . .

A strengthened ABM Treaty would allow the Geneva negotiations to address the primary objective of offensive arms control: increasing the stability of deterrence by eliminating the perceptions of both sides that the other has, or is seeking, a first-strike capability. . . . Both sides have such immense forces that they should concentrate on quickly reducing the most threatening components—those that stand in the way of stability and much lower force levels.

—Robert S. McNamara[1]

Although the Limiters favor counterforce targeting to limit damage, as well as specific weapons and plans that are central to the Extenders' strategy, they do not believe that such details are likely to make much difference. The basic analytical root of their disagreement is the belief that once a nuclear exchange is initiated it is likely to escalate rapidly out of anyone's control, no matter what plans have been laid. "MAD" is therefore an unalterable condition, not a policy; the fear of where a nuclear exchange might end deters its start. No plans are going to change that, and it is perilous to depend militarily and politically on the basis of precise

[1]McNamara, 1986, pp. 34–130.

discrimination and control. Moreover, the threat of a first strike in times of crisis, implied by a thoroughgoing counterforce posture as well as the immense size of the nuclear forces of the opposing superpowers, is destabilizing and dangerous. Arms control agreements are vital to reduce such threats; in addition, some Limiters favor a policy of no first use of nuclear weapons as a measure of unilateral arms control.

ANALYSES

The two basic analytical propositions of the Limiters mirror those of the Extenders:

- Deterrence is based on the existence of nuclear weapons and the uncertainty of what would really happen if they were used, not on any specific plans for their use, which is fortunate because such plans would be unlikely to work if implementation were ever attempted.
- Although the Soviet Union is still capable of great mischief, it is far too prudent to attempt such mischief in ways that would threaten our vital interests. The Soviets neither possess nor aspire to "strategic superiority" over the United States, and they are as anxious as we are to reduce the momentum of the nuclear arms race.

The key to the Limiters' theory of nuclear dynamics is McGeorge Bundy's phrase "existential deterrence." Nuclear weapons exist and cannot be made not to exist. Nobody knows what would happen were a nuclear exchange to be initiated, but everybody fears the worst that could happen, "the end of civilization as we know it—if not of mankind itself," in Drell's description of our stake in the Faustian bargain. The existence of nuclear weapons plus this fear keep both sides far from nuclear initiation. As summarized by Bundy:

The terrible and avoidable uncertainties in any recourse to nuclear war create what could be called "existential" deterrence, where the function of the adjective is to distinguish this phenomenon from anything based on strategic theories or declared policies or even international commitments. . . .

Now that both strategic arsenals are redundantly destructive and amply survivable, we can say with still more confidence that existential deterrence is strong, and that its strength is essentially independent of most changes in deployment. Because no one can predict how

155

these arsenals might be used, because these uncertainties create an enormously powerful existential deterrent, and because this reality is essentially unaffected by any changes except those that might truly challenge the overall survivability of the forces on one side or the other, it makes no sense to base procurement decisions on refined calculations of specific kinds of force that would be needed for a wide variety of limited nuclear responses.[2]

Not all Limiters would agree with Bundy's contention that "existential deterrence is strong"; Drell is too conscious of the potential inferno to be optimistic even in this sense, for example. But common to all the Limiters is the concept that the deterrence we do have, and that is all we have, is existential.

Existential deterrence is the Limiters' answer to the Extenders' accusation that they espouse the morally "MAD" strategy of wanting to target innocents. McNamara's description of mutual assured deterrence as "a grim fact of life" takes the issue head on, and it is difficult, at least in recent literature, to find a suggestion from any Limiter that threats to population are necessary for deterrence. French analyst Pierre Hassner is close to the American Extenders. Nonetheless, he suggests that it is

[not] entirely fair to accuse the MAD bombers of actually wanting to bomb innocents or even of claiming that they can deter only by threatening cities. Actually, I think that what they are saying is that threatening cities is the only way to deter without provoking, i.e., without raising the suspicion that you are preparing a first strike and hence increasing the danger of preemptive or launch-on-warning from the other side.[3]

In fact, the Limiters' own writings do not contend that "threatening cities is the only way" to do anything; their central point is the existential one that threats to cities and populations are implicit in the uncertainties surrounding nuclear warfare, and that suffices.

Indeed, Halperin says that Secretary McNamara quantified MAD merely as

a management device to justify turning down requests for increases in strategic forces. The doctrine was *not* used to prohibit the development of strategic forces capable of attacking Soviet military targets.

---

[2]Bundy, 1964, p. 4.
[3]Hassner, 1983, p. 8.

The United States already had that capability and would continue to develop and expand it.[4]

But on the face of it, the Extenders' discriminating strategy is not inconsistent with existential deterrence. Why then do the Limiters oppose it? Although they do not oppose counterforce rather than countercity targeting, they do disagree with the overall posture because they believe that the discriminating strategy will not work as intended; rather, its pursuit will lead to military and political instability and will preclude the achievement of several Limiter goals, particularly meaningful arms control agreements.

The detailed discriminating counterforce strategy cannot work, according to the Limiters, for four major reasons: It will lead to preemption; it is virtually impossible to control, militarily or politically; it will lead to unintended escalation; and collateral damage will be so great as to render the counterforce discrimination meaningless.

Preemption

According to an article in the *Atlantic Monthly* signed by ten leading Limiters, including Bundy, Halperin, and McNamara:

Decision-makers would be under great pressure during a crisis. There would be a strong incentive to fire off nuclear weapons before they could be destroyed on their launchers.[5]

Failure of Control

The *Atlantic* article goes on to say:

Command, control, and communications would deteriorate once a nuclear war had begun, leaving decision-makers with incomplete information on rapidly changing battlefield conditions. These factors make it likely that authority to use nuclear weapons would have to be delegated to field commanders soon after the onset of a nuclear conflict, or perhaps even before it began. Such a policy offers little room for error and leaves little time for rational response. ... As a 1983

---

[4]Halperin, 1987, p. 20.
[5]McGeorge Bundy, Morton H. Halperin, William W. Kaufmann, George F. Kennan, Robert S. McNamara, Madalene O'Donnell, Leon V. Sigal, Gérard C. Smith, Richard H. Ullman, and Paul C. Warnke, 1986, p. 36.

report by the North Atlantic Assembly stated: "Few experts believe that the NATO political consultation process could possibly function effectively in time of crisis."[6]

Escalation

Halperin expresses the Limiters' doubts about the possibility of stopping the nuclear spiral once it has begun:

Once a single nuclear weapon was used the pressure to respond and to use additional weapons before they could be destroyed would be great indeed. Military commanders are likely to feel that the prohibition on using nuclear explosive devices was removed once a single nuclear warhead had been exploded; political leaders would come under enormous pressure to authorize military commanders to use the nuclear explosive devices at their disposal according to military judgments. In hours, if not minutes, much of Europe would be destroyed and nuclear explosive devices would have exploded on Soviet territory. It is difficult to see how the exchange could be ended short of both sides firing all of their warheads including those that the United States labeled "strategic."[7]

Collateral Damage

Desmond Ball summarized many estimates of civilian casualties in many counterforce exchanges. The numbers ranged from zero (for U.S. attacks on Soviet targets chosen for their isolation from populated areas) to 50 million (for a major Soviet counterforce strike against the United States). The modal estimate seems to be from 20–30 million each for the United States and the Soviet Union,[8] but Ball had three major doubts about the validity or utility of such numbers, even for the low end of his range of counterforce attacks:

First, the figures can only be considered "limited" by comparison with those that might result from direct nuclear attacks on urban-industrial areas. In the U.S. case, the damage caused even by a counterforce

---

[6]Ibid., pp. 36–38.
[7]Halperin, 1987, p. 106.
[8]Ball, 1981, pp. 27–28.

exchange would be unprecedented. . . . In the case of a U.S. counter-force attack against the Soviet Union, the fatalities could well approximate those of the Second World War. . . .

Second, the figures are almost certainly underestimates of the actual casualties that would be produced in the situations postulated. . . . For example, the estimates described above do not include casualties caused by fires ignited by nuclear blasts . . . [and] the effects of nuclear war are generally calculated by summing the consequences of particular effects, and there is no methodology for assessing the synergistic effects, even though these would be substantial. . . .

The third point . . . concerns the overall magnitude of the uncertainty that surrounds all estimates of the effects of nuclear war. This uncertainty is inevitable.[9]

These reasons doom the detailed counterforce strategy to failure. But the strategy is also unnecessary. Historically, Bundy points out, "In all of our most serious confrontations, and in our avoidance of such confrontations—in Berlin as in Cuba, in 1985 as in 1960—it has been nuclear *danger* and not nuclear *superiority* that has been decisive."[10] This does not mean that we can ignore all details of nuclear posture and strategy; Bundy goes on to say:

It is a grave mistake to underrate the importance of both quality and quantity in the maintenance of deterrence, and particular attention must always be given to making sure that the strategic deterrent as a whole is amply survivable. There is also good reason for maintaining both plans and capabilities for appropriate replies to all kinds of nuclear attack—large or "small," general or local. My argument should not be confused with any assertion that a couple of hundred city busters are enough, or with any suggestion that we should not constantly attend to any new weakness or vulnerability that appears. . . . I have never heard a remotely persuasive argument that the world would be a better place if the Soviet government *did* possess a usable nuclear advantage.[11]

That the Soviets do not possess such an advantage is one conclusion of the other key Limiter analysis. More generally, the Limiters believe that the United States bases its attitudes and strategies toward the Soviet Union on vast misunderstandings of their intentions as well as their capabilities.

[9]Ibid., pp. 28–29.
[10]Bundy, 1986, p. 10.
[11]Ibid., pp. 12–16.

According to British historian Michael Howard, writing well before Gorbachev's access to power:

My own firmly-held belief, however, is that the leadership of the Soviet Union, and any successors they may have within the immediately foreseeable future, are cautious and rather fearful men . . . above all conscious of the inadequacy of the simplistic doctrines of Marxism-Leninism on which they were nurtured to explain a world far more complex and diverse than either Marx or Lenin ever conceived. Their *Staatspolitik*, that complex web of interests, perceptions and ideals which Clausewitz believed should determine the use of military power, thus gives them no clearer guidance as to how to use their armed forces than ours gives to us.[12]

Indeed, if anything, Soviet actions and attitudes are based on fear of us. According to John Steinbruner:

In recent years, Soviet leaders have repeatedly expressed fears that U.S. strategic programs are designed to provide the capacity to initiate attack on Soviet strategic forces in the event of war, with sufficient success to establish some meaningful form of military victory.[13]

In the afterglow of Reykjavik, McNamara absolved the Reagan administration of Steinbruner's deliberate creation of a "capacity to initiate attack on Soviet strategic forces," but put the Soviet fears into even sharper focus as lit by SDI:

What they fear is that we will deploy SDI say five or six years from now when we are even farther ahead. They would face a period of years before they caught up to us. During that period they would fear that we had a first-strike capability. They have every reason to be afraid of that. However, I am certain that is not the President's objective.[14]

Further, Soviet strategic fears are set on a base of general deterioration of their system. Zbigniew Brzezinski puts it similarly to his Harvard colleague and fellow National Security Council alumnus Richard Pipes, but with a very different policy twist from Pipes's "don't help them 'preserve the Stalinist system'" quoted above. According to Brzezinski:

---

[12]Howard, 1981, pp. 6–8.
[13]Steinbruner, 1986, p. 158.
[14]Interview with Robert S. McNamara, *Los Angeles Times*, October 17, 1986, Part II, p. 5.

160

I think the Soviet Union realizes that what they were predicting in the 1970s, namely the general crisis of capitalism, is not coming to pass, and that we are witnessing instead the general crisis of communism. . . . My own view, in the light of the foregoing, is that we can be quite sanguine about the next phase in the American-Soviet negotiations. . . . Eventually, I feel quite confident we will end up with greatly reduced offensive strategic forces and with both possessing some minimum strategic defenses, each thereby gaining additional security against each other, and also against third-party threats.[15]

Brzezinski was one of the first to suggest that the Gorbachev radicalism was in reponse to a "general crisis of communism," a belief that has since become conventional.

The Limiters suggest further that the details of Soviet strategic nuclear doctrine on which Extender Sovietologists and strategists put substantial weight, are being misread and misinterpreted. Marshall Shulman, who was principal advisor on Soviet affairs to the Secretary of State during the Carter administration, contends that:

The belief that Soviet doctrinal writings imply an acceptance of limited nuclear war as an advantage to the Soviet Union stems from a confused and superficial reading of that literature. In practice, Soviet military preparations have assumed that a credible deterrent must be underpinned by a capability to deal with various levels of possible conflict. . . . A careful reading of Soviet military and political writing gives no support for the belief that Soviet leaders accept the possibility that a limited nuclear exchange could reasonably be expected to remain limited.[16]

In the light of these beliefs about Soviet fears and military conservatism, how does one understand Soviet weapons procurement and strategic doctrine? David Holloway interprets the Soviet procurements that the Extenders claim are giant steps to surpass us as being, instead, catchup efforts to achieve parity:

[T]he Soviets refused to acquiesce in strategic inferiority and built up their offensive forces, attaining rough parity with the United States by the early 1970s. . . . Brezhnev and his colleagues were not willing to resign themselves to second place in the symbolism of greatness. They may have hoped in the mid-1960s, as they were to do in the

---

[15]Interview with Zbigniew Brzezinski, *Los Angeles Times*, October 16, 1986, Part II, p. 5.
[16]Shulman, 1982, p. 88.

1970s, that strategic parity would bring the Soviet Union economic and political benefits in its relationship with the West. . . . Soviet policy has been deeply rooted in the urge to compete with the United States and guided by the belief that any inferiority would have harmful military and political consequences.[17]

These views of the Soviet Union lead to another crucial difference between the Limiters and the Extenders, their interpretation of the causes and significance of the "arms race." The Extenders do not discuss it very fully because they do not take it very seriously. Their "We build, they build; we stop, they build" viewpoint argues that we can stop only our side of the race because Soviet actions are autonomous from ours anyhow. To the Limiters, however, this is a fundamental error, and the arms race is a crucial issue. McNamara picks up on the interpretations of the Soviets provided by such Sovietologists as Shulman and Holloway, together with his own experience as Secretary of Defense, to present a picture of the arms race in which each side conditions its actions on the other's:

Many Americans are under the impression that while the United States expands its nuclear forces at some times and shows restraint at others, the Soviet Union pursues a relentless, inexorable buildup. . . . From this it is argued that the United States must continue to expand merely to catch up.

The reality of the matter is much more complex than such misperceptions suggest. Soviet decisions about the forces that they will build are not simply the result of an internally motivated drive for power and superiority. Many of their force increases over the past twenty years can best be understood as reactions to American developments. In reverse, the same applies to many American developments. I have referred to this as the "action-reaction phenomenon." It is a fundamental force driving the nuclear arms race.[18]

A question less frequently discussed by the Limiters is: What's wrong with an arms race, anyhow? For the most part, the race is treated as being bad on the simple assumptions that more weapons are worse than fewer and increases in numbers worse than decreases. Some Limiters treat these assumptions essentially as first-order value judgments rather than basing them on any analyses contending that large and increasing numbers of weapons lead to war. McNamara does link the current arms race more specifically to increased likelihood of nuclear war, with his concern that

[17]Holloway, 1986, pp. 138–141.
[18]McNamara, 1986, pp. 52–53.

now we appear on the verge of an escalation of the arms race that will not only place weapons in space, but will seriously increase the risk that one or the other of the adversaries will be tempted in a period of tension to initiate a preemptive nuclear strike before the opponent can get in the first blow.[19]

The most detailed and balanced recent discussion by a Limiter, however, is by Joseph Nye of Harvard, also a Carter administration alumnus:

In a world with 50,000 nuclear weapons, many people believe cutting their numbers seems self-evidently good. Yet, many strategists are skeptical. Although they share the public's concern about avoiding nuclear war, they doubt that the number of weapons determines the probability of use—fewer, they argue, is not necessarily better. Moreover, some of the most popular reasons for cutting are not compelling.

Contrary to conventional wisdom, unless one assumes major political changes, nuclear reductions may not save much money. . . . There is also the belief that reducing the number of nuclear weapons reduces the odds of accidental use. However, the sheer number of weapons is not the major factor governing the odds of nuclear war. . . .

The more compelling arguments for reducing nuclear weapons tend to be political. Reductions may help maintain or restore public confidence in nuclear deterrence both at home and among U.S. allies. . . . Reductions could also reassure the American public about Soviet intentions, and reassure the Soviets about U.S. policies. . . .

The largest gains are likely to come in the political area, both in terms of reversing the sense of momentum that worries the public and in improving U.S.-Soviet relations.[20]

In addition to the arms race, many Limiters put an exchange starting with a nuclear accident or other "unintended wars" at the center of their worries. As Professors Michael Intriligator and Dagobert Brito, following a path similar to Nye's, contend, "The most dangerous aspect of the current arms situation is not the presence or the level of weapons, which, in fact, create the stability of mutual deterrence, but rather the danger of accident and especially the possibility that either or both of the superpowers has a

---

[19]Ibid., p. 6.
[20]Nye, 1986a, pp. 6–13.

launch on warning system."[21] The *Atlantic Monthly* article by the ten Limiters puts the matter into a more political context and suggests that undue confidence in "the stability of mutual deterrence" may, in fact, lead to war by accident:

> [E]ven if the specter of "nuclear accidents waiting to happen" instills a greater measure of caution in Soviet leaders, it cannot guarantee that the East and the West will never stumble into war. . . . There are many examples throughout history of wars beginning not through a rational calculation of mutual benefit and cost but through a miscalculation at the height of a political crisis.[22]

Stable "existential" deterrence is still central, because it is all we have, but even it is not dependable.

VALUE JUDGMENTS

Nuclear war by miscalculation, probably on the part of those who thought they could control it but couldn't, is at the analytical core of the Limiters' fears; avoiding nuclear war is at their value core. It is not the only value; if it were, unilateral disarmament would be an easy way out. In contrast to the Extenders, Limiters believe avoidance, not damage limitation and not prudent political use, is central.

The Extenders' two differentiating value propositions concerned the importance of damage-limiting control and the worth of defending against Communism. For the Limiters, one central value judgment drives their thinking about nuclear strategy:

- Nuclear war must be avoided;

but the single proposition is conditioned by another value judgment that is not stressed:

- Of course we must assume some risks to defend our own freedom and help defend the freedom of our close allies.

It is conditioned also by the analytical belief that neither avoiding war nor defending freedom is very easy. Damage limitation is not among the important values of the Limiters, not because they don't like it, but because analytically they believe it is not possible.

---

[21]Intriligator and Brito, 1984, p. 5.
[22]Bundy et al., 1986a, p. 38.

Thus far, this discussion of the Limiters has set forth their views and contrasted them to the Extenders. In taking up their value judgments, however, attention must be paid to the other boundary, that between the Limiters and the Disarmers. Whereas the Disarmers are unwilling to contemplate the actual use of nuclear weapons in *any* circumstances, the Limiters reject this absolute criterion. The Limiters thus must consider trade-offs between their two primary value judgments—opposition to Red as well as dead—and the relationship of deterrent threats to their potential implementation.

Father Hehir, the drafter of the Catholic Bishops' statement, is classed as a Disarmer under the definitions used here because of his contention that nuclear deterrence of nuclear attack may be moral but use of nuclear weapons even to execute the deterrent threat cannot be.[23] The Bishops themselves, however, fall within the Limiter consensus because they suggest not only that deterrence can be acceptable under some conditions, but that "proportional" use of nuclear weapons may also be permissible. As summarized in their statement:

Catholic teaching begins in every case with a presumption against war and for peaceful settlement of disputes. In exceptional cases, determined by the moral principles of the just-war tradition, some uses of force are permitted.

Every nation has a right and duty to defend itself against unjust aggression.

Offensive war of any kind is not morally justifiable.

It is never permitted to direct nuclear or conventional weapons to "the indiscriminate destruction of whole cities or vast areas with their populations." The intentional killing of innocent civilians or noncombatants is always wrong.

Even defensive response to unjust attack can cause destruction which violates the principle of proportionality. . . . No defensive strategy, nuclear or conventional, which exceeds the limits of proportionality is morally permissible.

"In current conditions 'deterrence' based on balance, certainly not as a step in itself but as a step on the way toward a progressive disarmament, may still be judged morally acceptable." (Pope John Paul II.)[24]

---

[23]At least that is the Wohlstetter interpretation of Hehir's view.
[24]National Conference of Catholic Bishops, 1983, pp. 4–5.

The Bishops' sentence in their summary, "The intentional killing of innocent civilians or non-combatants is always wrong," sounds like the words of the anti-MAD Extenders, but lest such a confusion be made, the body of their statement adds:

> But "counterforce targeting," while preferable from the perspective of protecting civilians, is often joined with a declaratory policy which conveys the notion that nuclear war is subject to precise rational and moral limits. We have already expressed our severe doubts about such a concept. Furthermore, a purely counterforce strategy may seem to threaten the viability of other nations' retaliatory forces, making deterrence unstable in a crisis and war more likely.[25]

For most of the Limiters, the acceptance of deterrence as the best available alternative for avoiding nuclear war is less agonizing—reality is reality. Schelling makes it a normal fact of life, and not only nuclear life:

> Most of what we call civilization depends on reciprocal vulnerability. . . . It is often said that terror is a poor basis for civilization, and the balance of terror is not a permanently viable foundation for the avoidance of war. Fear can promote hostility and fear can lead to impetuousity in a crisis. I agree, but I do not equate a balance of deterrence with a balance of terror.[26]

Most of the Limiters remain fairly terrified, however, although they stay away from the language of terror; and those who have been in the decision-making position substitute the language of pragmatics for that of outraged morality. McNamara quotes Bundy as saying:

> Think-tank analysts can set levels of acceptable damage well up in the tens of millions of lives. They can assume that the loss of dozens of great cities is somehow a real choice for sane men. They are in an unreal world. In the real world of real political leaders—whether here or in the Soviet Union—a decision that would bring even one hydrogen bomb on one city of one's own country would be recognized in advance as a catastrophic blunder; ten bombs on ten cities would be a disaster beyond history; and a hundred bombs on a hundred cities are unthinkable.[27]

---

[25]Ibid., p. 49.
[26]Schelling, 1985–1986, p. 233.
[27]McNamara, 1986, pp. 137–138.

Elsewhere, Bundy comments on the Bishops' report: "They think it will never be morally right to be the first to cross the nuclear threshold, thus joining those of us who have argued, as a matter of political prudence, that it is time to move away from reliance on that suicidal threat."[28] "Political prudence" feels more comfortable than morality, but the outcome is the same.

It is also more comfortable for the Limiters to assume than to discuss in detail the existence of other objectives, for which conventional conflict and nuclear risk may be appropriate, but these other objectives remain, and remain important. Harvard Professors Joseph Nye, Graham Allison, and Albert Carnesale name their book *Hawks, Doves, and Owls*. They do not class themselves even as owls, but in the terminology used here, they are Limiters, concentrating much more on avoiding nuclear war than on minimizing damage. At the beginning of the book, however, they make clear that war avoidance must be understood in a complex setting of multiple objectives. They ask of U.S. nuclear policy, "What are we trying to do?" and reply:

> Our one-line answer is: To protect U.S. values and institutions, which requires avoiding nuclear war between the United States and the Soviet Union. The United States must manage the political competition with the Soviet Union so as to avoid a major nuclear war. American policymakers will pursue other objectives as well, but this is the necessary condition that must be satisfied if we are to have the opportunity to pursue any other goal.[29]

And Bundy falls back on existential deterrence to reunite the avoidance of nuclear war with other foreign policy objectives: "We can draw a further conclusion which the Russians might not wish us to reach. Where existential deterrence is strong, where there is an informed fear of nuclear war on both sides, the threat of nuclear blackmail can be contained."[30]

A more comprehensive Limiter discussion of values in a nuclear context, however, has been presented by Nye, subsequent to his contribution to the *Hawks, Doves, and Owls* volume. He divides nuclear morality into three components—motives, means, and consequences. Although he assigns some weight to each of these, his own stress is on consequences:

---

[28]Bundy, 1983, p. 6.
[29]Allison, Carnesale, and Nye, 1985, p. 15.
[30]Bundy, 1983, p. 8.

Given the enormity of the potential effects, moral reasoning about nuclear weapons must pay primary attention to consequences. In the nuclear era a philosophy of pure integrity that would "let the world perish" is not compelling. But given the unavoidable uncertainties in the estimation of risks, consequentialist arguments will not support precise or absolute moral judgments.[31]

Thus, even the defense of freedom (motives) and even the distaste for the morality of nuclear threats (means) must give way to the examination of the consequences of a specific threat or action, particularly the consequences of risking an actual nuclear exchange as an outcome. And Limiter as well as Extender analysis of deterrence indicates that the nuclear threat may well be the best way to avoid the nuclear outcome. Potential consequences include the political as well as the nuclear, however, and Nye does not shy from these, but attempts to put them in context:

Sometimes political perceptions of a delicate nuclear balance of power are invoked to justify far-fetched or marginal foreign policy goals. But to resort to nuclear threats in order to protect low stakes is a morally and politically nasty bluff. Fortunately, prudence reinforces virtue in helping to limit such threats, since in deterrence a particular move is likely to succeed only if it is sufficiently proportionate to crucial values that it will appear credible.[32]

Such proportionality governs Limiter value judgments on matters other than the avoidance of nuclear war. But the weight put on avoidance is such that it must be a crucial value indeed that would invoke any calculated increase in the risks of this war. For some Limiters, the defense of Western Europe is that crucial. Whether the threat and potential actual use of nuclear weapons should be used for that defense is at the heart of the "no-first-use" controversy, over which Limiters divide in their policy recommendations.

POLICY RECOMMENDATIONS

Like the Extenders, the Limiters set forth a wide variety of policy recommendations. Three sets, corresponding to the three discussed above to characterize the central policy thrusts of the Extenders, illustrate the major

---
[31]Nye, 1986b, p. 91.
[32]Ibid., p. 47.

directions in which the Limiters want to move and the differences between the two schools.

- *Nuclear Strategy and Planning.* Move away from any use of nuclear weapons other than for deterrence of nuclear attack. To implement this, retain a nuclear force that is well enough protected to preclude a successful enemy first strike; and continue counterforce targeting on a strictly second-strike basis. In any case, existential deterrence will continue to deter Soviet aggression in Europe, as it has thus far. Limiter views here range from "no-first-use" (McNamara and others) down to "Maintain the first use threat, but don't plan for it and do everything to avoid its implementation" (Allison, Carnesale, and Nye).
- *Arms Control.* Strive for explicit arms agreements with the Soviet Union as an essential part of overall deterrent stability and arms control.
- *The Strategic Defense Initiative.* Confine SDI to laboratory research well within the bounds of the existing ABM treaty, retaining the option of using missile defense as part of a more comprehensive offensive and defensive deterrence-stabilizing agreement with the Soviets.

As has been noted, the Limiters' views on these matters, particularly on nuclear planning and on SDI, differ from those of the Extenders somewhat more in words (declaratory policy) than in actual targeting and other plans. A major practical manifestation of the differences, however, lies in budgetary choices: The Limiters would not only spend less on SDI, they would devote little of the defense budget to nuclear-option-proliferating hardware, compared, for example, with conventional readiness.

The most drastic Limiter recommendation on the use of nuclear weapons—a declaratory policy and a strategy that forswears their use unless or until someone else has used them against us—was set forth, tentatively, in 1982 by McNamara, Bundy, Kennan, and Gérard Smith:

The one clearly definable firebreak against the worldwide disaster of general nuclear war is the one that stands between all other kinds of conflict and any use whatsoever of nuclear weapons. To keep that firebreak wide and strong is in the deepest interest of all mankind. In retrospect, indeed, it is remarkable that this country has not responded to this reality more quickly. Given the appalling consequences of even the most limited use of nuclear weapons and the total impossibility for both sides of any guarantee against unlimited escalation, there must be the gravest doubt about the wisdom of a policy which asserts the effectiveness of any first use of nuclear weapons by

169

either side. So it seems timely to consider the possibilities, the requirements, the difficulties, and the advantages of a policy of no-first-use.[33]

McNamara's own view was less tentative, and, by his own account, had been for some time. In a 1983 article he wrote, in words repeated in his 1986 book:

I do not believe we can avoid serious and unacceptable risk of nuclear war until we recognize—and until we base all our military plans, defense budgets, weapon deployments, and arms negotiations on the recognition—that *nuclear weapons serve no military purpose whatever. They are totally useless—except only to deter one's opponent from using them.*

This is my view today. It was my view in the early 1960s.

At that time, in long private conversations with successive Presidents—Kennedy and Johnson—I recommended, without qualification, that they never initiate, under any circumstances, the use of nuclear weapons.[34]

The 1986 *Atlantic Monthly* article, signed by the four authors of the initial no-first-use piece and six others, lays out a path to no-first-use through an intermediate stage, no-early-use of nuclear weapons.

In the short run the United States can and should move toward a diminished reliance on nuclear weapons by reducing and relocating vulnerable nuclear forces currently deployed near the NATO-Warsaw Pact border. We believe that eventually the United States, in concert with its NATO allies, should formalize its commitment not to initiate the use of nuclear weapons and should alter its deployments, war plans, and attitudes accordingly....

As an initial measure, the Western alliance could adopt a policy of no early use.... Those weapons that raise the most serious problems relating to release authority and early use...could all be rapidly

---

[33]Bundy et al., 1982, p. 757. The "firebreak" concept, although recognized implicitly by many since the first use of nuclear weapons (e.g., by President Eisenhower but not by those advisors who recommended use of nuclear weapons at Dien Bien Phu), was formalized by Schelling, *The Strategy of Conflict*, App. A. It has been *the* central criterion for Extenders as well as Limiters in considering the use of nuclear weapons, ever since.

[34]McNamara, 1983, p. 79, repeated (without the italics) in McNamara, 1986, p. 139.

withdrawn and their storage facilities secured against conventional and other forms of non-nuclear attack.[35]

In his own book, however, Halperin, one of the signers of the *Atlantic* piece, goes further in terms of restructured posture: "NATO's conventional military forces would be completely separated from the specialized units designed to deliver nuclear explosive devices should the political leadership of the Alliance ever decide to employ them,"[36] but he does not go quite so far in absolute renunciation of first use:

[W]hat I am suggesting is not, strictly speaking, a no-first-use policy for Europe. It is a somewhat different proposal—one that focuses not on a public promise never to use nuclear weapons first, but rather on the forces and operational plans for nuclear and conventional weapons in Europe.[37]

Allison, Carnesale, and Nye also decline to go as far as absolute no-first-use. High among their policy prescriptions is:

DON'T adopt a no first use policy. Rhetorical removal of the threat of intentional escalation to nuclear war in Europe, the Persian Gulf, or Korea would (if believed) psychologically enhance Soviet advantages in general purpose forces and increase the risk that the Soviets might attempt a conventional attack. . . .

So long as nuclear forces are deployed in substantial numbers, they present an inescapable risk that any conventional war might escalate by design or by action to a nuclear one.[38]

Their rejection of no-first-use is in agreement with the Extenders, but the last sentence invokes existential deterrence, and their prescriptions differ substantially from the Extenders' detailed options. They surround their conditional acceptance of first use with such Limiter recommendations as:

DON'T seek a first-strike capability.

DON'T plan for a nuclear demonstration shot in Europe.

DO reduce reliance on short-range theater nuclear weapons.

DON'T use nuclear alerts for political signalling.

---

[35]Bundy et al., 1982, pp. 36–40.
[36]Halperin, 1987, p. 95.
[37]Ibid.
[38]Allison, Carnesale, and Nye, 1985, pp. 227–230.

DON'T multiply crises . . . by initiating another crisis in which [we have] the advantage.

DON'T decapitate [by targeting] Soviet political and military leaders and their C³ network.³⁹

Given all this, Allison, Carnesale, and Nye rejoin the recommendations of the ten authors of the *Atlantic Monthly* piece (among whom they are not numbered):

DON'T plan for early use of nuclear weapons.⁴⁰

The stress of the Limiters, on whichever side of the no-first-use issue they come down, is thus on *moving away* from the use of nuclear weapons, rather than on the Extenders' *control* of the use. This does not imply that the Limiters are unwilling to try for controlled counterforce. Rather, they want to make sure that such control is part of a second-strike strategy, not a cover for a concealed first-strike option. Halperin, for example, contends that:

American strategic forces [should] be capable of destroying only a small portion of the Soviet strategic forces quickly in a first strike. . . . It is sometimes suggested that this strategy would necessarily mean that American strategic forces would be targeted solely or primarily on cities. This is not so. The United States could maintain the capability to attack a range of targets including theater forces, industrial capacity, and even missile silos. All that would be eschewed is that ability to attack all or most of the Soviet strategic forces quickly.⁴¹

The Limiters' main instrument both for deemphasis of nuclear weapons and their control, however, is the explicit arms control agreement. Allison, Carnesale, and Nye's recommendations also include:

DO preserve existing arms control agreements.

DO pursue crisis stability through arms control.

DO reduce uncertainties through arms control negotiations.⁴²

Before we examine the Limiters' views on arms agreements, however, it is necessary to present one piece of recent historical context. Just as

³⁹Ibid., pp. 232–236.
⁴⁰Ibid., p. 236.
⁴¹Halperin, 1987, pp. 76–77.
⁴²Allison, Carnesale and Nye, 1985, pp. 242–243.

President Reagan's vision of a "hard-shell" SDI put a new and difficult twist into the Extenders' long-run recommendations for ABM, his performance in the Reykjavik talks with Gorbachev put a new and difficult twist into the Limiters' arms agreement recommendations. At Reykjavik, Reagan outran his staff preparations and his own previous positions to accept and even propose measures—e.g., zero ballistic missiles and/or zero nuclear weapons after ten years (depending on whose version of Reykjavik one accepts)—that had been around for a while as symbolic goals but were too radical even for many Limiters when put into a context of timetable reality. As put by Kissinger, "At Reykjavik, the Soviets took advantage of the weakness in the American decision-making process by suddenly agreeing to American positions put forward over the years primarily to paper over departmental differences."[43]

Politically, American Limiters could not reject this sudden "breakthrough"; substantively, many of them joined Kissinger in his doubts. For the Limiters as well as the Extenders, the problem introduced by the Reykjavik symbolism is characterized by Schelling's (pre-Reykjavik) contention that "hardly anyone who takes arms control seriously believes that zero is the goal," and his decrying of "'arms control' for its own sake, not for the sake of peace and confidence."[44] The Limiters' doubts were largely resolved, however, when the zero-weapons symbolism of Reykjavik became the 50-percent-reduction reality of the START negotiations. In effect, President Reagan had joined the Limiters, to the substantial discomfort of some of his Extender backers, some of whom left his administration. It *was* the president who changed, however; the Extenders and Limiters remained much as before, adapting their opposing theologies to the new Reagan/Gorbachev reality.

Schelling's "peace and confidence" is a broad statement of what the Limiters hope to get out of arms agreements. Somewhat more specifically, unlike the Extenders, they believe in Drell's terms that "the first and overriding goals of arms control negotiations should be: To enhance strategic stability based on a balance of highly survivable and secure deterrent forces."[45] Different writers stress various aspects of this objective:

Brzezinski:

[I]n any future negotiations, the issue would be what mix of offensive and defensive strategic forces would achieve mutual strategic security. That is the matter that ought to be negotiated with the Soviet Union—

[43]Kissinger, 1986d, Sec. V, p. 6.
[44]Schelling, 1985–1986, pp. 226–228.
[45]Drell, 1983, p. 37.

not largely theological discussions about the respective merits of a total Strategic Defense Initiative or a totally nuclear free world.[46]

Lieutenant General Glenn Kent (USAF, ret.):

The United States must therefore seek agreement with the Soviet Union on the fundamental principle of survival of strategic forces: that both countries seek stability and eschew the capability for a successful first strike.[47]

Bundy, Kennan, McNamara, and Smith:

In its underlying meaning the [ABM] Treaty is a safeguard less against defense as such than against unbridled competition.[48]

Walter Slocombe (Deputy Undersecretary of Defense in the Carter administration):

Historically, the objective of arms control has been to regulate and make more predictable the nuclear competition, not to purport to abolish it.[49]

Nye:

[O]nly a long-term political strategy of societal engagement and a jointly managed balance of power offer a real promise of escaping the dilemmas of deterrence.[50]

Steinbruner:

The United States is primarily interested in reducing the level of strategic force deployments in order to alleviate a perceived threat to the U.S. intercontinental ballistic missile forces and a politically sensitive imbalance in weapons deployed in Europe. The Soviet Union is primarily interested in restricting the process of technical improvement in order to alleviate what it perceives as an emerging threat to Soviet ICBMs and ultimately to the entire structure of Soviet military forces.[51]

All of these provide different angles on the central stress of most Limiters—the use of arms agreements to provide strategic stability through mutual deterrence adapted to the needs and postures of both the United States and the

---

[46]Brzezinski, 1986a, p. 27.
[47]Kent, 1984, p. v.
[48]Bundy et al., 1984, p. 274.
[49]Slocombe, 1985, p. 207.
[50]Nye, 1986a, p. 15.
[51]Steinbruner, 1985, p. 1036.

Soviet Union. In addition, however, several Limiters stress arms agreements to avoid "accidental" war. Intriligator and Brito have been quoted above. And Drell, after putting stable deterrence in the "first and overriding" position, adds "a second goal of negotiations. . . . To initiate significant, timely, and verifiable reductions in the nuclear forces and destructive potential of both nations."[52]

Not all Limiters would agree with Drell's stress, even though it is secondary, on reducing numbers of weapons. Many would subscribe to Schelling's complaint that:

> The main difference between pre-1971 and post-1972 arms negotiations has been the shift of interest from the *character* of weapons to their *numbers*. In the United States, this is the common interest that has joined left and right, leaving almost no room in between. . . . The last two administrations have been intent on matching hard-target capabilities, number for number, almost without regard to whether denying strategic-weapon targets to the enemy—such as deploying untargetable weapons—was a superior alternative to matching hard-target capability.[53]

Schelling's contention is that the Reagan administration as well as Carter's had adopted the numerical emphasis of some Limiters as an easy political path, leading to what he believes is the absurdity of the Reagan preference for the heavy apparently-first-strike multiple warhead MX missile over the mobile protected-retaliation single-warhead Midgetman because the latter would not only be more expensive per warhead but would also mean "more" missiles in an arms control agreement that counted vehicles rather than warheads.[54]

Halperin makes another use of the concept of the different "character" of nuclear weapons, emphasizing the need to increase the distinction between the nuclears and the others:

> [T]he United States [should] focus its efforts on stigmatizing nuclear weapons worldwide without raising concern that such efforts would undercut key components of American security. The United States would not only deny the utility of first use but would stigmatize the second use of nuclear weapons if such use was intended to be effective on a battlefield. . . . Though not eliminating the use of nuclear weapons as a tool of international diplomacy, the United States would want . . . to

---

[52]Drell, 1983, p. 37.
[53]Schelling, 1985–1986, pp. 225–226.
[54]Ibid., p. 228.

stigmatize these devices and emphasize the fundamental gap between them and instruments of war.[55]

Also, like Kissinger but unlike the Reagan administration and most Extenders, the Limiters put the issues of verification of arms control agreements and Soviet compliance with the agreements into a context that weighs the military and political significance of violations and ambiguities rather than asking the single question: Did they violate or didn't they? Nye argues that:

> What is striking is that the opponents of arms control have managed over time to move issues with minor military significance from the margin to the center of the U.S.-Soviet relationship. By treating these issues as a litmus test of Soviet intentions and establishing their rectification as a condition for continued adherence to the numerical SALT limits (which both sides have observed), the skeptics have progressively narrowed the President's options. This does not mean the alleged violations should be ignored; it means that the President should have insisted that they be seriously negotiated in the Standing Consultative Commission (as they merited), rather than politicized and implanted at the heart of the relationship.[56]

Their emphasis on arms agreements leads the Limiters to a wide variety of specific proposals for such agreements. The following list of examples illustrates the range of the proposals. Some of the variation in the list is due to the specificity of the proposed measures; they relate to the state of actual negotiations at the time that author put forth that proposal. What is notable throughout is that the Limiters pay as much attention to the details of proposed arms agreements as the Extenders do to the details of weapons and target discrimination.

- I recommend that we include a direct limit on the numbers of nuclear warheads on the long-range bombers and missiles in any future treaty negotiation. (Sidney Drell.)[57]
- The U.S. proposal is the one that would limit all strategic ballistic reentry vehicles to 5000.... The Soviet proposal is the one that would limit launchers for strategic ballistic missiles plus heavy bombers to 1800....

---

[55]Halperin, 1987, pp. 138–139.
[56]Nye, 1986a, p. 17.
[57]Drell, 1983, p. 38.

Taken together, these two proposals make particularly good sense. (Michael May, Associate Director, Lawrence Livermore Lab.)[58]

- In both [U.S. START negotiating] approaches, the reductions of the three principal commodities—ballistic missile weapons, ballistic missile throwweight, and bombers—would be negotiated separately. We propose a third approach: to aggregate the three commodities and negotiate constraints on them collectively. . . . If the United States and the Soviet Union are to seek a trade-off and a freedom to mix between throwweight and bombers, they must find a common currency. We propose such a currency: the standard weapon station. This currency expresses the throwweight of missiles in units of 400 kilograms. (Lieutenant General Glenn Kent.)[59]

- Arms control agreements should, therefore, be designed to improve the overall survivability of the nuclear forces of *both* sides. This can best be done through a combination of steps: by reducing the overall number of nuclear weapons and particularly of ballistic missile warheads; by permitting certain kinds of modernization (e.g., mobile missiles); by allowing the rebasing of ICBMs; by regulating the introduction of new missiles; and by phasing out or preferentially reducing certain kinds of older systems (e.g., MIRVed missiles). (Former Defense Secretary Harold Brown and Lynn Davis.)[60]

- Now a new approach has arrived in the idea known as "build-down." In essence the build-down principle says that no new weapons should be deployed unless a larger number of existing weapons are destroyed. (Alton Frye.)[61]

- Thus, a cooperative U.S.-Soviet limited strategic defense system might be a useful subject for consideration at the Geneva summit—not only as a compromise between the U.S. and Soviet positions, but as a positive step that is feasible, timely and in the interest of both nations in reducing the chances of nuclear war. (Michael Intriligator.)[62]

Many of these proposals entered the START negotiations. Their very variety indicates where the Limiters put their thought and their weight.

The emphasis on arms agreement provides the primary reason that the Limiters oppose SDI. The title of the 1984 article on SDI by Bundy, Kennan, McNamara, and Smith sets forth their thesis: "The President's Choice: Star Wars or Arms Control." They contend that:

---

[58]May, 1983, p. 1.
[59]Kent, 1984, pp. vi-vii.
[60]Brown and Davis, 1984, p. 1159.
[61]Frye, 1983/84, p. 293.
[62]Intriligator, 1985, p. 5.

The President's program, because of the inevitable Soviet reaction to it, has already had a heavily damaging impact on prospects for early progress in strategic arms control. It has thrown a wild card into a game already impacted by mutual suspicion and a search on both sides for unattainable unilateral advantage.[63]

Later, however, the Reykjavik talks led these four senior Limiters to concede that:

The Strategic Defense Initiative has proved to be a powerful bargaining lever. If indeed the Soviet government can have satisfactory constraints on strategic defense, it seems ready to conclude agreements greatly reducing offensive forces.[64]

They then went on to endorse a form of SDI, but it was very different from either the President's hard-shell population defense or the military-site-defending aid to deterrence favored by many of the Extenders. They suggest instead, "In Iceland, President Reagan spoke of needing a defense for 'insurance' even after all American and Soviet missiles have been dismantled. That is apparently a quite different 'minimal' enterprise."[65]

For other Limiters, however, even after Reykjavik, SDI remains the obstacle rather than the lever for arms agreements. Former CIA Director William Colby and David Riley contend that:

President Reagan made a clear choice in Iceland to move ahead with his Strategic Defense Initiative at the expense of the Antiballistic Missile Treaty of 1972. The decision is wrong for two basic reasons. It ignores the nuclear realities that make such a defense both practically impossible and politically destabilizing, and it ignores the major contribution the ABM treaty has made, since it was signed in 1972, to dampening the nuclear arms race and reducing the threat of nuclear war.[66]

These words summarize most of the reasons Limiters have opposed SDI until now. A good deal of discussion has focused on technical feasibility, but most Limiters, like most Extenders, admit that nobody can yet know; most Limiters have favored a vigorous research program to find out and to hedge against Soviet breakthrough on missile defenses.[67] Worry about the effect of SDI on the existing and future arms agreements on which the Limiters put so

---

[63]Bundy et al., 1984, pp. 273–274.
[64]Bundy et al., 1986b, p. 23.
[65]Ibid.
[66]Colby and Riley, 1986, p. 31.
[67]See Levine, 1986, pp. 24–27.

much weight, however, together with the action-reaction model of the arms race, have produced strong opposition to both the President's vision and the military-site-defense version of many of the Extenders. To the extent that Reykjavik has changed this, it is, as Bundy, Kennan, McNamara, and Smith say, in favor of a "quite different 'minimal' enterprise." In 1988, Senator Sam Nunn (Dem., Ga.), the powerful chairman of the Senate Armed Services Committee, suggested a similar "anti-accident" ballistic missile defense. As technical, budgetary, and political obstacles to SDI grew, this seemed the likely direction for the effort under the new administration.

As with the Extenders, the school of thought I call the Limiters contains a group of people with many different views. Nonetheless, they come together on several major common themes:

- Stable deterrence has prevented nuclear war, and it is all we have at this time to continue preventing it.
- Deterrence is largely existential, and the discriminating postures and strategies proposed by the Extenders have little to do with the matter.
- Although we should plan for counterforce rather than countercity targeting, the prospects for meaningful damage limitation are slim indeed.
- Nuclear accident is possible and we should take steps to avoid it.
- The way out in the short run is to enhance stable deterrence through arms agreements with the Soviet Union; in the long run, such agreements may get us off the merry-go-round, but we have to get through the short run in order to reach the long.

13. The Disarmers

We know that a holocaust may not occur at all. If one does occur, the adversaries may not use all their weapons. If they do use all their weapons, the global effects, in the ozone and elsewhere, may be moderate. And if the effects are not moderate but extreme, the ecosphere may prove resilient enough to withstand them without breaking down catastrophically. These all are substantial reasons for supposing that mankind will not be extinguished in a nuclear holocaust, or even that extinction in a holocaust is unlikely, and they tend to calm our fear and reduce our sense of urgency. Yet at the same time we are compelled to admit that there *may* be a holocaust, that the adversaries *may* use all their weapons, that the global effects, including effects of which we are as yet unaware, *may* be severe, that the ecosphere *may* suffer catastrophic breakdown, and that our species *may* be extinguished. We are left with uncertainty.

Once we learn that a holocaust *might* lead to extinction we have no right to gamble, because if we lose, the game will be over, and neither we nor anyone else will ever get another chance.

Therefore, although, scientifically speaking, there is all the difference in the world between the mere possibility that a holocaust will bring about extinction and the certainty of it, morally they are the same, and we have no choice but to address the issue of nuclear weapons as though we knew for a certainty that their use would put an end to our species.

—Jonathan Schell[1]

The Disarmers are a diverse group, more diverse than the other schools because in the classifying schema set forth here they go from a boundary near the more worried of the Limiters—the bishops and Drell, for example—to the theoretical infinity of unilateral and absolute disarmament. Yet in the 1980s there are few if any unilateral Disarmers among those who write on the subject.

---

[1]Schell, 1984, pp. 27–28.

It was not always thus. It would be difficult in the 1980s to find disagreement with Nye's conclusion that consequences must dominate moral reasoning about nuclear weapons, but in the 1950s and 1960s, many Disarmers agreed with the American Friends Service Committee pamphlet favoring unilateral disarmament: "Here I stand. Regardless of relevance or consequence I can do no other."[2] Thirty years later, however, it is the presumed consequences of postures and strategies that govern the writings of the Disarmers as much as the other schools; and the world is recognized as being too complex for simple unilateral disarmament to be advocated seriously on moral or other grounds.

The Schell statement with which this chapter began turns entirely on potential consequences of nuclear war, and the enormity of these consequences is one theme uniting the Disarmers. This theme would bring in many Limiters and even some Extenders, however. What distinguishes the Disarmers is the feeling that so long as nuclear weapons exist extinction is possible, which leads them to concentrate on getting rid of the weapons one way or another. They therefore dismiss deterrence as no more than a state we must move through as quickly as possible on the way to more permanent solutions.

This discussion of the Disarmers is structured somewhat differently from those of the other two schools. The next subsection examines their two major analytical propositions, but no discussion is presented on value judgments, because the Disarmers' single overwhelming judgment—any chance of nuclear war is intolerable—is explicit in the opening quote from Schell and is implicit or explicit in everything else set forth. The final subsection therefore takes up several Disarmers and discusses their policy recommendations and how they got there.

ANALYSES

The Disarmer's two basic analytical propositions, matching those of the two other schools, are:

- The existence of nuclear weapons, and their use, even for deterrence, will lead to nuclear war and holocaust.
- The Soviet Union wants to get off the nuclear bandwagon at least as badly as we do.

---

[2]American Friends Service Committee, 1955, p. 68.

The Schell statement illustrates one aspect of the unusability of nuclear weapons: If they are used at all, there is a chance that the use will escalate to the extinction of the race, and any such chance is intolerable. The statement itself, however, is worded to make an *a fortiori* case: "Even if we accept all of the most optimistic premises, the residual chance of extinction is intolerable." The Disarmers, of course, do not accept these optimistic premises, but agree rather with the Limiters who fear nuclear escalation and uncontrollability (but unlike the Disarmers believe that stable deterrence is the best way to avoid the first step toward holocaust).

Logically, one initial premise precedes the one that connects use of nuclear weapons to ultimate extinction of the race. It is the analytical connection from the existence of weapons to their use. Schell's existentialism, unlike Bundy's, suggests that the existence of nuclear weapons leads not to deterrence but to use:

> [T]he truth was that there was nothing wrong with the doctrine of deterrence which was not wrong simply with the possession of vast nuclear arsenals—with or without the doctrine of deterrence. The reason that no repair of the doctrine was possible was that the problem did not lie in doctrine. It lay in the world's possession of nuclear arsenals—in their "existential" features, if you like. For, whatever government spokesmen might say about possessing nuclear weapons only to prevent their use, the inescapable truth was that possession inevitably implied use.[3]

A similar view is expressed quantitatively and slightly less pessimistically by Professor George Rathjens of MIT:

> Some years ago, I concluded that 90% reductions in 1985 levels would likely mean reductions in fatalities in the event of large-scale nuclear war by factors of around two to ten, depending on the scenario. Reductions on this scale would hardly be a solution to the nuclear problem, but should they be denigrated as meaningless?[4]

And Randall Forsberg turns around the Extenders' concept of the counterforce strategy as limiting damage: "The quest for improved counterforce capability has driven the arms race far past the point where each contender can destroy the other's society and much else besides."[5]

---

[3]Schell, 1984, pp. 84–85.
[4]Rathjens, 1985, p. 11.
[5]Forsberg, 1982, p. 52.

The chief analytical point of the Disarmers is that it is not the plans for the use of nuclear weapons that determine what happens—counterforce plans and weapons will lead to the destruction of society, not military targets—but the existence of the weapons. Existence leads to use leads to extinction, and larger numbers lead to higher probabilities of use and extinction.

None of this is necessary, however, because the Soviets want to get away from the nuclear threat as badly as we do. The fault now lies more with us than with them. In two newspaper pieces preceding the November 1985 Geneva summit meeting between Reagan and Gorbachev, Princeton professor and *Nation* columnist Stephen Cohen analyzed successively the Reagan administration's approach to the Russians and the limited American criticism of that approach on the one hand, and the reality of Soviet needs and views on the other.

[N]ot one influential group or institution has mounted a sustained opposition to Reagan's militarized approach to the Soviet Union, either by rejecting its underlying political premises or by offering the only alternative, a broad policy of détente. As a result, mainstream discussion of U.S.-Soviet relations is narrow and superficial . . . avoiding fundamental questions about the long-term goal of American policy. Is it to live peacefully with the Soviet Union as a superpower? To roll back Soviet power in the world? To destroy the Soviet system? No coherent policy is possible without answers to these and other questions.[6]

In reality, everything indicates that Gorbachev is the first reform-minded Soviet leader since Nikita S. Khrushchev came to power in the 1950s. . . . Gorbachev needs détente-like relations with the United States if he is to become any kind of strong reform leader in the deeply conservative system. . . . [He] must overcome widespread objections from the party elite and state bureaucracy that even modest forms of decentralization and liberalization are too dangerous because of "the growing American threat."[7]

And a year later, after Reykjavik, Fred Neal of Claremont Graduate School and the American Committee on U.S.-Soviet Relations expounded on the same theme of American need to work with Gorbachev against the bad guys in the Kremlin:

[6]S. Cohen, 1985, p. 5.
[7]Ibid.

There are three main points of view among Soviet decisionmakers about how to deal with the United States. One is to continue urging arms control agreements, and making concessions toward that end, as at present. A second is that it is impossible to "do business with Reagan" and thus Soviet approaches should wait for a new administration. A third holds that the United States is irrevocably oriented to cold war hostility and that any accommodation is impossible, no matter who is President. Mr. Gorbachev has up to now opted for the first view, but in the face of what Moscow considers repeated rebuffs, this is unlikely to prevail for very long.[8]

These statements were fairly radical at the time they were written, in 1985 and even 1986. Limiters would have hoped that the Soviet Union was really changing but would have prudently reserved judgment. The rush of events in the late 1980s, however, has been such that a year or two later, most Limiters would accept Cohen's and Neal's descriptions of Gorbachev as descriptions of reality, and even some Extenders might hope.

In any case, the two analytical points are basic to almost all Disarmers: that the line from the existence of nuclear weapons to the extinction of mankind is too direct to be tolerable and that we can appropriately work out solutions with the Soviets, who increasingly share these same perceptions. These two points plus the value judgment that any chance of nuclear war is intolerable lead to no agreed set of specific recommendations, however.

POLICY RECOMMENDATIONS

Where the Disarmers want to get is clear: a world without nuclear weapons. Having rejected the simplicity of unilateral disarmament and "I can do no other," however, Disarmers recognize the extreme difficulties of getting from here to there in the real world, and they set forth many possible measures. Those discussed here are merely illustrative.

Schell's recommendations are substantially beyond those of the Limiters. He himself makes the differentiation in discussing the Catholic bishops' statement:

Having made . . . firm and far-reaching moral judgments, the bishops do not go on to make equally firm and far-reaching recommendations for action on the basis of them. Rather, they subscribe to such moderate

---

[8]Neal, 1986.

and partial proposals as the nuclear freeze[9] and no first use. Like the peace movement as a whole, the bishops are diagnostic radicals but prescriptive moderates.[10]

Having opted for radical prescription as well as diagnosis, Schell dismisses as impractical several common solutions such as world government. Unlike some of his confreres, he separates peace from justice and admits that his solution for peace leaves and even perpetuates injustice:

> Our first step would be to accept the political verdict that has been delivered by deterrence, and formalize the stalemate. . . . We can, in a manner of speaking, adopt our present world, with all its injustices and other imperfections, as our ideal, and then seek the most sensible and moderate means of preserving it. . . . The next question is whether, after formalizing the status quo, we can reduce our reliance on the extreme means by which we now uphold it, and how far that reduction can go. . . . But . . . we actually rely on the doomsday machine to serve another end: the preservation of our sovereignty. We still exploit the peril of extinction for our political ends. . . . Given this political reality—which shows no sign of changing soon—it appears that, in one form or another, our reliance on the nuclear threat cannot be broken. Nevertheless, even under these terms we have far more flexibility than we have thought. It is a flexibility that, I believe, extends all the way to the abolition of nuclear arms. On the face of it, there appears to be a contradiction between the two goals we have set for ourselves. It appears that we want to keep the stalemate but to abolish the weapons that made it possible.[11]

The paradox set forth in the last two sentences makes Schell appear to be writing the whodunit of nuclear strategy: "The room was locked from the inside. How did the murderer make his escape?" His answer is worthy, if not of Conan Doyle or Agatha Christie, at least of the better of the modern mystery pulps. It is a four-part world agreement, in which the first part is the objective and the fourth the hidden solution to the mystery.

> The key is to enter into an agreement abolishing nuclear arms. Nations would first agree . . . to have not world government, in which

---

[9]The freeze is treated here as a Disarmers' proposal. It is, however, close to the line between the Disarmers and the Limiters.

[10]Schell, 1984, p. 90.

[11]Ibid., pp. 140–143.

all nations are fused into one nation, but its exact opposite—a multiplicity of inviolate nations pledged to leave each other alone.

[A] second provision of the agreement would stipulate that the size of conventional forces be limited and balanced.

[P]robably as a separate, third provision of the agreement—anti-nuclear defensive forces would be permitted. . . .

However, none of these defensive arrangements would offer much protection if the agreement failed to accompany them with one more provision. The worst case . . . is not mere cheating, but blatant, open violation of the agreement by a powerful and ruthless nation that is determined to intimidate or subjugate other nations, or the whole world, by suddenly and swiftly building up, and perhaps using, an overwhelming nuclear arsenal. . . . Therefore a fourth provision of the abolition agreement would permit nations to hold themselves in a particular, defined state of readiness for nuclear rearmament.[12]

Schell's argument is that the power to rearm is the deterrent, parallel to today's deterrent, but at a zero level of existing nuclear weapons. He has received substantial, although not universal, praise in the Disarmers' community for getting the murderer into and out of the locked room.

Other Disarmer recommendations take directions different from Schell's. In his Introduction to the *Bulletin of the Atomic Scientists* book in which some of the Disarmers' material quoted here (and some of the Limiters' as well) appears, the late Harrison Brown, then editor of the *Bulletin*, wrote that:

Although I am not so naive as to suppose that a full-fledged world government can be created in the near future, it should nevertheless be possible for the nations of the world to agree upon a legal code covering the more critical elements of war and peace and to establish the necessary enforcement machinery.[13]

This view is much more common among the Disarmers than is Schell's rejection of world law. Its roots go back to the period immediately after World War II, when the World Federalists, reacting to the failure of the League of Nations and the perception that the United Nations promised little additional strength, formed their serious but small movement for a world federal government patterned on that of this country. The seminal work in the field, and

---

[12]Ibid., pp. 146–150.
[13]Harrison Brown, 1986, p. xvi.

perhaps still the best because of the lack of opportunity to test or change the concepts, was the 1960 book, *World Peace Through World Law*.[14]

George Rathjens, an MIT political scientist and an alumnus of the Harvard-MIT seminar of the 1950s and 1960s, is more pessimistic than Schell or Brown and, in the end, perhaps more radical. He paints a very different picture of the failures of the 1970s from those of Nitze and Schelling, quoted at the beginning of this report. Nitze blamed them on the Russians, Schelling on the loss of concept and the stress on counterforce. For Rathjens, however, the problems are much more fundamental:

> What accounts for the dismal record? . . . The overwhelming point is that all of these efforts have focused on constraining the development and/or deployment of the weapons themselves . . . rather than on the reasons nations want to acquire weapons. Focusing on weapons is not likely to be a very useful approach when they are so easily acquired. Moreover it is deceptive almost to the point of being a gigantic fraud: there is the implicit suggestion that controls of weapons of the kind that have been tried will solve the problem—or at least make a big difference—when there is no real reason for so believing. . . .

> There is a widespread belief that successful negotiations are possible only "from positions of strength." Whether true or not, the assumption leads to accretion of weapons in order to bargain effectively. . . .

> Negotiations relating to strategic weapons have been predicated, at least on the U.S. side, in large measure on the assumption that a major objective should be to give impetus to changes in strategic force postures that could make disarming "first strikes" against land-based missile forces less feasible. A result has been to exaggerate grossly the importance of this particular "scenario" relative to virtually all others that could lead to catastrophe. . . .

> While some . . . proposals imply modest reductions in numbers of strategic weapons and even selective reduction in "counterforce" weapons, it is hard to believe that they can lead to a reduction in either the probability of nuclear war or the level of damage should one occur, much less to the elimination of the nuclear threat. . . . [The] levels of weapons will remain so high as to make likely the near-total destruction of the major combatants.[15]

---

[14]Clark and Sohn, 1960.
[15]Rathjens, 1985, pp. 8–10.

This is actual pessimism, not the *a fortiori* "it could happen" reasoning of Schell. Rathjens also rejects Schell's deterrence by threat of rearming as being overly optimistic, contending that under Schell's scheme:

(1) The time required for nations to assemble weapons would vary enormously from one country to another. . . . (2) The time required for weapons production could be shortened by advance preparation. . . . (3) The time could be lengthened by destruction of weapons production facilities using "conventional weapons."[16]

Rathjens's own recommendations come out somewhere between world government and a world police force maintained by the larger powers and with some apparent doubt that either would work:

In [the] long term, I have visions of two alternative world order arrangements.

One is a world where nuclear weapons would have no use; a world in which no nations (or groups) that could acquire them (or that might have squirrelled away a few) would have grievances or concerns that could plausibly justify their wanting them (or using them). This implies universally acceptable means for the peaceful adjudication of differences that might arise between nations or groups. . . .

In my alternative vision, there would be at least some nations or groups with plausible motives to acquire (or keep) nuclear weapons. That could not be tolerated, so the implication is a police authority that could effectively prevent it anywhere that it might be a feasible or worrisome possibility.

I fear that my second model is more realistic than the first.[17]

If Schell, Brown, and Rathjens represent different aspects of Nye's "morality of consequences" built upon the Disarmers' analyses and value judgments, psychiatrist Robert Jay Lifton returns to the morality of motives and means more common in the 1960s. His article, "Toward a Nuclear-Age Ethos," is not explicitly intended as a set of political or strategic recommendations; yet the clear implication is: Were individuals to adopt this ethos, that fact would change the world. Lifton lists "ten principles . . . already adopted by a growing number of people."

---

[16]Ibid., p. 11.
[17]Ibid., pp. 13–14.

We face a new dimension of destruction—not a matter of disaster or even of a war—but rather of an end: an end to human civilization and perhaps humankind.

That nuclear end must be rejected. We must commit ourselves to the flow and continuity of human life and to the products of the human imagination.

We either survive or die as a species. Nuclear weapons create a universally shared fate—a technologically imposed unity of all humankind.

Collective human power can bring about change, awareness, and ultimately human survival.

A key to that life power lies in the renunciation of nuclearism—of the dependency on, and even worship of, nuclear weapons.

A world without nuclear weapons is possible—a world that directs its energies toward more humane goals and looks to more genuine human security.

The step must be taken away from resignation—from "waiting for the bomb"—toward commitment to combatting it.

In these personal, individual efforts, one's everyday working professional existence and creative concerns may be connected with the struggle against nuclear weapons.

This struggle does not call one to embrace hopelessness and despair, but rather a fuller existence.

The struggle to preserve humankind lends a renewed sense of human possibility; one feels part of prospective historical and evolutionary achievements.[18]

Most of the Disarmers tend to concentrate on the long-run vision, whether personal like Lifton or political like Schell, Brown, and Rathjens. Some take short-run positions close to the Limiters, but more, like Rathjens, dismiss short-run arms control negotiations as having little effect even if successful. One exception is the Nuclear Freeze movement, the concept of which was initiated by Randall Forsberg. The freeze recommendations *are* short-run, and they thereby contrast with the far more radical long-run recommendations set forth above. The movement itself is thus close to the boundary between the

---

[18]Lifton, 1986, pp. 353–359.

Disarmers and the Limiters. It is discussed under the Disarmer rubric because its primary objective is other than the stable deterrence most of the Limiters see as the best situation obtainable in the foreseeable future, and because it sees the freeze as a concrete step toward a better long-run solution. According to Forsberg,

> To end the danger of nuclear war the nations must not merely freeze nuclear weapons but abolish them. The freeze represents a modest but significant step toward abolition. It would terminate the technological arms race and shut down entirely this wasteful and dangerous form of human competition.[19]

Her description and rationale for the freeze is that it

> goes beyond other arms-control measures proposed in the past 25 years to put a stop to the production, testing and, implicitly, development of nuclear weapons as well as their deployment. By the same simplicity that has given it wide popular appeal[20] the freeze proposal responds directly to an ominous turn in the arms race. The bilateral freeze would preclude the production of a new generation of "counterforce" weapons by the U.S. and the U.S.S.R. . . .

> The time is propitious for a bilateral freeze. Today the U.S. and the U.S.S.R. are closer to parity in nuclear arms than they have been at any time since World War II. . . . The bilateral freeze would preserve this parity. It would prevent the emergence of a new, destabilizing U.S. advantage in counterforce capability. . . . And it would forestall the inevitable effort by the U.S.S.R. to match U.S. developments.

> As spelled out in the "Call to Halt the Nuclear Arms Race," a freeze on both sides would stop the following: the production of fissionable material (uranium 235 and plutonium) for nuclear weapons; the fabrication, assembly and testing of nuclear warheads; the testing, production and deployment of missiles designed to deliver nuclear warheads, and the testing of new types of aircraft and the production and deployment of any additional aircraft designed primarily to deliver nuclear weapons. . . .

---

[19]Forsberg, 1982, p. 61.

[20]At the time of Forsberg's article, November 1982, and subsequently, the freeze concept won a number of local advisory referendums. More recently, however, it has apparently disappeared politically.

A strictly enforced freeze that includes production and testing as well as deployment could lead after some years to a decline in the reliability and readiness of existing nuclear armaments. . . . [Even] though reduced confidence in the nuclear arsenal may decrease the likelihood of nuclear war and make nuclear weapons seem less relevant to security, uncertainty in this regard is bound to make most people feel less secure rather than more so. Hence a freeze should be defined to allow the maintenance of existing nuclear forces until reductions can be agreed on with due deliberation.[21]

The Limiters' views toward the freeze are ambivalent. Drell would like to like it, but can't quite:

I wish to be clear that as a technician I find difficulties with a comprehensive freeze as literal policy. . . . I have, however, supported the freeze campaign and I continue to support it as a mandate for arms control.[22]

Halperin favors a freeze, but within the context of his overall plan to separate and stigmatize nuclear weapons:

[A]daptation of a freeze would symbolize the acceptance by both sides of the precept I propose here: Nuclear devices are not weapons with which wars can be fought. Hence the details of the balance are of little importance and both sides can stop at whatever point they happen to be.[23]

Even so, the diversity of the Disarmers' policy recommendations matches or overmatches that of the Limiters. What differs is the objective for which these proposals are intended. For the Limiters, the theme is *Stabilize*. For the Extenders, it is *Control*. For the Disarmers, it is:

• Get rid of these things; nothing counts unless it is a step toward that goal.

---

[21]Forsberg, 1982, pp. 52–61.
[22]Drell, 1983, p. 27.
[23]Halperin, 1987, p. 141.

14. Conclusions: The Past and the Future

Plus ça change, plus c'est la même chose.

—Alphonse Karr, *Les Guêpes*

This time, the old French proverb fits the case. Through the past 30 years of debate over strategic nuclear arms, some of the debaters have changed, many have not. Some of the players have changed sides, or at least have moved across the arbitrary borders between the schools defined here. But the ideas have remained remarkably steady in the face of major technological and political change. As has been suggested above, one reason for this is the inherent untestability of strategic nuclear policy. Another is that the policy recommendations made by the debaters are logical conclusions stemming from strong premises—from fundamental value judgments and from analyses of factors in the real world that change even more slowly than technology and surface politics.

This is true of the past; it is likely to be true of at least the near future. For the future, the major potential technological change of a magnitude that might bring about a discontinuity in strategic thinking would be the proving out of a version of SDI close to President Reagan's perfect population defense; but few really believe that will come to pass. The major potential political change is a real redirection of the Soviet Union, led or begun by Gorbachev. This may well be happening, but few if any Western analysts are willing to suggest that it would go so far as to affect the basic equations of deterrence. Except for the Disarmers, the dominant facts are

192

the existence of nuclear weapons and the continuing need for some kind of deterrence as the ultimate guarantor against the use of these weapons.

The one best prediction for the future is that the unpredictable will occur, and it will make a difference. The remainder of this section takes up the past roots of the current debate and uses the past and current debate as a basis for a discussion of the future—my own synthesis and suggestions.

THE PAST: ROOTS OF THE CURRENT DEBATE

In *The Arms Debate*, I constructed five schools of thought for the early 1960s. These are detailed in Chapter 22. The relevant point here, however, is that in that earlier time the policymaking center was encompassed entirely by a single school called the "Middle Marginalists." In the late 1960s and the 1970s, that school broke in two; and the major division now, the focus of the current strategic arms debate, is down the middle of the old consensus.

- McNamara's movement from the strategic consensus to the Limiters' doubts about the strategies of the early 1960s has been described. Others who made the same shift as the consensus fractured (and who also signed the no-first-use *Atlantic Monthly* article) include Bundy, Halperin, and William Kaufmann.

Before these moves, the antecedent school to the Limiters[1] had something of an anti-establishment academic coloring to it; many of its members were non-Cambridge professors of such non-policy disciplines as sociology and psychology (rather than the economics and international relations of the establishment academics). Among the hard-nosed insiders of the Kennedy and Johnson administrations, these soft academics were a bit beyond the pale. With the inclusion of the ex-Secretary of Defense, the ex-Director of the National Security Council, and others with unquestioned credentials for pragmatism and experience, however, the new weight of the Limiters has changed the debate from the "establishment" versus the "softs" to a much tougher one within the policymaking center itself. The Limiters were "outs" under the Reagan administration, but they (more accurately, their political counterparts) are electable "outs."

---

[1]Called the "Antiwar Marginalists" in the earlier book.

Nonetheless, the *ideas* of the Limiters are very similar to those that had been held by the earlier nonestablishment group. McNamara, Bundy, and their colleagues, having helped initiate the various consensus concepts of counterforce and other forms of nuclear control, and then having examined these concepts both intellectually and from decisionmaking positions where it sometimes appeared that they might have to implement them, found the concepts wanting and opted instead for existential deterrence and arms agreements.

- The other part of the early-1960s strategic consensus—Wohlstetter, Nitze, Iklé, Herman Kahn before his death—stayed with the central concepts of controlled counterforce and suspicion of the Soviets and became the core group of the Extenders. They have been joined by some who had been further "right" in the earlier period. The drive to extirpate Communism even at substantial risk of nuclear conflict was already rather weak by the early 1960s, but many of the milder "protracted conflict" concepts discussed in Part One have also tended to fade. Worldwide communism has fractured and divided even if in the view of the Extenders Soviet aggressiveness has not moderated; further, as some of them took posts in the Nixon administration, they ran up against the limits of the possible. At the same time, many of those who had been in the middle moved perceptibly toward making their anti-Communism more explicit (Wohlstetter's earlier writings, for example, tend to assume rather than describe the litany of Soviet leaders' sins against their own people quoted above from his 1983 piece). These converging moves have made it possible to include both parts of the early divergency comfortably under the Extenders' rubric.

The changes in the schools from the early 1960s to the late 1980s have thus involved some rearrangement of the chairs in which various individuals sat, and some shifts in political power and relevance. The ideas associated with the extremes of unilateral disarmament and protracted conflict have atrophied. In the middle, however, in spite of the individual rearrangements, the concepts have remained remarkably constant. Table 2 is reproduced from the relevant portions of two tables in *The Arms Debate*.[2]

What is notable about the table is that the key views of the 1963 schools transmute themselves almost whole into those of the late 1980s. On the "left," the concepts of stable deterrence, the impossibility of melioration or control of nuclear war, the need for arms control, and the tractability of the Soviet Union all move to the Limiters without change. On the "right," the

---

[2]Levine, 1963, Table 1, pp. 212–213, and Table 2, p. 278.

earlier stress on control and melioration and the trepidation about the Soviet Union, together with the emphasis on the importance of nuclear weapons and threats in political conflicts, all map directly into the Extenders' current views.

Even the words seem familiar. For the Limiters:

Arthur Waskow (1962):

Rational control must rest on extremely effective communications, and communications would surely be one of the first casualties of a thermonuclear war. . . . Assuming that an American government is still functioning after the attack, it will have to try to give orders without knowing its own surviving defenses, the power left to its own striking arm, or the targets still requiring destruction in the enemy's territory. In fact, such a government may have great difficulty in delivering its orders at all. . . . The careful, second-by-second control that would be absolutely necessary to keep a counter-force war actually directed against forces would be impossible, and the counter-force war would degenerate into a completely disordered nuclear disaster.[3]

Amitai Etzioni (1962):

[E]scalation can take us not only from cold war to hot, from limited war to world war, and from conventional conflict to nuclear attack—it may also lead us that one step further to nuclear cataclysm.[4]

Wiesner (1962):

While a system of mutual deterrence is less attractive in many ways than properly safeguarded total disarmament, it may be somewhat easier to achieve and could be regarded as a transient phase on the way toward the goal of total disarmament. . . . [In the case of] a stable deterrent system used as a component of an arms-limitation arrangement . . . instead of completely eliminating nuclear weapons and delivery systems, a small number will be permitted to remain. While this situation is not as desirable as would be the actual elimination of all such weapons, it must certainly be preferred to the present unlimited arms race and actual elimination probably cannot be achieved.[5]

---

[3]Waskow, 1962, pp. 26–27.
[4]Etzioni, 1962, p. 57.
[5]Wiesner, 1962, pp. 215–218.

Table 2

1963 VALUES, ANALYSES, AND RECOMMENDATIONS

	Schools		
	Anti-War Marginalists	Middle Marginalists	Anti-Communist Marginalists
Values	Prevention of war	Prevention of war Melioration of war	Defense of freedom against Communism Forcing Communist retreat
Analyses: War	War will be thermonuclear Weapons can only be used to prevent war if anything War starts by accident, irrationality miscalculation "Limited Wars" escalate Arms races cause wars Once war starts control and melioration are impossible	War tends to become thermonuclear Weapons are primarily to deter war but we may have to strike (first or second) Rationality can exert substantial control over irrationality; accidental war requires both an accident and a wrong response; the "Paradox of Deterrence"; war can be self-generating Escalation can be controlled through proper attention to tactical nuclear weapons, conventional forces, etc. The arms race can perhaps be controlled Control and melioration of war may be possible, particularly in those cases where we strike first	War is a spectrum Weapons are political instruments War starts primarily for political reasons Nuclear weapons dominate war and conventional forces are important mainly for "psychology" The arms race can be exploited Control is possible and is necessary for the political exploitation of war

Table 2—continued

		Schools	
	Anti-War Marginalists	Middle Marginalists	Anti-Communist Marginalists
Opponent	USSR is becoming consolidationist in order to conserve its successes; clashes of interest are psychological USSR is moving away from military means to achieve its objectives	USSR is still carefully aggressive in the short run but perhaps it may change in the long; clashes of interest are real USSR uses military means for political ends, but is willing to take little nuclear risk	USSR is implacably aggressive and out to bury us, with no sign of change USSR is carrying on a "protracted conflict" with all means, although it now shies away from high nuclear risk
Recommendations Strategic; Arms Control	Short run: stable deterrence Long run: world peace through universal disarmament to be gained by negotiations which may start with unilateral initiatives	Short run: make war less likely and/or terrible by controls over numbers and/or uses of armaments to be gained by unilateral steps and/or tacit or explicit multilateral agreements Long run: a series of short runs	Short run: unilateral control over warfare to make war thinkable as a political tool Long run: agreement with Communists delineating areas of conflict and common interest
Deterrence	Only as a part of short-run stable deterrence	Various mixes of arms control and political deterrence; of controlled counterforce and/or countercity targets; of second and first strike	Controlled deterrence as a political weapon; "win strike second" as a shield against enemy escalation

Charles Osgood (1962):

[T]he Russians would accept an unambiguous opportunity to reduce world tensions for reasons of good sense *even* if not for reasons of good will. . . . Recent travellers to Russia . . . have been impressed by the "mirror image" of our own attitudes that they find among both the people and the leaders there.[6]

And as for the Limiters, so for the Extenders:
Wohlstetter (1961):

As for efforts to control the violence of nuclear war, whether by making some distinction between military and urban targets, or by controlling the application of force within each category, or as part of a bargaining process to force termination of the war on more favorable terms, they become a rather remote possibility with nuclear diffusion.[7]

Herman Kahn (1961):

[M]any strategists, and even some arms controllers, overlook the important requirement that a failure of stability should result in limited and "acceptable" consequences.[8]

Richard Fryklund (1962):

This strategy also relies upon our long-range weapons to deter attacks on the United States and its major allies, but it would control the use of these weapons to give us the maximum chance of winning with the minimum amount of death and destruction. . . . Deterrence would be continued *during* the war.[9]

Harry Willets (1961):

The Soviet leaders, to judge by their behavior to date, are unlikely to accept as in their national interest any major measures of disarmament or arms control that do not give them substantial strategic or political advantages. They may well be interested in reducing the dangers of war and the burden of armaments. But they apparently do not regard either of these tasks as so urgent that it cannot be com-

[6]Osgood, 1962, p. 207.
[7]Wohlstetter, 1961, p. 383.
[8]Kahn, 1961, p. 102.
[9]Fryklund, 1962, pp. 40–41.

bined with and made dependent on achievement of broader political objectives.[10]

The point is not that nothing has changed over 25 years. The Limiters are more likely now to take stable deterrence for the foreseeable future as a goal than as Wiesner's step on the way to total disarmament; control of the violence of nuclear war has become much more central to Wohlstetter's thinking than it was in his reference to proliferation. But the specifics illustrated by the quotations from the early 1960s, together with the familiar general thrusts set forth in Table 1, indicate how similar the current debate is to the earlier one.

The similarity of the arguments is particularly striking because they have remained constant in the face of truly major technological, political, and strategic changes over the quarter-century.

- Technologically, although ABM had been thought of by the early 1960s, it hardly came up in the debate. Even more important, however, MIRV, which has turned on end the basic strategic balance, changing it from the stable "it takes more than one to kill one" to the unstable "one shot kills many," is not mentioned at all in the literature of the early 1960s.

- Politically, the West was beginning to recognize the Soviet-Chinese rift in the early 1960s, but that had not yet affected strategic discussions. Most Sovietologists did not expect the diffusion of multicentric Communism, and only a few saw the loosening of Soviet bonds on the East European satellites. Internally, the Soviet Union was thought to be strong and vigorous, in contrast to the current Western perception that it is in severe internal economic and political trouble. True, Khrushchev then was thought of by some Westerners as Gorbachev is now, but Khrushchev did not last.

- Strategically, after the missile-gap scare of the late 1950s, which had wound down by the end of 1961, it was recognized that the United States was still far ahead of the Soviet Union in nuclear delivery capabilities. Today, parity is recognized by all; Soviet superiority is feared by a few.

One reason for the invariant strategic nuclear debate in the midst of radically changing circumstances is its theological character: The premises remain untestable, and it is therefore easy to believe or rationalize almost anything. In the debate over arms policy for the Third World, by contrast,

---

[10]Willetts, 1961, p. 172.

Vietnam conclusively disproved many previously accepted premises—e.g., that an American administration could operate a foreign and military policy without regard for domestic public opinion.

Perhaps more basic to the constancy of the debate is that even such radical changes as MIRV, the breakdown of Communist centralism, and the onset of strategic parity fail to shake the two truly fundamental and invariant premises of strategic nuclear policy and the strategic arms debate:

- Nuclear weapons *are* different and their dangers represent an unprecedented discontinuity in human history. No school of thought disputes this.
- The Soviet Union remains an enemy and an adversary and an opponent and a competitor of the United States; the likelihood of establishing relations approximating those we have with Canada, Western Europe, and Japan seems close to zero. However, the same could have been said of Germany and Japan 45 years ago.

The same fundamental premises are likely to hold for the foreseeable future, and they will continue to constrain and direct future strategic nuclear policy and the debate.

THE FUTURE: A PERSONAL SYNTHESIS ON WHERE WE GO FROM HERE

In fact, the world may be changing, in two ways that can be basic to policy and the debate. One could be a turning point, the other is a trend that has been continuing for a while and should be recognized.

- Gorbachev may really be different enough to represent a true turning point. At the beginning of his tenure, Western analysts generally stressed that his differences with his aged predecessors were primarily stylistic. More recently, the Sovietological consensus is pointing out that he may really mean it but he is having great difficulty with the massive Soviet *apparat*. The next increment may move on from there; predictably, it will also have many "buts" in it. One necessary "but," however, parallels that in the early 1960s: We have no guarantees that Gorbachev will last. The fundamental Soviet economic problems will. (Part Three goes into more detail on Western views of ongoing Soviet change.)
- There has been no real threat of nuclear conflict, or of military confrontation between the United States and the Soviet Union, certainly for 16

years, probably for ten more than that. Many authorities argue that the Yom Kippur War of 1973 never presented a real danger of a U.S.-USSR clash. The Cuban Missile Crisis of 1962 and the Berlin confrontations of the previous year surely did present such dangers, but the relative relaxation since then may be due in part to the fears created by those events.

Both of these changes or potential changes are profound. Neither, however, is likely to change the two fundamental premises for strategic policy: Nuclear knowledge will not be unlearned, and the weapons will remain unprecedently dangerous; U.S. relations with the Soviets will remain very different from those with Canada or France or Japan.

Strategic nuclear policy will continue to be based on deterrence. And deterrence brings with it the paradox highlighted by the Catholic bishops and their critics from both sides: The threat to use nuclear weapons is basic to peace, stability, and well-being; implementation of that threat would, with a high probability, be immoral and self-defeating.

This is the paradox that the Extenders have attempted to solve by designing nuclear postures and planning nuclear tactics with such careful precision and control that death and destruction would be kept to levels that, while horrible, would be within the range of historical human experience. Such control could not only limit damage; by making response certain, it would enhance deterrence and make even less likely the initial events leading to nuclear confrontation.

I agree with the Limiters that the inherent uncertainties make such control impossible to depend on. With Bundy, I believe that deterrence is existential, depending on uncertainty, not on certainty. It follows that I disagree with Wohlstetter that such plans and weapons can be meaningful in the way that he intends. But what Wohlstetter points out, and has been pointing out since "The Delicate Balance of Terror" in 1959, is that deterrence is neither easy nor automatically based on the mere existence of nuclear explosives. Making it too simple will make it too solvable. Such ideas as limiting nuclear weapons to 200 single-warhead hardened land-based missiles on each side are too easy to get around. So is sole dependence on submarine-based weapons.

What it comes to is that if deterrence is based on uncertainty rather than certainty, then the kinds of complex weapons and plans recommended by the Extenders are crucial for deterrence *not because they engender the kind of certainty claimed by their advocates, but because they are necessary to maintain uncertainty.* The Extenders' postures are necessary for the Limiters' existential deterrence.

The physical basis of U.S. deterrence is the Triad of land-based missiles, submarine-based missiles, and aircraft now equipped with gravity bombs and cruise missiles. The Soviets cannot attack all of these simultaneously and successfully, and their consequent uncertainty about the outcome of such an attack is central to its deterrence. What I am suggesting, then, is that the Extenders' postures lead logically to a "Niad," an N-dimensional Triad, which leaves the enemy and ourselves so uncertain as to what would happen if nuclear war began that neither side can contemplate using nuclear weapons. Existential deterrence will be preserved into the indefinite future. Wohlstetter's tactics are necessary for Bundy's strategy.

As one example, the likelihood of SDI fulfilling President Reagan's dream of a near-perfect population defense is generally conceded to be close to zero. It may not work for area and population defense at all; it probably can work at least to some degree for point defense of missile sites and other military targets. But making SDI one more tactic within our overall strategy is bound to complicate the enemy's problem and thereby enhance uncertainty and existential deterrence.

What remains to be asked is: What are the costs, in budgetary and other terms? SDI is expensive, so are the other weapons in the Extenders' proposed armory. And here, leaving aside the political issues of military versus other expenditures, my own feeling is that neither SDI efforts going beyond research nor other strategic weapons, even though they might enhance existential deterrence somewhat, should be granted first claim on the marginal military dollar. Military as well as other budgets are limited, and conventional capabilities need priority. Although these capabilities increased under the Reagan administration, not enough improvement has taken place either in NATO or worldwide response forces. As the new administration and the Congress predictably cut back on defense expenditures, too many of the cutbacks are likely to weigh on force readiness—spare parts, maintenance, training. Whether the fault is with the cutbacks or with Secretary Weinberger's Defense Department's failure to plan reallocations in advance of inevitable cuts is moot and not crucial. Restorations and improvements here are more important to U.S. security, NATO posture, and ultimately to world peace than are major SDI efforts or other nuclear furbelows and curlicues.

Further, costs are not only fiscal. I agree with the Limiters that arms agreements are important for stabilizing deterrence. But if they are badly handled, various aspects of the Extenders' detailed strategy may exact costs in terms of arms agreements or other stabilizing arms controls. Properly treated, however, carefully planned nuclear postures and strategies may enhance agreements, both as levers in helping to obtain them and as integral portions of the agreement, as suggested not only by many Limiters but by Kissinger as well.

For myself, then, I come out with many of the Limiters, favoring:

- An austere, detailed, discriminating counterforce strategy, excluding neither anti-ballistic-missile defenses nor, at this time, first use of nuclear weapons,
- set forth in such a way as to enhance the possibility of arms agreements, by careful design aimed at assistance in negotiating those agreements (but not as a "bargaining chip" to be simply traded away at the proper point),
- and ultimately to be integrated into the arms agreements themselves so that both the strategy and the agreements will enhance stable deterrence.

These thoughts will probably not end the strategic nuclear debate.

PART THREE
NATO, THE SUBJECTIVE ALLIANCE

15. Introduction

> I don't know what effect these men will have upon the enemy,
> but, by God, they frighten me.
>
> > —attributed sometimes to the Duke of Wellington
> > and sometimes to George III

> Arguments about logical consistency and conceptual neatness
> become the currency for intra-alliance bargaining in a manner
> which may exacerbate disagreement and transform difference
> in emphasis to disputes about theological absolutes. Fears
> abound that doctrinal positions have been thrown up as
> camouflage for disengagement, decoupling, or centralization of
> control. Thus NATO has at times been absorbed in great
> debates of strategy in a manner which has generated tensions
> of an order that the Russians have been hard put to emulate.
>
> > —Johan Jorgen Holst[1]

There are few objective truths about the North Atlantic Treaty Organization—the Atlantic Alliance. One fact is that the Alliance was armed in 1953 in response to what was seen as a substantial Soviet military threat to Western Europe. That is history, however; although the nations of the Alliance still believe the threat to exist, it has faded and changed substantially over the intervening years. NATO today is shaped primarily by the political needs of its member nations and by the members' perceptions of the Soviet Union and of each other. For British troops two centuries ago, and perhaps for NATO today too, as Johan Holst suggested some years before he became an active participant as Norwegian Defense Minister, it is not always clear who is most frightened by which perceptions.

The Alliance is in this sense very much a subjective one, engaged to a substantial degree in analyzing itself. A broad consensus (including myself) believe its continued existence to remain essential to Western well-being and to world peace, because without NATO the Soviets might still attempt to dominate Europe, militarily or politically. But the military as well as the political shape of the Alliance is based more on national and Alliance

---

[1]Holst, 1977, pp. 267–268.

politics than on imminent military threats. This has been true for many years; at the beginning of the 1990s, it is almost beyond question.

Such subjectivity leads to a debate over NATO's present policies and future structure that is complex and quite difficult to follow. Issues in the debate are mixtures of military and political factors; participants are officials and analysts within the member nations.[2] In the last half of the 1980s in particular, but more generally since at least the mid-1970s, the confusions of the debate have led to some policies that nobody liked even as compromises, and to intra-Alliance suspicions and hostilities that have presented unnecessary threats to the organization itself. The object of this study is to sort out the issues and the participants and to analyze the premises and logic leading to varying policy conclusions, not in order to evaluate which are "right" or "wrong" but to make clearer than at present what the debaters disagree about, and why. As changes in the Alliance accelerate, new postures will be based on the response of old positions to new pressures. Better understanding of underlying viewpoints may help direct change toward the preservation of NATO's strengths and halt internal erosion based on correctible misperceptions of the views of others.

The remainder of this chapter enlarges upon the initial assertion about military and political perceptions, sets forth the four "schools of thought" into which I divide the debaters for purposes of detailed examination, categorizes the issues on which the schools agree or disagree, and concludes by outlining the substantive themes.

This chapter is followed by a brief history of NATO and thinking about NATO. The next four chapters examine in detail the views presented by the members of the schools of thought.

In the late 1980s, NATO may be beginning a major transformation, initially induced by apparent extraordinary changes in its Soviet and Warsaw Pact opponents, as symbolized by the 1987 agreement. Rather than trying to capture these changes in mid-flight, the final chapter of this Part describes some of the major directions of change and suggests the ways in which the debate and the Alliance may move.

MILITARY AND POLITICAL PERCEPTIONS

NATO started as a fairly simple concept. It was created in the late 1940s to enable "us"—the West, clearly led by the Marshall Plan and military big brother the United States—to resist aggression by "them"—Stalin's

---

[2]The material is drawn almost entirely from individual writings. Although the essay provides political context, the analysis concerns the logic of ideas, not the politics of pressures and policy determination.

USSR. Such aggression may or may not have been a real possibility, but it most certainly was a real fear in Western Europe. The fear was based on the military and political hegemony the Soviet Union had imposed on Eastern Europe, reinforced by the Berlin blockade, and soon put by the North Korean attack on South Korea into terms of very concrete possibilities of military invasion of Western Europe, perhaps by Soviet proxies. NATO was thus initially presented with a conceptually simple problem, mostly military (although the role of formerly Nazi Germany presented intra-Alliance political problems from the start) and only two-sided. And almost since the beginning of the Alliance, the explicit solution to the problem has involved both conventional and nuclear military power, with nuclear weapons being the ultimate sanction against superior Soviet conventional forces as well as Soviet nuclear threats.

Forty years after the creation of NATO, and 35 after the decision to man and equip it as a multination armed alliance, the fear of direct military attack by the Soviets has faded. The Soviet *capability* for such an attack, conventional or nuclear or both, still exists, however; were all Western forces opposed to such aggression to disappear or the ultimate nuclear sanction to be withdrawn, the attack, or its more likely Platonic political shadow Soviet domination of West Europe without actual invasion, could again be seen as a major danger.

The danger is not inherent in geography or political economy. Achieving a zero fear of the Soviet Union by Western Europeans is possible; such a change is not unprecedented. Canada, for example, does not fear the overwhelming military might of the United States, nor do the French worry about a German attack. In terms of a millenium of accumulated European history that is no less remarkable than would be a peaceful and permeable border between East and West Europe say 20 years from now. Were this to come to pass, there would be no more perceived need for the West to resist Soviet political pressure than there is for Canada to mount a military defense against the "American Way," or for France or Germany to bow to the other. And there would be no need for the Western military alliance; NATO would probably disappear.

That time is not yet; perhaps it never will be. Throughout the West the Alliance is seen as remaining quite necessary. The difficulty that dominates the debate, however, is that with the fading away of the simple and direct military threat that engendered NATO initially, the military and political issues of the Alliance depend more and more on national and individual perceptions of the quality of a much more subtle Soviet threat: The troops and tanks in East Germany, Czechoslovakia, Poland, and the Soviet Union itself are not *likely* to move west; but still and all, in the absence of good defenses, they could. Western defenses, particularly nuclear, remain the necessary deterrent against Warsaw Pact attack; were the West to lack such defenses, it might be best not to upset the Great Power that controls the Pact's troops and tanks. The Soviets could thus extend political and economic constraints around the free nations of NATO, as they have around Finland.

It is "Finlandization" rather than military occupation that NATO Europe has worried about for two or more decades. The concept of a nation operating under a democratic system in the best European sense but nonetheless making its decisions in the belief that it cannot afford to irritate a far more powerful neighbor is a difficult one. Finland is the only current example; perhaps history can provide others among nations that existed on the periphery of Nazi Germany in the 1930s (Czechoslovakia in particular), but these had only brief lives because Hitler soon regularized their status by conquering them. Nonetheless, the concept remains. Western fears tend to be confirmed by Soviet doctrines related to the "correlation of forces," which assert that greater conformity to the wishes and needs of the USSR *should* in fact follow its preponderance of power. It is these fears, supported by the still-perceived possibility of the actual use of force by the Soviets, that motivate the nations of Western Europe and the United States to stay together in an alliance strong enough to deter the potential political and military threats from the East. Because of the evanescent nature of the political and military threats, however, and because of the lack of concrete and current evidence bearing on them, the debate tends toward the theological, although not so much as the debate over nuclear deterrence, where no real evidence is available.

The various Soviet threats are latent, however. More important to the shaping of the Alliance of the 1980s, and more difficult to deal with than external threats, are each member's perceptions of the other members of the Alliance and of the other members' perceptions. The issue around which most of the debate rages is that:

> Americans have committed themselves to the defense of Western Europe by nuclear means if necessary, but to deter aggression the Soviets must believe that commitment, and to keep the Alliance together the West Europeans must believe it, and believe that the Soviets believe it.

For Europeans, this issue is one of survival of their nations and their civilization; it is central to their security concerns. Most American officials and analysts, however, tend to take their own commitment for granted, and they talk about it less.

The difference in vital interests is not the only one, however. NATO's military posture consists of both military and political elements, and Americans and West Europeans differ over the balance between them. The most important example concerns the question of the threshold at which defense will change from conventional to nuclear. Americans treat this as being a military issue of threat, escalation, and combat; deterrence is made credible to Soviets and West Europeans because the United States maintains the *rationality* of nuclear response as a final alternative to defeat. West Europeans treat the same problem as a political issue of U.S. will; deterrence is made credible to the Soviets and other Europeans by the *visibility* of the American deterrent force, as a manifest of that will. As a result of these and similar differences, Americans tend to raise military issues within the Alliance, Europeans react; Europeans tend to raise political issues, Americans react.

In 1967 the Alliance came forth with two basic doctrinal pronouncements. One was Flexible Response, which provided for a spectrum of conventional and nuclear responses to Pact attack. Although intended to satisfy Europeans on the ultimate connection of the American strategic capability to deterrence of aggression on the continent, Flexible Response was largely an American military-style concept; deterrence lies in the power to respond. The other statement was the Harmel Report, named after the Belgian Foreign Minister who conceived the idea and headed the NATO commission that produced the report. The Harmel Report was a European-style political document, making clear that the Alliance was in fact a political as well as a military one and setting forth an objective of stability and détente in Europe as well as deterrence and defense. Flexible Response and the Harmel Report coexisted easily, but they exemplified the American and European styles in NATO.

The military-political distinction raises another problem, however. It is very difficult to justify vast military expenditures on mainly political grounds, particularly on the basis of satisfying one's allies. In 1965, Norman Jones and I wrote that:

> To preserve the Alliance . . . a [military] posture should try to satisfy (or at least not violate) the felt needs of the members, and we thus can arrive at a set of political criteria, based on these needs. . . . Since [such] political imperatives . . . will not suffice to obtain popular and governmental support for a posture, however, some military rationale is still needed, as a binding force for the chosen posture. . . . The

threat of an all-out Soviet invasion of Western Europe seems to have outlived its usefulness as a rationale, primarily because few governments or people still believe it to be realistic.[3]

Our crystal ball was clouded in one respect: After more than 20 additional years of implausibility, the all-out Soviet invasion still lives as the primary military rationale for the political Alliance. Nonetheless, the need for a military rationale to justify steps taken to satisfy political requirements continues to affect the NATO debate, and sometimes to dominate it.

The tendency of the Alliance to be more concerned with itself than with the threat from its Warsaw Pact opponents has, if anything, been increasing over many years. Ironically, what might change this introspective orientation is the possibility that the Soviet Union under the new leadership of Mikhail Gorbachev, or after Gorbachev, might swing radically in one direction or another; and the NATO West might be forced to concentrate again on the precise nature of the threat or nonthreat from the East.

One French analyst, writing in 1986, stated that: "In the bundle of factors that have, since 1954, determined the evolution of the Franco-German dialogue on matters of security, the Soviet Union has appeared, without doubt, as the only constant."[4] Although Soviet constancy has not been invariant in its expression—after the end of the Berlin crises of the early 1960s, for example, the possibility of direct use of military force seemed to decrease substantially—the USSR has remained a hostile opponent. Soviet hostility and opposition could be counted on, even if implemented differently under Khrushchev than under Stalin, and in still other ways under Brezhnev. Should this underlying constancy now change radically one way or another, the NATO debate could shift focus back to the Soviet Union instead of the member nations of the Alliance.

In fact, rapid change on the Soviet side has already begun. It will not be clear for many years how radical or how permanent it is—how far Gorbachev wants to or can push internal liberalization, or, for that matter, how long he will be in a position to keep trying. Equally unclear for at least as long will be the extent to which the new international approaches of the Soviet Union represent a difference of tactics rather than a fundamental shift of objectives. What is clear is that the USSR in the late 1980s appears very different from what anyone on either side of the East-West border predicted in the early part of the decade. Almost as certain is that whether the future direction is toward openness and international cooperation or repression and hostility, the Soviet Union of the 1990s will be far different

[3]Quoted in Levine, 1972, pp. 121–122.
[4]Gnessoto, 1986, p. 11.

from that of the 1970s. Technology, economics, and demographics will preclude simple reversion to the past, just as when Brezhnev retreated from the proto-*perestroika* of Khrushchev, the resulting Soviet Union of the 1960s and 1970s was quite different from Stalin's Soviet Union of the 1940s.

One way or another, the North Atlantic Alliance will have a new-style opponent; one way or another the Alliance will have to adapt. The Epilog to this part suggests that the NATO organism is likely to internalize the external stimuli stemming from Soviet change, shifting relationships within the Alliance rather than either breaking up or creating a radically different relationship with the Warsaw Pact. Such adaptations have begun in the late 1980s, as the Alliance and its members reacted to radical-seeming Soviet arms control and related proposals and tried to come up with proposals of their own designed to maintain and improve the security of Western Europe. Yet predictions going beyond the immediate future of NATO are no more certain than those attempting to lay out the future direction of Soviet change. The only certainty is change itself, with the change on both sides likely to occur much more rapidly than we have been accustomed to for at least the last two decades.

SCHOOLS OF THOUGHT

The major schools in the NATO debate are grouped around various American and European policy recommendations, based in part on different analyses but perhaps even more on different value weights put on potential gains and risks. To be sure, none of these differences are clean-cut: Europeans differ widely among themselves over NATO policy, and so do Americans. Further, some Americans tend to argue like Europeans, some Europeans argue like Americans; in particular, lines tend to blur because some arguments on each side of the Atlantic are based on resonance, conscious efforts to placate the other side.[5] Nonetheless the European-American distinction stands up as the crucial one for understanding this very complex debate because European debaters start out with the preservation of Western Europe as their central value; and how to maintain the essential American deterrent role in their preservation is the major

---

[5]The NATO debate is subject to one additional complexity absent from the other two segments of the American arms debate. In the Third World and strategic nuclear debates, the recommendations are made to a single government, that of the United States. In the NATO debate, they are addressed to 16 sovereignties, and what is a recommendation to one—"Our government should do this"—is an analytical issue for the others—"Will they do it?"

analytical issue they debate about. American debaters start out assuming the U.S. role, but how to balance deterrence of Soviet aggression against Western Europe with avoidance of strategic nuclear war is much of what they debate about. All this results in diverging European and American policy recommendations in spite of similarities on some specific issues. This European-American difference is based more on variously weighted value sets leading to different choices of salient issues than it is on major analytical or value differences on specific issues.

This Part divides the NATO debaters among four schools of thought, major and minor ones (defined in terms of their effect on policymaking) on each side of the Atlantic. Most American officials and analysts come together into one major school.

- *The Maintainers.* The members of this school stress the importance of maintaining the commitment of the United States to European defense. They converge on three propositions:
  - *No Early Use of Nuclear Weapons.* Recognizing that nuclear weapons are part of the overall scheme to deter Soviet aggression in Europe, and that this implies an inherent possibility that we might have to use them, nuclear defense should be a last resort, not a first. Almost all American officials and analysts espouse a doctrine of "No Early Use" of nuclear weapons in Europe: Do everything else possible first, even though such a high conventional-nuclear threshold might conceivably be taken as an unwillingness to use nuclear weapons at all and could thus downgrade deterrence. (It might, however, strengthen deterrence by making *any* initial American response more likely.)
  - *Increased Conventional Capabilities.* To make No Early Use as plausible as possible, substantial stress should be placed on improving NATO's conventional capabilities and strategies. A corollary-by-omission of this proposition is that not much is said about how to pay for such improvements. Both the desire for increased conventional capabilities and the economic-budgetary conundrum have deep roots in NATO's history.
  - *Continued U.S. Commitment.* As noted, Europeans question this, or at least fear its erosion. Most Americans do not. They desire no diminution of the historic U.S. commitment to the defense of NATO Europe and believe that no substantial weakening has yet occurred at either the conventional or nuclear levels. Although the commitment has lacked the certainty of a doomsday machine, it has sufficed to deter Soviet adventurism in Europe for 40 years,

and can continue to do so in the future in much the same manner. Commitment, measured as the *probability* of appropriate U.S. response, however, is not synonymous with the *size* of the U.S. forces in Europe, conventional or nuclear, representing that response. No consensus exists on these matters, and some Americans believe that the same commitment can be expressed more cheaply or differently.

To stress the consensus on these three propositions does not imply that the Maintainers form a single tight-knit school. On other issues in the overall arms debate, Americans divide into diverse schools. And there are important differences over NATO also, although they relate only in part to those on non-NATO issues. For example, the 1987 negotiations over zeroing out Soviet and American Intermediate-Range Nuclear Forces in Europe caused substantial controversy among American Maintainers, as well as between Americans and Europeans and among Europeans. Such differences among the Maintainers are tactical and temporary, appearing more on the surface than along deep fault lines based on substantially different value judgments or analytical conclusions. Many of the Americans who opposed the INF agreement did so primarily because they were worried about the reactions of European NATO members, rather than themselves fearing that it would substantially weaken deterrence or defense, an example of transatlantic resonance based on perceptions of perceptions. Tactical differences are the reason why the INF controversy threw together such unusual bedfellows: Former President Reagan and enthusiastic arms controllers favoring the zeroing out of INF, former President Nixon and Democratic Chairman Les Aspin of the House Armed Services Committee opposing it. On future issues, tactics may sort the sides out differently.

The split between the Maintainers and the other, much smaller American school that in recent years has spun off the right wing of this pro-NATO consensus is more fundamental:

- *The Withdrawers.* They want the United States to effectively withdraw from NATO. Most of them believe that Western Europe is fully capable of defending itself, is decadently unwilling to to so, and in any case is flirting far too seriously with the Soviet Union. Most Withdrawers are strong anti-Communists including many of the same individuals who want to confront the Soviet Union throughout the Third World, but they believe that the threat of Western Europe actually "going Communist" is slim, so the United States should apply its limited military and other resources to areas where the danger is more real, as well as to such

215

regions of growing economic importance as Japan and the rest of the Pacific Basin. *Public Interest* editor and NYU Professor Irving Kristol is one prophet here; Professor Melvin Krauss, also of NYU, is another. In addition, although most American radical Disarmers of the left concentrate on strategic nuclear weapons and do not treat with NATO as such, the few who do enter the European thicket make policy recommendations similar to those coming from the right; and they are included in this school, as are some strong-Navy partisans who want to concentrate expenditures on seaborne capabilities rather than land forces anywhere.[6]

The Withdrawers can be considered a "minor" School of Thought in that there are few of them and their influence in the United States is small. But they influence the NATO debate in at least one important way: Many of the European debaters take their views seriously as an indication of a future American trend toward withdrawal from the Alliance, and this conditions the views and arguments of these Europeans.

The European school most closely corresponding to the American Withdrawers comes from the "peace movement." Logically aligned with the American nuclear disarmers, they no longer have the same close political relationship as existed in the early 1960s when the British Campaign for Nuclear Disarmament (CND) and the American Committee for a Sane Nuclear Policy (SANE) worked closely together, and Bertrand Russell and C. P. Snow were prophets of both movements.

- *The Removers.* What they want to remove is nuclear weapons from Europe. They include the majority of the British Labour Party, the Green Party and an important portion of the Socialists (SPD) in the Federal Republic of Germany, and sizable contingents in most of the smaller NATO nations. The School is larger relative to the total electorates of these countries than are the American Withdrawers (or the American peace movement). Nonetheless, its *direct* influence on national policies has been small: The peace movement participates in none of the major European governments, and political arithmetic and the electoral calendar make such participation in the next several years unlikely; it does affect the governments of some of the smaller NATO members, but it controls none of them. Indirectly, however, the movement's ability to influence public opinion on specific issues by its arguments and by mobilizing large numbers of demonstrators keeps

---

[6]The different premises from which various groups of Withdrawers arrive at similar conclusions are so widespread that, were the group more influential on policymaking, it might be divided more rigorously into subschools.

216

governments and oppositions, particularly in Germany, looking over their shoulders, thus affecting the positions of the larger European School of Thought.

The Removers fear the U.S. nuclear commitment to the old continent. The more extreme members of the school believe that the United States, at least under President Reagan, was "morally equivalent" to the Soviet Union, at least under Chairman Gorbachev, although the movement began to gather strength when Brezhnev was still Soviet leader. They want East and West Europe to solve their own problems in a nonnuclear way.

The more moderate Removers, including most of those in the British Labour Party and the German SPD, remain pro-NATO. They just want to get rid of nuclear weapons in Europe and substitute conventional "defensive defenses" incapable of mounting offensive operations across the East-West border. The British Removers want to get rid of the British independent nuclear deterrent as well as the U.S. nuclear forces based in the United Kingdom, but the movement is not important in France, the owner of the other European independent deterrent force.

The more important of the two European schools of thought encompasses the governments of almost all the European NATO members and segments of the opposition parties as well.

- *The Couplers.* This school includes a broad range of mainstream European officials and analysts, including many in opposition as well as those in power, all of whom have some concern about the U.S. commitment. This school puts the greatest stress on mutual perceptions, starting with the perception of American intentions. In contrast to the American Maintainers, who take the continued U.S. obligation for granted, the Couplers focus on the question of whether in fact the American commitment can be taken for granted any more. They are particularly concerned about "decoupling," a weakening of the commitment that "couples" American strategic nuclear forces to the defense of Western Europe and thus provides the ultimate deterrent to Soviet aggression. The first two American propositions, on No Early Use and stronger conventional capabilities, are examined and reexamined to see whether they reveal any structural flaws in the third proposition favoring continued American commitment. For a few Europeans, particularly among the French, the question has been whether the commitment ever could be taken for granted.

217

Coupler viewpoints on all issues do not vary clearly by nationality. The major nations do differ on the key issues of the U.S. commitment to Europe and on the relationships among the European members, however; and the general *gestalt* of each of the big three European nations can be described, as can some of the roles in the NATO debate of the smaller members.

— The French, as *philosophes*, are the most concerned and the least troubled. Since de Gaulle, they have expressed the greatest doubts about the reliability of the American commitment, but most of the doubters also concede that the potential of their own independent deterrent stems in large measure from the possibility that its use may invoke the far larger U.S. nuclear force. French doubts about the quality and endurance of the U.S. commitment lead them, philosophically and perhaps pragmatically, toward more purely European defense concepts, in which their perceptions of the Germans in particular play a central role. So far as France's own defense policy is concerned, consensus is far stronger than in the other major NATO nations: There is broad national agreement on the need for continued independence of the French nuclear deterrent; there is no sentiment for reintegration into the military structure of NATO; and the Remover peace movement is trivial. After François Mitterrand's reelection as president and the concomitant election of a friendly National Assembly, in 1988, he relaxed some of the more extreme French doubts about American abandonment and moved France a bit back toward the Alliance, but without in any way abandoning either nuclear independence or nonintegration.

— The British agree on the need for a better coordinated European defense effort, strategically and technologically, but they base this more on its positive desirability than on any fear of U.S. withdrawal of the commitment to NATO. Unlike the French, the British are divided: Although the Removers are in a distinct minority in the United Kingdom, they form the majority of the main opposition party, Labour. The British Coupler consensus, including the Conservative government and most of the members of the smaller opposition parties in the middle, is that NATO is evolving gradually, as always, and a substantial American conventional and nuclear commitment is likely to be a feature for a long time to come.

— The West Germans have more disagreements within the Coupler establishment than do the French or British, as well as a substantial debate between the establishment and the Removers of the Green Party and the SPD left wing. Within the governing coalition, most of the Christian Democrats (CDU), and their sister party the Bavarian Christian Socialists (CSU) still tend to hold to the American nuclear deterrent as the key to German security. The long-time Foreign Minister, however, a leader of the Free Democrats (FDP), has increasingly downstressed the nuclear role. The major basis for these divisions is that, far more than the French and the British, the Germans are pulled in three directions: by the close Atlantic tie to the United States, by the European stress emphasized by the French, and by the Soviet ability to vary the political and military climate on the eastern border. The Federal Republic's situation is complicated by its front-line geography, by its dependence on the strength, particularly the nuclear strength, of others, and by the existence of a Soviet-dominated country with the same language and heritage, the German Democratic Republic. In addition, the residual guilt and suspicions left over from the Nazi era place constraints, now largely self-imposed, on German military policy. The result of all of these pulls is that German NATO politics frequently appear to the allies of the Federal Republic as being somewhat erratic. In the last year, however, almost all factions have come together on the symbolism of German foreign policy being set in Bonn, not Washington.

— Perhaps the only valid generalization that can be made about the smaller member nations—Canada, Scandinavia, the Low Countries, southern Europe, and Turkey—is that they differ from one another. They recognize that their choices, including the possibility of simply opting out of NATO (which might force them to leave the European Economic Community as well) are constrained. Given this, most of the smaller members tend toward the relaxed side of the concerns over U.S. reliability. In addition, however, they contribute several specific items to the debate. One is the reminder that NATO confronts the Warsaw Pact elsewhere than on the German central front; the "flank" nations, Norway and Turkey, are the only ones having land borders with the Soviet Union.[7] Another reminder is that the Alliance has severe internal problems unrelated

---

[7]The other NATO member bordering directly on the Soviet Union is the United States, across the Bering Strait.

to the Soviets or the Pact, the strong hostility between Greece and Turkey being the chief case in point. In addition, although the governments of the smaller members, except perhaps for Greece, remain firmly in the Coupler consensus, several of the nations have Remover contingents strong enough to be taken into consideration both as potential threats to some of the national contributions (e.g., of conventional forces in key sectors and of territory for military sites and supply lines) and as advocates of some military strategies based on static "defensive defenses."

ISSUES

The eight issue categories into which this essay divides the subject matter of the NATO debate range in a continuum from the almost completely political to the almost strictly military. The European Couplers stress the political end, and the issue they treat as central, that of the American commitment and nuclear coupling, is largely political—a question of will and willingness. These obviously depend in some measure on the military factors that would determine the outcome if the United States were to use its forces to fulfill the commitment.

- *The U.S. Commitment to NATO.* European analysts and authorities in the Coupler school believe that it has been the U.S. commitment in general and the nuclear commitment specifically that have deterred the threat of Soviet attack and continue to do so. Although most of them would prefer to deemphasize the nuclear aspects, American Maintainers tend to agree that the ultimate risk of nuclear war plays a central role in NATO deterrence.

The detailed strategic questions raised under this rubric include: What are U.S. policies with regard to nuclear deterrence of conventional or nuclear attacks in Europe that may involve American troops but not the American homeland? Are these policies changing drastically? How do the policies and stated U.S. commitments fit with other U.S. commitments in other parts of the world? Particularly in the light of changing nuclear balances, how willing is the United States and how willing will it be to stand itself hostage against attacks on allies? And how long will current commitments last, how dependable are they, and how reliable, particularly in the light of the idiosyncrasies of some recent American commanders-in-chief? All of these are matters of perceptions and perceptions of perceptions.

In addition to such matters of strategy and high policy, economic issues play a large role in transatlantic relations. One of these, burden-sharing within the Alliance, is within the purview of this book. Others, particularly issues of international trade, are peripheral here even though they may be the real determinants of the future course of the military alliance.

Closely related to the U.S. commitment is the issue of

- *The Europeans' Commitments to Themselves.* Even though "Europe and (or versus) the United States" is common phraseology, Europe is not a unit, at least not yet. Throughout the history of the North Atlantic Alliance, but increasingly now, the possibility has been discussed of a more specifically European role. This classical issue includes two rather different components: the possibility of a more indigenously European strategy, perhaps putting more weight than now on British and French nuclear weapons, and the effort to produce weapons cooperatively.

A more recent addition to the long-running discussion of a general drawing together of the European members of NATO has concerned the potential for Franco-German military cooperation. Issues that have come into serious discussion include the extent to which the interests of both countries dictate that France's defensive frontier should be at the Elbe rather than the Rhine and the implications of such a change for both French nuclear strategy and French and German conventional forces.

One political issue is potentially more important than any of the others, even that of U.S. commitment.

- *The Soviet Role.* It is still widely believed that without NATO, the Soviets would dominate Europe militarily and politically. Most military measures are justified in terms of a much more specific threat, however: a massive Warsaw Pact attack across the Iron Curtain. Since the end of the Berlin crises of the early 1960s, the likelihood of such an attack has been increasingly difficult to take seriously. As a result, justifications have had little to do with real military steps, and this dissonance has distorted the debate. The perceived Soviet threat remains the *raison d'être* for NATO, but because the perception that Soviet hostility was low and prudent has been constant over many years, *variations* in the Alliance and in the debate have depended more and more on members' perceptions of one another. Were this to change—if Gorbachev were to

221

convince the West that the Soviets are really substantially less hostile than in the past or, conversely, if the internal turmoil brought about by Gorbachev were to make Soviet hostility less prudent—then the USSR might replace the United States as the central consideration for NATO. In the late 1980s, such changes are beginning to have a considerable effect on the debate.

Closely related is an issue that in the early days of NATO could not even have been described in a separate paragraph.

• *Eastern Europe.* At the start of the Alliance, the Soviet bloc was the USSR and a collection of satellites subdued militarily and tamed by brutality. Yugoslavia broke loose early but was considered a special case. Western failure to intervene in East Berlin in 1953, in Hungary in 1956, and in Czechoslovakia in 1968 definitively demonstrated the irrelevance of NATO military force; this was the Soviet sphere of influence, and violating it was assumed to run too great a risk of starting the big war. The post-Stalin period, however, saw the beginning of a phenomenon contemplated earlier by only a few Western Sovietologists, the gradual if uneven relaxation of Soviet dominance, to the point where almost all of the satellites have exhibited some degree of autonomy in domestic systems or foreign relations. To some extent, loosening of the Soviet grip has been allowed by NATO *non*interference in the East; once the Soviets understood that we would not actively abet "disruption" in the satellites, they may have been more willing to allow small fires without fearing Western contributions of more fuel. In the specific case most important to the West and probably to the Soviet Union too, however, that of East Germany, West German Chancellor Willy Brandt's *Ostpolitik* initiated a set of policies much more active than before in encouraging a degree of Communist exchange with the West. The Federal Republic is literally and figuratively central to NATO, so that in that case at least, Eastern European issues assume substantial importance to the Alliance.

The final political issue in the NATO debate is one that has never dominated the discussion but has occasionally loomed large.

• *NATO and the Rest of the World.* Throughout the years of the Alliance it has been understood that the United States has had continuing security responsibilities in regions of the world other than Europe. Occasionally other members, notably France and Britain, have projected military power to other areas. Indeed, one major change from the beginning to the present has been the shift from the gradual decolonialization by the older powers

222

encouraged by the "anti-imperialist" United States, to the more recent outcries in Europe about U.S. activities in Vietnam, Central America, and other parts of the Third World. One question raised in the debate of the 1970s and continuing strongly into the 1980s has been the role of the United States and the rest of NATO in protecting the flow of oil to the industrial nations from the Middle East. After Reagan was elected, doubts were expressed as to whether global anticommunism weakens the American commitment to Europe.

The more military issues include the crucial link between conventional and nuclear warfare, as well as questions more specifically concerned with conventional weapons and strategies. Because American Maintainers think more in military terms than do the European Couplers, the link is as central to them as is the U.S. commitment to the Couplers.

- *The Conventional-Nuclear Link.* This is the military side of the political question about the reliability of the U.S. commitment, particularly the commitment to use nuclear weapons if necessary. Militarily, the coupling question is that of the "threshold." At what level of conventional violence, under what conditions of imminent defeat, how, tactically, will the U.S. president permit or order NATO's Supreme Commander to use American nuclear weapons? The before-the-event planning issue here is that of Deterrence versus Defense: To what extent are conventional forces intended to defend against conventional attack by the Warsaw Pact, compared with the use of those forces, particularly American troops, as a "tripwire" for U.S. nuclear weapons? Some members of the Coupler school suggest that deterrence is everything; modern conventional defense would be more traumatic than conventional World War II and would thus be little preferable to nuclear devastation. These issues are covered by NATO's "Flexible Response" doctrine, but the doctrine is so flexible and necessarily vague about what defense will be put up against what aggression that it permits a full panoply of views in the debate.
- *Conventional Weapons.* These issues include the size and deployment of forces, their sustainability over time in battle, and the quality of the Warsaw Pact armies they will face. They cover types of weapons and roles of new "Emerging Technologies." The issues also emphasize strategies: forward defense, offensive versus defensive tactics, Follow-On Forces Attack (FOFA), AirLand battle, "defensive defenses," and the like, each one of which has deep roots in NATO history and debates, and political as well as military dimensions. Much less discussed is the

constraint that has inhibited resolution of each of these issues throughout the history of the Alliance—the budgetary constraint of who's to pay. Another underlying issue is whether a conventional war fought on NATO territory (mainly West German) would be much less destructive than a tactical nuclear war.

One additional issue that falls under the conventional weapons rubric is the defense of NATO's flanks—Norway and Turkey, which border on the Soviet Union; and Greece, which has a common boundary with Bulgaria. NATO defense plans for these areas are primarily conventional; indeed, Norway has explicitly eschewed the presence of nuclear weapons on its territory. For the most part, however, the flanks are ignored in NATO dialogue, except by the flank nations themselves.

Finally, on one set of issues, political and military considerations are not only well-mixed, as they are in all of the categories, but also almost equally balanced.

- *Arms Control and Disarmament.* On one side of the national and international debates on arms control and disarmament in Europe is the contention that mutual East-West arms reductions will in themselves assist in maintaining peace and European stability. On the other side are considerations of the effects of various measures on the military balance between NATO and the Warsaw Pact, the effects of changes in this balance on the chances of Soviet attack, and the political shadow of such an attack. The common NATO belief in overwhelming Warsaw Pact conventional superiority has raised questions about any form of nuclear arms control that might sacrifice the Alliance's capability to deter a conventional attack or oppose it with nuclear weapons. More recently, however, the possibility of using conventional controls to improve the balance has begun to appear serious, and the realities of alternatives have entered the debate, substituting for some of the symbolism that had dominated when nobody believed that anything was possible anyhow.

THEMES

Cutting across the schools of thought and the specific issues are several themes brought out by the analysis and referred to throughout the discussion. They are presented here to help tie together the potential 32 boxes created by four schools and eight issue categories.[8]

- *Changes always appear radical when you are in the midst of them.* This theme begins with the next chapter on the history of the Alliance. NATO has frequently appeared to be changing drastically and, more often than not, alarmingly. Most of the time such changes have turned out to be routine.
- *Views on Alliance policy are based on members' perceptions of the Soviet Union and of each other.* This has already been discussed and will recur.
- *Interests and perceptions differ among members of the Alliance, and, in particular, between the European members and the United States.* That interests differ is obvious; the paramount interest in self-preservation differs according to whose self is being preserved. In large measure, different perceptions are based on these different interests. One crucial transatlantic difference is not interest-based, but stems from historically different world views: Europeans tend to treat the world in general and the Soviet threat in particular as being political; Americans think much more in military terms.
- *Some positions in the debate are taken in order to reconcile other debaters.* The essay terms this "resonance." All of the member nations and most of the debaters value the Alliance highly and fear its erosion stemming from the disaffection of others. Thus positions are often based neither on national interests nor on considered views of the common interest, but on a desire to reconcile the assumed interests or perceptions of Alliance partners. Frequently this is constructive; the metaphor of marriage has been used. Sometimes, however, fear-based resonance leads to a crescendo of misunderstanding and self-fulfilling prophecies. The metaphor may apply here too.
- *Fading fears of direct Soviet military attack have accentuated intra-Alliance differences, political considerations, the role of perceptions, and negative resonances.* Hence the functioning of NATO as a "subjective alliance" and the substitution of fear of "Finlandization" for fear of military aggression. Were the East-West border characterized by massed forces on high alert, life would be simpler but a lot more dangerous.
- *Potentially major changes in the Soviet Union are inducing potentially major changes in the Alliance.* These changes, particularly those in Soviet external policy most relevant to the West, are perceived as being

---

[8]The issue categories are not used in the discussions of the two minor schools, the Removers and the Withdrawers, so the actual number of boxes is somewhat smaller. The whole thing remains very complicated, however.

far more radical than those of the preceding quarter century. If they were seen as militarily threatening, they might recreate the dominance of military over political considerations in the Alliance. Because they are apparently moving in the opposite direction, they are more likely to affect NATO's political structure.

16. History

> I can recall, from the early days of NATO, an air force colonel who kept on his desk a rubber stamp that said: "In this perilous moment in the history of the alliance. . . ." He used that stamp with great frequency.
>
> —James Schlesinger[1]

In retrospect, the history of NATO has moved along a fairly smooth curve, even though the retrospective curve may be made up of the stringing together of what seemed at the time to be recurrent perilous moments. In its three and a half decades, however, the Alliance has undergone one substantial change in character, with the change taking place mostly in the 1960s.

NATO was created to cope with two problems—the potential for future Soviet aggression in Europe, and the history of past German aggression. These problems dominated throughout the 1950s; but with the ending of the Berlin crises in the early 1960s, Europe and the world began to settle into safer patterns. The Soviet military threat perceived by West Europeans changed from active to latent; German aggression became a matter of record and memory but no longer a menace for the future.

The Berlin Wall solved the problem of population flight for the Soviets and East Germans and ended the perennial confrontations around that city; the Cuban missile crisis and the subsequent disappearance of the unpredictable Khrushchev stabilized U.S.-Soviet military relations. Later in the decade, West German Socialist Willy Brandt, first as Foreign Minister and then as Chancellor, had two major effects: His *Ostpolitik* openings to the East confirmed the settling down of relations with the Soviets and the East Germans; his impeccable and active anti-Nazi record finally put to rest

---

[1]J. Schlesinger, 1984.

227

most Western fears of the future reverting to the past. In addition to these two major changes in the Soviet and the German problems in the 1960s, the American entrapment in Vietnam signalled the shift within NATO from a reactionary Europe whose decolonization needed prodding by an anti-imperialist United States to something that appeared to be 180 degrees away.

At the same time, an issue that had been germinal at most in 1951 when the U.S. commitment of troops cemented the military alliance, the connection between conventional defense and nuclear deterrence, by the late 1950s and the 1960s grew to become the dominant question in the NATO debate. The building of the British and French nuclear deterrents in the same period, and the 1966 departure of France from NATO's military structure, were based in large measure on the issue of the nuclear threshold and U.S. commitment.

By the 1970s, then, NATO had changed from an Alliance about the Soviet Union of the present and the Germany of the past to an organization that was operationally much more concerned with itself and the specific needs of its individual members although still based on the perceived need to counter the Soviet military threat and its political consequences. It had become the "subjective" alliance. The key issue toward which the NATO debate was oriented became, as it remains today, the certainty or uncertainty of the American commitment and how the United States and the other nations cope with this less-than-perfect guarantor of West European security.

THE 1950s: INITIATION

Within NATO, the organization, put together in the late 1940s as a somewhat symbolic response to Soviet pressures, became a military alliance with the commitment of American troops in 1951, in substantial measure as a response to fears created by the North Korean invasion of South Korea. The recognition that West German troops would be needed for defense of the West led to the creation of the European Defense Community (EDC), intended to create a European army that would include German soldiers under the command of others; but the 1954 failure of the French to ratify EDC put West German forces directly into NATO. The 1952 Lisbon conference set forth conventional force goals so high (96 active and reserve divisions) as to be far out of the reach of NATO wills and budgets, and the recognition of this unreality led to a belief in overwhelming Soviet conventional superiority as a permanent matter. As a result, nuclear deterrence of Soviet aggression in Europe became the central emphasis of the Alliance. In 1954, the MC 14–2 plan put into NATO doctrine the concept of (American) massive retaliation, but British and French unwillingness to bet their existence on the American commitment led to the start of the two independent deterrents.

Among the member nations, the strong leaders were Eisenhower (and John Foster Dulles) and Adenauer. The British shifted between the two major parties and the French drifted. American nuclear strategy consisted of massive retaliation; and the United States, after finishing the Korean War, was economically comfortable if frequently mildly depressed. Boosted by the Marshall Plan, European economies recovered rapidly led by the German economic miracle; by the end of the decade Germany was able to make a major military contribution to the Alliance. In 1957, the Treaty of Rome initiated the European Economic Community (EEC), the Common Market, but without Britain. Within several NATO nations, notably France and Italy, Communist parties were large and considered a real threat.

The Soviet Union moved from Stalin through Malenkov to Khrushchev, who, while more personable and less ominous than Stalin, proved to be just as hostile in different ways. Although the Russians agreed to a peace treaty permitting a free Austria, the suppression of the Hungarian revolt in 1956 confirmed both the willingness of the Soviets after Stalin to preserve their East European hold and the unwillingness of the West to intrude into the Soviet sphere of influence. The initiation of the Warsaw Pact formalized the Soviets' multinational response to NATO multinationalism, but no doubts were allowed about who was in absolute control of the Pact. The launching of Sputnik in 1957 demonstrated to the West that it could not depend on technology to outrace the Soviets militarily.

Outside of Europe and North America the major relevant trend was the rush of the nations of West Europe to decolonize their possessions and contract their spheres of influence. Frequently this was voluntary, as it had been for the British in India in the 1940s, but Dienbienphu and Suez illustrated some less willing withdrawals.

THE 1960s: REFORMULATION

Within NATO, the decade of change began with the Soviet testing of Western wills as they tried to use military pressures to end the Western occupation and free status of West Berlin and finally gave up when the building of the Wall staunched the flow of East German refugees to the West. With the continuation of economic growth, the termination of the Berlin crises strengthened the Federal Republic of Germany, and by the end of the decade it was a "regular" member of the Alliance, emotionally as well as juridically. France, however, became much less regular, as de Gaulle in 1966 withdrew his nation from NATO's integrated military structure, revising both force plans and lines of communication and pushing Alliance headquarters from Paris to Brussels. By the end of the decade, the Alliance had adapted to this partial French withdrawal. American troops in Europe were increased for the Berlin crises and then decreased as they were withdrawn for Vietnam; some of Defense Secretary McNamara's American systems analysts endeavored to show that NATO could match Soviet conventional capabilities at acceptable costs. The British nuclear deterrent developed as part of NATO, and the French *Force de Frappe* came into being as a more independent entity; but these did not satisfy the felt needs of the Europeans for a stronger connection to American strategic forces, certainly not the needs of the West Germans who were proscribed from owning nuclear weapons. Various devices attempted to fill these needs, the most notorious of which was the Multilateral Force (MLF) by which Polaris-carrying ships would be manned by multinational NATO crews, although the American president would retain final control of the nuclear warheads. The scheme collapsed of its own political weight and implausibility.

Later, in 1967, MC 14–3 replaced the massive retaliation of MC 14–2 with "Flexible Response," with its spectrum of potential replies to various Warsaw Pact aggressions. Although the specific responses to specific provocations were not set forth, nuclear responses played an important and explicit role, including a role in opposition to initial nonnuclear Soviet attacks. In the same year, the Harmel Doctrine broadened NATO's role from a purely military alliance to one that could also search, organizationally, for disarmament and détente. At the end of 1969, the Alliance was perhaps no less strong, but it was very different from what it had been at the beginning of 1960.

Among the member nations, the leadership of the leader nation began with John Kennedy, who, centrally interested in NATO, played a major personal role after a false start in his Vienna meeting with Khrushchev and after the Cuban missile crisis showed his real strength. Lyndon Johnson, however, turned his foreign interests (always secondary to his domestic ones) to Vietnam, as did Robert McNamara, the strong Secretary of Defense through most of the two administrations. By nearly monopolizing

American attention through most of the decade, Vietnam worried the other NATO nations both because it distracted from Europe and because, having withdrawn from colonialism themselves, the Europeans disapproved of what they saw as American neocolonialism. U.S. Senate Majority Leader Mike Mansfield worried the West Europeans even further by pushing his resolutions to reduce American troop levels in NATO, putting more of the burden on the now-well-off European members. In the meantime, McNamara, in spite of his growing preoccupation with Vietnam, did find the time to put forth two changes in strategic nuclear doctrine, both highly relevant to NATO deterrence. The first, set forth in his 1962 Ann Arbor speech, moved the United States from Dulles's massive retaliation toward a discriminating counterforce strategy; the second, five years later, qualified the first by restressing the crucial deterrent nature of the (perhaps inevitable) nuclear risks to cities. The new flexibility on both counts was embedded for NATO in MC 14–3. The dominant figure in European NATO was de Gaulle, who took France on its almost independent way militarily while keeping Britain off the continent by refusing it entry to the Common Market, but the de Gaulle era in France ended with the student riots of 1968, as it had begun with the Algerian riots of 1958. In the Federal Republic of Germany, meanwhile, the change over the decade was symbolized by the shift of the Chancellorship from Konrad Adenauer, a strong and strongly anti-Soviet and anti-Communist leader, through several weak successors to Willy Brandt, another strong leader who initiated the *Ostpolitik* rapprochement with the Soviets and the East Germans. One facilitating factor for *Ostpolitik* was that the internal Communist party was never serious in the Federal Republic, but by the end of the decade such parties were no longer considered as serious threats to stability even in Italy and France.

The Soviet Union got rid of Khrushchev after, and in part because of, the Cuban missile crisis. Even before the Cuban affair, however, the ending of the Berlin crises with the building of the Wall marked a step back from the overhanging threat of real military aggression in Europe. Under Brezhnev, the Soviet Union built its military strength with MIRVs at the strategic level and adventured throughout the world; but after Berlin, it refrained from hostile gestures across the European curtain. In Eastern Europe, however, Prague in 1968 reiterated that there had been no change from Budapest in 1956. Within the communist world as a whole, the very major change was the shift from the Soviet-Chinese alliance, which many in the West in the 1950s had thought of as worldwide monolithic communism, to implacable hostility by the end of the decade. This was not only strategically important in itself, it presaged similar but lesser changes in the face of communism in Europe.

Outside of Europe and North America, the 1960s saw the end of European colonialism. More important, Vietnam signalled major changes in the American relation to the Alliance. Together with the changes in NATO itself and in the other nations, it meant that by the end of the decade, U.S. leadership of NATO was much weaker than it had been at the beginning, thus setting the stage for the difficulties of the 1970s and the 1980s.

THE 1970s: DOUBTS

Within NATO, the membership structure remained stable and the threat of Soviet aggression in Europe remained minimal, but the 1970s were characterized by growing questioning of fundamental tenets, particularly of the quality of American leadership of the Alliance (or, perhaps, the basic stability allowed the luxury of such questioning). The decade started with the SALT and ABM agreements on U.S.-Soviet strategic arrangements, which, although they were approved of by the West Europeans, began to throw additional doubts on America's ability or willingness to put its own homeland at risk by using nuclear weapons against the Soviets in response to aggression in Europe. These doubts increased substantially through the period, as the Soviets gained effective strategic parity—the ability to put the United States at about as much risk as the USSR in any nuclear exchange.[2] Politically, Watergate, the defeat in Vietnam, and the weak presidencies of Gerald Ford and Jimmy Carter eroded U.S. international as well as domestic leadership. Carter began his administration by pushing the neutron bomb on European governments made reluctant by domestic opposition, and then backing off the bomb. As a result mainly of this and of worries about strategic parity, Helmut Schmidt, who had succeeded Brandt as Chancellor after having been his Defense Minister, took a proposal initiated by NATO's Nuclear Planning Group to reinstall American intermediate-range nuclear missiles in Europe, and made it into a political test for the United States and the Alliance. At the end of the decade, the Schmidt proposal resulted in the two-track decision: to install in Germany, Britain, Italy, and the Low Countries the Intermediate Nuclear Force (INF) of Pershing II ballistic missiles and cruise missiles but (mainly as a bow to peace movement Removers in Europe) to negotiate with the Soviets over the mutual reduction of INF and the corresponding SS-20 force, which the Russians had begun to install.

Among the member nations, the United States had a weak presidency from the beginning of Watergate in 1973 to the end of the decade.

[2]See Nitze, 1985a, p. 5.

Particularly after the deflation of Nixon, the dominant figure in American foreign policy through 1976 was Henry Kissinger, but the ultimate fiasco in Vietnam together with decade-long economic problems weakened both foreign and domestic policy. In Germany, without discontinuing Brandt's *Ostpolitik*, Schmidt added an Alliance-oriented personal military expertise. Giscard d'Estaing was a somewhat charismatic but not strong French leader. The British Labour leadership of Harold Wilson and James Callaghan remained pro-NATO. For Britain and for the other European members of the Alliance, the major event was that the United Kingdom finally committed itself firmly to Europe by joining the Common Market. For Western Europe as for the United States, however, the 1970s were filled with bad economic news, mainly because of the rapid increases in petroleum prices as the OPEC cartel took hold. In spite of economic sourness, however, the internal communist threat, which had decreased in the 1960s, virtually disappeared. In Italy and in Spain, which had moved toward NATO after the post-Franco democratization, communist parties became "Eurocommunist," under partial control from Moscow at worst. The French party became so tame that François Mitterrand initially included it in his Socialist government with little distress in NATO.

The Soviet Union remained firmly under the leadership of Brezhnev, with little internal change. The confrontation with China continued, exacerbated by the rapprochement between the United States and China. The European satellites began to differentiate themselves, within limits, from the Soviet Union and from each other, culminating in the birth of the Solidarity movement in Poland. Militarily, as noted, the Soviets achieved effective strategic parity, which, together with the installation of the SS-20 missiles in Europe, upset NATO considerably. At the end of the decade, the occupation of Afghanistan poisoned East-West relations, although NATO came to no agreement on how to treat with it.

Outside of Europe and North America, the major phenomenon was OPEC's taking control of petroleum markets and prices. The consequent many-fold increase in the world price of oil dominated the decade economically and was largely responsible for the overall political sourness of the period as well. Additionally, the rapid growth of the Japanese economy presented substantial competitive problems for the West.

NATO thus entered the 1980s in a state of some disarray and a mild degree of psychological as well as economic depression. The politics of depression led to major political changes in the Western nations. Because the previous leadership had been to the left, the new leaders were almost all conservatives: Ronald Reagan for Jimmy Carter in the United States;

Margaret Thatcher for James Callaghan in Britain; and Helmut Kohl for Helmut Schmidt in Germany. The major exception was France, where the Socialist François Mitterrand replaced Giscard as president, but after a few years Mitterrand was forced to accept the conservative Jacques Chirac as Prime Minister. In the Soviet Union, Brezhnev was followed by two short-lived successors, and then came Gorbachev and major change.

In NATO, initial installation of INF commenced over substantial domestic opposition. The political ability to actually install the INF missiles was taken as a successful test of NATO's manhood, a perception that set the stage for the debate later in the 1980s about negotiated removal of the missiles. The initial basis for the removal negotiations of 1987 was that to mute the internal political opposition in 1981, NATO had offered the Soviets the zero option of removing the entire INF in return for removal of all Soviet SS-20s, in the sure belief that Brezhnev would turn it down. He did turn it down, but Gorbachev accepted it, throwing the Alliance into disarray. The disarray had begun, however, when as president of the United States and nominal leader of the Western Alliance, Ronald Reagan, alone and then in combination with Gorbachev, went through a series of events—the "Evil Empire" speech, SDI, the Libyan raid, Reykjavik—that left the Europeans muttering about unpredictability and lack of consultation.

Until Gorbachev, discussion of most of these issues had changed very little since the Alliance reformulation of the 1960s. Two of the issues, in fact, changed hardly at all since the early 1950s. The first of these concerns *The Soviet Role*. This debate might be characterized, slightly unfairly, as George Kennan versus George Kennan. In his seminal 1946 paper, "The Sources of Soviet Conduct," prepared as a commentary for Secretary of Defense James Forrestal and then published over the nom de plume, "X," Kennan wrote:

> [I]t is clear that the main element of any United States policy toward the Soviet Union must be that of a long-term, patient but firm and vigorous containment of Russian expansive tendencies. . . . Soviet pressure against the free institutions of the Western world is something that can be contained by the adroit and vigorous application of counterforce at a series of constantly shifting geographical and political points, corresponding to the shifts of Soviet policy, but which cannot be charmed or talked out of existence.[3]

Kennan contends that the Soviet pressure against free institutions he discussed was not military. "In no way did the Soviet Union appear to me, at

---

[3] X, 1947, reprinted in *Foreign Affairs*, Spring 1987, pp. 861–862.

that moment, as a military threat to this country."[4] And a careful reading of the "X" paper bears him out; but from the point of view of the debate, what is more important is that the analysis was widely interpreted as calling for military containment, and this interpretation was a major influence on subsequent American policy. It provided the intellectual backing for the Truman Doctrine, which was used initially to defend against Soviet-backed incursions in Greece and Turkey, and for the subsequent extension of the Doctrine to other areas. In Europe, it formed the basis for the military alliance, particularly after the Berlin Blockade, and then the Korean invasion demonstrated that Soviet pressure could indeed be explicitly military as well as political. This interpretation of Kennan's "containment" concept governs one Western view of the Soviet Union down through the debates of today; the opposing view, however, is the one Kennan himself has taken for many years and takes now:

It is entirely clear to me that Soviet leaders do not want a war with us and are not planning to initiate one. In particular, I have never believed that they have seen it in their interests to overrun Western Europe militarily, or that they would have launched an attack on that region generally even if the so-called nuclear deterrent had not existed. But I recognize that the sheer size of their armed forces is a disquieting factor for many of our allies. . . . For all of these reasons, there is now indeed a military aspect to the problem of containment as there was not in 1946; but what needs most to be contained, as I see it, is not so much the Soviet Union as the weapons race itself.[5]

In any case, these two positions on containment have governed the two major views of the USSR incorporated into the NATO arms debate since the start of the Alliance—from Stalin through Malenkov, Khrushchev, Brezhnev, Andropov, and Chernenko; through cold war, crisis, blockade, and détente. But the growing belief that Gorbachev is different enough from his predecessors that the Soviet Union will *really* change this time has begun to affect the debate.

The second issue that has changed but little is that of *Conventional Weapons*. The Lisbon conference of 1952 called for 96 divisions, some 60 of them active, to defend Western Europe conventionally against overwhelming Soviet troop strength. Neither the wealthy United States nor the poor nations of Europe were willing to pay for them; the NATO conventional force has consisted of roughly half those numbers ever since.

---

[4]Kennan, Spring 1987, p. 885.
[5]Ibid., pp. 888–889.

Those numbers have long since gone by the board, but every NATO supreme commander since Lisbon has asked for substantially more than he had to enable him to fulfill his conventional defense responsibilities; and many analysts in a position to be more objective have called for similar increases. But neither the wealthy United States nor the now-wealthy nations of Europe have been willing to pay.

The first force goals of the 1950s were not closely linked to the threshold at which conventional defense would have to be abandoned in favor of nuclear weapons, but by the early 1960s the connection had been established, and the issue of *The Conventional-Nuclear Link* has remained a constant in the debate ever since. Two statements from 1960–61 apply almost as well in the late 1980s.

> From [the Russian] standpoint the problem of successful aggression in Europe is to find a level and kind of attack large enough to be useful, but small enough to be well below the threshold risking American nuclear response. . . . It is becoming more and more widely accepted among critics of NATO that the most important task for the alliance today is to raise by conventional means the threshold of attack that the Russians would have to launch in order to be successful.[6]

and

> If NATO is not willing to make the effort required for a conventional defense, its other option would be to rely more heavily on tactical nuclear weapons. . . . Deterrence would be achieved not by protecting against every contingency, but by confronting the Soviets with the prospect of a conflict with incalculable consequences.[7]

The authors of the two statements, both still members in good standing of the Maintainer school in the current NATO debate, would not necessarily take the same points of view today, but both would agree that the issue of the conventional-nuclear link remains central. So would those in the other schools who might want to treat the link differently (the European Couplers) or do away with it entirely (the American Withdrawers and the European Removers).

Indeed, for the Couplers, the issue is less that of the precise conventional-nuclear threshold than of the feared attenuation of the link connecting American strategic nuclear weapons to European defense and deterrence—the issue of *The U.S. Commitment to NATO*, which for them

---

[6]Wohlstetter, 1961, pp. 381–382.
[7]Kissinger, 1960, p. 526.

remains central to the NATO debate. Pierre Lellouche, one of the leading prophets of the end of the American commitment, quotes François Mitterrand (before Mitterrand was elected president of France) as saying: "The Alliance rests on a fiction: American intervention in Europe in case of Soviet aggression."[8] Lellouche himself stresses the role of strategic parity in weakening this commitment:

> This new menace of a Soviet counterforce strike (rather than solely anti-city) has for the moment no more than a limited effect on the security of the American continent as such. This is because of the conjectural character of a Soviet surprise attack against American silos, and the second-strike capacity which the Americans would retain even after such an attack. In contrast, this menace would have different consequences for American *extended* deterrence in Europe. The risk of seeing its ICBMs preventively destroyed adds to the already great uncertainty that already weighs on the employment of strategic systems by the American president in case of conflict in Europe.[9]

But (as Lellouche points out) the French expressed almost identical doubts long before strategic parity. General Pierre Gallois, the theorist of de Gaulle's independent deterrent, wrote in 1961:

> And how believe that the Strategic Air Command would use its weapons of massive destruction for the sake of a third party, if America thereby risked, in reprisal, a setback of two centuries from the extent of the damages suffered! Then what becomes of the indispensable credibility of the reprisal against aggression?[10]

The point is not that nothing has changed. Rather, it is that although much has changed in 25 years, the debate over the crucial issue of the U.S. commitment has changed very little. The European Couplers have always been afraid that fear of opening the Pandora's box of nuclear war might prevent the Americans from using nuclear weapons in behalf of even their closest allies. The quarter-century of changes, including strategic parity, has added only one more element to the mutual fears and doubts that have resonated across the Atlantic almost since the beginning of the Alliance.

Four of the issues—*The American Commitment, The Conventional-Nuclear Link, Conventional Force Levels,* and *The Soviet Role*—are thus

---

[8]Lellouche, 1985, p. 39.
[9]Ibid., pp. 68–69.
[10]Gallois, 1961, p. 191.

old ones, having been debated in much their current form since the beginning of the Alliance in the 1950s or at least since its reformulation into its present shape in the 1960s. The other four issues are somewhat newer, at least as they are now discussed.

Discussions of *The Europeans' Commitments to Themselves* might have moved into their current form in the 1960s, as fears of Germany past faded in the minds of the other NATO members. But de Gaulle's difficulties in reconciling a *Europe des Patries* with a more unified version under distinct French leadership postponed such changes, and the debate did not really take its current form until the suspicions of the United States induced by Carter, Reagan, and strategic parity grew stronger in the late 1970s and the 1980s.

Before and after the Soviet suppression of the Prague spring in 1968, the primary assumption about *NATO's role in Eastern Europe* was that NATO did not have a role in Eastern Europe. Militarily that remains the case, but from *Ostpolitik* through the rise and fall of Solidarity, it has become increasingly clear that NATO members and to some degree the organization itself can and want to play a political role in the differentiating world of what are now seldom called the "Soviet satellites." This role has become the subject of a changing debate.

The issue of *NATO and the Rest of the World* has taken on many different shapes, from the American involvement in Vietnam, through the rise and decline of OPEC, to the terrorism and Persian Gulf scenarios of the 1980s.

Arms Control and Disarmament have been debated throughout the period. In the early 1960s proposals related to Europe took the form of "disengagement" of NATO and Warsaw Pact forces in central Europe. This was not taken very seriously by the American Maintainer and European Coupler establishment, and it faded. From the mid-1960s to the mid-1980s, "serious" arms control discussions concerned the strategic weapons of the two superpowers and eventuated in the ABM treaty and SALT I and II. So far as European arms control was concerned, the establishment used ongoing negotiations to provide a political sop to the Remover peace movement. The second track of NATO's 1979 INF two-track decision—the offer to negotiate down the levels of intermediate missiles being installed—and the 1981 offer to zero them out if the SS-20s were also removed, were offered in the belief that they were not serious because the Soviets would never agree. When Gorbachev did agree in 1986, the issue and the debate became very serious indeed and turned out to have an intimate relationship to the central issue of the American commitment.

The NATO debate of the late 1980s thus turns on the old issues, in somewhat but not very new forms. The American commitment remains pivotal; the nuclear-conventional link, nuclear weapons issues, the Europeans' commitments to themselves, and the arms control-disarmament debates all depend in greater or lesser degree on understandings of what that commitment is and beliefs about what it should be. The debate over levels of conventional forces is also related to the commitment issues, but proceeds on even more ancient premises.

Two issues may change the direction and the quality of the debate substantially, however. One has already begun to have a major effect, reflected in the analysis here: The question of how much and how fast Soviet policy toward the West is changing has become the wild card that may well start all the other debates off in very new directions. The other new issue, which has not yet had a major role but may achieve one, is that of economics, both in the West as the Common Market's 1992 "Year of Europe" approaches with its threat of a transatlantic trade war, and as increased East/West trade relations show some possibility of affecting security relations. These economic issues are foreshadowed by some of the "burden-sharing" and other discussions covered below, but the shadow is pale compared with the role economics may play in the future.

17. The Couplers

> For Germans and other Europeans whose memory of the catastrophe of conventional war is still alive and on whose densely populated territory both pacts would confront each other with the destructive power of modern armies, the thought of an ever more probable conventional war is terrifying. To Germans and other Europeans, an ever more probable conventional war is, therefore, no alternative to war prevention through the current strategy, including the option of a first use of nuclear weapons.
>
> —Karl Kaiser, Georg Leber, Alois Mertes, and Franz-Josef Schulze[1]

> For de Gaulle, the fate of the American nuclear guarantee was sealed. Sooner or later, he predicted, an "equilibrium of deterrence" would replace American superiority, and this "equilibrium" would protect only the two superpowers "and not the other countries of the world, even though they found themselves tied to one or the other of the two colossal powers."
>
> —Pierre Lellouche[2]

NATO is about Europe, and the Couplers are the mainstream European School of Thought. The first of the two quotations, by four Germans, including spokesmen for both the Christian Democratic and Socialist parties, summarizes succinctly the major common European value judgment, one sometimes forgotten by Americans: Europeans value their own self-preservation, and their historical experience leads them to fear the conventional war they have experienced almost as much as the nuclear war they can imagine.

The European dilemma, however, is based on the belief that the nuclear threat is needed to deter conventional war. The ultimate nuclear deterrent for the West is the American strategic force, and, as Lellouche's quote from a 1964 de Gaulle press conference illustrates, West Europeans have been nervous for many years about the reliability of the commitment of this force to their defense. Issues of commitment—the commitments of

---

[1]Kaiser et al., 1982, p. 1164.
[2]Lellouche, 1985, p. 47.

European nations to each other as well as that of the United States to Western Europe as a whole—and of how these commitments might be implemented are central to the European portion of the debate. Indeed, this more than anything else distinguishes the European Couplers from the American Maintainers.

The eight issue categories are analyzed in four groups:

- *Alliance Political Issues*, including the U.S. Commitment to NATO, the Europeans' Commitments to Themselves, and the Rest of the World;
- *Military issues*: the Conventional-Nuclear Link, and Conventional Weapons;
- *The Opponent*: the Soviet Union, and Eastern Europe;
- *Arms Control*, as one output of the East/West interaction.

ALLIANCE POLITICAL ISSUES

The U.S. Commitment

The French, since de Gaulle, have been the most concerned about the strength of the American commitment. Lellouche, until recently a member of the *Institut Français des Relations Internationales* (IFRI), is at the forefront of those who contend that de Gaulle was prescient in his "sooner or later" prediction of the erosion of the American nuclear commitment. Lellouche believes that the time has come and that France and the rest of Europe must recognize this and plan accordingly:

> General de Gaulle's defense system which we have inherited was essentially conceived by him at the beginning of the 1960s. Another world. A world marked by the incontestable nuclear superiority of the United States and by an unprecedented economic boom, with these elements assuring the stability of Germany and of Europe at the heart of the Atlantic Alliance, and permitting the birth of the process of European construction. . . . Nuclear arms technology hardly hinted at its first great revolution: intercontinental missiles had only just appeared, the conquest of space had no more than begun, and guidance precision was measured in kilometers.

> On all of these points, we almost live today on another planet. Not only has the USSR put an end to American nuclear superiority, but it has

established in Europe an absolute superiority as much nuclear as in conventional forces, thus creating political instability at the heart of NATO.[3]

And, as a result:

. The famous American "umbrella," though it may still retain an important political value, has lost its strategic significance. Without doubt, America will fight for Europe—but it will fight with conventional armies, without risking uncontrollable escalation to the nuclear level.[4]

Complementing Lellouche's strategic thinking, Jimmy Goldsmith, the Anglo-French publisher of the largest French weekly newsmagazine, L'Express, added an analysis of American demographic and economic change, and then echoed a series of arguments for reduced commitment that he had heard within the United States. In an article widely discussed in France, he wrote that:

San Antonio, Texas, is now largely Mexican. Miami is a sort of capital of Latin America. Los Angeles aspires to become the same for the Pacific. The European sensibility and heritage is on the decline. The volume of American commerce with the Pacific region has exceeded that of commerce with Europe. . . .

The debate is not limited to the left or the right; neither to isolationists nor internationalists. . . . The reasons for change are identifiable: (1) Americans have the conviction that chronic assistance to those who do not need it is injurious. . . . (2) Americans think that Europe potentially has all that it needs to defend itself. . . . (3) The softness [toward the Soviets] of European foreign policy is considered a "polluting" element for American foreign policy. . . . (4) When an alliance is made up of a dominant partner and a number of weaker ones, the distortions are evident. . . . (5) At a time when Europeans criticize the budget deficit ($221 billion in 1986) and the balance-of-payments deficit ($140 billion) of the United States, the cost of participation in NATO is an argument well-used by partisans of retreat.[5]

Lellouche and Goldsmith expressed a common French view of the erosion of the American commitment, but they expressed it somewhat more

---

[3]Lellouche, 1985, pp. 28–29.
[4]Ibid., p. 88.
[5]Goldsmith, 1987, pp. 37–38. In his role as Anglo-French financier, Jimmy Goldsmith is Sir James Goldsmith.

extremely than many of their countrymen. François Heisbourg, an influential French analyst and official who has become Director of the International Institute for Strategic Studies (IISS) in London, for example, contended in a review of Lellouche's book that less has changed than he implies: "That the American guarantee was categorical is not new, and France, in its time, had considered this situation sufficiently disquieting to create a national deterrent force."[6] And several writers suggested that many of the problems were based more on the idiosyncracies of the Reagan administration than on any fundamental American tendencies.[7]

In any case, most French analysts and officials agree that either fundamental strategic changes or current ideologies will cause the United States to reduce its commitment to NATO, although a few argue that American vital interests will continue to support the commitment.[8]

This discussion began before the suddenly serious U.S.-Soviet negotiations in 1987 over NATO's nonserious (in 1981) "zero-zero" proposal to remove all U.S. and Soviet INF missiles from Europe. Zero-zero caused additional consternation, with worries centering on whether it was the first step down "the slippery slope" to full denuclearization of Europe and thus full abrogation of the American commitment. Even before the 1987 negotiations, these concerns had received a major boost from the November 1986 Reagan-Gorbachev Reykjavik meeting, where Mr. Reagan's failure to consult the allies, and his apparent tendency to present proposals without having thought them through, added greatly to West European insecurities. One post-Reykjavik statement, by then French Prime Minister Jacques Chirac to the Western European Union, shows both the extent of disquietude and the degree to which official France was willing to put this tactfully on the record. Discussing potential removal of the intermediate range missiles, Chirac said:

If one could only be grateful for the declared intention of the Soviets to dismantle most of their SS-20s, one could but hope to avoid the possibility that the eventual removal of the American missiles would not begin a weakening of the tie between Europe and the United States. . . . We can never repeat frequently enough that the danger to our existence presented by the formidable nuclear, conventional, and classical arsenal of the East must always be seen in its totality. Considering the inherent superiority of the Soviet Union in conventional and chemical forces on the European continent, security over the long

[6]Heisbourg, 1985.
[7]See, for example, Hassner, 1986b, p. 7.
[8]For an example of the latter, see Boyer, 1987.

243

term will continue to require the presence in West Europe of a sufficient number of American nuclear arms.[9]

In addition to its audible whistling in the dark over continuation of the American commitment, Chirac's statement is notable for the continued public agreement by a French official that, even with its own independent nuclear deterrent, France still must count on American weapons as well. It should also be noted that President François Mitterrand, Chirac's political opponent but resident (at that time) of the same political home in the French constitutional "cohabitation," appeared far more relaxed about the same matters.[10] After Mitterrand's 1988 reelection, achieved by a victory over Chirac, this relaxation in the Elysée began to wean French thinking from the kinds of fears expressed by Goldsmith.

The British Couplers,[11] although concerned with the same issues, differ in tone and substance from the French. If the French have been tensely worried about a diminishing U.S. commitment and believe the diminution to be the result of such objective changes as strategic parity and changing American ethnicity, the British continue relaxed, feeling that much of the apparent erosion is subjective and should be approached under the banner of "Come, let us reason together."

The prevailing British view has been expressed in a series of articles by Frederick Bonnart, a retired Army officer who edits *NATO's Sixteen Nations*, an unofficial journal published in Brussels. Bonnart is clear on both the need for maintaining the Alliance in something like its current state, and the cooperative way in which this should be done:

[H]owever well matched Soviet conventional power in Europe may be—and at present it is not—there can be no security for Europeans in the long term without the presence on their continent of sizable American nuclear and conventional forces.[12]

Marriages are for better or for worse, for good or for evil. Alliances may be a little more flexible. But both stand to gain by a mature attitude of each partner toward the other. As in any cooperative human endeavor, the cost to each should be considered less important than

---

[9]Chirac, 1986a, pp. 164–165.

[10]See for example, Hoagland, 1987, p. A2.

[11]Politically, this School includes the Conservatives and a few remaining "right-wing" members of the Labour Party, although mainstream Labour is in the Remover category. The Liberal-Social Democratic Alliance has also been largely Coupler and has taken official positions consistent with this viewpoint, but much of the Liberal segment has stayed substantially on the Remover side. At this writing, however, with the merging of the two parts into a single party, which some Social Democrats are leaving, the ultimate position is not clear.

[12]Bonnart, 1987b.

the common benefit to both. In a matter of life and death, it is only that which counts in the end.[13]

This is not to say that the British believe that no movement is taking place. Historian Michael Howard sees substantial change happening, with more needed, but nothing like an end to NATO or a fundamental restructuring that might, for example, shift the Alliance to a primarily European rather than an Atlantic basis. Howard stresses a common British theme—that the Alliance has been slow in adapting to change—quite different from the French idea that the world has begun to fall down around our ears as the American nuclear commitment comes into doubt. He suggests that, starting with 1949:

> The American presence was wanted in Western Europe, not just in the negative role of a *deterrent* to Soviet aggression, but in the positive role of a *reassurance* to the West Europeans. . . . There can be little doubt that since 1949 changes have occurred, both objective and subjective, on a scale comparable to those between 1815 and 1854, or 1870 and 1914. . . . What is needed today is a reversal of that process whereby European governments have sought greater security by demanding an ever greater intensification of the American nuclear commitment; demands that are as divisive within their own countries as they are irritating for the people of the United States. Instead we should be doing all we can to reduce our dependence on American nuclear weapons by enhancing, so far as is militarily, socially and economically possible, our capacity to defend ourselves.[14]

Howard's last sentence brings up another central theme in the transatlantic debate over the U.S. commitment to NATO, that of burden-sharing. This is not much talked about by the French who, because they consider their own contribution to NATO to be an independent one, are reluctant to either criticize the contributions of others or defend their own. Many in the United States, though strongly pro-NATO, believe that the Europeans should be bearing much more of the economic and other weight; and this is much on the mind of the British. But Foreign Secretary Sir Geoffrey Howe, after suggesting that sudden unilateral attempts by the United States to "equalize" burdens could turn out to be quite negative from the American as well as the European standpoint, contends that they are not badly balanced in any case:

---

[13]Bonnart, 1987a.
[14]Howard, 1982–1983, pp. 310–322.

[T]he most likely result of withdrawing the American "prop" might well not be to spur the Europeans to stand on their own two feet and multiply their own defense efforts. It could be more likely to make them question whether their own commitments to each other were still worth the sacrifices involved. It would certainly strengthen the platform of those (happily a small minority at present) who have always argued for European neutrality and/or accommodation with the East. . . .

Overall, the non-U.S. NATO allies do appear to be shouldering roughly their fair share. (This paragraph will not, I hope, be taken as European special pleading. Every sentence in it is taken from Defense Secretary Caspar Weinberger's report to Congress of March 1984 about the balance of allied contributions.)[15]

And finally, many of the British agree with other Europeans that the problems of the role and commitment of the United States, whatever their fundamental basis, were substantially exacerbated by the policies and style of the Reagan administration. The British, like the French and all other West Europeans, were deeply distressed by President Reagan's nonconsulting unilateralism at Reykjavik. Whatever remains of the "special relationship" encourages British writers to comment more directly and pungently on American politics than do the French. Even before Reykjavik, David Watt, former Director of the Royal Institute of International Affairs, wrote:

Let us put our cards on the table. There are two basic views about President Reagan's foreign policy. One, the Administration's, appears to be accepted (if the opinion polls are to be believed) by the majority of Americans. It is that the United States, after years of weakness and humiliation, has once again faced the challenge of an aggressive, expansionist Soviet Union, revived the global economy, rescued the Western Alliance and generally reasserted true American leadership in the world. The other view is shared to a greater or lesser extent by much of the rest of mankind, with the possible exceptions of the Israelis, the South Africans, President Marcos of the Philippines and a few right-wing governments in Central and South America. It is that the Reagan administration has vastly overreacted to the Soviet threat, thereby distorting the American (and hence the world) economy, quickening the arms race, warping its own judgment about events in the Third World, and further debasing the language of international

---

[15]Howe, 1984–1985, pp. 333–334.

intercourse with feverish rhetoric. A subsidiary charge, laid principally by the Europeans, Canadians and many Latin Americans, but frequently endorsed in the Arab world and the Far East, is that in a desperate attempt to rediscover "leadership," the United States under Reagan has reverted to its worst unilateral habits, resenting and ignoring, when it deigns to notice, the independent views and interests of its friends and allies. It is in my experience almost impossible to convey even to the most experienced Americans how deeply rooted and widely spread the critical view has become.[16]

Or, put with perhaps more typical English restraint by an even stronger pillar of the Establishment, Field Marshall Lord Bramall, retired Chief of the General Staff:

The question therefore that we should perhaps be asking ourselves is whether . . . the somewhat erratic content of some of the policies that sadly have recently been evident across the Atlantic, should somehow be changing what we do. In general terms, I am sure that the answer to the . . . question is emphatically no.[17]

Even after Reykjavik, and even after the reappearance of zero-zero, not "changing what we do" as a West European response to actual or potential changes across the Atlantic has been the standard British response. Over the long run, moves in the direction of self-reliance are inevitable and desirable, but, as Howard points out, they should be gradual and constrained.

The German Couplers cover a broader spectrum in their views on the U.S. commitment than do the French or the British: some German views resemble the French tension of Lellouche, others the British calm of Bramall. To be sure, most of the German Couplers—the governing coalition of the Christian Democrats (CDU), Bavarian Christian Socialists, and Free Democrats (FDP), plus a large portion[18] of the opposition Social Democrats (SDP)—do all agree on the crucial importance to the Federal Republic of the continued American nuclear commitment. Opposition was widespread, for example, to the suggestion for No First Use of nuclear weapons by NATO, tentatively put forth in the early 1980s by the

---

[16]Watt, 1983, p. 521.

[17]Bramall, 1987.

[18]How large a portion is unclear on two grounds: First, estimates vary on how many of the Social Democrats in the Bundestag or elsewhere are "moderates" like several quoted in this discussion of the Couplers; second, it is not clear how immoderate the "left wing" is. The SPD remains committed to NATO and to the U.S. commitment to NATO, but how to weigh this against various SPD antinuclear stances is less well defined than for, say, the British Labour Party.

American "Gang of Four" (McGeorge Bundy, George Kennan, Robert McNamara, and Gerard Smith).[19] The four Germans quoted at the beginning of this section—Karl Kaiser (Director of the *Deutsche Gesellschaft fur Auswartige Politik* or DGAP), Georg Leber (an SPD Bundestag Deputy and former Defense Minister), Alois Mertes (a CDU Deputy), and Franz-Josef Schulze (a retired general and NATO commander)—wrote:

> The tight and indissoluble coupling of conventional forces and nuclear weapons on the European continent with the strategic potential of the United States confronts the Soviet Union with the incalculable risk that any military conflict between the two Alliances could escalate to nuclear war. . . . Not only the inhabitants of the Federal Republic of Germany but also American citizens help bear the risks, the conventional as well as the nuclear. The indivisibility of the security of the Alliance as a whole and of its territory creates the credibility of deterrence.

> [T]he proposed no-first-use policy would destroy the confidence of Europeans and especially of Germans in the European-American Alliance as a community of risk, and would endanger the strategic unity of the Alliance and the security of Western Europe.[20]

In fact, however, this 1982 statement of principle papered over deep German worries about the U.S. commitment that antedate the No-First-Use proposal, let alone Reykjavik, and cracks in the German Coupler front, which the 1987 zero-zero revival turned into widening fissures. In 1981, Uwe Nerlich, Research Director of the major German defense analysis institute, the *Stifftung Wissenschaft und Politik*, expressed great doubts about U.S. policy as it had manifested itself in the 1970s:

> Given the leading role of the United States in Western affairs, the most distressing aspect of the current political reality is that the United States no longer propounds a concept of world affairs within which Western Europe could play roles at all commensurate with its inner dynamics. In fact, U.S. policies no longer follow any design; they are guided by crisis behavior as the occasions arise, without sufficient instruments to control the outcomes. . . .

> If during the first Nixon term a more complex American approach put the Soviet Union temporarily on the defensive, the primacy of

---

[19]See Chapter 12.
[20]Kaiser et al., 1982, pp. 1159–1162.

American domestic affairs imposed itself again with the end of the Vietnam war and the climactic events of Watergate. To make matters worse, the Carter administration painfully demonstrated that competence is the key element in all relations with the Soviet Union.[21]

The invidious comparison between Carter and Nixon might lead some Americans to believe that this is a right-wing diatribe against American softness, but Nerlich was no right winger in any conventional sense. Six years later, he was even darker in his views of the conservative governments that then ruled all the major NATO nations:

[T]he alliance tends to be engaged in a vicious circle: The weaker the political leaderships, the more security policies are victimized by domestic policies, which in turn overburdens democracies and often lowers their quality, and, of course, this exacerbates the need for political leadership, etc. The INF debate since 1986 is a case in point. Friedrich Nietzsche stated 110 years ago: "Those who aim publicly at something too large and beyond their capacity will also lack the capacity to disavow their aims publicly."[22]

A part of the 1981 paper was devoted to the contention that "the only way the Atlantic Alliance can persist is through social democratic support."[23] This was apparently a shot in the civil war to save the soul of the social democratic SPD for then-Chancellor Helmut Schmidt's strongly pro-NATO, pro-nuclear policies. Schmidt lost the war and the chancellorship, the SPD lost the government for at least a decade, and the cracks in the Coupler consensus have become gulfs. Although many members of the SPD remain Couplers in that they continue to support NATO—perhaps a majority, depending on the precise line used to delineate the School—even the moderates differ substantially on nuclear issues from the CDU and from Nerlich, as will be seen below in the discussion of German attitudes toward the zero-zero and subsequent arms control proposals.

One reason for the SPD civil wars is that the West German Couplers must keep on looking back over their shoulders at the Remover peace movement, with its profound distrust of everything American and nuclear. This is discussed in a 1983 analysis by Christoph Bertram, former Director of IISS, now political editor of *Die Zeit* of Hamburg:

---

[21]Nerlich, 1981, pp. 71–83.
[22]Nerlich, 1988.
[23]Nerlich, 1981, p. 81.

While the [German] antimissile movement had acquired an unprecedented depth and articulation, it nevertheless remained the manifestation of a minority. The efforts within the SPD to prevent the party from drifting into opposition to the Atlantic Alliance reflected this. They were motivated not only by the conviction of the leadership that there was no alternative to NATO, but also by the realization that no party opposed to the security link with the United States would stand a chance with the conservative, security-minded German electorate.[24]

In any case, by 1987 the zero-zero negotiations caused, or revealed, the great gap between the two sides of what had once been the German Coupler consensus. Both sides remained committed to NATO, to dependence on the United States of the Alliance in general and the Federal Republic in particular, and to the crucial role of the American nuclear deterrent. But whether to endorse zero-zero, what would happen if and when it was adopted, and what to do next were all subjects of major contention. On a political level, the issue divided the government coalition, with FDP Foreign Minister Hans-Dietrich Genscher favoring the zeroing out of all intermediate-range missiles; and CDU Chancellor Helmut Kohl, who strongly opposed the removal of the 500–1000 kilometer-range weapons (the Short-Range Intermediate Nuclear Force, or SRINF), being dragged into acquiescence by Genscher and by American pressure. By 1989, the oncoming (probably in late 1990) federal elections had driven the situation into even greater confusion, with all West German parties agreeing with each other (and disagreeing with most of the Federal Republic's allies) on the need to negotiate with the Soviets over *short-range* nuclear weapons (SNF), but disagreeing among themselves over the desired outcome of those negotiations. The SPD wanted a "third zero"—no SNF—most of the CDU wanted a floor above zero, and Genscher was not clear.

With regard to the treaty's effect on coupling, the anti-zero-zero view is expressed analytically by Nerlich, who contends that the withdrawal of American INF missiles would so weaken the link with the United States that European deterrence would have to depend on French and British nuclear weapons:

> The zero option—a treaty agreement not to deploy U.S. intermediate-range weapons in Western Europe for some quid pro quo—raises fundamental questions about the maintenance of NATO's deterrence strategy and for the foreseeable future can in no way be justified on strategic grounds. However, were such an agreement, a treaty of whatever kind

---

[24]Bertram, 1984, p. 627.

resulting in a withdrawal of the American INF, nevertheless to come about, then the French and British nuclear forces would have to acquire completely new functions.[25]

But Gert Krell, the Director of the Peace Research Institute of Frankfurt (which, in spite of its name, is not part of the Remover peace movement), believes that the effects of zero-zero on the U.S. commitment have been vastly overblown:

It is very difficult to understand that there should still be resistance against this package in the West. . . . The objections are . . . not credible. They sound schizophrenic when raised by French leaders who complain about what they see as decoupling by the United States, but who hold on to France's own and long-standing decoupling from the defense of Europe. . . . Coupling the United States to Europe through nuclear escalation linkage is not a question of hardware but of deterrence politics and metaphysics. Security through extended deterrence cannot be enforced by the deployment of nuclear weapons—of which there will be an abundance even after LRINF withdrawal on European soil or in the adjoining waters. More important are the political unity of the alliance and the presence of U.S. troops.[26]

The initial zero-zero controversy has been replaced by the SNF controversy, but the basic issue remains the same for the Germans. Being fully dependent on the United States nuclear deterrent, Germans of whatever viewpoint may just have thought about these issues more thoroughly and more pragmatically than the philosophers in the other major European members of NATO.

The Europeans' Commitments to Themselves

It has been abundantly clear since the beginning of the Alliance that no member other than the United States had any individual capability to stand up to Soviet military power. The independent nuclear forces of France and Britain might enable those two nations to keep the Soviets on the proper side of the Rhine and the Channel by mounting essentially suicidal threats behind the deterrence of "the strong by the weak," in the phrase used by the French. But implementation of the threats would be a fatal remedy for a fatal disease, and for that reason use of the independent nuclear forces for

---

[25]Nerlich, in Kaiser and Lellouche, 1986, p. 187.
[26]Krell, 1987, mimeo., pp. 13–14.

national purposes was uncertain; pledges for Alliance purposes were even more uncertain in the case of Britain, unmade in the case of France. These deterrents were thus of little comfort to the rest of NATO, particularly to the Federal Republic of Germany, the only large European nation bordering on the Iron Curtain.

It has been equally clear since at least the 1960s, when Western Europe became economically strong, that if the nations to the west of the Elbe became a unity instead of a loose confederation, they could command enough economic and military power to deter the Soviets, defend against them, and probably, if need be, defeat them.

Western Europe remains confederal at best, which Americans frequently ignore when thinking in terms of "the European contribution." In recent years, however, European uncertainties about the U.S. commitment, American prods to share more of the burden, and economic incentives to produce more weapons in Europe have combined to bring various steps toward defense unity into consideration. Discussions have concentrated on a broad West European "alliance within the Alliance," or at least more of a common contribution and strategy; and the narrower possibility of a specifically Franco-German arrangement at the center.

For *the Germans* and *the French*, it is this central arrangement that dominates the debate, even though few of either nationality would dissent from the longer-run objective set forth by Peter Schmidt of the *Stifftung Wissenschaft und Politik*: "the renewed interest of France in cooperating more closely with the Federal Republic of Germany could be used as a 'moving force' to improve the state of European integration."[27] More recently, in 1987 after zero-zero turned serious, French analyst Jean d'Aubach set forth a far-reaching conclusion of the line of thought that begins with fear of U.S. abandonment:

> The probability of a diminution of the American commitment in Europe is not negligible. . . . This is the reason why Europe has no alternative solutions in the next three decades: *it must possess nuclear weapons* to guarantee its security. . . . It seems that the "juxtaposition" *of the French and British capabilities* could reach this result.[28]

Few French or British—or Germans—would go that far, however.

On the other side (and somewhat earlier) former Chancellor Helmut Schmidt grumbled:

---

[27]P. Schmidt, 1984, p. 34.
[28]D'Aubach, 1987, pp. 1–9.

On balance, I have come to think that General De Gaulle was right in his belief that the British are not really prepared to cast their lot with the rest of the European nations. . . . The British will join the club only if they cannot prevent it from being successful. (If this sounds harsh, I apologize to the British.)[29]

Such harshness would command less than a consensus in Germany or France.

In any case, what is more important than the specific view of Britain is the fact that that view is not very important in the debate, nor is d'Aubach's Franco-British nuclear melding: Most German and French debaters are intense about their own relationship, vague about its extension to "Europe" as a general entity, and don't think any more than do Americans about the other specific nations making up this general entity.

Virtually all the debaters hope for a stronger Franco-German relationship as a reinforcement of their mutual defense. Lellouche puts it strongly:

[O]ur defense—of our survival as well as our liberties—begins on the Elbe and not on the Rhine. . . . But in that case, let us be clear with ourselves, with Germany, and with the adversary. The only way to transmit this signal consists of *redeploying our forces, massing them no longer on the Rhine, but on the Elbe.*[30]

This is particularly important to Lellouche because of his fears that a weakened American commitment will leave the Franco-German alliance as the mainstay of French defense.

The hope for stronger military ties has not been father to the relationship, however. The Germans and the French had been trying for many years. In the 1970s, Schmidt, as Chancellor, became so disgusted with President Carter's eccentricity (see Nerlich's comments above) that he tried to substitute a German-French core for American leadership of the Alliance. The concept faded when Giscard was replaced by Mitterrand and Schmidt by Kohl; but in 1984, he urged it on these two successors:

Cooperation began to decline during the administration of President Carter. He confronted his European allies with surprising "lonely" decisions, taken without consultation. The situation was not eased when he made a number of subsequent corrections, since some of these were put into effect just as surprisingly. . . . [The] vacuum in transatlantic leadership was filled in considerable degree by the close

---

[29]H. Schmidt, 1985, pp. 52–53.
[30]Lellouche, 1985, p. 281.

cooperation on foreign and economic policy between Giscard d'Estaing and the German Chancellor [Schmidt]. With Giscard's departure in the spring of 1981 and the accession to office a few months earlier of Ronald Reagan, the situation worsened again. . . .

Valéry Giscard and I had it in mind to establish a considerably closer link between, on the one hand, France's nuclear power and its conventional army and, on the other, conventional German military forces and German economic power. This goal today is a task for Mitterrand and Kohl.[31]

At about the same time, he made all this much more concrete in a Bundestag speech, where he proposed 18 German and 12 French divisions, under French command, with some financial support for the French effort coming from Germany. French-born Harvard Professor Stanley Hoffman reported that "The speech was barely discussed in France."[32]

In fact, starting in 1982, two years before the Schmidt proposal, Chancellor Kohl and President Mitterrand had begun a formal attempt to move their two nations' security structures and strategies closer together. It did not work well; Pierre Hassner evaluated the results of this effort, much more modest than Schmidt's proposal, in a terse phrase: "Never so much talk, never so little progress."[33]

The summary statement of a joint volume sponsored by the German and French institutes DGAP and IFRI illustrates the problems and the issues in this or any substantial Franco-German defense arrangement, as seen from both sides. As put by the editors:

Four years after the "new start" in cooperation in the realm of security, it must be conceded that the Franco-German defense partnership is still a long way from achieving real substance. . . .

From the French side, the dominant impression is that the major French initiatives toward the Federal Republic, in principles, in political platforms, and more concretely in technological, military, and space policy, have paid hardly any return. . . .

From the German side, the same impression of frustration dominates. In spite of the positive movement seen by the French, the feeling of distrust and deception lives on, reinforced by French defense concepts

---

[31]H. Schmidt, 1984, pp. 25–27.
[32]S. Hoffman, 1984, p. 647.
[33]Hassner, 1986a, p. 171.

254

still viewed as nationalistic. . . . While France has taken a substantial step to fill German needs for consultation on French tactical nuclear weapons . . . it is clear that rather than tending toward greater cooperation on nuclear matters, forward movement has come up against a barrier created by the convergence of psychological pressures (on both sides), and by military considerations concerning the conditions for employing French forces and tactical nuclear weapons, as well as the political fallout of Soviet-American arms control negotiations.[34]

Why these frustrations? Perhaps the general answer is that put by Dominique Moisi of IFRI: "France and West Germany have deeply different visions of the world. France at heart is a status quo power; West Germany belongs to the revisionist camp."[35] This worries the French.

What the Germans want from the French, as summarized by CDU Bundestag Deputy Markus Berger, is that:

We must assume in common—and, in the interests of the Federal Republic, as long in advance as possible and under the best possible conditions—a tight joining of Alliance contingents for a forward defense [of Germany's Eastern border].

France must participate there with all its forces. Any distinction between a zone protected and defended by the global power of France, the French homeland for example, and a strategic rampart defended by conventional forces, where France will participate only on its own decision and with selected contingents, is in the interests neither of the Germans nor of French security.[36]

Former Prime Minister Chirac, however, maintained the distinction between the inner and outer zones, taking the French commitment to the Federal Republic as far as it could be taken in words alone, but making clear that it did consist largely of words:

[I]f the survival of the nation rests at the frontiers of our land, its security rests at the frontiers of its neighbors.

---

[34]Kaiser and Lellouche, 1986, pp. 311–312. *Le Couple Franco-Allemand et la Défense de L'Europe* provides an excellent binational multivoiced treatment of the history and possibilities of Franco-German defense cooperation.
[35]Moisi, 1987a, p. 4.
[36]Berger, 1986, p. 198.

But

> Crisis situations for which we must prepare so that deterrence remains strong are, in truth, largely unpredictable. That is why France attaches so much importance to conserving her freedom of action—to avoid the deterioration of her forces in automatic engagements for which they are badly adapted.[37]

Soon thereafter, Chirac told the West Germans that if they were attacked by the Soviets, France would come to their aid "immediately and without reservation,"[38] which was a stronger statement but still left French forces under French command and retained the decision to use nuclear weapons for the president of France, as President Mitterrand pointed out at the same time. One French battalion has joined a new Franco-German brigade, but that is far short of the 12 French divisions contemplated by Schmidt, or of the French redeployment desired by Lellouche. (And even the mild step-up of symbolism marked by the Chirac statement and the brigade have caused visible upsets to other member nations, particularly Italy, one more obstacle to real movement.)

Conserving freedom of action by maintaining the independence of the French deterrent and by keeping out of NATO's integrated command structure is nearly unanimous among the French. The Germans and the French understand that this is essentially unchangeable, that it is inconsistent with the German goals as outlined by Berger, and that these facts put a severe constraint on strengthening the Franco-German coupling.

A strong German central premise puts an equally binding constraint on the coupling, and it is equally well recognized by the French: the need of the Federal Republic for maintenance of the full NATO and the full American connection. As put by Lothar Ruehl, a Minister of State in the Ministry of Defense:

> It must be impossible for the Warsaw Pact to mount an attack that will allow it to isolate German forces and to seize German territory without immediately engaging the entire Alliance, and, in particular, American and British forces. . . . The allied defense within the NATO framework thus has the *absolute* priority over all other military cooperation.[39]

---

[37]Chirac, 1986c, pp. 13–14.
[38]Quoted in the *Boston Globe*, December 23, 1987, p. 9.
[39]Ruehl, 1986, p. 38.

Although the German-American tie thus constrains Franco-German possibilities, it is understood by the French who recognize that they too depend in part on the American strategic deterrent. The German emphasis on the Alliance as a whole and the United States in particular is why Nerlich can write: "The French nuclear force remains for the Federal Republic a second-order question."[40]

Added to the French strategic disagreements are concerns over a perceived lack of German cooperation in coproduction of weapons. Heisbourg is generally upbeat about Franco-German cooperation in weapons production, but the title of his chapter in the Kaiser-Lellouche book, "Cooperation in Matters of Armaments: Nothing is Ever Achieved," reveals certain doubts,[41] and in another piece published about the same time, (1986), his exhortation for the future exhibits some signs of pessimism:

There is little time for Europeans to put their act together, both in terms of organization and of funding, if they wish to be true partners in developing the combat systems of the 1990s—this is especially true for West Germany. Even though the Federal Republic's military R&D funding has increased by close to 30 percent in 1985, it will take several years for Bonn to catch up with the French or the British in this realm.[42]

These military problems are in substantial measure based on a political issue seldom publicly expressed by the French but sometimes deeply felt, that of German ties to the East as they might some day supersede German ties to the West. Benoît d'Aboville of the French Foreign Office perhaps cuts closest to the real issue in writing that "for a large fraction of French opinion, it is the Germans who, in the name of *Ostpolitik*, insist on the pursuit of dangerous chimeras."[43] This makes cooperation more difficult; the other side of the same phenomenon is a core French fear expressed by Helmut Schmidt as a German: "In the long run the Germans will remain on the Western side only if the French help them and bind them to the West."[44] Schmidt's statement shows why cooperation remains necessary.

The meaning of the Germans not "remaining on the Western side" is somewhat difficult to make concrete. Nobody in Germany and few in France take seriously the "Rapallo" model by which the weak German Weimar Republic tried to tie itself to the young but powerful Soviet Union.

---

[40]Nerlich, 1986, pp. 175–176.
[41]Heisbourg, 1986b, pp. 117–130.
[42]Heisbourg, 1986a, p. 99.
[43]d'Aboville, 1986, p. 248.
[44]H. Schmidt, 1985, p. 56.

The situation now is reversed; one French fear is of the strong Federal Republic profiting by dealing with the weak Soviet Union and the East bloc, leaving the French economy floundering in the wake.

Other French fears go deeper than that; a thousand years do not dismiss easily. Cooler voices, however, echo Thierry de Montbrial, Director of IFRI, who suggests that:

> Those who, already seeing a neutralized and more or less unified Germany, deduce from this in the name of their interpretation of Gaullism that we must retire into our stronghold, manifest a singular inferiority complex, as if France were a spectator in the history of Europe.[45]

In any case, it is the concatenation of the felt need for strong ties with the Germans, and the difficulties of establishing such ties, that lurk at the core of the French dilemma. The summation of the Franco-German debate over the Europeans' Commitments to Themselves is that it is positive and limited. The flirtation warms and cools but, as is inherent in a flirtation, it is essentially symbolic; both sides understand that it remains far from a consummation. In the same 1987 issue of *L'Express* in which Jimmy Goldsmith mentioned his doubts about the American commitment, staff writer Jérome Dumoulin started off an enthusiastic article about the future of the Paris-Bonn defense arrangement by quoting the next-to-last sentence in Kaiser and Lellouche's summary of their Franco-German volume: "The hour has come to make the great leap toward tying together the destiny of the two lands."[46] What he does not quote is the next sentence—the very last of the book—"It remains to be seen if the occasion will be seized."[47]

The British, properly enough, do not write about the special Franco-German relationship; they certainly do not seem to fear it. Rather, unlike the Germans and the French, they devote some attention to the more general and abstract concept of a broader European military alliance within (or in the limit as a substitute for) the North Atlantic Alliance.

One motivation, far less ubiquitous in Britain than among continental writers, was fear of American withdrawal, particularly after Reykjavik. Lord Gladwyn, a long-time high-level British diplomat, exhibits a perceptible sense of panic about:

---

[45]de Montbrial, 1987–1988, pp. 653–654.
[46]Dumoulin, 1987, p. 39.
[47]Kaiser and Lellouche, 1986, p. 325.

retreat as it were, into Fortress America. . . . In such distressing circumstances, short of having arrived at a credible form of European political unity, there is every reason to suppose that Western European governments would be found willing and able to enter into some arrangements which would leave the Soviet Union in a position to exercise a sort of hegemony over the whole Continent. . . . There are elements in Germany which might favour such a solution. Indeed we should probably dismiss the classic German *Drang nach Osten* as they call it, at our peril. The only way to eliminate this danger is for us to favour the genuine embodiment of Western Germany in an operative European political union which, at the moment and unlike the French, we seem as a government to be far from favoring.[48]

Most British officials and analysts take the American aberrations of the mid-1980s more in stride, as being transitory. British interest in greater unity on defense is longer run and lower key. Hedley Bull, an Australian turned Oxford Professor, had an early-1980s vision of the need for greater West European defense unity that was taken as a possibly appropriate direction for the long run; it still is by many Britons:

There are three reasons why the countries of Western Europe should explore a Europeanist approach to their security. First, the old formulas of North Atlantic unity do not adequately recognize the differences of interest, both real and perceived, that divide the United States from its European partners. . . . Second, the policies advocated by the [European peace movement], while they are based partly on a correct perception of the differences of interest between the United States and Western Europe, would expose the latter to Soviet domination. . . . A third reason why Western Europe should explore this new course relates to what may be called its dignity. . . . [It] is demeaning that the rich and prosperous democracies of Western Europe in the 1980s . . . should fail to provide the resources for their own security and prefer to live as parasites on a transatlantic protector increasingly restless in this role. . . .

[A] Europeanist policy is not viable unless the nations of Western Europe can develop some appropriate form of unity. This is the greatest uncertainty of all. . . . The object should be a West European military alliance—an alliance within an alliance, preserving the wider

---

[48]Lord Gladwyn, 1987.

259

structure of NATO. There might ultimately be a European alliance without NATO.[49]

For other Britons, however, more pragmatically oriented toward the short run, such an alliance, within or instead of NATO, is more of a fantasy than a vision of the future. As put by Bonnart, a few years after Bull's piece:

> When the [European Community] has overcome the problems of the common agricultural policy, the integration of new members, Irish neutrality, growing unemployment, industrial stagnation, and a few others, it might well, in the next century, be ready to tackle its own common defense. . . . Before such an EC defense could be created, however, the [NATO] alliance would likely disintegrate rapidly, with its members falling like ripe plums, one after the other, under the domination of the one superpower then left on the Eurasian continent.[50]

The Common Market's move toward 1992 has begun to overcome some of these problems, but Bonnart's Europessimism is more typical of the British than Bull's optimism. Even in regard to 1992, Prime Minister Thatcher has resisted any effort to put political rather than purely economic content into the unity. Within the defense realm as such, the most serious part of the debate over the Europeans' commitments to themselves continues to take place on the continent and to concern the Franco-German connection. And unless the American commitment goes as sour as Lellouche predicts, both the French and the Germans recognize that progress is likely to be slow.

The Rest of the World

The debate over the appropriate relationship of the Alliance to the "rest of the world"—the two-thirds of the earth's population living south of the Mediterranean, the Caucasus, Siberia, and the Rio Grande—has undergone a sharp reversal since the beginning of the Alliance. In the early 1950s, the French, Portuguese, and Belgian empires were still close to their pre-World War II sweeps; so was the British, except that it had lost the jewel in the crown and the *raison d'être* for the rest, India; and the Dutch alone had shed their imperium, the Dutch East Indies having become Indonesia.

---

[49]Bull, 1983, pp. 875–892.
[50]Bonnart, 1986, p. 4.

Before the Vietnam war—the American Vietnam war of the 1960s, not the French war of the 1950s—the NATO debate consisted in large measure of anti-imperialist nagging from west of the Atlantic, and the debate within the United States centered on the question of how much risk we should take of weakening NATO in the name of anticolonialism. In 1959, for example, former Secretary of State Dean Acheson wrote:

> The most important objective today . . . is to hold together those sources of strength we possess. These sources are North America and Western Europe. . . . This . . . immediately draws the usual objections: "But you will throw in your lot with the colonial empires. . . ." If we would approach life from the point of view of formal moralistic rules, this caveat may be interesting. But if we approach our problem from the point of view of solving it, then these considerations are not at all important.[51]

The combination in the 1960s of European shedding of most of the remnants of empire and American fiasco in Vietnam reversed the direction of moralizing and condescension. By 1987, Frenchman Jimmy Goldsmith could be as understanding of American interests in the Third World as Acheson had been of European interests 28 years earlier.

In fact, the question of NATO's role outside of Europe—and, even more important, the American role as it affected the commitment to the Alliance—while on such occasions as the American bombing of Libya it may have weighed more heavily on public opinion on both sides of the Atantic than it did on officials and analysts—was a serious one. Like other issues south of the Mediterranean, however, it did not preoccupy most West European officials and analysts.

Peter Stratmann of the *Stiftung Wissenschaft und Politik* does take the issue up in order to caution that it ought not misdirect NATO:

> Many statements made by defense and foreign-policy experts in the current Western and, in particular, American, debate on strategy convey that Soviet strategy may have undergone a significant change. . . . [T]he focus of Soviet political ambitions and strategic preoccupation has shifted to third-world regions outside the NATO area. . . . Many analysts are so fascinated by the challenge to "prepare for the unexpected" in the Third World that they tend to neglect or deemphasize the all-too-familiar "eurocentric" scenarios of "Soviet aggression against NATO." The indisputable fact that the Soviet Union

---

[51]Acheson, 1959.

261

continues to accord priority to the enhancement of its offensive capabilities directed against NATO has apparently had little effect on their views.[52]

And Former Chancellor Schmidt picks up another common European strand, that the United States oversimplifies and knows not what it does in the Third World. To the south:

West Europeans have a clear interest in peaceful solutions in Central America. If the problems cannot be solved peacefully, then, in the European perception, the danger might arise that the traditionally good and close relations between Europe and Latin America might be jeopardized. The credibility of the United States as the Western leader might also be damaged in the eyes of a considerable part of the West European public, and this would add a strain to the European-America relationship.[53]

To the east—the Middle East:

In my view there is no chance that the West, or the United States, can bring about a "solution" for this troubled region that could possibly bring about a stabilized peace. The truth is that no one in the world can defend the Persian Gulf oil. . . . The best we can do is to try from time to time to shift our weight a little bit to one side or the other.[54]

The questions of the appropriate Third World role of the Alliance and of the United States within or outside the Alliance have continued unsolved and indeed not even completely defined. In themselves, they remain an abrasive rather than a major determinant of European NATO policies or of the European side of the NATO debate; but they provide another indicator of European fears of American desertion, or at least distraction. The prevailing view is Stratmann's—keep your eye on the center ring of the circus—but European Couplers are aware that events in the Third World or American reaction to those events could pull the action into the outer rings, particularly in the Middle East, and that European or American public opinion could concentrate there no matter what is going on in the center.

---

[52]Stratmann, 1986, pp. 35–47.
[53]H. Schmidt, 1985, p. 83.
[54]Ibid., pp. 93–95.

MILITARY ISSUES

The Conventional-Nuclear Link

The conventional-nuclear link represents the military side of the issue of the U.S. commitment. The political question discussed above was: How strong is the American commitment to use nuclear weapons if necessary? The military question is: How will the commitment be implemented if necessary? European positions on the conventional-nuclear link, unlike positions on the more political aspects of the debate, do not fit easily into national categories. The major disagreement on the link is the one *between* Europe and the United States, and even that is more a distinction in ways of thinking about the issue than in recommended solutions.

The European-American difference can be described in the terminology of operations analysis as a question involving two variables: The Europeans want to maximize one variable subject to constraints imposed by the other; the American Maintainers consider the second the variable to be maximized, the other as the constraint.

- The West European Couplers want a strategy that will maintain the credibility of the link between any potential conventional war on their continent and the American nuclear weapons that are counted on to deter the war's outbreak in the first place. The constraint is that the link to American nuclear forces cannot be so automatic as to scare the Americans away from the initial engagement.
- The Americans want a strategy that will avoid invoking nuclear weapons. The constraint is that this must be done without breaking the link completely, so that the nuclear deterrent to Soviet aggression in Europe will remain credible enough to do its job.

The two major American schools in the strategic nuclear debate contain those who, like Wohlstetter, stress the controlled use of nuclear weapons for deterrence, damage limitation, and warfighting; and those who think it likely that such control will fail and that deterrence is, in Bundy's term, "existential," depending on the uncertainties associated with the very existence of nuclear weapons. Parallel to the American nuclear-control school are those Europeans who recognize the distinction between conventional and nuclear weapons and the importance of the threshold between the two, but espouse a carefully conceived strategy including controlled nuclear use as a potential defense and hence as a deterrent. Stratmann argues:

Given the comprehensive nature of the Soviet military challenge, it is unfortunate that the Western debate on force development programs has been based on a purported dichotomy between conventional and nuclear options. What is required in my view is a more complementary, integrated approach rather than the sweeping rejection of the utility of nuclear weapons which is in fashion now. Of course, in order to reduce NATO's current dependence on early employment of nuclear weapons stronger conventional capabilities are mandatory. But the availability of capable nuclear forces can significantly contribute to the stability of conventional defense.[55]

And Lellouche adds an argument for the doctrine closest to the hearts of the American nuclear controllers, targeting of nuclear strikes on the enemy's military forces rather than trying to deter him by threatening his cities.[56]

This contrasts with Norwegian Johan Holst's view of NATO deterrence, which draws on Bundy's existentialism:

The need to preserve a system of conventional denial and residual nuclear deterrence in Europe . . . does not imply the elimination of nuclear weapons, only a strengthening of the presumption against inevitable use. As long as nuclear weapons exist and are deployed in survivable and controllable fashion, no aggressor could have high confidence that he could push his conventional advantage with impunity. The residual capacity for nuclear response provides a kind of existential deterrence.[57]

From a similar point of view, SPD Bundestag Deputy Karsten Voigt echoes the American arms controllers' doubts about the deterrent utility of controlled counterforce strategies: "So long as it is even faintly conceivable that a threat of selective nuclear strikes could lead to a major nuclear war and thus to mutual destruction, the threat itself [of a controlled response]—by rational standards—is not credible."[58]

The European debate has many layers. NATO's "Flexible Response" doctrine, official Alliance policy since 1967, is summarized succinctly by the German foursome whose statement about Europeans' indifference

---

[55]Stratmann, 1984, p. 13.

[56]Lellouche, 1986, pp. 259–260. Atypical among Europeans, Lellouche's nuclear concept is close to that of the Americans of the Wohlstetter school, who contend that their opponents favor counter-city targeting. Americans of the Bundy school deny this, asserting that the threat to the cities is an existential fact of life, not a preferred policy. See Levine, 1987b.

[57]Holst, 1986c, p. 69.

[58]Voigt, 1984, p. 103.

between conventional and nuclear war waged on their territory headed up this chapter:

> The strategy of flexible response attempts to counter any attack by the adversary—no matter what the level—in such a way that the aggressor can have no hope of advantage or success by triggering a military conflict, be it conventional or nuclear. The tight and indissoluble coupling of conventional forces and nuclear weapons on the European continent with the strategic potential of the United States confronts the Soviet Union with the incalculable risk that any military conflict between the two Alliances could escalate to nuclear war. The primary function of nuclear weapons is deterrence in order to prevent aggression and blackmail.[59]

But of course the simple military statement covers a host of political as well as military subtleties.[60] Flexible Response was as much a response to the allies' inability to agree on a precise strategy as it was to the Soviet threat as such. Voigt points out that:

> The contradictions and conflicting interests inherent in the strategy of flexible response have never been fully discussed. They have been covered over by a NATO doctrine that views the resulting strategic ambiguity as an added factor of risk and thus an additional element of deterrence against the Warsaw Pact. But this is of dubious value for Alliance politics: it presents the Soviet Union with the opportunity to exploit unresolved conflicts of interest among the Atlantic allies thereby causing considerable strain in the Alliance.[61]

The Kaiser-Leber-Mertes-Schulze statement and that of Voigt exemplify the pattern of European discussions of the conventional-nuclear link: Explicit agreement is expressed in military terms centered on the Flexible Response doctrine; the explicit agreement, however, papers over implicit political disagreements that can frequently be detected around the edges.

The central example is the question of *the threshold* at which NATO might make the choice to turn to nuclear weapons in order to avoid defeat at the conventional level. In the writings of recent years at least, it is

---

[59]Kaiser et al., 1982, p. 1159.

[60]One such subtlety apparently lies in international semantics. The ordinary rendering in French of "Flexible Response" is "*Riposte Graduée.*" The primary English-language meaning of *graduée* is not surprisingly, "graduated," but that is not synonymous with "flexible." Graduation implies, for example, always starting at a low level of violence, which is not implicit in flexibility. None of this seems to be commented on in the literature, however.

[61]Voigt, 1984, pp. 101–102.

difficult to find disagreement with the 1983 expression of French diplomat François de Rose, "The key task is to create the capabilities that can lift from the Alliance, in the event of a crisis, the incubus of early resort to nuclear weapons in order to avert certain defeat on the conventional battle-field."[62]

NATO Information Director Wilfried Hoffmann, however, expresses doubts about too high as well as too low a threshold:

If NATO were to have too few conventional forces, the East could come to the conclusion that the West no longer seriously contemplated a military defense because its failure to take steps to avoid an early recourse to *nuclear* weapons could be seen as a reluctance to undertake any kind of self-defence, by either nuclear or conventional means. If however, NATO were to build up its conventional forces beyond a certain limit, the East could conclude that the West was in fact deterred by its own nuclear weapons, and at least secretly no longer relied on them.[63]

More frequent is an agnostic but conservative position, "Why Change?" as expressed, for example, by Heisbourg's statement that "one could conclude that NATO's present force posture in Europe is reasonably satisfactory because it provides a relatively cost-effective mix of nuclear weapons (for deterrence) and conventional forces (destined to lend credibility to the threat of nuclear deterrence and to deal with limited contingencies)."[64]

Former French Prime Minister Raymond Barre, while advocating a high threshold, brings up another key point in European doubts about the concrete steps needed to raise it—the cost:

West Europeans should aim to raise their overall defence capability and strengthen their immediate capacity for resistance. This concerns the whole of the Alliance and, in particular, my own country. It is difficult for a medium-size power such as France, as Britain well realizes, to do everything: simultaneously to maintain a nuclear deterrent at the best level possible, to keep conventional defence forces capable of acting alongside our allies on the European continent, to secure civil defence, and to maintain the forces needed to honour commitments outside Europe. And yet, this must be done![65]

---

[62]de Rose, 1983, p. 23.
[63]W. Hoffman, 1984, p. 7.
[64]Heisbourg, 1987a, pp. 48–49.
[65]Barre, 1987, p. 298.

As Americans have discovered in other contexts, however, exclamation points provide no clear solution to budgetary problems. Kaiser, Leber, Mertes, and Schulze run into a similar dilemma: "an energetic attempt to reduce the *dependence on an early first use* of nuclear weapons must be undertaken. . . . In sum, we consider efforts to raise the nuclear threshold by a strengthening of conventional options to be urgently necessary."[66] But earlier in the same article, "We believe that the authors [of the No First Use proposal] considerably underestimate the political and financial difficulties which stand in the way of establishing a conventional balance by increased armament by the West."[67]

The No First Use proposal marks a conceptual upper bound on the threshold: Never use nuclear weapons unless the Warsaw Pact uses them first. As discussed in the chapter on the Maintainers, few Americans take No First Use literally as a current policy proposal. (The initiating article by the American "Gang of Four" proposes discussion of the concept, aimed at possible future implementation.) For many West Europeans, however, it is taken more seriously, as a threat. In addition to their fears about its effect on the American commitment, the German four who answered the Americans expressed a broad West European consensus in regard to the effects of a No First Use doctrine on the Russians and on the Alliance. Were the doctrine adopted by NATO:

> Even in the case of a large-scale conventional attack upon the entire European NATO territory, the Soviet Union could be certain that its own land would remain a sanctuary as long as it did not itself resort to nuclear weapons. . . . [Thus] the proposed no-first-use policy would destroy the confidence of Europeans and especially of Germans in the European-American Alliance as a community of risk, and would endanger the strategic unity of the Alliance and the security of Western Europe.[68]

Their manifesto opposing No First Use is not a right wing or militarist document; Leber has been an SPD deputy; and Voigt, a sometime SPD spokesman on defense policy, advocates no more than "a Western defense strategy capable of renouncing the early use of nuclear weapons,"[69] thus avoiding endorsement of No First Use in all cases. This is not to say that the entire SPD would accept Voigt's implicit residual First Use strategy; but those members who remain in the Coupler consensus rather than being

---

[66]Kaiser et al., 1982, pp. 1169–1170.
[67]Ibid., p. 1163.
[68]Ibid., p. 1162.
[69]Voigt, 1986, p. 39.

part of the more radical Remover school (not only No First Use, but No Nuclear Weapons) do not completely disown first use.

Indeed, it is difficult to find a current West European endorsement of No First Use, except by the Removers. Within the Coupler consensus, Holst has consistently advocated a high nuclear threshold, and in 1983 he came close to an endorsement of No First Use: "An NFU pledge [by NATO] could contribute to stability provided both sides take steps to reduce the vulnerability of their nuclear postures in Europe and to withdraw weapons that are likely to exert pressures for early and massive use."[70] But by 1986, shortly before he became Defense Minister of Norway,[71] he qualified it a bit more: "The marginal arms-control benefits of a no-first-use doctrine—as compared to a doctrine of no early use—must be considered in relation to possible marginal costs in terms of deterrence and Alliance cohesion."[72] And, as Defense Minister, he has taken a step farther back, although Norwegian policy is strongly antinuclear. In describing this policy, which eschews nuclear weapons for Norway or in Norway, he nonetheless makes it clear that:

> NATO's strategy neither prescribes nor rules out the use of nuclear weapons. Norway places emphasis on developing a credible conventional defence system which would transfer to her opponent the burden [that] consideration of the possible employment of nuclear weapons would represent. Such employment is deterred by the Alliance's capacity to retaliate.[73]

The Couplers' approach to the Conventional-Nuclear Link was further illuminated by their attitude toward INF. The zero-zero negotiations leading to the removal of INF will be taken up under the Arms Control heading. The discussions about initial installation, before the zero-zero proposal was taken seriously, however, throw light on the European primacy of political thinking over military, particularly the role of INF in maintaining the U.S. commitment, for this strategic issue as elsewhere.

A military justification for INF is very difficult to find in European writings. University of London Professor Lawrence Freedman came closest:

---

[70]Holst, 1983, p. 194.

[71]In several places throughout, this report uses the phrase "officials and analysts" to describe the participants in the arms debate. Holst is one of the few individuals describable as an "official and analyst." American Under Secretary of Defense Fred Iklé is another, as is his predecessor in office Robert Komer, and House Armed Services Committee Chairman Les Aspin.

[72]Holst, 1986c, p. 69.

[73]Holst, 1986b, p. 3.

[The] location of the new NATO missiles dispels any Soviet illusion about containing the consequences of a nuclear strike in Central and Western Europe and as such performs a valuable function. There really does seem to be some substance to the idea that the physical presence of U.S. weapons on European soil not only provides reassurance to the Europeans but also significantly affects Soviet calculations.[74]

This argument, however, is not based on the utility of the missiles for carrying out some military mission better than other weapons; it is rather that they strengthen U.S. coupling to NATO deterrence. As put by Freedman: "LRTNF [Long Range Theater Nuclear Force] modernization was thus requested by West Europeans to increase the risk to the United States."[75]

And the official German position on INF installation, as presented by Ruehl, makes clear several national political imperatives in addition to the demands of coupling:

The government of the Federal Republic of Germany focused on three demands regarding TNF modernization: 1) the emphasis of the TNF structure may not be placed on tactical nuclear weapons and tactical options; 2) the modernization may not effect massive additions to long-range delivery systems; 3) the Federal Republic of Germany may not occupy a special position in Europe. The first two demands together produced the third. However, this third demand, the *central demand* of TNF policy, as determined by strategic-operational as well as psychological factors, surpassed in its breadth the combined effects of the first two: It has as its goal the distribution of the burden within the Alliance and in particular among the NATO partners on the European mainland: The burden of LRTNF deployment should not rest on German soil.[76]

The zero-zero dispute faded, but fear of "singularity"—the belief that the "burden of" not just LRTNF but any nuclear deployment "should not rest on German soil"—became central to all German views in the debate. The zero-zero debate was followed in Germany by the "modernization" issue: What kind of newer weapons if any, under the treaty limits, should or could be brought in to replace nuclear deterrence "lost" by the treaty? Like zero-zero, modernization was more important as a symbol than as a military issue, and the symbolism was made particularly acute by the German feeling that it was being pushed on them by Americans insensible to German needs. In 1989, the same symbolism united most West Germans in

---

[74]Freedman, 1985, p. 63.
[75]Freedman, 1986, p. 65.
[76]Ruehl, 1987, p. 180.

the belief that NATO should at least ease the FRG's dilemma by negotiating with the Warsaw Pact over reducing nuclear weapons in both halves of Germany. This unity included Germans with very different views on the posture and the coupling mechanism that should come out of the desired negotiations.

The modernization and negotiation issues, *are* at least as important for their political symbolism as for their military reality, however. For the Germans, they have come to represent their sovereign right to assert their own national interest; and this asasertion is all the stronger as a highly competitive federal election approaches. For many other Europeans, this assertion of independence carries with it overtones of a romantic German desire to once again dominate *Mitteleuropa* politically and economically (although not militarily.) For some Americans, the German attitude represents a basic challenge to the Alliance bargain that has maintained the American presence and the coupling of the nuclear deterrent. And yet, coming around the circle, but not yet completing it, the majority of Germans still recognize the centrality of coupling for their own security. *It is this complex dilemma that has begun to dominate the subjective politics of the Alliance as, and because, Gorbachev's changes have radically altered the external threat.*

Unlike INF, President Reagan's SDI proposal was on its face an American rather than a European issue, but for Europeans it has raised similar threshold questions. West Europeans oppose SDI in part for economic reasons because they believe that it will give American research and development a boost that Europe cannot match. On the strategic side, many European analysts, like many Americans, have doubts about the feasibility of SDI as much more than a partial defense against missiles; nonetheless, they must take a potential strong ABM capability seriously, just in case.

Freedman, for example, is concerned with the effects on the Alliance of the shift toward American withdrawal that SDI seems to signal:

> Governments, which have spent much of the 1980s trying to reassure their voters that nuclear deterrence not only worked effectively in preserving the peace but could endure for many decades, have been irritated to find the President echoing the claims of the anti-nuclear movement that nuclear deterrence is immoral and unstable.... To the West European governments, the President's rhetoric could be viewed as an indication of a desire to release the United States from risks attendant on

its nuclear commitments. If the "technical" fix of SDI failed, was not the logical next step to withdraw from the commitments?[77]

This summarizes succinctly the Couplers' political-strategic fears about SDI. The West European opposition to the ABM system invokes a tighter consensus than do most threshold issues, uniting debaters across the range, from such low-threshold writers as Heisbourg to such high-threshold advocates as Holst and Voigt.

One final question in regard to linkage between conventional and nuclear warfare, although of concern to West Europeans in general, is primarily French. American nuclear weapons are not the only ones that might be invoked by combat in Europe; French and British weapons are also of direct concern. The concern is primarily French (the British, linked as they are into the NATO military structure, are less involved in separate strategic calculations), but the effect of independent deterrence on NATO strategy must also be considered, because escalation by NATO to nuclear levels will not necessarily be differentiated nationally by the Soviets.

The role of nuclear weapons in French doctrine has been made quite clear. As put by President Mitterrand in a formal statement on French defense policy highlighted as being definitive throughout the French policy community:

> Prestrategic arms are not intended to extend conventional arms. They are placed by definition at the front end of the nuclear process. They will not become theater or battlefield weapons; we can permit no ambiguity on this. The concept is one of an ultimate and unique warning. There can be all sorts of diplomatic or political warnings. But there can be only one nuclear warning; that is the ultimate.[78]

Indeed, the function of the smaller, shorter-range weapons is made clear by calling them "prestrategic" rather than "tactical," which is the term NATO uses for corresponding systems that under Flexible Response might possibly be used for war-fighting. One current problem is that the short range of the existing French tactical missile, Pluton, means that it must be integrated into otherwise conventional military units, but this may be solved in the future when the greater range of the oncoming Hades missile will at least make it possible to regroup nuclear weapons into their own formations.[79]

---

[77]Freedman, 1986, p. 252.
[78]Mitterrand, 1988.
[79]See, for example, Heisbourg, 1987b, p. 4.

The Germans, although they appreciate being covered, if still somewhat ambiguously, by the umbrella of French as well as American nuclear deterrence, are worried by French nuclear doctrine. One concern is with the effects on the allied armies defending German soil. As put by German General Schulze, former NATO Central European commander:

[F]or the possible employment of French tactical nuclear weapons to support a counteroffensive by French units, preservation of the interests of a state which is "directly concerned" is not an issue that involves German security interests alone.... American, Belgian, British, German, and Canadian troops would all be "directly concerned." It is thus not a question of coordination with the Germans alone, but of coordination with the Central European command.[80]

Integration is not the only issue for the Germans, however; "singularity" again becomes highly relevant. The greater range of Hades than Pluton takes care of the problem of prestrategic weapons being able to reach only West German soil, but West German soil is not the only problem, as pointed out by French journalist Alfred Valladao, quoting from an interview with Mitterrand:

Hades, for him, is an arm destined not for battle, but as the last "nuclear warning"—no more than very classical deterrence doctrine. But there remains a problem: the German Federal Republic. "This country, our ally, needs to know that it will not be the target of the ultimate warning," says Mitterrand. Not a word, however, on East Germany: unless Hades is placed on the Elbe, its range implies that the final warning will fall on the German Democratic Republic—which is no more to the taste of the German Federal Republic.[81]

Franco-German issues pervade Coupler thought. In this, as in many other matters, the European Couplers do not all think in the same way. But they all think about the security of NATO Europe, against the military threat of conventional or nuclear war as well as against the political threat of Soviet constraints on their liberties, and that distinguishes them from the American Maintainers.

---

[80]Schulze, 1986, p. 165.
[81]Valladao, 1988, p.4.

Conventional Weapons

German fears of being abandoned are exacerbated by the knowledge that the Federal Republic is a narrow country running north and south; an even partly successful attack from the east could capture most of the German population and economy in short order. As a result, NATO's commitment has always been to the *forward* defense of West Germany—the Warsaw Pact cannot be allowed any substantial penetration—which greatly complicates the already difficult problem of conventional defense of this long border.

The debate over the appropriate level of conventional capabilities for NATO is the oldest in the Alliance. It began with the setting forth of the Lisbon force goals in 1952, and with the subsequent ignoring of the goals, and it has changed little since.

The United States wants greater conventional capabilities for NATO, and has since the beginning. Americans also reach a consensus on wanting a greater European contribution to these capabilities. Many Europeans have agreed, at least in principle; but others have disagreed, some on the principle and some on the burden of such increases in conventional capabilities. In addition, most Europeans express doubts about the hopes held by many Americans that new high technology weapons will help restore the conventional balance, and about new "deep" strategies based in part on new technology. In this case, however, many Americans share the doubts as well.

West European agreement to the need for improved conventional capabilities is not a national matter. Briton Jonathan Alford, until his death Deputy Director of IISS:

[T]hree factors lead to the conclusion that NATO in general and NATO Europe in particular must contribute more at the conventional level. The first derives from the change in the Soviet-American nuclear relationship. If the nuclear component of Western deterrence is generally acknowledged to have become less credible and if deterrence in Europe is the sum of nuclear risk and conventional denial, it is necessary to improve NATO's conventional ability to deny the Warsaw Pact all possible conventional objectives. Second, the Warsaw Pact in general and the Soviet Union in particular have shown no sign of reducing the rate of increase of their investment in conventional forces, reflected less in quantitative than in qualitative terms. Third, the United States, by assuming a wider conventional security burden outside Europe, tends to shift a somewhat greater security load onto European shoulders.[82]

German General Wolfgang Altenburg, Chairman of the NATO Military Committee:

> Because the use of nuclear weapons could lead to utter destruction, we need a greater conventional capability in Allied Command Europe in order to buy time and become less reliant upon nuclear retaliation.[83]

Ambassador de Rose, who also suggests specific roles for his nation in the conventional buildup:

> A buildup of NATO's conventional forces would therefore be a double action move: it would remedy one of our weaknesses and increase one of the Soviet Union's.
>
> For if the Alliance, or rather the integrated forces under SACEUR [Supreme Allied Commander, Europe], are to upgrade their strength, it would be of considerable importance, if French forces are to play their role of general reserve, that they be able to hold on in conventional operations as long as those fighting alongside them.... Equally important would be the role that France would have to assume in the logistic field. If the Western conventional posture is to provide for a greater capacity to stem a Warsaw Pact offensive, full use of French territory, facilities, lines of communication, etc., would be required.[84]

Even in principle, however, Europeans are far from unanimity on a conventional buildup. Ambassador de Rose (who is retired from the active French diplomatic corps) may favor the buildup, but former Prime Minister Chirac put conventional forces in an explicitly secondary position:

> To guarantee nuclear deterrence, the keystone to our system of security, is the first mission of our defense.... But nuclear deterrence is not everything. For many responses, France must use conventional forces—when tensions or even conflicts menace our interests or those of our friends.[85]

And, going beyond principle to pragmatics, Dutch analyst Jan-Geert Siccama suggests that technological progress means that the number of civilian

---

[82]Alford, 1983, p. 104.
[83]Altenburg, 1986, p. 20.
[84]de Rose, 1983, pp. 142–148.
[85]Chirac, 1986b, p. 29.

casualties in any future conventional war in Europe would dwarf the 23 million of World War II. He lists as reasons the urbanization and suburbanization of Western Europe; the proliferation of poison-producing chemical factories and depositories; and the centralization of the supplies of electricity, water, and other public services.[86]

Some European advocates of greater dependence on conventional defense assert that the conventional balance is not really as bad as is frequently pictured. The contention that NATO is almost able to defend against Warsaw Pact aggression has a long history, almost as long as the Lisbon-and-thereafter fear that the Alliance was nowhere near able. An entry on the optimistic side comes from the defense correspondent of the *Economist*, James Meacham. In the conclusion of a long analysis written under the headline, "Can the line be held? Yes, but," Meacham writes:

> There is little doubt that the central front could be held against the first echelon of a conventional attack by the Warsaw Pact powers. But then the question marks begin to appear. Would the French lend their weight in time? Would the congestion caused by West German mobilization and the massive American and British reinforcements become unmanageable? Would the allied air force be able to give direct support to the ground battle or would it break its back pressing home attacks deep into Eastern Europe? Would the air defenses stand up to the pounding they would be sure to receive? ...
>
> NATO's armies and air forces would have some chance of defeating a sudden surprise attack completely and could almost certainly last for more than a few days against an attack by partially mobilized forces ... [and] it is a fair guess that if NATO's conventional forces could hold out for two weeks they could hold out forever.[87]

The more conventional view on NATO's conventional capabilities, however, is that expressed by Alford, Altenburg, and de Rose at the beginning of this section—more effort is needed. And almost as conventional, at least in Europe, is the belief that it will be awfully difficult to get there from here. Heisbourg lists as major problems budgetary constraints, demographic factors leading to sharp reductions in the numbers of men of military age, and political differences among the European allies.[88] The budgetary doubts about substantially increased expenditures for conventional capabilities are precisely as old as the Lisbon demands for such

[86]Siccama, 1984, pp. 32–33.
[87]"NATO's Central Front," *The Economist*, August 30-September 5, 1986, p. 22.
[88]Heisbourg, 1986a, pp. 72–78.

capabilities; this is *the* classical NATO issue. The political constraints change over time, but in one form or another they antedate the Alliance. The demographic issue is fairly new.

Given these constraints, NATO has long looked for a way in which to strengthen its conventional defense substantially without many (or perhaps any) increases in costs. Starting in the 1960s, the search has led to considerable interest in new military technologies based primarily on new guidance systems. In the earlier years the systems of greatest interest were those that it was hoped would allow an infantryman to destroy a tank with so high a probability that the Warsaw Pact's offensive armored capability could be defeated from NATO's defensive foxholes. By the 1980s, however, the "Emerging Technologies" (ETs) stressed long-range guidance systems precise enough to allow missiles to destroy deep enemy targets with conventional rather than nuclear munitions. This has led in turn to consideration of new NATO strategies based on conventional-weapons interdiction of Pact lines of communication and follow-on reserve echelons. One of these, "Follow-On Forces Attack" (FOFA) comes from Supreme Headquarters, Allied Powers, Europe (SHAPE); another version is embodied in the U.S. Army's "AirLand Battle."[89] In addition, a proposal for defending the West by mounting a counteroffensive toward the east, put forth by Harvard Professor Samuel Huntington,[90] has been widely discussed.

These technological and strategic concepts are primarily American and will be discussed in the chapter on the American Maintainers. Most West Europeans are highly skeptical, and the European support that does exist is tentative and qualified. For example, although Heisbourg is optimistic on the technological possibilities for major improvements in the accuracy of individual weapons and in electronic battlefield control, he suggests that the Soviets are capable of keeping up technically well enough to maintain the current balance. In addition he cautions that in "practice it usually is unsafe to build vast doctrinal edifices as long as the relevant technology has not been, to some extent at least, proved in the field," which he sees as a standard American tendency.[91] The comment itself represents a standard West European criticism.

Beyond the feasibility of the new technologies, many Europeans voice substantial political doubts about the deep strategies. Krell expresses the

---

[89]What the difference is between FOFA and AirLand Battle is in itself the subject of some controversy, which, fortunately, is not highly relevant to the overall NATO debate. This report draws such distinctions as necessary from Sutton et al., 1983, pp. 65–76.

[90]See, for example, Huntington, 1982. This is discussed below in the analysis of the American Maintainer school.

[91]Heisbourg, 1986a, p. 94.

fears of those Germans who are concerned about defending West German territory without appearing to renew historical German aggression toward the east, as well as about arms control. On Huntington's counteroffensive proposal, he comments:

> Samuel Huntington has asked the question, why NATO should observe operational restraint, when the Soviet Union threatened the West with a large-scale ground offensive. NATO should react in a similar way.... [But this would have] disastrous consequences for military and political stability.... A NATO strategy which threatens to put Soviet control over Eastern Europe at risk *militarily* would not only be the end of détente, but of the NATO alliance. It would run counter to the logic and the course of development in West German security policy and *Ostpolitik* since the early 50s, whatever its purely military rationale (asymmetry of options, e.g.) may be. In the German debate, respect for recent European history and Germany's terrible contributions to it are inseparable from such calculations.[92]

He provides similar criticisms of FOFA and AirLand Battle, suggesting that they are both provocative and easy for the Soviets to counter and thus would increase tensions in central Europe without increasing Western security.

It is not only nonofficial analysts in Germany who worry about these issues. The 1984 Defense White Paper, submitted by Defense Minister Manfred Woerner, a government and CDU mainstay who has since become Secretary-General of NATO, says:

> The maxim of limited goals for NATO's strategy radically excludes the option of offensive defense. Neither preemptive war nor offensive or preventive operations, which lead into enemy territory in order to gain space for one's own defense, are politically acceptable or militarily feasible concepts for NATO.... National tactical-operational guidelines such as the U.S. AirLand Battle doctrine as laid down in the Field Manual 100–5 are valid in Europe only to the extent to which they are compatible with the principles of defense in NATO.[93]

On the opposite side from the various proposed "offensive" solutions to the conventional imbalance are several suggestions for a "defensive defense," designed to strip away all offensive capabilities and instead strengthen the

---

[92]Krell, 1986a, p. 25.
[93]Ministry of Defense of the Federal Republic of Germany, *Weissbuch*, 1985, p. 30, quoted in English translation, ibid., p. 29.

capability to repel the enemy by holding in place in a fairly static area defense. These originated primarily with European Removers. Briton David Gates of the University of Aberdeen provides a series of Coupler criticisms of the concept: It precludes tactical counteroffensive as part of the defense, it is too easy for an enemy to figure out and counter, it is too dependent upon high technology as well as massive manpower and materiel. But then he suggests that it may have a place (e.g., in "enclosed and forested areas"), although nowhere near as important a one as its advocates believe.[94]

Neither "offensive" nor "defensive" defenses find many adherents among Couplers. German analyst Joseph Joffe sums up the ordinary skeptical response to this entire range of proposals for radical change of NATO doctrine:

> In the end the three conventional complements/alternatives to forward defense—no-first-use, forwardism and rearwardism—fall down where the logic of politics meets the logic of strategy. There is a reason why the messy and uncertain tenets of "flexible response up front" have survived so many powerful challenges. With all its shaky compromises between manpower needs and manpower yields, between the conventional and the nuclear, flexible response is the thin red line separating two logical alternatives that are even more unattractive.[95]

Nonetheless, as potential negotiated arms reductions and pressures on defense budgets have come together to force consideration of radically reduced NATO conventional forces, defensive defenses have taken on a new interest among European Couplers as well as Removers.

All of the discussion of conventional weapons thus far presented has concerned the Central front, the West German border with East Germany and Czechoslovakia. In fact, the Germans on the Central front and the French right behind them do concentrate almost entirely on that area, to the exclusion of NATO's flanks—Norway, Turkey and Greece. Yet the flanks, both by NATO's will and by the will of the flank nations themselves, are to be defended conventionally, with no reason to believe that that defense will be easier than on the Central front.

Stratmann, in spite of the title of his paper on "NATO Doctrine and National Operational Priorities: The Central Front and the Flanks: Part II," devotes slightly less than one page out of 20 to the flanks. (Part I by an American does emphasize the outlying regions.) In it, he makes clear the prevailing central European view of the secondary nature of the flanks:

---

[94]Gates, 1987, pp. 309–315.
[95]Joffe, 1984, p. 145.

Initial operations on the *Northern Flank* would primarily be directed at protecting the strategic assets of the Northern Fleet and securing and winning its passage through the G-I-UK [Greenland-Iceland-United Kingdom] Gap into the Atlantic. In the course of this campaign, Soviet forces would certainly attempt to neutralize and, if possible occupy NATO airbases and other assets in Northern Norway.... As for NATO's *Southern Flank*, major Soviet offensive operations are not to be expected during the initial phase of the war....

In the view of Soviet planners, the overall strategic success will probably be determined by the rapid advance of the landfront in the [Central] area. The key objective is to penetrate NATO's forward defense and reach the Rhine and the North Sea ports within a few days.[96]

The Southern flank presents substantial problems for NATO—Greek and Spanish pressure to remove American bases, Greek-Turkish tensions, and the role of Turkey in an all-out Soviet attack in Europe being chief among them—but these seldom enter the public debate, least of all in northern Europe. In 1988, when Spain forced the United States to withdraw its fighter aircraft from the Torrejon air base, the major concern expressed by Europeans to the north of the Pyrenees was the policy precedent they feared was being set for NATO's Central front.

The same tendency to set the issue aside might be true for the Northern flank were it not for the fact that Norwegian Defense Minister Holst is a member in excellent standing of the North Atlantic community of strategists, and a prolific writer. His assessment of the importance of Norway to the rest of NATO, primarily in its location astride Soviet routes to the Atlantic, is not dissimilar from Stratmann's; but Norway is not secondary to Norwegians, and Holst goes beyond Stratmann to complete the circle on his nation's role:

If Norway should fall into hostile hands the ability of the Western alliance to maintain the integrity of the sea lanes of communication—or the "sea bridge"—linking North America to Western Europe would be seriously impaired. If the Western alliance should prove unable to secure the trans-atlantic sea lines of communication, NATO's ability to hold the central front in Europe would be seriously impaired. If NATO's ability to hold the central front should be seriously questioned, the Western powers would find their negotiating position vis-a-vis the Soviet Union seriously impaired. Similarly, if NATO should not appear

---

[96]Stratmann, 1986.

279

capable of controlling the process of escalation on the central front in the event of war, the credibility of the commitment to reinforce Norway would be seriously impaired. Without credible reinforcement from her allies Norway's ability to defend herself against aggression would be seriously impaired. Hence Norway's participation in NATO is based on shared and reciprocal interests reflecting a basic condition of interdependence.[97]

To pursue these ends, Norway and the Alliance have designed a rather intricate strategy. Holst's description of Norway's strong policy against basing or hosting nuclear weapons, which nonetheless "neither prescribes nor rules out the use of" such weapons, has been discussed above. Other restrictions are also imposed on NATO activities, but an extensive program of joint exercises is carried out with the nation's allies, including Canada, which shares with Norway the military problems imposed by a harsh northern climate.

Holst points out elsewhere that "Norway, Denmark and Iceland are allied with the Western powers in a much more encompassing and committed manner than Finland is tied to the Soviet Union."[98] In a sense, nonnuclear Norway may provide an illustration of what NATO Europe would be if all nuclear weapons were withdrawn from Europe *but* the Alliance and the ultimate American strategic nuclear guarantee remained. The picture is far more encouraging than that implied by the term "Finlandization," but no one can guarantee that the result of such a nuclear withdrawal would be Norwegianization rather than the more constrained state in which the Soviets force Finland to exist.

THE OPPONENT

The Soviet Union

This discussion of the Couplers' views of the Soviets begins by repeating the statement by Nicole Gnessoto, the French analyst quoted in the Introduction to this NATO study: "In the bundle of factors which have, since 1954, determined the evolution of the Franco-German dialogue on matters of security, the Soviet Union has appeared, without doubt, as the only constant."

---

[97]Holst, 1986a, p. 3.
[98]Holst, 1987, p. 3.

The sentence was published in 1986; as soon as a year later, the constancy had disappeared as the world wondered whether Chairman Gorbachev's high-wire act was as radical and real as it seemed, or whether it was done with mirrors and smoke concealing the same old hostile Soviet Union, and if real, could it last? Two years after that, it was apparent that the changes in external policy, as well as those internal to the Soviet Union, were radical; if they can last, they will affect all aspects of the NATO debate, not only the direct analysis of the Soviets themselves. In particular, they are likely to change the focus of the debate from our perceptions of ourselves to our perceptions of the opponent.

Some Europeans who near the far right end of the political spectrum describe the Soviet Union in terms akin to Ronald Reagan's "Evil Empire." Jean-François Revel, for example, in a book much admired by the American right, states flatly, "It is natural for communism to try with all its might to eliminate democracy, since the two systems are incompatible and communism's survival depends on its rival's annihilation."[99]

Most Couplers see the Soviet Union as hostile and opportunistic but prudent; the debate is over the particular mixture of these factors and how the Russians translate them into doctrine and operating practice. No matter what the Soviets do in the next several years, the Couplers will continue to observe the mixture and argue over the particulars; the arguments set forth here will not disappear, nor will they change much, although their relative weights may.

One point of consensus is as unanimous as a political or military belief can get. No European official or analyst in the last 20 years, nor any American for that matter, has believed that the Soviets were planning a military attack on the West in any near-term period. But this is far from a statement that military power is irrelevant. Almost as unanimously, European Couplers and American Maintainers have believed that the primary reason for the comfortable premise about the Russians is that they have been deterred by NATO power. Given this constraint, then, the Couplers believe that the Soviet intention is to use military power to exert political pressure without ever having to go to war.

Hannes Adomeit, a Sovietologist at the *Stiftung fur Wissenschaft und Politik* explains the underlying basis for Soviet military-political policy:

Perhaps the most important concept for the theory and practice of Soviet foreign policy is that of the "correlation of forces." . . . Lenin constantly pointed to the necessity of taking into account "all the forces, groups,

---

[99]Revel, 1983, p. 7.

parties, classes and masses operating in a given country.". . . All this is not merely of historical interest. It is to suggest that trust in the effectiveness of combined external military and domestic political pressure to achieve Soviet objectives has characterized Soviet foreign policy in Eastern and Western Europe without interruption ever since Stalin. . . . Soviet conventional superiority in Europe and the offensive strategy connected with it have remained one of the most important military and political facts of life in Europe. Their utility as a political instrument with which to influence American and Western European perceptions and policies has never really diminished.[100]

Potential Soviet exploitation of the "correlation of forces" covers a broad range of possibilities and engenders an equally broad range of Coupler views. Lellouche details the worst of West European fears based on this Soviet doctrine, arguing that the Soviets use military power "to extract political advantages, little by little"; "the USSR *must* control Western Europe"; this in turn will determine "the victor in the historic struggle between socialism and capitalism"; strategic parity has helped them to "put in train a new phase of external expansion"; and European conventional arms control negotiations in Stockholm have assisted "the establishment of an overall 'pan-European' system of collective security controlled by Moscow." His summary is that:

> their European strategy is traditionally arranged around three axes: . . . to cut the nuclear umbilical cord connecting Europe to the United States . . . to progressively transform this nuclear "disconnection" to a political decoupling . . . to create sources of diversion for the United States (around the periphery of that nation—in Latin America and the Pacific).[101]

On the other end of the Coupler spectrum, in 1982 West German Foreign Minister Hans-Dietrich Genscher, well before Gorbachev, saw a change—not at that time in Soviet objectives—but a change in tactics and constraints profound enough to engender an important change for the West. He discussed:

> a fundamental change in communist doctrine, a first breakthrough in a Manichaean concept that normally regards non-Communists as nothing but class enemies. Leonid Brezhnev developed the principle of avoidability of nuclear war into a strategy of "peaceful coexistence." This does not mean that the Soviet Union has foresworn its goal of a world

---

[100]Adomeit, 1985, pp. 72–79.
[101]Lellouche, 1985, pp. 96–105.

282

revolution. Rather, a policy of peaceful coexistence serves to promote Soviet predominance (effectively domination) in such a way that a major war between East and West is avoided and economic cooperation with the West is made possible. Hence a Soviet leadership that can expand its arms arsenal without encountering any corresponding efforts on the Western side . . . will do so in keeping with the role it has ascribed itself. . . . But how would a Soviet leadership behave which, in pursuing such a policy, was faced with an adequate response by the West, involving a correspondingly high risk? . . .

The concept of a dual strategy provides the most effective response to the challenge posed by the Soviet strategy of "peaceful coexistence": one part of this strategy, a policy of equilibrium, is designed to bring home to the Soviet leadership that it is futile to pursue a policy of predominance. The détente part of the strategy at the same time affords the Soviet Union an alternative.[102]

Later in his article, Genscher took up an economic issue of the early 1980s that was germane to NATO if only because it upset some Americans, including several in the Reagan administration: West European assistance to a pipeline bringing Soviet natural gas to Western Europe, which many Americans believed gave the Soviets a strategic hold over Western Europe, financed by credits from the West Europeans themselves. Genscher contended that the net effect might actually decrease German primary energy imports from the Soviet Union.[103]

The pipeline furor has died, but the question of economic cooperation with the Soviet Union remains. More recently, Willy de Clerq, External Relations Commissioner of the European Economic Community, the Common Market, said:

Improved trade could also, in a more general way, improve the climate of relations between Eastern and Western Europe. I sometimes feel that some Americans look at Eastern Europe from such a distance that they are only able to distinguish black and white. Here, at close quarters, we can see the various shades of gray.[104]

By 1989, EEC/NATO members led by Germany and Italy were beginning to probe deeply into the possibilities and political implications of increased trade with the Soviet Union and the other nations of the Warsaw Pact.

---

[102]Genscher, 1982, p. 47.
[103]Ibid., p. 56.
[104]Quoted in "Western European Considers Formal Trade Ties with Soviet Bloc," *Washington Post*, August 5, 1987, p. 16.

Among some Couplers, however, severe doubts remained. Lellouche's comment on economic détente was that it would lead to "an unprecedented expansion in transfers of technology and capital from the West to the East, with no return whatever in either the foreign policy of the USSR or the internal development of the regimes of Eastern Europe."[105]

What difference would Gorbachev make? At the outset of his regime, Lellouche had substantial doubts:

> Intuitively, I think that these new men, while they certainly will be younger, will not necessarily be "newer," in the measure that they have been molded by the same bureaucratic/ideological machinery. The powerful inertia of the system (that of the Party) to act to curb, even to block, any attempts at innovation, should not be underestimated. From all evidence, the succession crisis which has occupied the Kremlin since Brezhnev is far from over.[106]

Experience since this passage was published in 1985 would necessarily moderate it somewhat; the evidence indicates that the Party has at least "curbed" some of Gorbachev's attempts at innovation, but it has "blocked" very few. Nonetheless, many West Europeans as well as Americans retain their suspicions of the directions and actions of the Soviet Union. One reason is suggested by Helmut Schmidt, in his book published about the same time as Lellouche's:

> [T]he key point I want to stress is the deep historical roots, and resulting steadiness, of the Grand Strategy of Soviet Russia itself. It is worthwhile to look at historical maps to see how small the Grand Principality of Moscow was some five hundred years ago.... And look at the map of today. Russia has grown and grown and grown.... For over five hundred years, all the Tsars pursued a policy known as "Gathering of the Russian Lands," which, practically speaking, meant conquering other people's land and afterward russifying the inhabitants. This Grand Strategy of cautious but continuous expansion has been continued and carried forward by the Soviet leadership of Russia.[107]

Traditional Russian history looms large among West European analysts. Even so strong an anti-Communist ideologue as Lellouche starts his chapter on Soviet expansionism with a quote from the Tsar's Prime Minister of

---

[105]Lellouche, 1985, p. 107.
[106]Ibid., p. 109.
[107]H. Schmidt, 1985, pp. 24–25.

1905.[108] Although Americans come out at about the same place, they tend to stress the Communist roots of Soviet behavior rather than the Russian roots. In any case, a 500 year perspective like Schmidt's, which makes Peter the Great and Lenin into blips on a long-run trend, is likely to reinforce doubts about a Gorbachev turn in the trend.

Nonetheless, Gorbachev has made a difference in Coupler thinking about the Soviets. One of the most upbeat statements came from Lord Carrington, retiring Secretary General of NATO:

> Whatever may be said about Mr. Gorbachev's public relations, his remarkable capacity for dealing with the press and his new style, it is equally evident that he is, in substance, seeking a different path, a more modern path for the Soviet Union. This is not of course a non-Marxist path, but a new route to Marxism through greater efficiency and the better use of resources. To achieve that, he will wish to spend less on defence and to transfer resources to the civilian sector.... We witnessed some remarkable developments at Reykjavik. Remarkable, because only a few weeks before it would have been unthinkable for concessions of the kind proposed by the Soviet Union to have been made.[109]

In a later piece, in which he worried about the effect of the then-imminent zero-zero agreement on the Alliance he had shepherded so long, he qualified his earlier enthusiasm: "But there is also room for skepticism about Mikhail S. Gorbachev's foreign-policy goals."[110]

Earlier in 1987, former French Prime Minister Barre also exhibited substantial skepticism:

> Mr. Gorbachev has broken sharply with his predecessors on several major issues: a younger generation of political leaders, better social discipline, the drive for improved economic efficiency, the many steps taken to reduce intolerance and promote greater freedom of speech, and the start made in the release of political prisoners. We must welcome these changes and not belittle them, while suspending judgment as to whether they will ultimately turn out to be marginal or fundamental....
>
> It should also be borne in mind that in the field of foreign policy, Mr. Gorbachev has essentially taken up where his predecessors left off.... New disarmament plans are being advanced in rapid succession, but in fact seem to be inspired by the traditional Soviet objectives going back to

---

[108]Lellouche, 1985, p. 93.
[109]Carrington, 1986, pp. 34–35.
[110]Carrington, 1987, p. 1.

the 1950s. And above all, Soviet military capacity...continues to grow.[111]

The Couplers' perception is that the Soviet Union is changing. The degree, the speed, and the permanence of the change are highly uncertain; and until these are clearer, the change cannot be fully factored into the debate. What may have hastened its inclusion for a time was that while the perception of Gorbachev moved one way in 1987–88, the Couplers' perception of Reagan moved the other. As put by Dominique Moisi of IFRI:

In the East-West confrontation, images are as important a part of reality as the objective factors such as the arms race. On this count the Soviet Union lately has fared better than the United States. Here in France the combination of Reykjavik and the Iran arms scandal has helped revive an old negative image of the United States. At the same time, the Soviet Union is enjoying a new and more positive image under the impulse of an energetic and dynamic leader who is beating Ronald Reagan at his own game of public relations.[112]

This has been changed by the INF treaty (although not the way it was initially negotiated), the Moscow summits, and the end of the Reagan administration in a bath of warmth. But transitory feelings related to leadership images form the short-run aspect of the longer-run issue, raised by some Removers, of the "moral equivalence" of the United States and the Soviet Union. Moral equivalence is not accepted by the Couplers; if it were, the debate would change profoundly. For now, and seemingly into the future, the Coupler assessment of Gorbachev is agnostic. As put by Bertram:

Gorbachev is the first Soviet leader to talk of "common security" (unlike Stalin), to abstain from saber-rattling and dramatic Third World adventure (unlike Khrushchev) and to emphasize the Soviet need for international stability as a function of his desire to promote domestic reform at home (unlike Brezhnev). Indeed if the statements made by the general secretary were to come to reflect a committed, sustained policy, this would be the kind of attitude that the West has always sought....

The problem is that even if these expressions of intent are genuine, Soviet power will be of a profoundly ambiguous nature for a very long time to come.[113]

---

[111]Barre, 1987, p. 293.
[112]Moisi, 1987b, p. 5.
[113]Bertram, 1987a, pp. 944–945.

It is the potential change in the Soviet Union, real as well as perceived, that may change the Alliance and the NATO debate even more rapidly than any perceived change in the United States.

Eastern Europe

The Couplers' discussion of Eastern Europe provides one of the clearest illustrations of the NATO debate as depending as much on different emphases as on different views. In this it resembles many of the differences between the Couplers and the American Maintainers.

There are, in fact, few differences among Coupler views in regard to the bloc of Soviet satellites. Nobody believes either that they can be "liberated" or that they are any longer simple microcosms of Soviet Russia, unable to vary because of fear of the Red Army. The consensus picture is somewhere in between: NATO policy can affect the nations of the Warsaw Pact and within strict limits can help increase their autonomy and their internal ease. But until very recently few in most of the European NATO nations have cared enough to write about it; indeed, the multi-ethnicity of the United States leads more Americans than West Europeans to concentrate on Eastern Europe.

Except for Germans. The German Democratic Republic (GDR) is in many ways the second most important member of the Soviet Bloc; although it is exceeded in population by Poland, it has a far stronger economy and an apparently more loyal tie to the USSR, and it lies along most of the East-West border. It also shares a language, a culture, and a history, as well as the border, with the Federal Republic of Germany. West Germans are acutely aware of the very different situation of their relatives across that border; indeed, the goal of reunification is written into the constitution of the Federal Republic.

The West Germans of today are also comfortable realists who recognize the limits of cross-border brotherhood and the risks of too much of it. Reunification as such sometimes comes up on special occasions—in May 1987, for example, pique at the pressure being put on the Germans to agree to zero-zero led a CDU Bundestag deputy to call for negotiations on the issue with the Soviets—but the occasions are rare, and what little sound and fury there are quickly disappear. Rather than political reunification, the operational goals of most West German officials and analysts tend toward liberalization of the East, economic cooperation, and relaxation of border-crossing restrictions. Krell describes the breadth as well as the substance of agreement within the Federal Republic to subordinate or ignore reunification:

[F]or a long time the idea of reunification was the framework in which the other issues were defined. . . . Gradually the primacy of reunification has lost its force. Hope for restoration of the territories east of the Oder-Neisse [now in Poland] has waned almost completely, as has the support for legitimacy of that hope. As for reunification with East Germany, no political group sees it as a near-term prospect. There is a broad consensus that living with and improving the *status quo* between East and West is the order of the day. And it is now also widely accepted that any chance for improving the political and economic situation of the Germans in the GDR requires the active support of that *status quo*. Working for more freedom for the East Germans (and East Europeans) on the basis of a definite territorial *status quo* has gained priority even over the long-term prospects of reunification. Even the non-desirability of reunification can now be discussed. The Germans are rediscovering that throughout most of their history the German nation has lived in separate states, and that this may have advantages, not only for the international order, but for the Germans themselves.[114]

True, the basic consensus receives different expression from different portions of the German political spectrum. On the right, Walther Kiep, a leader of the CDU, starts off with a manifesto, but moves quickly to realism:

The German question is unresolved. It will remain on history's list of unfinished business until all Germans have had a chance to freely exercise their right of self-determination. Until then, we in the Federal Republic will maintain our unswerving view that the German question must be resolved by achieving unity through peaceful means. Keeping the question open, Germany's legal status must not in any way be placed in question or otherwise rationalized away. . . .

For West Germans, however, the yardstick of the quality of relations with the G.D.R. continues to be the measure of the freedom of movement that can be attained for the people in both parts of Germany. . . . It will only be possible to reduce . . . tensions by bringing about a steady improvement within divided Germany. This is the specific contribution the two states in Germany must make in support of the détente and peace process in Europe as a whole.[115]

Professor Richard Lowenthal takes more account of the internal motivations of the GDR, suggesting that their political mood is growing more similar

---

[114]Krell, 1986, pp. 32–33.
[115]Kiep, 1984/85, pp. 317–318.

to that of the Federal Republic, accepting the division of Germany, and with at least the leadership valuing superpower protection of their status. He sees, on both sides of the border: "a common acceptance of both the achievements and the recognized horrors of a common past and . . . a growing pride in a common contribution to détente and peace—expressed in the phrase, used equally on both sides of the border, that 'no war must ever arise again from German soil.'"[116] That is not only a German slogan. It still rises to the surface on occasion when other NATO nations consider German reunification. In 1984, for example, Italian Foreign Minister Giulio Andreotti, in the midst of a fight over the use of the German language in the Northern Italian provinces bordering Austria, contended sharply that "There are two German states now, and there should be two in the future."[117]

At its core, the question remains a German one. Nonetheless, other Europeans, notably the French, have begun to take more notice of political and economic possibilities in Eastern Europe. Mitterrand in a 1988 interview made some statements that the editors thought important enough to put into the leaders for his entire wide-ranging discourse on French foreign policy:

> I have met four times with Mr. Gorbachev. . . . I have gone to Hungary and seen Mr. Kadar three times; Mr. Honnecker, president of the German Democratic Republic, has come to see me in Paris as has the Polish prime minister, Mr. Jaruzelski. . . . It is not their internal situations that bring me there. But what is happening today calls on us . . . the rapprochement between the two Europes constitutes for us, the Europeans, the great happening of the end of the century. . . . We can revive the cultural ties that have united France and the nations of Central Europe and the Balkans. . . . Our civilization springs from the same sources and spiritual affinities are worth more than trade.[118]

The reasons for this do have to do with trade as well as spiritual affinity. Perhaps they have most to do with the fear that German ties to "Central Europe and the Balkans" might leave France out, economically as well as culturally and politically. Some Frenchmen in positions of less responsibility than the President of the Republic—and indeed, some other Europeans too, including Britons—have begun to express fears of German ambitions for *Mitteleuropa*. That virtually no Germans take this seriously does not fully allay the suspicions of their allies in a time of rapid change. As noted

---

[116]Lowenthal, 1984/85, p. 303.

[117]Quoted in Haltzell, 1986, p. 2.

[118]"Une Interview du Chef d'État: Mitterrand Fait le Tour du Monde," *Libération*, November 23, 1988, pp. 5–6.

above, what Germans see as their simple right to sovereignty and independence can be interpreted by others as hegemonic ambitions. The word
"nationalism" has had both connotations, historically; it still does.

ARMS CONTROL AND DISARMAMENT

The *incremental* policy edge of all these discussions is the gradual change
of weapons systems, strategies, budgets, and arrangements within the Alliance. Potentially much less incremental is the chance of substantive and
substantial arms control agreements affecting weapons and postures in
Europe. This section primarily examines the debate over the zero-zero
agreement as it suddenly became real in 1987. That agreement led to far
more serious consideration than before of potential subsequent European
arms control measures, both conventional and nuclear. Future arms control possibilities are discussed in Ch. 21, the epilog on NATO.

When Gorbachev picked up the dormant NATO zero-zero proposal, and
when U.S. Secretary of State Shultz negotiated it to near reality in Moscow
and then brought it back to NATO in Brussels, the reactions of most European Couplers were between qualified and negative. To be sure, one reason
was the process by which it had come about, beginning with American unilateral and apparently not thought through negotiations at Reykjavik, and
continuing with the failure to consult meaningfully until Shultz returned
with a putative agreement. But Coupler doubts centered also on the substantive effects of the agreement on nuclear deterrence in Europe; and both
the process and the substance led to the fear that this would be merely the
first step toward full denuclearization and withdrawal of the American
guarantee.

The doubters included almost all French analysts and many German
Couplers. In March 1987, when the negotiations were beginning to be
understood as being quite serious, former French Premier Barre expressed a
series of doubts:

> *First*: implementation of the zero option could weaken . . . NATO's
> ability . . . to offset the conventional and chemical superiority of the
> Warsaw Pact. . . . *Second*: also to be avoided is the probability that the
> zero option, by removing an intermediate stage of escalation, could
> weaken NATO's capacity for Flexible Response, thereby bringing about
> the dilemma, if not "all or nothing," at least "all or too little.". . . *Third*:
> . . . just as the credibility of extended deterrence by the United States
> implies the physical presence of American forces, those forces can only

stay in Europe so long as they remain protected by extended U.S. deterrence.... All this suggests that it would be far preferable, as a first step, to achieve a substantial reduction of *both* strategic nuclear forces and medium-range missiles. This would avoid the decoupling of Europe's defense from the United States.[119]

This was a standard French view. The Germans were more divided. Genscher had been Foreign Minister in the government of SPD Chancellor Schmidt when the two-track option was agreed to and the zero proposal for INF extended; he was still Foreign Minister in the government of CDU Chancellor Kohl when the negotiations became serious; and he still backed them, as did many other German politicians, including some in the CDU. The defense analysts (and appointed officials, particularly in the Ministry of Defense) were far more concerned with the loss of NATO's INF missiles, however. Joffe treated it as a Soviet conspiracy:

Needless to say, Gorbachev knows what he is doing. First, in offering double-zero, he invited NATO to get rid of its most modern weapons, the Pershing II and cruise missiles, and to forgo deployment on the next level down.... The second catch is conceptual. Nuclear weapons in Europe, especially those that could pierce the Soviet sanctuary, represented the core of Western Europe's defenses.... The third catch is psychological. In the age of "parity"... the Europeans have always sought safety in nuclear arrangements that obliterate the distinction between local and global war. Pershing II and cruise missiles standing in the path of a Soviet advance might just go off (whereas a Minuteman III stationed in Montana might not), destroying along with Kiev any dream of a war neatly confined between some Central European "firewalls."[120]

Joffe's view was particularly bitter; the more typical attitude of the French and German Couplers was summarized in the headline over an editorial in *Le Monde*, "Euromissiles: the resigned "yes" of Europeans."[121]

The British were, in general, more relaxed than the French and the CDU Germans. Lord Bramall, former Chief of the General Staff, expressed a common view:

As someone who has been connected with the problem for seven or eight years, I firmly believe that in the light of Mr. Gorbachev's so-called initiative—which only seems to say what many in the West have been

---

[119]Barre, 1987, p. 295.
[120]Joffe, 1987, pp. 17–18.
[121]*Le Monde*, May 28, 1987, p. 1.

wanting for some time—it makes considerable sense to start by mutually reducing or eliminating medium-range missiles, which have always had more useful political and bargaining potential than real military value.[122]

Other Britons favored other starting points, and most had substantial doubts about the process, beginning in Reykjavik, that initiated the negotiations culminating in the zero-zero agreement. University of Southampton Professor Phil Williams's negative summary, however, described continental fears more closely than those of British Couplers:

> There are several aspects of the process which bother many Europeans. The first is that there was little or no consultation about the negotiations. . . . Another aspect of the process which worried the European allies is that the Soviet Union seemed to be far better prepared for the negotiations than the United States. . . . West European concerns about the negotiating process are accompanied by alarm about the assumptions that President Reagan brought with him to the negotiations. The European allies see a growing trend in U.S. thinking toward the deemphasis of nuclear weapons. . . . The president's Strategic Defense Initiative and, in particular, his emphasis on the transition from an offense-dominant to a defense-dominant world, is seen in Europe as destabilizing and decoupling. . . . What makes the zero-zero option even more unpalatable to European governments is that it was accompanied at Reykjavik by President Reagan's proposal to eliminate all ballistic missiles over a 10-year period. . . . Although the United States would still be able to deter attack on its own territory, there would be additional question marks over extended deterrence.[123]

When zero-zero became a *fait accompli*, acceptance, at least on the official level, became general and even enthusiastic as the debate moved on to next steps. Ongoing developments will be discussed in the Epilog; but one basis for such developments, in addition to zero-zero, will probably be a series of proposals produced in Europe in the early 1980s when any real agreements with the Soviets looked unlikely, but some arms control and disarmament advocates kept on trying.

Their major proposal, for a nuclear-free zone in central Europe, is associated with the Coupler wing of the German SPD. In 1984, Bundestag Deputy Voigt first made clear that he was not a Remover unilateralist:

---

[122]Bramall, 1987, Column 195.
[123]Williams, 1987, pp. 39–42.

Even if the United States were to renounce unilaterally the deployment of land-based, intermediate-range weapons in Western Europe, the West would still possess a sufficient nuclear deterrent. But for primarily *political* reasons NATO should not agree to renounce such deployments until the Soviet Union is ready to reduce its nuclear arms adequately.[124]

And then he went on to discuss the nuclear-free zone:

Theoretically, it is conceivable that a devastating war could be fought in Central Europe with only conventional and short-range nuclear weapons without any greater risk of escalation. From the perspective of deterrence, anti-demolition munitions and nuclear artillery contribute little to NATO's military capability.... The Palme [late Swedish Prime Minister] Commission proposed a nuclear weapons-free zone extending approximately 150 kilometers in each direction from the border between NATO and the Warsaw Pact. Agreement on such a zone should be sought even if compliance with it, particularly at a time of rising tensions, would be difficult to control.... [This] proposal reduces the risk of a nuclear war restricted to Central Europe.[125]

Other segments of the Coupler community in Germany or elsewhere have not favored this proposal. Recently, however, it has surfaced again in the context of renewed conventional arms control negotiations.

Among the Couplers in general, nuclear arms control is looked at skeptically because of the fundamental belief that nuclear arms remain the essential deterrent against Soviet conventional as well as nuclear power. Increasing exceptions to this generalization, however, can be found among the Germans; even many of those who consider the coupling of the American deterrent to remain essential believe that nuclear arms negotiations may be useful, at least in terms of FRG politics going into the 1990 election.

The fear of Soviet conventional preponderance, however, has made conventional arms controls of even greater interest, as the Soviets' unilateral reductions as well as their willingness to negotiate on the basis of asymmetry has made such controls appear far more serious than they did in 15 years of negotiations in Vienna. In the wake of zero-zero and the fears that the removal of nuclear weapons will accentuate the conventional imbalance in Europe, the Couplers are taking such controls very seriously indeed.

---

[124]Voigt, 1984, p. 106.
[125]Ibid., pp. 114–115.

SUMMARY: COUPLER RECOMMENDATIONS

One thing this section has demonstrated is that the Couplers do not form a close-knit School of Thought, nearly unanimous on all matters; far from it. It is remarkable, then, that in spite of the wide differences and vigorous disputes within the school, they do reach consensus—but not unanimity—on several broad policy recommendations:

- Europe should move at "all deliberate speed" toward forming a stronger second pillar for the Alliance. This is agreed upon both by those most frightened by the prospect of a weakened U.S. commitment and those most relaxed.
- It may be necessary to spend *some* more on conventional capabilities, if for no other reason than to satisfy the United States, but not a lot more. And when the finance ministers say "No," the answer is acceptable.
- Nuclear deterrence, particularly American nuclear deterrence, is what keeps the bear from the border, and must be maintained, although perhaps deemphasized.
- The "rest of the world" outside of Europe is important but not very important, and the United States should not be diverted from the preservation of Europe.
- Arms control is A Good Thing, which we should all favor, but we should also all be suspicious, particularly when the superpowers agree between themselves on nuclear arms controls. Conventional arms controls, however, may offer real possibilities.

These all stem, one way or another, from the central value judgment that the preservation of Europe is the most important objective for Europeans, and the central analytical premise that the American commitment continues to be necessary for that preservation. The corresponding policy recommendations of the American Maintainer school stem from different premises and turn out considerably different on each count. And all the premises and recommendations on both sides of the Atlantic may change, given enough real change on the other side of the Elbe.

Before crossing the Atlantic to the American Maintainer mainstream, this analysis turns to the two minority schools that help define the mainstreams—the European Removers and the American Withdrawers.

18. The Removers

At our 1986 Annual Conference, my Party once again committed itself—by an overwhelming vote of 5 to 1—to our country's full membership and participation in NATO.

The size and location of our country means that using nuclear weapons would always be pointless or self-destructive, or both.
— British Labour Party Leader Neil Kinnock[1]

This confession of our faith is incompatible with the development, deployment and use of weapons of mass destruction. Such weapons are capable of exterminating the human race which God has loved and elevated, and of devastating all of Creation.
— Reformist Federation (German Reform church)[2]

The views of the European peace movement, the Removers, cover a broad range. On the moderate end are the politicians who, both by conviction about the requirements for defense and because they are striving for electoral success with an electorate that can be both antinuclear and pro-NATO, argue for change within the Alliance. On the more radical end are the church and other peace movements, which, like the American disarmament movement, simply want to do away with nuclear weapons. But it is the central desire to move away from nuclear defense and deterrence, within the Alliance or outside of it, slowly or rapidly, conditionally or unconditionally, that defines the Remover school.

The Removers form a considerable minority in Britain, where they have dominated Labour, the main opposition party, and also include many Liberals; and in West Germany, where they include the environmentalist Green Party with up to 10 percent of the electorate and are strong, although not dominant, in the SPD, which leads the opposition. Their minority status in both countries was confirmed by elections in 1987, and electoral arithmetic and calendars make it extremely unlikely that they will have another chance at gaining power until at least late 1990. Further,

---

[1]Kinnock, 1986, pp. 3–11.
[2]*Das Bekanntis zu Jesus Christus und die Friedensverantwortung der Kirche. Eine Erklarung des Moderamens des Reformierten Bundes*, quoted in Risse-Kappen, 1984, p. 209.

public opinion surveys as well as voting data in both Britain and Germany imply that the prospects for both Labour and SPD (or a still unlikely federal-level coalition between the SPD and the Greens) are directly proportional to the degree of their moderation on defense issues. The voters in both countries have strongly and consistently favored the Alliance and the American tie.[3]

Nonetheless, public opinion can change. And votes in these countries (as in the United States) are ordinarily swayed more by domestic conditions than by international relations. Major economic difficulties before the next election, for example, could bring to power in either Britain or Germany governments dominated or at least substantially influenced by Removers. Whether or not events move in this direction, the Remover minorities are strong enough to keep the Coupler governments looking back over their shoulders.

The 1979 decision to deploy INF, for example, added the second track—the offer to the Soviets to trade INF reductions for SS-20 reductions—because European governments wanted to keep the peace movement at bay. In the event, when the INF missiles were brought to Europe, the movement took to the streets and commons, but failed to prevent entry; had it not been for the second track, the Removers might have been strong enough to impede installation of the weapons. As has been discussed, the price the INF Couplers paid for the second track was the turmoil caused by Gorbachev's unexpected acceptance of the offer to trade down.

Moreover, in addition to the United Kingdom and the Federal Republic, the Removers are strong in some of NATO's smaller member nations, notably in parts of Scandinavia and the Low Countries. They have been in the minority there too, but in multiparty situations that are sometimes quite volatile. And each of these countries, although not contributing major military power to the Alliance, is important because of location and politics.

For all of these reasons, the European Removers are politically far more important in the NATO debate than is the radical opposition in the American debates over strategic nuclear issues and Third World policies. The following discussion does not analyze the Removers' views in the same categories (e.g., U.S. Commitment, Conventional-Nuclear Link) as have been used for the Couplers and will be for the American Maintainers. With the Removers as with the other schools, the choice of issues is as important as the viewpoints on these issues. This analysis follows the natural contours of the Removers' discourse, taking up first their negative

---

[3]See, for example, Flynn and Rattinger, 1985; and Schweigler, 1986.

arguments—what they are against, particularly nuclear deterrence and defense in Europe—and why; and then moving to their positive proposals for "defensive defense."

The German Reformist church statement at the head of this section is radical in the religious pacifist mode that has informed part of the international peace movement since the invention of nuclear weapons and, indeed, long before. As a statement of personal faith it stands with the eloquent words of the American Quakers' precept expressed in their uncompromising position on nuclear and other war-peace issues: "Here I stand. Regardless of relevance or consequence I can do no other."[4] As an argument on policy, the Reformist statement is part of the religious debate on nuclear morality centered in some measure around the more equivocal statement of the American Catholic bishops, who reluctantly endorsed continued nuclear deterrence while arguing against almost all uses of nuclear weapons. The German Catholic bishops took a similar stand as did the Evangelical Church, much the largest Protestant denomination.

Political radicalism within the West German peace movement is expressed as advocacy of "nonalignment of the German states, withdrawal of all foreign troops from Western and Eastern Europe, dissolution of the NATO and Warsaw Pact military blocs," and sees these policies not only as leading to elimination of the nuclear threat but also as a step toward German reunification:

> In this way the German question will become an instrument of peace for Europe; a withdrawal of the two German states from the military blocs will create a real détente zone and at the same time facilitate closer cooperation between the two German states. . . . A confederation between the two German states would be conceivable as a state in the process of attaining national unity.[5]

This is by no means an expression of the views of all the German Removers. The more moderate wing—perhaps a majority depending on where one draws the line between the moderate Removers and the more radical of the Couplers within the SPD—wants to remain within NATO while moving away from nuclear deterrence. In its 1986 resolutions, the SPD, as political parties do, balanced its platform between its two wings. On one key statement, however, concerning removal of the INF missiles (which had been brought in initially at the urgent behest of former SPD Chancellor Schmidt), the Removers clearly won out:

---

[4]American Friends Service Committee, 1955, p. 68.
[5]Both of these are quoted in Kiep, 1984/85, p. 319.

[T]he SPD: appeals to the United States immediately to stop delivery of further Pershing II and Cruise missiles and to remove those already deployed; appeals to the Soviet Union to remove the missiles counter-deployed in the GDR and Czechoslovakia and drastically to reduce its SS-20s to the 1979 level. With a view to achieving these aims an SPD federal government will . . . [reverse] the Bundestag decision of 22 November 1983 in order to remove the parliamentary basis for the deployment of such weapons for which permission was granted by the present conservative government.[6]

The seeming symmetry of language on Eastern and Western missiles does not really obscure the facts that not only are the Western missiles to be eliminated while the Eastern ones are to be reduced to former levels, but that the Soviet Union is *appealed to*, whereas the Bundestag, were the SPD to gain control, would *require* the removal of the American missiles. Indeed, when, some months later, Gorbachev agreed to a treaty eliminating all of his SS-20s in return for all of the Western Pershing IIs and cruise missiles, the SPD was left in the embarrassing position of having to "retreat" from unilateral Western withdrawal to bilateral withdrawal, which would remove the Soviet missiles as well.

Nonetheless, the SPD firmly endorsed the Federal Republic's links to the West:

The Federal Republic of Germany is politically and militarily integrated into the European Community and NATO. For as long as the Soviet Union remains an excessively armed superpower in Europe the West Europeans will need to be linked with the military counter-balance of the United States.[7]

And in several other ways—for example forward defense and continuation of conscription—it shows itself to be far from pacifist or other radicalism.

The British political left is quite similar. Labour Party Leader Kinnock's balance, set forth in his statement quoted at the head of this chapter, is expressed in terms of strongly antinuclear policies backed by strongly pro-NATO arguments:

Britain must choose between effective conventional defense and its own nuclear weapons, and we in the Labor Party hope that it will choose conventional defense even if Britain has to take unilateral

---

[6]Social Democratic Party of Germany, 1986, p. 13.
[7]Ibid., p. 2.

action to renounce the nuclear program. Moreover, a careful strategic assessment of United States nuclear weapons systems in Britain leads us to the conclusion that these nuclear systems should be withdrawn. . . .

Our entire effort in the Labour Party is dedicated to ensuring that our country is effectively defended and that our alliance with our fellow democracies remains strong. To those ends, we want to make the transfer of precious funds from expenditure on Polaris and Trident nuclear forces to improved conventional capabilities, thereby enhancing both our domestic defense and the quality of our NATO contribution. Moreover, we want to insure that real progress is made toward changing the "first use" NATO strategy which currently contradicts the interests of common security between East and West.[8]

Kinnock's then-Shadow Foreign Secretary and former Labour Defense Minister Denis Healey, after presenting a similar set of arguments for the same positions, concluded on a rather different note:

The main objective of a Labour government in NATO would be to persuade its allies to cooperate in building an effective conventional deterrent in Europe. . . . Yet we recognize that we cannot change NATO strategy unilaterally and that NATO strategy must be indivisible. So we shall continue to cooperate in the existing strategy until we succeed in changing it, as the Kennedy Administration did in the 1960s.[9]

The last passage sounds very much as if, had Labour won the 1987 election, the plank about ousting American nuclear weapons from Britain would have been implemented very slowly indeed. In any case, more recently as Kinnock and his followers have attempted to convert the electoral rout of 1987 into victory in 1991/2, they have tried to nudge the party from pure nuclear unilateralism to negotiated multilateral nuclear disarmament. The issue remains to be finally resolved within the Labour Party.

Much of the analytical basis for Labour's Remover political policies has stemmed from a study entitled *Defence Without the Bomb*, prepared in 1983 by the Alternative Defence Commission made up of academics, clerics, union officials, and others. As in the German case, the intellectual base is far more radical than the political cutting edge represented by Kinnock. The study is, in fact, a rather radical analysis with a few members of the

---

[8]Kinnock, 1987, p. 31.
[9]Healey, 1987, p. 726.

Commission being even more radical than the consensus that wrote the document. In sharp distinction to Healey's "we will teach them patiently."

The Commission is unanimous that a nuclear disarmed Britain could not accept NATO's current nuclear-based strategy. It debated at length whether it would be better for Britain to stay in NATO and seek to influence its policy in a non-nuclear direction, or to leave the Alliance altogether. The majority reached the conclusion that Britain should seek to initiate a process of nuclear disarmament in Europe by staying in the Alliance subject to the condition that NATO does move decisively toward abandoning any reliance on a nuclear strategy. The goal of de-nuclearising NATO strategy implies the following steps: (1) Acceptance by NATO of a policy of no-first-use of nuclear weapons. (2) Withdrawal of short-range, "battlefield," nuclear weapons. (3) Withdrawal of "theatre" nuclear weapons. (4) The decoupling of the U.S. strategic deterrent from NATO by ending reliance on U.S. nuclear weapons as an element in NATO strategy. . . .

If NATO was not willing to renounce nuclear strategies, Britain should withdraw from the Alliance. It could then explore the possibility of alternative approaches to collective security in Europe, or adopt a non-aligned position. Some Commission members thought that from the outset Britain should adopt a non-aligned approach.[10]

The study provides a variety of arguments and proposals in its 300 pages. One thing it does not go in for is America-bashing. Although it is obviously quite critical of American nuclear policies, the nearest it comes to hostility is in terms of future possibilities, and slightly shamefacedly at that: "If Britain went non-nuclear and left NATO, we would be less directly threatened by Soviet nuclear strategy, but we might also need to ask whether the USA posed any kind of military threat,"[11] a theme not expanded upon. In fact, although peace-movement hostility to the United States and belief in the "moral equivalency" of the United States and the Soviet Union is a theme frequently written *about*, it is one that is hardly ever written down by those who espouse it.[12]

The Alternative Defence Commission volume provides little assessment, hostile or otherwise, of the United States. Its discussion of the Soviet Union is more extensive, falling within the "on-the-one-hand, on-the-

---

[10]Alternative Defence Commission, 1983, pp. 8–9.
[11]Ibid., p. 56.
[12]For a Danish third-person version, see Monitor, "SDP Successor Generation Less Sympathetic to U.S., E.C. Goals," *Berlingske Tidende*, April 28, 1986, p. 12.

other-hand" frame that was the most optimistic anyone was willing to get in the pre-Gorbachev era. One contradiction to a standard and central Coupler belief is set forth, however. It concerns "Finlandization."

> The term Finlandisation tends to be used in a way that oversimplifies the degree of control exercised by the Soviet Union over Finland. Though Finland is obliged to observe a neutrality which in some respects leans towards the Soviet Union, and limits its criticism of the Soviet Union, it undoubtedly retains independent democratic institutions, and its economic links with the USSR benefit Finland and do not prevent it from trading freely with the rest of the world. . . . A comparison with Panama's relationship to the United States . . . puts Finland's position into better perspective. As a country small in population bordering on a powerful neighbor, and occupying a position of strategic importance to it, Finland enjoys a reasonable degree of autonomy.[13]

Of course, Britain does not border on any such "powerful neighbor." West Germans may take less comfort from the "reasonable degree of autonomy," however.

The Alternative Defence Commission also takes up and extensively discusses the *positive* theme of the Removers—nonnuclear defensive strategy, centered largely on "defensive defense." The Commission advocates:

> preparations for military resistance which would deny an easy victory to an invading force. This aim might be met either by having the ability to hold an attacking force for several weeks by an in-depth deployment which would ensure serious attrition of advancing forces. It . . . means possessing few, if any, offensive missiles or long-range ground-attack aircraft, and limiting the number of tanks to those required for a mobile defense.[14]

Another exclusion (in addition to offensive missiles and long-range aircraft) suggested by a Danish analyst, contrasts sharply with the technological hopes of the Couplers: "Without entirely abandoning advanced weapons systems, we have to put the main emphasis on older and more primitive weapons which are not dependent on radar and which, therefore, are not as accurate but which, on the other hand, cannot be put out of action elec-

---

[13]Alternative Defence Commission, 1983, p. 76.
[14]Ibid., pp. 179–180.

tronically."[15] Coupler David Gates's previously cited critique of defensive defense, however, suggests that, in contrast to the Removers' ethos of militia defense of home and hearth, they would, in fact, also have to depend on high technology to be militarily effective.

The issue of defense on the continent is of more specific interest for the Germans (and for the Danes) than it is for the British. Andreas von Bulow, a defense analyst and spokesman for the SPD, admires Swiss and Swedish defenses and argues for a similar German system:

> A look at the Swedish and Swiss structures strikingly shows that these certainly not militarily incompetent nations put a considerable emphasis on the infantry.... For their defense the Swiss and the Swedes have thus set up relatively tight-knit configurations in order to stop attacking, highly-mechanized units; behind these stand defense forces with strong tank components that can be used at points of main effort where there is a danger of breakthrough. These forces are not sufficient, however, to be used for territory-taking operations. In contrast, at the center of NATO's armament is the great mass of tanks. . . .

> The Federal Republic will be able to maintain a balanced defense commitment in the 1990s only if military structures are radically changed. . . . A more static defense requires a great deal of manpower in case of war. This personnel, especially for a network that is strong on anti-tank defense, should by no means be manned by conscripts, but rather, as in Sweden and Switzerland, by reserves.[16]

Von Bulow's ultimate objective for Western defenses, aside from the denuclearization of Europe, is surprisingly like that of some of the French Couplers. He wants Western Europe to defend itself.

> By the turn of the century, at least, the conventional defense of Western Europe should be in the hands of the West Europeans. A certain reliance on the U.S. nuclear umbrella, possibly also a limited physical presence of conventional U.S. troops, for example, in geotactically precarious Berlin, might still be necessary. The East European communist regimes should by then be able to stand on their feet. Their own security system should no longer be dependent on the Soviet Union.[17]

---

[15]Koefoed, 1985, p. 9.
[16]von Bulow, 1986, pp. 136–147.
[17]Ibid., p. 151.

But a more radical projection of the promise stemming from installation of a defensive defense comes not from the German SPD but from a serving military officer of the Federal Republic, Rear Admiral Elmar Schmaehling, director of the Bundeswehr Office for Studies and Exercises:

> An increasingly faster process of mutual disarmament, and thus also of the reduction of conventional offensive weapons, will lead in all countries to defense structures that are purely defensive—that is to say, they are most efficient in defending their own territory. If this is mutually achieved, nobody will have an attack capability anymore and then the military alliances with integrated Armed Forces will able to be dissolved. This will lead to an end to the unnatural situation in which another state's armed forces are stationed on one's own territory.[18]

This statement was not popular in the Ministry of Defense, but free speech laws for the German armed forces, installed as a hedge against the return of classical German military discipline, made it difficult to do anything about it.

The Removers are at least a few years from power in the major European NATO nations, Britain and West Germany. (They are virtually nonexistent in France.) In some of the smaller member nations, notably Denmark and the Netherlands, the combination of the inherent political instability associated with large numbers of small parties maneuvering for position with each other and with vocal Remover contingents means that such issues as denuclearization and defensive defense loom quite large in the arms debates and sometimes in the national political debates. In Denmark in particular, former Social Democratic Prime Minister Anker Jorgensen took a stand in 1986 in favor of defensive defense:

> A nonthreatening nonoffensive defense structure is a defense system which by its structure demonstrates peaceable nonoffensive aims, but which at the same time possesses the capacity to work together with other nations in order to inflict on an attacker such losses in and from one's own sovereign territory that attack cannot be assumed beforehand to result in a successful outcome for the attacker.[19]

One of the ways that the Social Democrats proposed to implement this policy was to move the Danish NATO brigade in Schleswig-Holstein (West Germany) to Jutland-Funen (Denmark).

---

[18]Schmaehling, 1988, pp. 16–17.
[19]Quoted in *Berlingske Tidende*, June 17, 1986, p. 4.

More broadly, an organization called Scandilux, made up of the Social Democratic parties of Benelux and the continental NATO members of Scandinavia, has, according to Danish Professor Nikolaj Petersen, coalesced around a set of ideas that can serve as a summary of Remover recommendations. They are:

> the concept of "common security" . . . between the NATO and Warsaw Pact countries. . . .
>
> the concept of a larger and more independent European role in Western defence. . . .
>
> an alternative NATO strategy for the defence of Western Europe, including the following elements: (a) reduction of the role of nuclear weapons in NATO strategy, including a large-scale removal of . . . tactical nuclear weapons, the adoption of a no-first-use doctrine . . . and the establishment of nuclear-free zones . . . (b) opposition to "deep-strike" strategies . . . (c) formulation of a so-called "defensive" concept for the defence of Western Europe.[20]

It is not clear what the political prospects are for the Removers, either in Scandilux (where, for example, Norwegian Defense Minister Holst, a member of the Social Democratic government, remains a charter Coupler), or in the larger countries (where the possibilities before the 1991/92 elections are limited). What is clear is that the European Remover school has as complete and coherent a vision of policy and the future as any other. Its closeness to power (and, in the cases of Denis Healey and Anker Jorgensen at least, its experience of past power) and the depth of its support have enabled it to think through its ideas in a way not required of all radical factions in all aspects of the arms debate of the 1980s.

---

[20]Petersen, 1985, p. 11.

19. The Withdrawers

> Approaching the millenium . . . Americans are coming to real-
> ize that our front line is the skyline; America's primary
> national defense interest is to protect itself from the threat of
> incoming missiles. Our global mission is better served by
> investing money in a new nuclear shield than in manning old
> casernes in Germany.
>
> —William Safire[1]

> Abroad, an assertive American foreign policy meets with great
> resistance from our allies, most of whom are utterly risk-
> averse, and some of whom believe that a grudging appease-
> ment of Soviet power will mollify its messianic appetite. This
> is especially evident in Western Europe, where, under the
> American nuclear umbrella, national pride has softened into
> something that resembles national pique.
>
> —Irving Kristol[2]

The American Withdrawer school is newer and narrower, and therefore less complete in its ideas, than its corresponding (in a sense) European school, the Removers. The two correspond, even though the Removers come primarily from the "left" and the Withdrawers from the "right," in that they both favor a sharp drawdown of the American commitment to NATO. Further, they both have deep historical roots: the Removers in pacifism and post-World War II European anti-Americanism, the With-drawers in the pre-World War II American isolationism echoed by Safire and the post-war visceral anticommunism exemplified by Kristol. Indeed, although the American peace movement, on the left, pays little attention to NATO, the policy recommendations that they do make fit quite nicely with those of the right Withdrawers. They do not share the strong anticommu-nism, but they do share the isolationism; and they fit the defining charac-teristic: They want the United States to withdraw from Europe.

Avowed isolationism has been out of date in the United States since the early 1950s. True, one American undercurrent in the isolationist tradition—that, since the restoration of West European prosperity by the

---

[1]Safire, 1987, p. 21.
[2]Kristol, 1985, p. 14.

1960s, the Europeans have not carried a fair share of the responsibility for their own defense—provides an important basis for the Withdrawers' arguments. But it took cumulating feelings on the American right that the West Europeans were insufficiently anticommunist and insufficiently supportive of American anticommunism and other American global interests to reactivate their isolationism in the early 1980s.

The Withdrawers' view of insufficient European anticommunism had early roots in lack of NATO support for our war in Vietnam. In the late 1970s, some of the Withdrawers' feelings were based on the lukewarm (at best) support by our allies for President Carter's post-Afghanistan Olympic boycott; some were based on what was perceived as incomplete support for the Polish Solidarity movement; some on lack of support regarding Iran and the Persian Gulf; some, a bit later, on West European opposition to U.S. activities in Central America. A precipitating event in the early 1980s, though, took place within Europe—the bargain by the West European nations to bring in Siberian natural gas through a pipeline that some Americans contend was subsidized largely by concessions from these nations.[3] NYU Economics Professor Melvin Krauss, one of the most prolific of the Withdrawers, uses the pipeline as an instance to combine the insufficient-anticommunism theme with another used by the Withdrawers that the West Europeans are too willing to compromise principle for economic advantage:

> [T]he pipeline deal clearly is part of the overall European strategy of Soviet appeasement. But there is another important aspect of the deal. . . . The truth of the matter is that the Soviet pipeline deal probably had as much to do with increasing employment and profits in a severely depressed European industry as it did with paying tribute to the Kremlin.[4]

At another point, under the subhead "European Defense Free-Riding," Krauss asserts that "The reason we allocate a greater portion of our economic product to defense than the Europeans is not that we are more warlike than our allies, but that we subsidize Europe's defense needs,"[5] and he defends this analysis with numbers. Burden-sharing is a common American theme, and not only among the Withdrawers; as has been noted, Europeans cite other numbers to argue the point.

---

[3]See Genscher, 1982.
[4]Krauss, 1986a, p. 149.
[5]Ibid., p. 18.

Krauss and fellow NYU Professor Kristol, editor of the neoconservative *Public Interest* quarterly, are both cited by French publisher Jimmy Goldsmith as leaders of the American drive to cut the commitment to Europe.[6] The citation is essentially accurate, but Goldsmith also mentions Senator Sam Nunn; and Nunn, as well as Henry Kissinger and former National Security Advisor Zbigniew Brzezinski who are frequently grouped with Nunn, is quite different from both Krauss and Kristol. Nunn, Kissinger, and Brzezinski are not Withdrawers; they are interested in restructuring NATO or NATO strategy precisely to preserve the Alliance under what they see as new conditions. As such, they form an important portion of the American Maintainer consensus quite different from the Withdrawer viewpoint.

Kristol philosophizes historically on NATO interference with America's larger mission:

> When George Washington warned the young republic against any entangling alliances, the U.S. was a medium-size power, geographically distant from the Great Powers of Europe. . . . The U.S. today, however, is one of the Great Powers, not a middling power. The meaning for us, therefore, of an entangling alliance has changed. . . . In general, an entangling alliance for a superpower today is one that is more likely to inhibit or prevent its taking action that it deems to be appropriate or timely. The Soviet Union, of course, has no such entangling alliances. . . .

> [T]he NATO alliance, as now constituted, is not limited to the defense of Western Europe. . . . As things now stand, the U.S. would not even have the legal right to use any of the American bases in Western Europe to support military operations in the Mediterranean, Northern Africa or the Middle East. Several members of NATO have made it quite clear that they would feel free to deny us this right, should they disapprove of our action.[7]

And what may be worse yet, according to Krauss, is that the United States has softened in response to West European softness: "The Europeans said, in effect, 'You adopt détente, or else we won't let you defend us'—and they got away with it."[8] They also get away with opposing us in international forums: "Western Europe often votes against the United

[6]Goldsmith, 1987, p. 24.
[7]Kristol, 1986, p. 18.
[8]Krauss, 1986b, p. A17.

States on key strategic issues in the United Nations—Nicaragua, El Salvador, Grenada, and so forth."[9] His conclusion on the theme of collective European softness is in the form of a rhetorical question: "[C]an there be any doubt as to the long-range debilitating effect wrought by the American security blanket on European perceptions of the external danger?"[10]

Krauss's book has specific chapters on West Germany and France (although, surprisingly, neither a chapter nor even an index reference to Britain). On Germany: "The desire for détente is so strong in the Federal Republic that it transcends political parties and ideological allegiances."[11] This, however, is in large measure the fault of the United States:

> [T]he idea of keeping West Germany in a militarily inferior position by having a foreign power provide for its defense and basic security needs had considerable appeal after World War II, given Germany's dubious historical record. . . . When West Germany's commitment to democracy could no longer be challenged and its economy became the strongest in Western Europe, it should have been obvious that unless there was an adjustment of its status as a militarily inferior nation, West Germany increasingly would feel estranged from those responsible for its condition and particularly from that country most responsible and upon which it was most dependent, the United States. The appeal of neutralism to the West Germans should have come as no surprise, though it did to many.[12]

And as for France, in 1983 Krauss held up French independence as a model for what NATO should be, suggesting a separate German nuclear deterrent in addition to the French and the British.[13] By the time of his 1986 book, however, he was more dubious:

> Though the basics of official French defense policy have changed very little under Socialist Mitterrand . . . there is a new revisionism gaining credibility in France that threatens the entire Gaullist defense edifice. This new French revisionism has a most unlikely spokesman in Yves Montand, the popular French actor and chansonnier.[14]

If it was fair for Krauss to cite Montand as a spokesman for France, it was also fair a year later for Goldsmith to cite Krauss as a spokesman for the United States.

---

[9]Krauss, 1986a, p. 27.
[10]Ibid., p. 28.
[11]Ibid., p. 93.
[12]Ibid., p. 105.
[13]Krauss, 1983, p. 24.
[14]Krauss, 1986a, p. 130.

More recently, Krauss has put his argument for turning nuclear control over to individual West European nations into the context of the zero-zero negotiations:

As pointed out by Gregory Fossedal of the Hoover Institution . . . the president could respond to Mr. Gorbachev's offer to negotiate the zero-based option by announcing his intention to give control of all U.S. medium-range nuclear weapons located on European soil to the Europeans. . . . The Europeans may or may not accept the American lead in this matter; that is for them, not the U.S. to decide. For our part, we should offer the missiles to the nation-states in which the missiles currently are located. If the Europeans want an alternative arrangement, we should stand ready to accommodate them.[15]

Christopher Layne, an attorney writing in *Foreign Policy* quarterly, picks up the burden-sharing theme of the other Withdrawers and comes out with similar recommendations for getting the United States out of NATO. Layne, however, does not share the ideological anticommunism of most of the other Withdrawers:

Short of war, Europe's division can best be ended by a negotiated superpower disengagement. . . . The United States has a vital interest in lessening the tensions from Europe's division: Central Europe has been the focal point of superpower confrontation for 40 years. . . . Both superpowers have an interest in reconciling legitimate Soviet security concerns with Eastern Europe's desire for greater political autonomy. The goal of disengagement, therefore, would be not to induce states to leave Moscow's security orbit but to achieve Eastern Europe's Finlandization.[16]

Layne *is* of the right; the one affiliation he uses to identify himself for his published articles, for example, is with the Cato Institute, an organization devoted to very free-market economics and associated politics. But his arguments, lacking the anticommunist tone of Kristol and Krauss, are similar to those made by Richard Barnet of the Institute for Policy Studies on the left. Barnet, one of the few American analysts on that end of the spectrum to include NATO seriously in his military-disarmament writings, suggests that neither the Soviet threat nor the American deterrent are any longer very plausible to West Europeans and that, as a result, although Europe is capable of fielding its own stronger forces, "taxpayers on the

---

[15]Krauss, 1987, p. 30.
[16]Layne, 1987a, p. 34.

continent are not enthusiastic about supporting larger defense budgets or more conscription."[17]

The central policy recommendation stemming from this reasoning makes Barnet a Withdrawer:

Thus, the Europeans should bear the primary responsibility for their own defense. The United States should use its power to make the military environment in Europe less dangerous by negotiating the denuclearization of the military forces facing one another in Europe and by taking substantial steps toward the demilitarization of the Continent. . . . The reality is that Europe can be defended only by non-nuclear means, and the appropriate men and women to undertake that defense are Europeans.[18]

Layne, like the other right Withdrawers, does not share Barnet's desire for denuclearization; nonetheless, his recommendations sound similar. His withdrawal stance comes in two styles, bilateral and unilateral. The bilateral negotiated version revolves around the "reunification and neutralization of Germany" and the "dissolution of NATO and the Warsaw Pact."[19] The unilateral version, which is accompanied by a West German independent nuclear deterrent force rather than German reunification, proposes: "Washington should fix an ironclad timetable for the phased withdrawal over 4 years of all ground, air, and nuclear forces from Europe. At the conclusion of its pullout, the formal U.S. commitment to NATO would end."[20]

Not even Kristol would go quite as far as complete withdrawal of both forces and commitment. His object, like Layne's, is to put Europe on its own:

Obviously NATO—even a purely European NATO—would need a sufficiency of [nuclear] weapons . . . to deter a Soviet first use of them, regardless of any arms control treaties that might be signed. But reserving those weapons for this purpose would mean that Western Europe would finally have to face its moment of truth: the recognition that to deter the Soviets it would have to develop its conventional forces, and convincingly assert the will to use them.[21]

---

[17]Barnet, 1987, p. 80.
[18]Ibid., pp. 81–82.
[19]Layne, 1987b, p. 13.
[20]Layne, 1987a, p. 33.
[21]Kristol, 1987, p. 28.

The "even a purely European NATO" implies that he is still open to a transatlantic alliance, were that possible under acceptable terms. His recommendation for the United States is a reduced, but not completely dissolved, American commitment to Western Europe:

> This means that NATO, as currently structured, is an archaic institution, that the defense of Western Europe will become primarily a Western European responsibility, that Western Europe will have to gird itself to fight and (hopefully) win a conventional war against the Soviet Union—with American help, if needed, but not with a recourse to nuclear weapons.[22]

Krauss has a slightly different summary recommendation, close to Layne's but consistent with his own emphases on balanced contributions and global anticommunism:

> Washington should announce a phased withdrawal of U.S. troops over a period of, say, five years . . . [but] a distinction should be made between Europe's flank states and center. Clearly, in terms of resources and the potential to hold together under duress, Europe's center is far stronger than its flanks. Scandinavia is of sufficient concern to the core states of Western Europe that they could be expected to look after the northern flanks should the U.S. depart. . . . But what is to become of the flank states like Turkey, that do not shortchange their defense and have significant strategic value to the United States? Perhaps it would be wise for the U.S. to make a separate bilateral agreement with Turkey after we leave Europe to insure its security.[23]

Finally, mention should be made of a specifically naval version. Washington analyst Jeffrey Record, paralleling the reasoning of the other Withdrawers in a 1982 booklet he wrote with retired Admiral Robert Hanks, lists three recommendations:

> Withdrawal of nonnuclear U.S. ground forces from Germany and attendant alterations in the U.S. Army's size and force structure.

> A major expansion in U.S. naval power and seaborne force projection capabilities.

> Creation of a new global strategy based primarily on sea power and seaborne force projection capabilities, and oriented primarily toward non-NATO contingencies.[24]

---

[22]Kristol, 1985, p. 14.
[23]Krauss, 1986a, pp. 237–238.
[24]Record, 1982, p. 29.

Withdrawal of U.S. ground forces implies a different direction from Kristol's willingness to extend conventional help only, but otherwise the recommendations are consistent. The naval version differs from the other Withdrawer writings too in one additional and crucial particular: The stress on global seaborne force projection became part of the Reagan administration's military strategy for the United States, although certainly not accompanied by withdrawal from Europe.

The Withdrawers are not all identical, not even the pronuclear right-wing Withdrawers. But where they do come together is in their central recommendation to the United States: *Get out of Europe.* In this they are similar to most of the European Removers, but they differ from the mainstream American consensus, the Maintainers; some Maintainers want to restructure NATO and the American commitment, but they want to do it to strengthen both. "Maintaining and strengthening" is their theme, not "getting out."

20. The Maintainers

The message is that we want to be a part of NATO; that we are going to continue to be a part of NATO whether this amendment passes or does not pass; that we will even continue to be a part of NATO if our European allies do not comply with any of the provisions of this amendment; that we will continue to have hundreds of thousands of troops in NATO even if this amendment passes and even if the allies do not comply with any of its provisions or tests. We will still have a nuclear deterrent that will not only protect this Nation but explicitly help protect our European allies. We will continue to have theater nuclear capability and commitment to our European allies. We will continue to have naval commitment. . . .

But the amendment is designed to give NATO as an alliance every incentive to improve its conventional defense. The reason we need to improve conventional defense is that the continued reliance on the early use of nuclear weapons is diametrically opposed to the national security interests of this country and the security interests of our Western European allies. . . .

[I]f we do not have allies that are going to do their part, there is no need for the American taxpayer to continue to spend billions and billions and billions of dollars. . . . We can have a tripwire—that is, having our forces basically link the American nuclear deterrent to the defense of Europe—for a lot less money.

> —Senator Sam Nunn (Dem., Ga.), discussing his 1984 amendment to gradually withdraw some American troops from Europe unless the European allies made certain specified increases in their contributions to the Alliance.[1]

Just as their own preservation is the central value judgment for West Europeans and the U.S. commitment to the defense of Western Europe is the focus of their debate on how to preserve their existence and independence, preserving *itself* (and the rest of the world) from nuclear holocaust is the central American value, and the Conventional-Nuclear Link—the threshold—is the how-to on which the Maintainers focus.

---

[1]Nunn, 1984, p. S7721.

For the Americans as for the Europeans, the commitment and the threshold are two sides of a coin. Senator Nunn's ringing reaffirmation of the commitment to NATO defines the Maintainer school, but the commitment is not much debated; it is assumed rather than being dissected as it is by the Couplers. Nunn's desire to raise the nuclear threshold, however, also commands a near-unanimous Maintainer consensus, and how to do it absorbs much consideration by American officials and analysts.

The three points mentioned in the introductory chapter—No Early Use of nuclear weapons, the need for stronger conventional capabilities to support this, and the continued American commitment to NATO—are, in fact, matters of consensus among the Maintainers. That is not to say that they do not argue with one another; this chapter brings out wide differences of opinion. Almost all of these differences, however, turn out to be on overarching issues that concern NATO but are not primarily *about* NATO—SDI and arms control, for example. The analysis here covers the NATO-related aspects of these debates, but almost all the debates stop at the water's edge; the Maintainers all espouse approximately the same policies toward NATO Europe.

MILITARY ISSUES

The Conventional/Nuclear Link

General Bernard Rogers set forth the Maintainers' view of NATO's central military problem and the principle by which it should be solved, in one of the many statements he made as Supreme Allied Commander, Europe (SACEUR):

> NATO's current conventional posture does not provide our nations with adequate deterrence of Warsaw Pact non-nuclear aggression or intimidation derived from the threat of such aggression. If attacked conventionally today, NATO would face fairly quickly the decision of escalating to a nuclear response in order to try to cause the aggressor to halt his advance. . . . Credible deterrence requires NATO to attain a conventional capability that would give us a reasonable prospect of frustrating a non-nuclear attack by conventional means. . . . [This] "reasonable prospect" formula is compatible with Flexible Response.[2]

---

[2]Rogers, 1986, p. 6.

314

The Maintainer consensus on both the problem description and the need for its solution encompasses a broad range of officials and analysts. Whether or how the solution can be brought about commands much less of a consensus.

The consensus in favor of raising the threshold is a strong one, including debaters who disagreed greatly on other nuclear issues. On one end of the range, Wohlstetter, a leader of the group of American analysts who believe that deterrence, particularly in Europe, depends on our ability and willingness to use a variety of nuclear options,[3] is nonetheless clear that these options are last resorts that we should avoid by being equally prepared to meet conventional force with conventional defense. In a 1987 paper, for example, he repeated the conclusion of the report of the 1961 Acheson Commission in which he participated:

> It emphasized the raising of the nuclear threshold, not its removal. . . . It was more credible that we would use conventional force to repel a conventional invasion and, if our conventional forces were overwhelmed, that we would use nuclear weapons, if we could use them discriminately and for a military purpose.[4]

On the antinuclear end of the spectrum, the "Gang of Four"—McGeorge Bundy, George Kennan, Robert McNamara, and Gérard Smith—while advocating serious discussion of No First Use by the West of nuclear weapons,[5] recognized that they were suggesting an ultimate direction, not an immediate policy proposal. In the later article in which the four, as part of the larger gang of ten, espoused No First Use as a long-run goal, they endorsed No *Early* Use as an implementable step in current and developing policy:[6]

No Early Use is another name for the Maintainers' consensus goal, a threshold as high as possible. The terminology crosses the spectrum to those who remain far from the No-First-Use position. Ambassador David Abshire, for example, the Reagan administration's representative on the NATO Council, stressed that: "It is most important to improve conventional defense because we must never be forced to contemplate the prospect of too early use of nuclear weapons."[7]

Abshire's stress on conventional improvement to raise the threshold is also part of the Maintainer consensus, but many analysts contend that as

---

[3]See Ch. 11.
[4]Wohlstetter, 1987, pp. 53–54.
[5]See Ch. 12.
[6]See Ch. 12.
[7]Abshire, 1984, p. 7751.

NATO is currently postured, No Early Use is almost impossible; NATO will have to use nuclear weapons almost immediately if it is to fight at all. John Steinbruner of the Brookings Institution, for example, contended in 1983 that:

> As NATO forces have evolved, the capability to use nuclear weapons has been closely associated with conventional forces. Artillery and tactical air units that provide supporting firepower for the ground armies responsible for holding NATO territory can use both conventional and nuclear ordnance and are trained to do so. The elaborate management procedures necessarily associated with nuclear weapons inhibit flexibility in conventional operations and pose hard choices for NATO commanders. In net effect the presence of nuclear delivery systems in forward units introduces a strong bias toward their use in combat, if not actually first then certainly very early.[8]

Since 1983, nobody has suggested that the threshold has risen substantially, although Robert Osgood's fear, a year later, that it was dropping rapidly, was also unjustified.[9] Such ever-present fears of ever-worse conventional capabilities provide one more illustration of the ubiquity of James Schlesinger's colonel's rubber-stamp, "In this perilous moment in the history of the alliance. . . ."

Steinbruner and Osgood doubted NATO's conventional capability to postpone the decision to go nuclear in Europe. At about the same time, William Kaufmann, a one-time advisor to Robert McNamara, questioned the other end of the Flexible Response range, the potential use of American strategic nuclear forces:

> Whatever NATO's military guidance may say, it is highly improbable that the U.S. strategic forces would ever be ordered to launch a first strike against targets in the Soviet Union in response to a conventional invasion of Western Europe. Indeed, this probability has been close to zero for at least twenty-five years [as of 1983].[10]

He used the point to advance the cause he had been active in for most of those 25 years, raising the threshold by increasing conventional capabilities.

Kaufmann's expressed doubt about the use of strategic weapons exemplifies a belief likely to evoke the European Couplers' worst fears, and few of the American Maintainers would go that far. Nonetheless, it is not very

---

[8]Steinbruner, 1983, p. 3.
[9]R. Osgood, 1984, p. 82.
[10]Kaufmann, 1983b, p. 29.

surprising that a respected American analyst could make a statement potentially so shocking to West Europeans; the interpretations of the link remain very different on the two sides of the Atlantic. An American view (by Washington defense analyst Leon Sloss) of the European view highlights the contrast:

> Under the vague and sufficiently ambiguous formulation of Flexible Response, we witnessed the emergence of two distinct and, to a degree, contradictory objectives. Very briefly, the U.S. wants maneuvering room and options, while Europe wants to avoid thinking about a prolonged conventional war or limited nuclear exchanges at the theatre level by threatening a much bigger war which would entail the total destruction of Europe, the Soviet Union and the United States. If the only war is a general holocaust—so goes European reasoning—then there will be no war. From this vantage point, U.S. ground troops and U.S. theatre nuclear forces . . . would not be a "firebreak" as the U.S. envisaged. Rather they would be the "fuse" which would ignite the strategic arsenals immediately. . . . All this is highly dangerous in today's environment.[11]

The question here is not whether Sloss's analysis of the West Europeans is correct; it represents a common Maintainer view of the Couplers. The Maintainers' primarily military thinking about the link is lost on many of the European Couplers; the Couplers' primarily political thinking about the U.S. commitment—the political side of the same issue—is held in contempt by many of the American Maintainers.

In the view of many of the Maintainers as well as the Couplers, the whole thing has been exacerbated over time by the onset of "strategic parity." Sloss continues his argument on the danger of "today's [1985] environment":

> The enormous shift in the overall strategic balance of the last 20 years has had different consequences for the U.S. and for NATO Europe. While U.S. strategic forces have been able to maintain a rough parity with their Soviet counterparts, the same forces cannot be deemed equally able to buttress the U.S. commitment to a NATO strategy which implies first use of nuclear weapons to deter a conventional attack. And yet this is still the essence of NATO strategy and of the official role assigned to U.S. nuclear weapons.[12]

---

[11]Sloss, 1986, pp. 61–62.
[12]Ibid., p. 63.

It was in this context of a strategic balance perceived to be deteriorating that INF was proposed in the late 1970s and introduced in the early 1980s. The issue to the West Europeans was less the level of the conventional-nuclear threshold than it was the width of *any* gap in the chain of Flexible Response that led from conventional defense to the American strategic deterrent. If the failure of conventional defense led to the use of short-range nuclear weapons in Western Europe, the lack of an intermediate-range force might allow a pause after the West was devastated but before the homeland of the Soviet Union was involved. And if the Soviets were to foresee such a pause, this might bring about a failure to deter their initial conventional attack.

Americans were more inclined to describe the gap in military terms. General Rogers, for example, described INF's role in NATO strategy:

NATO decided to deploy land-based long-range I.N.F. missiles in 1979 to fill a gap in our spectrum of deterrence. The gap existed because American F-111 aircraft based in Britain were then the last remaining part of the theater nuclear system that could reach Soviet soil, provided the aircraft could penetrate Warsaw Pact air defenses. The fact that the Russians began deploying SS-20 missiles in 1977 made the NATO decision more urgent.[13]

The political-military issue raised by some Maintainers opposed to INF is whether the location of the missile launchers or their participation in the "theater nuclear system" (given that the president of the United States must release them to the theater commander before he can use them) make a difference for Flexible Response or anything else. Jonathan Dean of the Union of Concerned Scientists expressed doubts:

The decision of an American president as to whether to respond to an overwhelming Soviet conventional attack on Europe . . . with nuclear weapons would not depend solely on the pattern of deployment of U.S. missiles in Europe. Rather, such a decision would depend primarily on the president's assessment of the overall situation at the time. . . . The presence or absence of land-based American missiles deployed in continental Europe would be a secondary factor in this decision—and for that matter, in its execution; many other American delivery systems are available for the purpose.[14]

---

[13]Rogers, 1987b, p. E25.
[14]Dean, 1987a, pp. 26–27.

Neither Rogers's "gap in our spectrum of deterrence" nor Dean's doubts about this gap take up the question of what would be done with nuclear weapons if deterrence were to fail. The actual fighting of a nuclear war in Europe is not much discussed, at least not on the open record. Wohlstetter, however, together with his colleague Richard Brody, did build several scenarios to illustrate the point that NATO must pay attention to the detail of localized nuclear warfare rather than throwing up its hands in the belief that such combat would mean the destruction of civilization in the major population centers of Europe. Using as an illustration "contingencies involving a Soviet invasion of northwest Iran leading to the Gulf," and the concomitant "possibility that the Soviets might use nuclear weapons selectively to eliminate unexpected obstacles to such an invasion," they suggest that:

> The foregoing scenario offers a good example running counter to the conventional wisdom that the Soviets could not use nuclear weapons to accomplish military objectives of importance to them and to the NATO nuclear powers without doing so much damage to Western population centers that the NATO nuclear powers would have no stake in exercising prudence and control if they used nuclear weapons in response.[15]

And although the threat is more likely on the periphery, it is not absent from the Central front in Europe:

> Even Soviet nuclear strikes during an invasion through the center of Western Europe, if directed selectively only at military targets critical for the invasion, could confine damage to these targets much more extensively than is generally recognized. . . . Precisely delivered air bursts could destroy aircraft on main operating bases in Britain, France, and the Federal Republic. The collateral fatalities might be in the high tens of thousands. That would be an enormous disaster. But far less than the total destruction of Western European cities. And European leaders might anticipate that as the consequence of their own use of nuclear weapons if the expected nuclear destruction were to get out of control.[16]

As part of his desire for controlled Western nuclear options to use in (or deter) scenarios like this, Wohlstetter is a strong advocate of SDI. Among most European Couplers, SDI "is seen . . . as destabilizing and decoupling"

---

[15]Wohlstetter and Brody, 1987, p. 159.
[16]Ibid., p. 161.

in Briton Phil Williams's words, but Wohlstetter contends that this view is based on misunderstanding. He used a French publication to put his pro-SDI argument into NATO terms:

> Certain technicians favorable to President Reagan's Strategic Defense Initiative ... have envisaged Soviet attacks which utilize 30,000 warheads ... all directed against cities in an attack mounted as a total surprise. And they have given priority to the not very obvious objective of intercepting all the warheads used in such an absurd attack. It is more plausible, if the Soviets attack, that they will use their ballistic missiles to obtain a greater probability of destroying military obstacles (in the United States or Europe) in the way of their invasion. Faced with this menace, a more modest defense against ballistic missiles could be one of the effective elements of a solid Alliance posture, which would also have to include the offensive capacity to respond selectively against Warsaw Pact targets, including those in the USSR. . . . In this way, it would assist in deterring the Soviet attack.[17]

Wohlstetter's statement comparing the "30,000 warheads" to "more modest" interpretations of the demands on SDI helps explain why, on this even more than on other issues, West Europeans and Americans misunderstand each other. It is because Americans confuse the arguments in their own SDI debate. "Certain technicians" in Wohlstetter's words, but also President Reagan who proposed it, have talked about SDI as a universal hard-shell defense against all incoming ballistic missiles. Most military analysts dismiss this kind of defense as a dream, but some, like Wohlstetter, favor SDI for its role as part of a counterforce deterrent against a range of Soviet attacks against Europe as well as the United States. Some Europeans doubt the benefits they are to receive from this modest defense and accept the worst possible interpretation: Reagan came across louder than Wohlstetter, and these Europeans believed that he really wanted and could get his full hard-shell defense for the United States; but they doubted that he was really very interested in getting *them* one. Hence, they saw SDI as part of American decoupling, a retreat to a happy life under the shell, with all wars confined to Europe.

By no means do all Maintainers agree with Wohlstetter on the need for SDI or for "a counterforce deterrent against a range of Soviet attacks;" nor do they agree with Sloss on other effects of the onset of strategic parity. Kaufmann's suggestion that the probability of an American strategic nuclear strike in response to a conventional Soviet attack on Western Europe "has been close to zero for at least twenty-five years" implies that

---

[17]Wohlstetter, 1985–1986, p. 1013.

the shift to parity has been largely irrelevant for NATO deterrence and defense; things have been the same since the 1950s. And Bundy's statement that "What keeps the peace in Europe, then, is the whole range of consequences that aggression would entail"[18] contains no hint that he believes parity has changed that range in any important way.

It does not take existentialism to worry about the European reception of SDI. American opponents have been concerned about its effect on the Alliance. According to Stanford Professors Sydney Drell, Philip Farley, and David Holloway:

> The prospect of revival of ABM deployments thus brings Western Europe not reassurance, but uncertainties and perhaps greater dangers should it come about. In the short-term, American interest in ABM exacerbates other concerns—the American confrontational approach to the Soviet Union, an arms buildup which many see as seeking military superiority and a nuclear war fighting capacity, and a readiness to use military power and a scorn for negotiations and political processes.[19]

European discomfort is neither causal nor central to their case against SDI, but their statement is one of many transatlantic resonances heard among the Maintainers, arguments based on the need to reconcile and soothe our allies to preserve the Alliance. The European version discussed in the previous chapter was the willingness of many Couplers to try to placate the Americans by agreeing, in principle at least, to the need for stronger conventional capabilities, even though these Europeans did not really want to diminish deterrence by decreasing the likelihood of escalation to the nuclear level.

Nor is opposition to SDI among the Maintainers based on resonance alone. James Thomson of RAND questions both the president's and Wohlstetter's versions on military grounds:

> The SDI was supposed to have ushered in a new era, based on a concept of deterrence in which nuclear offensive threats would have played little if any role. . . . In the face of technological uncertainties, and perhaps European political objections, the U.S. administration appears to be scaling back its concept towards (or at least complementing it with) a concept in which the deployed SDI would contribute to deterrence by reducing the vulnerability of critical Western

---

[18]Bundy, 1983, p. 6. This was the article in which Bundy first used the phrase "existential deterrence."

[19]Drell, Farley, and Holloway, 1984, p. 76.

military assets. . . . But at the present time there are many open questions about the feasibility of this concept, as well as about the more ambitious original concept.[20]

How then do Maintainers hope to raise the threshold? Most of the proposals call for increased conventional capabilities discussed below. One set, however, centers on the No-First-Use discussion by Bundy, Kennan, McNamara, and Smith. In spite of the fears their initial article created among many West Europeans, it does fall short of a firm proposal. And the most thoroughly thought through of related proposals—by Morton Halperin, a member of the ten who signed the longer follow-on article but not of the original four—steered around No First Use as such. Halperin stressed instead the complete separation of nuclear "devices" and their stigmatization as being completely inappropriate as weapons of war.[21]

The distance of Halperin's proposal from some current military thinking is illustrated by a contrasting statement in a paper by five U.S. Army analysts writing in the publication of the Army War College:

NATO's conventional and nuclear capabilities are not separate entities, but synergistic components of an effective defense posture. One cannot replace the other and major deficiencies in one cannot be compensated for by improvements in the other.[22]

Although this provides a reasonable description of NATO's current posture, it is a view seldom defended in the explicit debate, particularly among Americans. Central to the argument of those who stress the link and worry about the threshold—virtually all of the Maintainers—is the "firebreak" between conventional and nuclear combat, a different metaphor for what might be termed the threshold with the door closed. A firebreak is a forest space denuded of vegetation so that a fire cannot cross it into the part of the forest that has not been burned; the metaphorical firebreak is to keep a conventional war from jumping the lines and consuming civilization in a general nuclear war.[23]

But for the West Europeans, a better metaphor might be the "fire door" at the threshold; fire doors are not locked, because people might have to escape through them. In this case, the people at greatest risk are the Germans. The American Four recognize German needs and fears as the

---

[20]Thomson, 1986, pp. 20–21.
[21]See Ch. 12.
[22]Sutton et al., 1983, p. 73.
[23]The firebreak concept has existed since nuclear weapons were first discussed publicly. It was formalized by Schelling, 1960, App. A.

322

potential Achilles heel of No First Use and as the key issue to be examined in their proposed study:

> In such an exploration, the role of the Federal Republic of Germany must be central. Americans too easily forget what the people of the Federal Republic never can: that their position is triply exposed in a fashion unique among the large industrial democracies. They do not have nuclear weapons; they share a long common border with the Soviet empire; in any conflict on the central front, their land would be the first battlefield. . . . Having decisively rejected a policy of neutrality, the Federal Republic has necessarily relied on the nuclear protection of the United States, and we Americans should recognize that this relationship is not a favor we are doing our German friends, but the best available solution of a common problem. . . .
>
> A policy of no-first-use would not and should not imply an abandonment of this extraordinary guarantee—only its redefinition. It would still be necessary to be ready to reply with American nuclear weapons to any nuclear attack on the Federal Republic, and this commitment would in itself be sufficiently demanding to constitute a powerful demonstration that a policy of no-first-use would represent no abandonment of our German ally.[24]

Again resonances, undoubtedly heartfelt ones.

Few Maintainers, aside from the ten including Bundy and McNamara who signed the follow-up article, take No First Use very seriously, even as a study proposal. One reason is resonance to the strong negative reaction from European Couplers. Even more important is the unlikelihood of increasing conventional capabilities enough to support it, a need the Four explicitly recognized. No First Use and related proposals, like Halperin's, depend on either an increase of conventional capabilities or an assessment that they are already sufficiently balanced. This is also true for virtually any means of raising the threshold; in order to work, they depend on conventional capabilities—improved, reassessed, or rebalanced through arms control. Without such improvements or reassessments, the Maintainer debate over the link and the threshold, although central, is also rather theoretical, and the five Army officers' description of the synergistic link between conventional and nuclear capabilities will remain an accurate description of current reality.

---

[24]Bundy et al., 1982, pp. 758–759.

Conventional Weapons

Senator Nunn's words, quoted at the head of this chapter, "The reason we need to improve conventional deterrence is that the continued reliance on the early use of nuclear weapons is diametrically opposed to the national security interests of this country and the security interests of our Western European allies," provide the central theme for the Maintainers' consideration of conventional weapons. The better we can defend conventionally, the higher the threshold, the less likely we will be to face the nuclear decision and, indeed, for the Maintainers more unanimously than the European Couplers, the stronger the deterrence of Soviet conventional aggression.

A few Maintainers contend that we are really in pretty good shape even now. Journalist Fred Kaplan sets up the standard view that "the Russians . . . have an overwhelming advantage in conventional weapons," and then goes on to claim disagreement by Kaufmann and others

> who conclude that the view is simply wrong, at least highly exaggerated. "It's one of the great hoary myths of all time," says William Kaufmann. . . . "I'm perfectly willing to say the balance of forces isn't as good as I would like. . . . But it's not nearly as bad as a lot of people say, and the problems that are there aren't that big a deal to fix."[25]

Kaufmann has long been associated with this position. His own highly detailed written analysis, however, was more carefully hedged and indicated what he meant by "problems that . . . aren't that big a deal to fix":

> [The] Pact's ground forces dwarf those of NATO in the number of divisions, tanks, armored fighting vehicles, and artillery pieces. If these numbers are approximately correct, what reasons exist for questioning the ability of the Pact to conquer NATO in a conventional war and to do so with great dispatch? One reason, quite simply, is that what are known as static comparisons, while not irrelevant to a military analysis, are only one factor among the many that must be taken into account. . . . Soviet strategists . . . may have little choice but to seek quick results through blitzkrieg tactics. Certainly the ground forces as presently constituted are not well suited to extended campaigns of offense or defense.[26]

---

[25]Kaplan, 1987, p. 2.
[26]Kaufmann, 1983a, pp. 44–58.

Kaufmann is more upbeat than most of those who assess NATO's ability to resist a conventional attack conventionally. It may be a case of half-full or half-empty, but the more frequent view is that expressed by Senator William Roth (Rep., Del.), co-sponsor of the Nunn Amendment:

> The current status of NATO's conventional defenses insures that, in the event of war, we, the NATO alliance, will be obliged to escalate quickly to the nuclear level. According to General Rogers, such escalation should be conceived in terms of days, not weeks.[27]

Roth's statement does not necessarily contradict Kaufmann's analysis. The military analyst says we need some fixes, but even without them we may well have enough strength to make the Soviets think hard about their prospects at the conventional level, and probably to deter them; the Senator's remarks suggest that without fixes, in a situation where the Warsaw Pact is not deterred and does attack, our conventional defenses are likely to crack quickly.

Both Kaufmann's analysis and the Senate debate stem from the first half of the 1980s, however. The Alliance has not stood still since then, but how much progress has been made is conjectural. Senator Carl Levin (Dem., Mich.), for example, had backed the 1984 Nunn Amendment to force the improvement of NATO conventional defenses; but in 1988, as Chairman of the Subcommittee on Conventional Forces and Alliance Defense, he released a report pointing out the uncertainties surrounding any measurement of conventional strength, and then stated as his own view: "I believe an uneasy conventional balance exists today in Europe." Uneasy as it was, he thought that the balance should suffice to deter Soviet conventional attack.[28]

Even so, the conventional belief about the conventional balance, not necessarily in contradition to Levin's view, is that NATO remains dangerously deficient. Part of the reason lies in the rubber stamp "In this perilous moment in the history of the alliance;" NATO's officials and analysts have *always* felt this way about conventional defense in the years since Lisbon. And part is explained by General Rogers's 1987 statement: "NATO has gotten stronger every year, because of commitments that have been met, but when one looks at the gap between our force capabilities and those of the Soviet Union and the Warsaw Pact, you find that the gap has widened in every area of measurement we have."[29] This throws into question the meaning of "getting stronger," but it describes a standard belief.

---

[27]Roth, 1984, p. S7728.

[28]U.S. Senator Carl Levin press release, announcing his report, *Beyond the Bean Count: Realistically Assessing the Conventional Balance in Europe*, Senate Subcommittee on Conventional Forces and Alliance Defense, Washington, D.C., January 20, 1988.

[29]General Bernard Rogers in conversation with Ian Davidson, transcript of a recorded documentary, British Broadcasting Corporation, London, May 13, 1987a, p. 14.

The primary problem, according to General Rogers is:

> our inability to sustain our forces adequately with trained manpower, ammunition and war reserve materiel. This major deficiency—lack of sustainability—is generally ignored by those persons who maintain that NATO can succeed conventionally. The problem is not that our forces will not perform admirably at the General Defensive Positions (GDP) (if appropriate advantage has been taken of warning times); they will. The problem is that they cannot fight long enough through lack of adequate sustainment.[30]

In recent years at least, lack of sustainability has been widely perceived as NATO's greatest weakness. Greater allied contributions to sustainability by increasing the stock of munitions available was the first of the two substantive demands of the Nunn Amendment (in addition to the financial demand of annual increases in defense spending, the burden-sharing issue, which will be discussed below). The second demand was for greater European support for U.S. tactical air reinforcement. Were the two not achieved according to numerical criteria specified in the Amendment, 90,000 U.S. troops (somewhat less than one-third of the total) were to be withdrawn from Europe in three annual increments.[31]

In addition to these enforceable requirements, the bill listed as specific needs to fill specific gaps in conventional capabilities: improvements in air base defenses; increased trained manpower levels, particularly reserves; increasing war reserve material; improvements in mine/countermine capability; and improvements in offensive counter air capability.[32] The amendment did not pass. It came close, but Senator Nunn did not press it after 1984. Three years later, he reported some improvement, but remained an armed agnostic:

> Although signs of progress in this area are encouraging, we must recognize that much remains to be done if NATO is actually to meet the goals it has set for itself. NATO has less than a superb record in following through on its force commitments, so I am in a sense still watching and waiting to see if my amendment should remain on the shelf.[33]

---

[30]Rogers, 1986, p. 6.
[31]The Nunn Amendment, *Congressional Record, Senate*, June 20, 1984, p. S7721.
[32]Ibid.
[33]Nunn, 1987, p. 7.

Each authority has his own set of NATO shortfalls, each time frame has its own. Kaufmann's come close to those of the Nunn Amendment,[34] as do those of three retired officers and one civilian expert who provided specific proposals in 1985 for a European Security Study sponsored by the American Academy of Arts and Sciences.[35] A year later, Washington analyst Philip Karber termed "marginal" with an "ominous trend" NATO's anti-armor capabilities and its ability to strike deep à la FOFA.[36] In 1987, Anthony Cordesman of the *Armed Forces Journal* paralleled Karber on NATO anti-armor deficiencies and long-distance strike capability, but also listed: maldeployment among national sectors on the central front; air and tactical missile defense capability; naval forces and anti-submarine warfare; lines of communication, logistics, munitions, and war reserves (although reporting recent progress); and C^3I.[37] And Reagan Defense Secretary Weinberger chose to stress the "disadvantage in the capability to generate adequately trained and equipped reserves quickly to stop a Warsaw Pact breakthrough along the East-West Border."[38]

Underlying it all is a general belief among Maintainers that it certainly would be nice to move a little way toward matching Warsaw Pact *numbers* in manpower and weapons, but that it simply is not going to happen. Thomson quotes another analyst: "Andrew Hamilton provides a rationale for an additional 20–45 equivalent heavy combat divisions which are stronger divisions than the average NATO division today,"[39] and without endorsing anything that substantial, then goes on to set aside the possibility for any such change: "In any case, conventional deterrence would require substantial force growth. That simply is not in the cards."[40] Thomson's own modest recommendations stress improvements in the NATO planning process as being at least as important as many of the proposed substantive fixes.

The point is not the disagreements among the officials and analysts; there is rather more agreement on specific deficiencies than one might expect. Rather, what is important here is the strong consensus that several things are wrong, and at least some of them must be fixed if we are to mount a conventional defense that is either going to stymie Warsaw Pact aggression or raise the threshold for the decision to go nuclear. The consensus includes such optimists as Kaufmann and Senator Levin.

[34]Kaufmann, 1983a, pp. 44–58.
[35]Goodpaster et al., 1985, pp. xv-xvi. Although both the overall group and the panel of experts are European-American, the study comes up in the Maintainer section because it was American-sponsored.
[36]Karber, 1986, p. 16.
[37]Cordesman, 1988.
[38]Weinberger, 1987, Part V, p. 5.
[39]From Hamilton, 1985.
[40]Thomson, 1986, p. 21.

If major conventional improvements are not in the cards, one reason lies in the questions: How much will it cost to fix these things? Will such sums be forthcoming? Who is to pay? Like the needs, these are classical issues dating back to Lisbon. The debate over burden-sharing will be discussed in the section on the U.S. Commitment. As for "How much?" the Nunn Amendment demanded a 3 percent per year increase, which was the ante agreed to by the NATO membership under Carter administration prodding in 1977, but hardly adhered to religiously thereafter. In 1982, General Rogers upped it a bit, asking a 4 percent increase per year for six years.[41]

The Nunn requirement can be estimated at slightly below $10 billion a year, the Rogers request at slightly more than $10 billion.[42] Other proposals for other packages price out at anywhere from $5 to $20 billion. None of these costing efforts is very meaningful, however. When Carter and Nunn's 3 percent a year has been reached only sporadically, and Rogers's 4 percent not at all, there seems little reason to expend major efforts to price out what is really needed. *The Alliance has known about and debated its deficiencies for 35 years, and for that length of time it has estimated what it would cost to fill the deficiencies, and neither the debates nor the estimates have been taken seriously enough for anyone to put up a major portion of the funds.*

Nor does any Maintainer believe that substantial increases are more likely now than in the past. Thomson's appraisal of why "it is not in the cards," in his words, would receive little dissent:

> The money and manpower will not be available, especially in Europe, which would have to contribute the lion's share of the resources needed for conventional deterrence. Although NATO nations reportedly did better in meeting the 3 percent real growth goal in 1984 than in the previous few years, the long-term trend in Europe is toward tighter defence budgets, including in Britain and Germany, the European countries with the largest defence efforts. . . . Prospects are slim to zero that Europe's continued economic stagnation will be ended by an extended period of great economic growth that would permit decisive increases in defence efforts. In any case, the second factor would militate against the defence sector becoming the beneficiary of economic gains. Despite all the efforts of the United States and of their own political leaders to "educate" them, European publics do not feel an imminent threat to their survival. Only an extended

---

[41]Rogers, 1982, p. 1155.

[42]This is based on Kaufmann's estimate of total NATO spending of $263.2 billion a year (Kaufmann, 1983, p. 79), raised to $300 billion for subsequent inflation.

period of substantially increased East-West tensions, clearly the fault of the USSR, is likely to change the situation.[43]

Since then, the Gramm-Rudman budget limitations have closed down what little chance there might have been of "decisive increases" on the part of the United States, Europe has not begun an "extended period of economic growth," and treaties, summits, negotiations, and unilateral drawdowns have all led in the direction precisely opposite of any "extended period of substantial East-West tensions."

Lacking the political or economic support to move straight ahead toward substantially stronger conventional capabilities, the Maintainers have been increasingly attracted to the technological and strategic devices that many European Couplers have questioned. They are also questioned by some Maintainers, but the support-to-skepticism ratio is higher west of the Atlantic. The debate over strategic expedients has a history going back almost as far as the other issues raised by the conventional balance; even the technological fixes have been discussed for nearly twenty years.

Richard DeLauer, former Under Secretary of Defense for Research and Engineering, believes that the time has come for the "emerging technologies" to play a major role in righting the conventional balance:

The new technologies have . . . now reached the point where their insertion into the military inventory of the NATO forces is readily at hand. It is only by the vigorous pursuit of these technologies and the related advanced warfare concepts that the Alliance can be expected to overcome the vast numerical superiority enjoyed by the Warsaw Pact forces.[44]

The enthusiasm is not limited to DeLauer, who had an official and professional responsibility for introducing the new technologies into the U.S. defense establishment. With the exception of Kaufmann, each of the authorities quoted above on the deficiencies of NATO's conventional capabilities included the new technologies as an important part of the solution; for the four experts of the European Security Study, and for Cordesman, the technological possibilities were central.

Washington defense analyst and former Army officer Steven Canby, however, expresses deep doubts about the new technologies, going far beyond the issues of timing and net contribution expressed by the European skeptics and some Maintainers as well:

---

[43]Thomson, 1986, pp. 21–23.
[44]DeLauer, 1986, pp. 42–44.

America's weapons have become too costly and too difficult to maintain because of systemic problems in the way they are designed and procured. Many are militarily questionable. . . . America designs its weapons for engineers and the Soviets design theirs for soldiers. . . . Our defense establishment is so fascinated by technology and one-on-one duels that it loses sight of real combat, and often of the laws of physics. Too many of our new systems are overrefined and unable to operate against adaptive opponents in unpredictable environments— the conditions that make war as much art as science.[45]

Canby mounts a heavy attack on SHAPE's FOFA strategy. The strategy itself is described by Sutton, Landry, Armstrong, Estes, and Clark (the five Army analysts quoted above with regard to conventional-nuclear force integration):

The SHAPE concept seeks to locate and track Warsaw Pact forces during their entire process of deployment, from garrison to battlefield commitment, and to attack them when and where they are most vulnerable. The concept aims at exploiting particularly critical enemy vulnerabilities in the reinforcement process, the rigidity of his planning for an echeloned offense, the density of forces along limited attack routes, and critical transportation facilities.[46]

Canby attacks it from all directions:

Emerging technologies applied to the deep attack of Follow-on Forces (FOFA) *cannot* be effective, in principle or practice. FOFA is a concept beyond the capabilities of technology. Its infeasibility transcends the many limitations of the specific equipment proposed. It is necessarily a preprogrammed, deterministic system. Such systems cannot operate in uncongenial, adaptive and unpredictable environments. . . .

[T]he new technologies fail on four counts: Technology can be a trap; The Soviet operational method has been incorrectly analysed; Technical and operational feasibility are not synonymous; Counter-measures exist. . . .

The concept rests on a survivable *"top-down"* command, control and communications system, plus *detailed pre-planning* and *timing* of reinforcements. . . .

[45]Canby, 1985a, p. 5.
[46]Sutton et al., 1983, p. 65.

For the deep attack technologies, five problems exist: Cost; Equipment Reliability; Equipment vulnerability; System complexity; Flawed logic.[47]

It seems probable that Canby's strictures would extend slightly less strongly to the Army's AirLand Battle, which the five Army analysts compare to SHAPE's FOFA. Both are "deep battle" concepts, depending on air strikes well behind the immediate area of ground combat, but AirLand Battle is less "top-down" than FOFA and might thus meet Canby's objections better:

> AirLand Battle thrives on the early allocation of airpower to support the ground commander, a process which reduces the extent of centralized control and application; the SHAPE concept, however, plans for more traditional use of airpower through centralized air allocation and application theater-wide.[48]

Jonathan Dean points out that AirLand "could involve use of nuclear as well as conventional weapons in strikes deep into Warsaw Pact territory in response to Pact attack," and therefore terms FOFA "less far-reaching." He also says that although FOFA calls for initial conventional deep strikes, "for the most part, their intended range would be considerably less than in the Air-Land Battle concept—100 kilometers or less."[49] In any case, Dean opposes both strategies: "Although they may be conceived by their supporters as a purely defensive response to possible Warsaw Pact attack, if deployed in large numbers, these weapons can be used for attack."[50]

The third in the triad of deep strategies is the "counteroffensive" of Samuel Huntington, Director of the Harvard Center for International Affairs. This differs from the other two in that it contemplates a distinct ground offensive against the East, with objectives that are more political than the other two purely military designs, and with the explicit intent to threaten the Soviets' East European bloc.

> A strategy of conventional retaliation in the form of a prompt offensive into Eastern Europe would help to deter Soviet military action against Western Europe. . . . The logical extension of the forward defense concept is to move the locus of battle eastward into East Germany and Czechoslovakia. . . . To date the Soviets have been free to concentrate all their planning and forces on retaliatory moves into

---

[47]Canby, 1985b, pp. 7–13.
[48]Sutton et al., 1983, p. 76.
[49]Dean, 1987b, pp. 63–64.
[50]Ibid., p. 66.

West Germany. A Western retaliatory strategy would compel them to reallocate forces and resources to the defense of their satellites and thus to weaken their offensive thrust.[51]

As has been discussed, the Huntington concept upsets many European Couplers on political grounds. Keith Dunn of the U.S. National Defense University and William Staudenmaier of the Army War College object to the strategy on military grounds as well:

> Whether considered in terms of suitability, feasibility, flexibility or acceptability, the concept of a conventional retaliatory offensive does not appear to offer a credible alternative to NATO's current strategy. As a war-fighting strategy it is unsuitable because it does not provide a decisive use of military force. . . . Nor is it feasible. . . . [By] neglecting to account for the Soviet second strategic echelon, it woefully underestimates the allied force required to implement it. . . . In terms of flexibility, the concept depends on the Warsaw Pact to launch its invasion in a specific way that will play into NATO's hands.[52]

This is followed by a summary paragraph quoted, with emphasis, by General Rogers, the progenitor of the FOFA alternative, himself:

> Besides, and possibly most importantly, if NATO were able to adopt all the force structure changes [to which this SACEUR would add "and sustainability needs"] that would be required to make the retaliatory strategy work, there would be no need to change NATO's strategy. Defence and deterrence would be ensured without the need to endorse a politically and operationally risky course.[53]

In sum, each of the three forward strategies has its advocates among the Maintainers, and each receives far more detailed military analysis than among the Couplers; but none commands a consensus. In case NATO's conventional defenses were actually called upon to resist a Pact attack, elements of FOFA in particular would probably be used, but in their current and prospective states, none of the three alternatives is viewed by any of the debaters as close to a complete substitute for the current strategy or even a major strategic change. Nor does a consensus view the emerging technologies themselves as bases for such a change, although these do have their strong advocates.

---

[51]Huntington, 1982, pp. 21–23.
[52]Dunn and Staudenmaier, 1985, p. 116.
[53]Rogers, 1986, p. 14.

332

The other end of the strategic spectrum, "Defensive Defense," has not been taken very seriously by the Maintainers. General Rogers disposes of it quickly:

> The concept is beset with inadequacies: it would leave the West vulnerable to blackmail from the threat of overwhelming conventional force, to say nothing of the nuclear threat; the concept provides no convincing deterrent to aggression; and it could take effect primarily after NATO territory had been occupied. Finally, this concept, with no means of ejecting the enemy from NATO territory, is void of hope for our people.... Once in possession of NATO territory, it is unlikely that the Soviet Union could be persuaded to leave by the very limited range of offensive options offered by the type of forces associated with this concept.[54]

And Thomson relates it to another concept in a way calculated to make both sides of the pair quite uncomfortable:

> All the suggested alternatives [to current NATO strategy] have greater military, technical or financial problems than the current concept. This includes some of the most recent popular notions, whether they be strategic defenses or their intellectual brother—"defensive defenses."[55]

Nonetheless, under arms control and budget pressures, American Maintainers, like European Couplers, have begun to take defensive defense more seriously.

What the conventional force debate comes down to in concept is that all the Maintainers stress a need for greater capabilities if the threshold is to be raised (and almost all are anxious to raise it); they recognize the economic and related constraints that make straight-line increases impossible; some see a way out through more or less radical fixes; but no such fix commands a consensus and perhaps not a majority. And their Coupler partners on the other side of the Atlantic are much less interested anyhow.

All of the Maintainers' conventional debate thus far examined, just as virtually all of the Couplers' parallel debate, concerns the Central front. The Americans, although sometimes concerned with the role of the Northern flank in protecting the sea lanes to central Europe, seldom bring it into explicit discussion, although Norwegian Defense Minister and analyst Holst does get at least as much attention in the United States as in central Europe.

---

[54]Ibid., p. 13.
[55]Thomson, 1987, p. 3.

One brief analysis of issues both north and south has been presented by Karber. His general conclusion about the importance of the Northern flank to NATO as a whole parallels Holst's:

> A successful defence in the North is a prerequisite for NATO's conventional prospects in the Centre. This area is more than a flank. It is the guardian of Europe's link to American reinforcement and supply.[56]

And he provides an upbeat analysis of the Norwegian and allied efforts in that country but contrasts it with the southern part of the Northern flank, where Danish efforts are weak and German defenses are diluted by other demands on both naval and land forces.[57]

So far as the Southern flank is concerned, he suggests that it too is primarily a naval problem, with the issues here being as much political as military, stressing particularly the problems raised by the Greek-Turkish dispute.[58] These views, presented at the IISS annual meeting of 1985, were generally confirmed at the 1987 annual meeting in Barcelona, the theme of which was the Mediterranean. In spite of all the political and other problems, however, Robert O'Neill's conference summary reported that: "The most important single observation of [the committee on Mediterranean security] was that the balance of forces between NATO and the Warsaw Pact in the Mediterranean favoured the West."[59]

The military issues on both flanks resemble watery reproductions of the issues on the Central front, but they demand much less attention. The political problems on the Southern flank are unique to that area. What they share with the rest of NATO, however, is that the political issues may well overwhelm military needs and strategies.

ALLIANCE POLITICAL ISSUES

The U.S. Commitment

Journalist Drew Middleton, long-since retired as military columnist for the *New York Times*, wrote in 1987:

---

[56]Karber, 1986, p. 16.
[57]Ibid., pp. 18–19.
[58]Ibid., p. 21.
[59]O'Neill, 1988, p. 67.

Should the United States lose Central America or the Middle East, military survival would be difficult but far from impossible. The loss of NATO Europe, on the other hand, would leave America virtually without powerful allies and the many billions of dollars invested in the area.[60]

This is the old-time religion. It reflects Dean Acheson's 1959 "The most important objective today . . . is to hold together those sources of strength we possess. These sources are North America and Western Europe." It is present in full evangelical strength in Senator Nunn's 1984 "we want to be part of NATO . . . we are going to continue to be part of NATO" no matter what our European allies do, quoted at the head of this analysis of the Maintainers. It underlies the cautions expressed by many Maintainers, exemplified by former Defense Secretary Schlesinger's "Therefore, all of our public comments should be carefully gauged according to the realization that the fundamental defense of Western freedom lies in preserving the cohesion of the alliance."[61]

This section examines the Maintainers' restatement of the U.S. commitment to NATO and the reasons for it, the resonance of their views as they reflect and try to calm West European fears, "burden-sharing" as a core issue, and various Maintainer proposals for restructuring the Alliance and the American role in order to preserve both.

In spite of the fears of many European Couplers, the importance and the preservation of the Alliance remain the central tenets of the Maintainers, and the Maintainers remain very much the majority of American debaters and American voters.[62] One underlying reason for this devotion is suggested by Schlesinger: "Europeans are, in the view of Americans, good people; thus they are deserving of our protection. That protection does not arise out of a sense of Realpolitik."[63]

Empathy does not make a strong political case for the spending of hundreds of billions of dollars, however, so former Ambassador to West Germany Richard Burt continued to depend on Realpolitik in his defense against both the Removers and those Maintainers who want to reduce the size of American forces in NATO:

They are wrong. Maintaining a free, independent and democratic Western Europe remains the pre-eminent strategic interest of the United States. In global terms, the loss of Western Europe would be

[60]Middleton, 1987, p. 28.
[61]J. Schlesinger, 1984, p. S7745.
[62]Surveys show that about two-thirds of the American electorate support NATO. The residual included "undecideds" as well as opponents.
[63]J. Schlesinger, 1984, p. S7748.

as significant as the Chinese-Soviet split—with America on the losing end.[64]

Even though the Nunn Amendment did not pass, the 1984 debate marked a trough in support for NATO. A few years later, the Congressional commitment seemed stronger. In December of 1986, NATO Ambassador Abshire reported that:

> The good news for NATO is that a new partnership has been formed with the Congress—after some Americans in the past had lost patience with the Europeans never coming to grips with conventional defense improvement. The new pro-NATO network feels that a new attitude at NATO and in the European capitals has emerged, built not only around the old-fashioned approach to arms cooperation of a two-way street, but on a new coalition approach toward better return on defense expenditures.[65]

And in 1987, Senator Nunn, the leader among Americans who in Abshire's phrase "had lost patience," used a few words quoted above to express conditional satisfaction with NATO efforts since his 1984 amendment nearly passed: "signs of progress . . . are encouraging . . . much remains to be done. . . . NATO has less than a superb record in following through." On the other side of Capitol Hill, the House of Representatives passed a resolution in the spring of 1987 opposing reduction of U.S. troop levels in NATO.

This new warmth undoubtedly stemmed in part from increased European efforts, although, as suggested by Nunn, they still had a very long way to go in 1987. Nonetheless, it may seem paradoxical that while Reykjavik and zero-zero raised West European fears of American abandonment to a crescendo, American Maintainers appeared surer of the U.S. commitment than they had for some time.

Rather than paradox, it is cause and effect. Because the Maintainers place the preservation of NATO near the top of their list of priorities, they respond rapidly in resonance to West European views that seem to threaten the Alliance: *It is in the American interest to preserve the Alliance; therefore it is in the American interest to satisfy the European interests in the Alliance.*

Georgetown University Professor Stephen Wrage, for example, resonated with the Europeans against the Reagan administration:

[64]Burt, 1987, p. 6.
[65]Abshire, 1986, p. 23.

Our actions set off the debate, yet now we are ignoring it. To the Reagan administration, Europeans' concerns are inconvenient obstacles in the drive toward and agreement with the Soviets. Reagan's advisers calculate that any agreement, no matter what its consequences for NATO, would be a foreign-policy triumph that would put the Iran-*Contra* debacle behind them and help them finish strong.[66]

And Schlesinger, having served in the cabinet under both parties, was in a position to resonate even more broadly: "Europeans, quite understandably, have been irritated by what appeared to be the erratic weakness of Jimmy Carter, and they have been almost equally irritated by what appeared to be the erratic strength of President Reagan."[67] And even traditional conservative eminence William Buckley took a stand 180 degrees away from neoconservatives Kristol and Krauss. They had turned from Europe, he still resonated:

So Secretary of State George Shultz told the NATO commander-in-chief to shut up about his objections to the INF agreement. . . . What General Rogers said . . . was that the projected swap means, very simply, that our deterrent force in Europe is weakened. . . . That [leaves] us to contemplate this single point implicit in the projected deal, namely that its purpose is not military but political, and that the advantages to be gained politically outweigh those lost militarily. On this point, General Rogers . . . tells us that many European leaders ruefully regret the treaty to which they are now committed but that they are "hoist on their own petard." . . . Our allies are left in a bind, and it is dismaying to contemplate with such icy detachment that, in the current controversy, Secretary Shultz is Neville Chamberlain, General Rogers, Winston Churchill.[68]

Buckley does not supply a 1930s analog for Ronald Reagan.[69]

Like Schlesinger's "Europeans . . . are good people," resonance has its limits as a prop for policy. The major limit in the United States is the feeling on the part of many Americans that the West Europeans are letting us pay for their defense, either refusing to carry their share or at least not volunteering to do so as long as "Uncle Sam" (an isolationist epithet from before World War II) is willing to pay it all. Although Senator Nunn avoided this theme in the Senate debate over his amendment, stressing instead the need to reinforce conventional capabilities to raise the threshold, many of his colleagues focused on

---

[66]Wrage, 1987, p. 5.
[67]J. Schlesinger, 1984, p. S7749.
[68]Buckley, 1987, p. 56.
[69]Edward VIII?

"burden-sharing." Senator Levin, for example, used several measures to estimate European contributions to the common defense:

> Despite their 1977 commitment to increase defense spending annually by 3 percent after excluding inflation [sic], our NATO allies had an average 2.8-percent increase in real growth in their defense budgets in 1981. In 1982, that average went down to 2.3 percent real growth. In 1983 it declined to about 2 percent real growth. In 1984, it is tentatively projected that the average real growth for non-United States NATO nations will be only between 1.2 and 1.7 percent. . . .

> On a per capita basis, the United States far exceeds all its allies in defense spending. We spent $819 per American citizen in 1982; . . . our nearest ally—financially—was the United Kingdom, which spend $467 per capita. . . . In 1982, we spent 6.5 percent of our GDP [Gross Domestic Product] on defense. Other economically strong allies spending far less were West Germany—3.4 percent; the Netherlands—3.2 percent; Norway—3 percent; Denmark—2.5 percent; and Canada—2.1 percent.[70]

Nunn's tentative agreement that at least they're beginning to try became more typical in subsequent years. Nonetheless, in 1987 Congresswoman Patricia Schroeder (Dem., Colo.) offered a bill similar to the Nunn Amendment, putting it into the context of the balance-of-payments deficit, which had become a major issue by that year:

> Of the $300 billion the United States spends on defense, something more than half, say, $150 billion, goes for NATO obligations. Our trade deficit is running at about $175 billion a year. What we are spending to protect our allies is about the same amount by which we are losing the trade war.[71]

Schroeder's effort was taken less seriously than Nunn's because she lacked both his authority as senior Senate Democrat on defense and his acknowledged expertise. And more generally, in spite of the trade problems of the late 1980s, post-Reykjavik resonance made the American burden-sharing attack much weaker in 1987 than in 1984. General Rogers, for example, without giving up his exhortation for more Alliance conventional support all around, told an interviewer in 1987:

---

[70]Levin, 1984, pp. S7768-S7770.
[71]Schroeder, 1987, p. 4.

The fact is that those nations in Western Europe within this alliance are not getting a just credit for the amount of the burden they do share. . . . On average . . . I find that the Western European nations are bearing a fair share of the collective security burden but the fact is, if we wish peace with freedom, we're going to have to spend more. And I can tell you, if we accept these agreements . . . go to both zero, zero, zero, zero, levels, there's a major cost associated with that.[72]

Perhaps the best-hedged statement on burden-sharing is that presented by *New Republic* editor Morton Kondracke:

The burden-sharing movement could lead to a stronger set of alliances and a stronger U.S. economy—if conventional forces are built up on our side or the Soviets can be induced to reduce theirs, and if Japan can be induced to spend its surpluses on economic development.[73] This will require sophisticated diplomacy on the part of the United States. Unjudicious ally-bashing, however, will only help Mikhail Gorbachev separate the United States from its friends.[74]

For the short run, this might well command a substantial consensus among the Maintainers, at least in their less cantankerous and political moments. Over a longer period, however, the bottom line may be that put forth by economist Charles Cooper, who was the Ford administration's Assistant Secretary of the Treasury for International Affairs. Cooper reflects that after the administration coming to power in 1989 has shaken down, a reduction of the U.S. commitment to NATO "seems to me almost inevitable. Some forty years on, the status quo in Europe looks increasingly anachronistic and unstable as U.S. worldwide and strategic commitments outstrip U.S. capacity to sustain them."[75]

The longer-run burden-sharing issue is also one of the roots of several proposals for a much more thoroughgoing restructuring of NATO, eventuating in a lesser American role. Two similar ones, from Carter administration National Security Advisor Brzezinski and Nixon-Ford administration Secretary of State Kissinger, have been taken very seriously in Europe—as a threat. They have been taken somewhat less seriously in the United States.

---

[72]"Rogers, 1987a, p. 9.

[73]The Japan theme frequently and the Third World economic development theme occasionally have appeared in the burden-sharing debates analyzed here, but they have been excluded from the analysis because they would take it off on tangents leading away from the NATO debate as such. Another irony of 1987 was that fear of a transatlantic trade war was muted somewhat when both sides of NATO joined in Japan-bashing.

[74]Kondracke, 1987, p. 17.

[75]Personal communication.

Although some West Europeans lump these two proposals together with the Withdrawers' efforts to get out of NATO entirely, and also with Senator Nunn's pressures for the Alliance to live up to its stated commitments and strategies, Brzezinski and Kissinger, Kristol and Krauss, and Nunn really suggested three quite different directions. Some similarities do exist: the Brzezinski and Kissinger proposals, like Kristol's and Krauss's to get out, are based in part on the belief that the European members of NATO are not carrying their fair share of either the burdens or the responsibilities of an Alliance that was conceived under vastly different economic and political circumstances. And, like Nunn, Brzezinksi and Kissinger are concerned about the U.S. nuclear deterrent, although perhaps more with the possibility that the American commitment is no longer sufficiently credible, and cannot be made credible, than with the Senator's fear that the threshold is too low.

But the two former executive policymakers differ from the Withdrawers in that they want a continued strong American commitment, conventional and nuclear, to Western Europe; and they differ from Nunn in that they want to restructure fundamentally rather than improve within the current apparatus.

In his 1986 book, Brzezinski started out sounding rather like the Withdrawers, but ended up quite differently:

> It is clear that the allocations for the defense of Western Europe represent a massively disproportionate share of the overall U.S. military budget. . . . These unbalanced global deployments have more to do with history than with strategy. They reflect neither the actual estimates of the Soviet military threat nor a measure of each area's relative geopolitical importance. . . .

> Until and unless the European members of NATO are prepared to raise and maintain enough conventional forces to fight those of the Soviet Union to a standstill, the U.S. strategic deterrent and the U.S. front-line forces that would become immediately engaged in combat remain a vital component of the overall Western effort to deter war in Europe.

> Undoubtedly, some Europeans will claim that any redeployment of any U.S. troops will weaken U.S. defenses . . . [but a] gradual reduction of approximately 100,000 troops would . . . free U.S. budgetary and manpower resources for the flexibility needed to respond to other geostrategic threats.[76]

And a year later, he made the strength of the commitment to NATO within his reduction proposal even more explicit:

_____
[76]Brzezinski, 1986b, pp. 171–181.

340

The U.S. commitment to the defense of Europe will remain as strong as ever strategically and politically, given the fact that large U.S. forces will continue to be deployed in Europe, even with some reductions. Moreover, the U.S. nuclear guarantee will also continue to provide a clear demonstration of that enduring commitment. In brief, in the years ahead U.S. and European security should and will remain organically insoluble and strategically coupled.[77]

Brzezinski's book is an analysis of the U.S. worldwide objectives and strategy. Kissinger's proposal focuses more specifically on NATO and is more detailed in both its analysis and its proposals. He first discussed it in 1979, and later laid it out systematically in a 1984 article in *Time* magazine:

Existing arrangements are unbalanced. When one country dominates the alliance on all major issues little incentive remains for a serious joint effort to redefine the requirements of security or to coordinate foreign policies. . . . An imbalance such as the one now existing cannot be corrected by "consultation," no matter how meticulous. . . . Those who governed Europe in the early postwar years were still psychologically of the era when Europe bestrode the world. . . . The new leaders were reared in an era when the U.S. was pre-eminent; they find it politically convenient to delegate Europe's military defense to us. . . . The change in the nature of European leadership has been paralleled in the U.S. Our new elites do not reject NATO any more than do their European counterparts. But for them, too, the alliance is more a practical than an emotional necessity, more a military arrangement than a set of common political purposes. . . .

A continuation of existing trends is bound to lead to the demoralization of the Western alliance. An explicit act of statesmanship is needed to give new meaning to Western unity and a new vitality to NATO.

Kissinger's proposed program includes European assumption of "the major responsibility for ground defense"; switching of the jobs of NATO Secretary-General and Supreme Allied Commander so that the political job of Secretary-General would become an American one whereas SACEUR would be a European; European responsibility for "arms control negotiations dealing with weapons stationed on European soil;" and redeployment of some, but by no means all, American ground forces to U.S. soil.[78]

---

[77]Brzezinski, 1988.
[78]Kissinger, 1984, pp. 20–23.

Whatever the perceptions of some European Couplers, Kissinger, like Brzezinski, is far from advocating any sort of withdrawal from NATO. Indeed, in Kissinger's case there is some irony in the fact that three years after his *Time* piece, when he feared that something rather less radical than his proposals—the zero-zero INF agreement—was about to hit NATO, he sounded all the alarms. In an article questioning zero-zero, written with former President Nixon, they warned that "If we strike the wrong kind of deal, we could create the most profound crisis of the North Atlantic Treaty Organization alliance in its 40-year history."[79] Of Kissinger's devotion to NATO there can be no doubt.

Not that the restructuring proposals go uncriticized by other Maintainers. An unspoken criticism is implicit in the fact that proposals by such eminent, experienced, and responsible people as Brzezinski and Kissinger are not widely discussed. They are feared by Couplers, but not discussed in detail in Europe; for better or worse, most American Maintainer officials and analysts have ignored them in favor of the immediate tasks and crises.

New York Times columnist Flora Lewis provides a summary that could be the last word in this particular variation of the structural controversy. In contrast to Kissinger's mourning "the change in the nature of European leadership" and parallel American leadership, she quotes retiring NATO Secretary General Lord Carrington, and goes on from there:

> "I am of the World War II generation. . . . [T]he next secretary general should be of the postwar generation." The observation goes beyond personalities to the heart of NATO's problems, reflected in an unusual outpouring of proposals from both Americans and Europeans for drastic change in the structure of the alliance. Practically all of the suggestions, from people such as Henry Kissinger, Zbigniew Brzezinski, former French President Valéry Giscard d'Estaing and former German Chancellor Helmut Schmidt, as well as less famous figures, are impractical, unreasonable, even outrageous. . . . NATO is not out of date. Nor is the organization and operation of the alliance. The conditions that led to its formation have not disappeared, and none of the ideas for structural change would improve it or probably work as well. What it needs is stimulation to thought and curiosity. What it gets from Western leaders is old rhetoric.[80]

The Maintainers share an unease about the state of the Alliance, although not necessarily an unease that goes beyond "this perilous moment in the

---

[79]Nixon and Kissinger, 1987, p. 1.
[80]Flora Lewis, 1987a, p. 19.

history of the alliance." They share no common analysis of causes or solutions. *But what the American Maintainers all do continue to share—which the European Couplers continue to doubt—is a firm commitment to American assistance in the defense of Western Europe.*

The Europeans' Commitments to Themselves

Most Americans skirt the question of closer ties among the European members of NATO, treating it as a matter for Europeans, within the overall issues of the U.S. commitment and the structure of the Alliance as a whole. Most Maintainers would welcome a shoring up of the "European pillar," some doubt the possibilities, and a few believe that creation of a truly European structure would strengthen the entire Alliance. Brzezinski and Kissinger fall into the last group; stronger European organization is necessary for the greater responsibilities they would like the West Europeans to assume.

Columnist Lewis expresses a typical Maintainer view. She observes "new talk about more defense cooperation among Europeans. This is all to the good, especially because there is little chance of an increase in conventional European defense."[81] General Rogers hopes for that conventional increase, but otherwise he comes out in about the same place:

> [T]he West Europeans have realized that they must take a greater interest in their own defence—try to keep the strategic nuclear umbrella of the United States tied to the security of Western Europe, but to do more to strengthen the West European pillar of the Trans-Atlantic bridge, and I think that's a good thing. And you see that in the WEU [West European Union]—you'll see it in the Euro-group, and you'll see it just in the bilateral meetings . . . between France and Germany and between France and the United Kingdom, and I think that's a good thing because all of that is contributory to a credible deterrent for NATO. . . . I don't think it's necessarily a divergence of interest. . . . But I do think that [Reykjavik] had a sort of an alarm clock effect here in Western Europe, it rang a few bells and made them think, you know we're going to have to do more for ourselves.[82]

Like the Couplers, most Americans focus on the Franco-German relationship. Analytically a few are upbeat. After interviewing Helmut Schmidt, Joan Bingham of the Atlantic Institute presented her own hopes:

---

[81]Flora Lewis, 1987b, p. 27.
[82]Rogers, 1987a, p. 12.

343

The "German question" sends tremors through the Elysée. The French fear German dreams of reunification will lead to neutralism. The time is ripe for a new unified defense system such as Helmut Schmidt described or another configuration with a Franco-German nucleus. As it is unthinkable that France would agree to be militarily reintegrated in NATO, this new entity would give her a chance for a dominant leadership role in Europe. Always suspicious of the Anglo-Saxon, de Gaulle would have applauded. A new American administration should welcome any strengthening of the European pillar of the Atlantic Alliance even if it should be outside U.S. military command.[83]

But columnist William Pfaff, himself an advocate in the Brzezinski and Kissinger mode of "a necessary reassessment of burdens and responsibilities in the alliance," is nonetheless skeptical about the prospects. Also having interviewed Schmidt, he says of Schmidt's proposal for a Franco-German alliance with a Frenchman in command:

The Schmidt argument that France and West Germany should combine to look after the defense of Europe is tenable as a military proposition. Is anyone going to do anything about it? The French might. The West Germans won't. At least they show no sign, thus far, of doing anything like this, or even of very seriously considering it.[84]

This assessment was made after the leaders of the Federal Republic had begun to squirm under the pressures of the imminent zero-zero agreement.

Particularly since zero-zero became real, West European cooperation has become of interest to several American newspaper columnists. Ernest Conine of the *Los Angeles Times* foresees an eventual separation of Europe from the United States. (He is not, however, a Withdrawer, anxious for it to come about. He just sees it coming as the result of existing trends.)

[T]here is a distinct feeling of unease among European political leaders and defense professionals, as well as among those with pacifist inclinations. The unease has several roots. For many young Germans it stems from an active dislike of the United States and a growing conviction that West Germany does not control its own destiny. Fundamentally pro-alliance leaders resent the fact that Western Europe's political influence has not grown in proportion to its economic strength, and they know it won't as long as Europe depends so heavily on the United States for its security. Perhaps most

[83]Bingham, 1987, p. 3.
[84]Pfaff, 1987, p. 6.

important, there is a loss of faith in the quality of American leadership. There is also concern, nourished by recent U.S.-Soviet negotiations on arms control, that America has begun a process of nuclear disengagement from Europe.

The bottom-line reality . . . is that present arrangements are no longer consistent with economic and political realities—including the fact that an economically strapped America may soon feel compelled to reduce its commitments to Europe for the simple reason that it can no longer afford them.[85]

Conine's reading of "European political leaders and defense professionals" is rather like French publisher Jimmy Goldsmith's reading of Americans ranging from Kristol to Nunn, and indeed setting Goldsmith's March 1987 column alongside Conine's July piece provides another example of resonance, moving in the opposite direction from the attempts on both sides of the Atlantic to bolster one another. The reverse resonance can be seen in the mutual reading of negative experts on each side, advocating separation in part because of fears of the other side advocating it. Conine's observation that the West Europeans are concerned "that America has begun a process of nuclear disengagement from Europe" provides an example of his reading of the European reading of an American movement—which most American Maintainers would contend is not taking place.

Conine does not believe that anything is going to happen soon. His lead sentence is "The 'Europeanization' of European defense is not yet an idea whose time has come." Most Maintainers are not likely to think much about coping with it until and unless its time does come.

The Rest of the World

In the summer of 1987, when the U.S. Navy recognized that minesweeping was not among its capabilities and the State Department appealed to our allies for assistance in the Persian Gulf, their initial rejection induced angry reactions from within the United States. The *Chicago Sun-Times* editorialized,

One after another, America's Western friends and allies have rejected the Reagan administration's request for help with minesweeping in the Persian Gulf, where last month a mine caused considerable damage to

---

[85]Conine, 1987, p. 5.

a tanker navigating under U.S. protection. The most severe blow, the hardest to take, is the one from Britain. Also on the naysaying list are France, West Germany and the Netherlands.[86]

The allies did ultimately assist, but the initial demurrer and the American reaction took their place in a string of such events dating from earlier Gulf incidents in the 1970s and going through the refusal of NATO members other than Britain to allow the use of bases or transit rights for the bombing of Libya. In 1989, the revelation of German assistance to the construction of a chemical warfare plant in Libya—and particularly the initial German resentment of the revelation—led to such bad tastes all around that it began to affect even the Alliance debate over Central European posture.

In general, the indeterminate role of European NATO members in supporting U.S. out-of-area activities has been an irritant, particularly when Americans felt that the activities were in the mutual interest of the members—e.g., the maintenance of the flow of Gulf oil, which went mostly to Europe and Japan, and the punishment of terrorism, which hit Europeans as much as Americans. The irritant, however, has had more of an effect on public opinion as exemplified by the *Sun-Times* editorial and on the Withdrawers than it has on the debate among the Maintainers.

Brzezinski's analysis sounds like a mild version of the Withdrawers':

Today, the United States is weakest where it is most vulnerable— along the strategic front that poses the greatest risk of either a major Soviet geopolitical thrust or an American-Soviet collision. . . . While American power is tenuous along the third strategic front in southwest Asia, the United States still allocates more than half its total military spending for the defense of the first front in Europe.[87]

But unlike the Withdrawers he wants only to readjust, removing 100,000 troops from Europe and allocating the budgetary savings to the areas he considers to be in greater danger.

Kissinger arrives at approximately the same point by a more political route. In contrast to the old days of European colonialism,

Now it is Europe that insists that the treaty's obligations do not extend to the developing world. And it is Europe that feels free to disassociate itself from U.S. actions where indigenous upheavals and Soviet efforts to out-

---

[86]"America Betrayed by its Friends," *Chicago Sun-Times*, August 4, 1987, p. 23.
[87]Brzezinski, 1986b, p. 175. The second strategic front is in the Far East.

346

flank the alliance produce contemporary crises. . . . This produces the following problems which must be solved if long-term paralysis is to be avoided: The United States cannot grant Europe a veto over its actions outside the NATO area unless it is ready to abdicate its responsibilities for the global equilibrium; but neither can it be in Europe's interest to undermine America's willingness to defend its vital interests, for the defense of Europe is part of these vital interests. . . .

The conclusion, I believe, is unavoidable: Some American forces now in Europe would contribute more to global defense if redeployed as strategic reserves based in the United States, able to be moved to world trouble spots. . . . [The] objective should be to distinguish clearly between those American forces earmarked exclusively for the defense of Europe and those available for other areas.[88]

Robert Komer, who, after his 1960s stint in Vietnam later became Under Secretary of Defense in the Carter administration, presents two cautions about such moves. The first relates to American interests: "We have to be more prudent about Third World use of military force on a scale that would seriously interfere with other higher priority U.S. commitments."[89] This appraisal balances Komer's Defense Department background when he was primarily concerned with NATO against his 1960s experience.

Komer's second *caveat* concerns the West Europeans. Rather than accusing them of shirking, we should understand that they evaluate and prioritize differently:

The Europeans realize that denial of Persian Gulf oil access would undermine the viability of NATO Europe without any Warsaw Pact attack. They also realize that the Soviet Union could exert great political pressures on them simply by turning on and off the flow of Middle East oil. But they are even more concerned that the Alliance still falls short of meeting even initial conventional defence requirements in Europe itself. . . . In effect, the U.S. seems to be focusing increasingly on third-area contingencies, whereas NATO Europe tends to regard this as a risky overextension of U.S. resources at the expense of adequate priority to European defence.[90]

Although Komer is, here and elsewhere, a strong advocate of increased West European contributions for conventional defense, he does not comment

---

[88]Kissinger, 1986f, pp. 1–6.
[89]Komer, 1984, p. 88.
[90]Komer, 1986, pp. 64–65.

further on the irony of Europe's difficulty in increasing these contributions while criticizing the U.S. lack of "adequate priority to European defence." This is what bothers the Withdrawers as well as the burden-sharing Maintainers.

Komer's own prescription is for specialization. In 1984, he argued for a "division of labor" in which the United States would be responsible for protecting the flow of oil "while the other affected allies concentrate on shoring up their own home-defense capabilities."[91] Two years later, he reported progress, in that the NATO Defense Ministers did accept "a new set of biennial force goals meant to provide compensation for possible U.S. deployments outside the NATO area," but he pointed out that "force goals are a far cry from actual forces.[92]

Komer, and Brzezinski and Kissinger, and the other Maintainers all provide answers to the question of allocation of responsibilities for NATO defense of joint interests in the rest of the world. Further, they recognize that not all interests are joint. An issue they tend to finesse, however, is the overall failure of Europe to join in the global anticommunist crusade so ardently desired by the Withdrawers and espoused in part by the Reagan administration. This is because few of the Maintainers outside of the administration espoused that crusade,[93] and those within, wherever they stood philosophically, had to balance it against the immediate needs of NATO.

Komer, however, did confront the naval version of the Withdrawers' global emphasis, which he believed to be the implicit strategy of the Reagan administration, as inevitable defense budget cuts imposed by the Congress would leave in place the substantial number of new ships being built together with the requirement to support them at the cost of other military expenditures.[94] And his own response strikes hard at the presumed strategy:

> Cutting the coat to fit the cloth by concentrating on a primarily maritime strategy cannot adequately protect our vital interests in Eurasia because it cannot adequately deter a great land-based power like the USSR. . . . Even if all Soviet home and overseas naval bases were put

---

[91]Komer, 1984, p. 86.

[92]Komer, 1986, p. 63.

[93]Kissinger is active in the debate over the Third World as well as NATO; although he was close to the Reagan administration on many issues, he was of a distinctly different view from its crusader contingent. See Part One.

[94]Komer, 1984, pp. 55–59.

out of action, and Soviet naval and merchant vessels swept from the high seas, this would not suffice to prevent Moscow from seizing or dominating the rimlands of Eurasia, including the two great industrial agglomerations of Europe and Japan, and cutting off their economic lifeblood—Middle East oil. . . .

Some advocates of a maritime strategy evade this issue by contending that Europe is now more than rich enough to provide for its own defense. . . . True, a stronger and more integrated European defense effort would be highly desirable, and has always been favored by Washington on strategic grounds. But to suggest that Europe alone would do what Europe plus America so far have not done is whistling in the wind. . . . Indeed, adoption of a primarily maritime strategy would have a devastating impact on the very network of alliances on which the United States is so dependent to maintain a credible deterrent or defensive balance vis-a-vis the USSR.[95]

Although the Maintainers agree with this continued European emphasis, they remain worried about both the strategic and burden-sharing issues, and about the effects of irritated American public opinion as well, and they look for various means to structure American and European responsibilities. To the extent that the United States backs off some extremes in defining its unilateral global interests—in the new administration, perhaps—the remaining issues between the Maintainers and the European Couplers will be no more divisive than those in most other areas. Resonance with our allies is possible here, as elsewhere. James Schlesinger may be the most understanding of all the Maintainers:

From time to time, Americans have been annoyed to discover that, for some reason or other, Europeans do not wish to see the cold war resumed in the heart of Europe—just because the Russians dispatched military forces into a country—Afghanistan in 1979—that they had politically taken over a year earlier—or because of conflicts in the Caribbean, Central America, the Horn of Africa or wherever. A gratuitous spillover of Third World struggles into Europe is unacceptable to the Europeans—and Americans simply have to accept this reality.[96]

But Schlesinger has not been in office lately.

---

[95]Ibid., pp. 67–69.
[96]J. Schlesinger, 1984, p. S7749.

THE OPPONENT

The Soviet Union

There is less difference between the Maintainers and the Couplers on their analyses of the Soviet Union than on any of the other issues. Although the interpretation of Soviet ends and means is basic to the design of NATO's political and military posture, the questions about the Soviets are intellectual ones; and the answers are intellectual and perhaps ideological, rather than being based directly on varying national interests. In the Western world, although Sovietologists' interpretations of objectives and strategies vary over a very wide range, the range is about the same on both sides of the Atlantic. The Maintainer range of recent interpretations of Gorbachev and his changes may be even broader than the Coupler range, but that could be a statistical phenomenon based on the fact that the United States turns out more Sovietologists than does Europe.

Even more than in Europe, there is an American far right with views on the Soviet Union exemplified by President Reagan's "evil empire" speech; but by the mid-1980s Reagan had dropped the phrase and apparently the viewpoint, much to the disgust of some of his more conservative supporters. Many of these had decided that the real struggle with communism was elsewhere than in Europe and had become Withdrawers; the remainder differed little from the more suspicious end of the narrow range of views held by virtually all Maintainers before Gorbachev.

Before Gorbachev—indeed, from the death of Stalin to the death of Chernenko, with some slight weakening during the Khrushchev era— American Sovietologists believed that the Soviet objective was to drive us out of Europe, that only their tactics varied over the years, but that their military power was always an essential instrument for those tactics. Almost alone as an exception among the Maintainers was George Kennan, who has contended for almost four decades that his "containment" doctrine had been badly misinterpreted and that he had "never believed that they have seen it in their interests to overrun Western Europe militarily."

More typically, Alan Platt of RAND has presented a succinct list of Soviet objectives, and a history of recent strategies and tactics they have used to reach these objectives, as of mid-1985. At that time, Gorbachev had been in command only a few months:

Throughout the postwar period, there has been a fundamental continuity in what the Soviet Union has sought in Western Europe—the transformation of the status quo in favor of Soviet interests. In trying to bring about this long-term objective, the Soviets have sought to: maintain a Soviet military advantage in the European theater; ensure continued East European responsiveness to Soviet interests; secure widespread acknowledgment of the Soviet Union as a superpower co-equal with the United States; expand Soviet access to Western technology and credits; loosen American political and military ties with Western Europe; transform West European political systems from within by aiding "progressive" elements.[97]

Platt then went on to describe Soviet policy through the first half of the 1980s as repeatedly attempting to achieve these objectives by tactics of wooing the United States, then Western Europe, then both, then neither. None of these worked; their failure set the stage for Gorbachev's more radical changes.

Such descriptions of Soviet fundamental objectives and of the opportunistic means of reaching those objectives commanded a substantial consensus among Maintainers at that time. As Helmut Schmidt did on the Coupler side, Brzezinski put it into a historical as well as a geopolitical context:

From time immemorial, Russian society expressed itself politically through a state that was mobilized and regimented along military lines, with the security dimension serving as the central organizing impulse. The absence of clearly definable national boundaries made territorial expansion the obvious way of assuring security.... Russian history is, consequently, a history of sustained territorial expansion.[98]

In a book whose subtitle, "Dismantling the East-West Military Confrontation," indicates its hope for a much more relaxed future, Jonathan Dean described the same recent events discussed by Platt, but with less of an air of Soviet inexorability:

There is a clear pattern in this record. It is one of repeated Soviet attempts to influence West European, especially Federal German, policy, using Soviet military power as a basis for these efforts—and of

---

[97]Platt, 1986, p. v. Although the report appeared in 1986, Platt's preface states that "It largely reflects information available as of August 1985."
[98]Brzezinski, 1986b, p. 17.

351

repeated failure of these attempts. This is the reality of the Soviet intimidation issue, and it seems likely to continue.[99]

Platt stressed the repetition of the attempts, Dean their failure; the distance is not great, but it spans the range of Maintainers' views before the recognition that Gorbachev was likely to make a difference, one way or the other.

Platt laid out five possible future Soviet policy alternatives as seen from his 1985 vantage point: attempted breakup of NATO by favoring Western Europe at the expense of the United States; the same by favoring the United States; defying both Western Europe and the United States, attempted renewal of détente by extending overtures to both; and "a purposefully confrontational policy toward the West."[100] His own estimate was that "short-term Soviet policy, despite public denials, is likely to proceed along the path suggested by the first alternative,"[101] the attempt to seduce the West Europeans away from the United States.

In fact, by the time 18 months had passed, the alternative chosen by the Soviets was recognized by the Maintainers, to the surprise of practically all of them, to be the pursuit of détente with both sides of NATO. But this recognition has not ended a debate, it has begun one—a far more fundamental debate over the Soviet Union than has taken place within NATO since its beginning. The two sides were laid out by Platt in his evaluation of what a Soviet move toward détente might imply:

[I]t might signify a major change in the way the Soviet Union sought to approach the United States and Western Europe. Or, on the other hand, it might just signify a continued long-term effort to loosen ties within the Atlantic Alliance, but through the choice of different short-term means to this end.[102]

Gorbachev has made a difference. That is accepted by Maintainer as by Coupler Sovietologists. Whether the difference is a "major change" in direction or a new and perhaps brilliant set of tactics, still designed "to loosen ties within the Atlantic Alliance," divides the Maintainers as it does the Couplers.

On the suspicious side, Harry Gelman of RAND asserted in 1987 that Soviet goals were unchanged:

---

[99]Dean, 1987b, p. 84.
[100]Platt, 1986, pp. ix-x.
[101]Ibid., p. 37.
[102]Ibid., p. 35.

The central core of [Soviet] goals remains the gradual reduction of American presence and influence in Western Europe, provided this happens under circumstances that do not promote the emergence of an effective substitute—a coherent West European offset to Soviet geopolitical weight in Europe.[103]

And he provided a scorecard of how well Gorbachev was doing as of mid-1987. On the pro-Soviet side, he counted narrowing West European popular support for nuclear deterrence, decaying consensus in West Germany, flexible Soviet adaptation to their failure to prevent INF installation, Soviet ability to exploit Western tensions over conventional arms control, the favorable effect on Western public opinion of Soviet internal reforms, the gap between the United States and Europe on Third World issues, and West European discomfort over American political erraticism.[104] On the debit side for the Soviets were the failure of the left to gain political power in West Germany or Britain, the anti-Soviet trend in French policy, a strengthening of West European political forces favoring security cooperation but not advocating greater independence from the United States, the possibility that *glasnost* might unleash uncontrollable forces within the Soviet Union, internal Soviet controversy over economic cooperation with the West, and the possibility that policies within the Soviet Union might decrease control over the satellite nations.[105]

By no means have all the Maintainers agreed with Gelman's assertion that the Soviets, as they have since Stalin's day, retain the objective of dominating Western Europe by driving the Americans out. Until Gorbachev, almost all did agree; after his first year, several diverged from the thinking that scored him purely on the old goals. William Hyland, the editor of *Foreign Affairs*, used his journal to take direct issue with those who see new means to old ends:

It is possible to see in Gorbachev's changes nothing more than shifts in tactics. It can even be argued that the wily old Gromyko would have arrived at similar conclusions about the position of the Soviet Union, but without resorting to Gorbachev's novel rhetoric. A more persuasive analysis, however, is that Gorbachev views foreign policy in much the same way he sees his domestic situation. That is, he still believes in the basic system but recognizes that radical changes are in order, and that this will involve paying a price in the near term to

---

[103]Gelman, 1987, p. vi.
[104]Ibid., pp. viii–xiv.
[105]Ibid., pp. xvi–xxiii.

achieve longer term aims. Thus he is introducing innovative elements into current Soviet foreign policies which are beginning to outweigh the elements of continuity.[106]

"Paying a price in the near term to achieve longer term aims" might be interpreted as new tactics with old strategy, but Hyland's next two sentences are:

In sum, the accession of Mikhail Gorbachev to the leadership of the Communist Party of the Soviet Union marks the beginning of a new historical period. The transition from Brezhnev to Gorbachev is a genuine generational change, unlike the transfer of power from Khrushchev to Brezhnev in 1964.

Professor Jerry Hough of Duke University and the Brookings Institution provides a historical-sociological explanation for the change. In opposition to the concept set forth by Brzezinski and Schmidt that Soviet expansion is the continuation of centuries of Russian history, he espouses the theory that interprets "the Communist revolution as an overthrow of Peter the Great's Westernized elite and a break with Russia's natural evolution toward constitutional democracy." In recent years, however, the elite has reasserted itself and is demanding not democracy but a "looser one-party dictatorship." The effect on external policy is a tradeoff:

The deal for the middle class is clear: a looser political system in exchange for the lash of foreign economic competition. . . . Moscow needs to focus foreign policy on improving relations with Europe and Japan. That means Moscow will have to make concessions to Europe and Japan and decrease the number of troops facing Europe to reduce fears about investing in the Soviet Union.[107]

And economist Charles Cooper agrees with Hough on attributing internal causes to Soviet change but turns the argument in an economic direction: "Gorbachev has indeed made a difference, but that difference reflects the 'fact' of Soviet economic deterioration."[108] The internal affects the external, however: According to Bush administration National Security Advisor Brent Scowcroft: "The cold war is not over," but Gorbachev's foreign policy changes reflect "a recognition on his part that he badly needs a period of stability if not definite improvement in the relationship, so he can face

---

[106]Hyland, 1987, p. 10.
[107]Hough, 1987.
[108]Personal communication.

the awesome problems he has at home in trying to restore the economy. That's his basic objective."[109]

Hyland's causal explanation is external rather than internal, and he ends up on the other side of the cold war metaphor from Scowcroft:

> For some reason we refuse to learn how to live with the undeniable success of American foreign policy since World War II. . . . We have won the ideological war; we are close to winning the geopolitical contest in the Third World, except for the Middle East. We long ago won the economic competition. As James Reston remarked in his final regular column for the *New York Times*, "I think we've won the cold war and don't know it."[110]

But mid-1989, much the same was being said by President Bush. But Bush would also agree with Hyland's conclusion: "Preserving the European alliance must remain the cornerstone of American policy."[111] Others, however, who have been pushing for U.S.-Soviet rapprochement for much longer, wax more enthusiastic. At the start of the 1987 zero-zero negotiations, Arthur Cox, secretary of the American Committee on U.S.-Soviet Relations, contended,

> Gorbachev is eager to reach an agreement with Reagan for deep reductions in all types of nuclear weapons. Despite the debacle of the Iran-*Contra* affair, Reagan still has an opportunity to salvage the integrity of his presidency by reaching a momentous agreement with Gorbachev to end the arms race and drastically reduce the nuclear arsenals.[112]

Abraham Brumberg, former editor of the journal *Problems of Communism* and something of a patriarch among Sovietologists, delineates the two extremes and a middle group and then stakes out a somewhat different middle position for himself:

> One school holds that the Soviet Union will inevitably be transformed into a genuine democracy. Its adherents include a sprinkling of "revisionist" historians, whose writings on the Stalin period would bring a blush to the cheeks of even their most orthodox Soviet colleagues. . . . A much larger group consists of those who claim that the Communist system cannot change, no matter what. . . . There is a third group,

---

[109]Quoted in the *Los Angeles Times*, January 23, 1989, p. 1.
[110]Hyland, 1987, pp. 14–15.
[111]Ibid., p. 15.
[112]Cox, 1987, pp. 1–3.

the skeptics, whose case is clearly more persuasive than the others. . . .
Mr. Gorbachev may mean well, they say, but how can he succeed in
efforts that strike at some of the most long-lived and tenacious
features of Soviet society?

Healthy skepticism is justifiable but not to the point of dismissing the
possibility of change. The reforms may yet fail, stall, or dissipate.
Yet nothing in our logic or experience supports the notion that the
Soviet leadership may be unable to change their country. Only our
assumptions tell us that.[113]

Most Maintainers take one version or another of this middle position.
Gelman, who in October 1987 centered his analysis on the unchanging
nature of Soviet objectives, a year later reiterated his previous views,
characterizing "the cynicism that has motivated all the Soviet peace campaigns to date, throughout the regimes of Stalin, Khrushchev, Brezhnev,
Andropov, and Chernenko,"[114] and repeated that "the Soviet political
offensive against the coherence of the NATO alliance has become much
more formidable under Gorbachev."[115] Yet even Gelman has moved and
writes movingly: "I wish to make it clear, despite everything else I have
said, that I think the possibilities for improvement of our relations with the
Soviet Union are indeed better now than they have ever been in my life-
time."[116]

All of which has led to a new and very central question for debate:
Should we attempt from the outside to assist Gorbachev overcome internal
opposition and economic problems? Whitney MacMillan, chief executive
of Cargill, Inc., a major American grain-exporting firm, and Richárd Ullman of Princeton contend "that it is very much in the interest of the goal
of American policy to help him," and propose both arms control measures
and economic assistance.[117] But Abraham Becker and Arnold Horelick, colleagues of Gelman at RAND, are skeptical:

The Soviet future is uncertain and we can have little confidence in
our ability to shape the Soviet course. . . . The U.S. policy problem is
not only how to remain open to possibilities for major improvements
in U.S.-Soviet relations but also how to limit the costs of adverse

[113]Brumberg, 1987.
[114]Gelman, 1988, p.6.
[115]Ibid, p. 12.
[116]Ibid, p. 20.
[117]MacMillan and Ullman, 1987, p. 23.

developments. We believe that a strategy of step-by-step engagement is the most appropriate instrument for achieving these goals.[118]

Step-by-step engagement is a broad enough umbrella to cover most Maintainers.

Eastern Europe

The Maintainers pay substantially more attention to Eastern Europe as a whole than do the European Couplers other than the Germans. One reason is that the larger number of American Sovietologists allows for more specialization. Another is that the fairly recent East European roots of many Americans lead to more of an interest in the Soviet satellite nations. For similar reasons, the Maintainers treat less with the "German question"; most German immigration to the United States was many generations back.

One American attitude toward the Eastern nations is that expressed by Huntington. The central thesis of his counteroffensive strategy is that it would compel the Soviets "to reallocate forces and resources to the defense of their satellites and thus to weaken their offensive thrust." More specifically,

[T]he adoption of this strategy should be accompanied with a clear invitation to Eastern European governments to avoid invasion by opting out of a Soviet-initiated war. At the very least, such an invitation would create uneasiness, uncertainty, and divisiveness within satellite governments, and hence arouse concern among the Soviets as to their reliability. In practice, the allied offensive would have to be accompanied with carefully composed political-psychological warfare appeals to the peoples of Eastern Europe stressing that the allies were not fighting them but the Soviets and urging them to cooperate with the advancing forces and to rally to the liberation of their countries from Soviet military occupation and political control.[119]

As has been noted, the counteroffensive strategy is opposed by most Maintainers and Couplers. Most Sovietologists (of which Huntington is not one) take another tack. As described by Milan Svec of the Carnegie Endowment for International Peace: "The principle behind United States policy toward Eastern Europe has for many years been 'differentiation'—in

---

[118]Becker and Horelick, 1989, p. ix.
[119]Huntington, 1982, p. 31.

357

effect, a promise to reward those governments that show greater tolerance, flexibility and independence from Moscow."[120]

One of the leading advocates of differentiation is Brzezinski, who pushed in this direction long before the "many years" during which it has been national policy, long before it became obvious. In 1961, writing with William Griffith, he called for:

a policy of what might be called peaceful engagement in Eastern Europe. This policy should: (1) aim at stimulating further diversity in the Communist bloc; (2) thus increasing the likelihood that East European states can achieve a greater measure of political independence from Soviet domination (3) thereby ultimately leading to the creation of a neutral belt of states which, like the Finnish, would enjoy genuine popular freedom of choice in internal policy while not being hostile to the Soviet Union and not belonging to Western Military alliances.[121]

Not that Brzezinski has been under any illusions as to the possibilities for rapid change. Writing a quarter-century later, after his stint as National Security Advisor and at a time when Gorbachev had just come into power, he points out that:

Despite forty years of forced indoctrination, all the Communist regimes in Eastern Europe remain in power through heavy reliance on severe internal police control, reinforced by the potential threat of Soviet intervention—and by Soviet troops on the ground in Poland, East Germany, Czechoslovakia, and Hungary. . . . At the same time, Moscow is determined to restrict the scope of East European independence in foreign affairs. . . . At the first Warsaw Pact meeting held under Gorbachev's chairmanship, the principle of tight coordination was firmly reasserted.[122]

Brzezinski's strategy for change in Eastern Europe fits into his overall schema to put more of NATO's responsibilities onto its European members. Marking the fortieth anniversary of the 1945 Yalta Agreement, supposed to have divided Europe between East and West (Brzezinski argues that the decision was made earlier), he emphasized that:

---

[120]Svec, 1987, p. 27.
[121]Brzezinski and Griffith, July 1961, p. 644.
[122]Brzezinski, 1986b, pp. 82–83.

the historic balance in Europe will be changed gradually in the West's favor only if Russia comes to be faced west of the Elbe rather less by America and rather more by Europe. Thoughtful Europeans realize, moreover, that the future of Europe is intertwined with the future of Germany and of Poland.[123]

His program included: NATO's "publicly repudiating...the partition of Europe," which he terms "the historic legacy of Yalta," while simultaneously "reconfirm[ing] its commitment to the Helsinki Final Act," which "confirmed the durability of the existing frontiers in central and eastern Europe," creating "the maximum number of opportunities for Eastern European participation in various all-European bodies," intensifying "aid to those East Europeans who are struggling actively for the political emancipation of Eastern Europe," and implementing his ideas for the restructuring of NATO.[124]

Two years later, after Gorbachev had begun to make his distinct mark, Brzezinski reiterated his central themes:

In the heart of Europe, we can see a revival of the old concept of *Mitteleuropa*. Today, the average Czechoslovak, Hungarian, or Pole openly professes that he feels closer to the typical Austrian, German, or further west the Frenchman than to his eastern neighbors. . . . We must exploit these trends and build on the confidence in the fact that the existing territorial status quo in Europe, as confirmed by the Helsinki agreements, is no longer subject to change. We must seek on that basis to shape progressively a new political reality in Europe.[125]

Ross Johnson of RAND (later Director of Radio Free Europe) analyzes the same issues from the viewpoint of the Soviet bloc itself—the governments of the East European nations and the pressures and constraints they put on the Soviet Union:

[At] the end of Gorbachev's first year [1985–86], the motives that impelled the East European leaderships to cultivate special ties with Western Europe in the wake of NATO's INF deployment remained as strong as ever and continued to complicate Soviet policies directed toward increasing discipline and cohesion in Eastern Europe. . . . Thus, since the mid-1970s, the Soviets have faced an increasingly pronounced dilemma in attempting to use control over Eastern Europe to promote greater Soviet influence in Western Europe while at the same

---

[123]Brzezinski, 1984/1985, p. 294.
[124]Ibid., pp. 295–299.
[125]Brzezinski, 1988, pp. 4–17.

time attempting to avoid the "reverse influence" from Western Europe that could threaten Soviet control of Eastern Europe.[126]

The constraints seen analytically by the Maintainer Sovietologists thus coincide substantially with the strategies recommended by Brzezinski and the others who want to differentiate among members of the Soviet "bloc": Gorbachev cannot allow too great a scope for autonomy, and the West should not push for it. The structure is fragile, and too much internal or external pressure in the wrong place might cause its collapse; few Maintainers would shed tears over that, except that too sudden a collapse might bring instability, confrontation, and combat. And no Maintainer wants to take that risk. The possibilities are thus quite limited.

All this leaves out Germany, on which the Maintainers concentrate less than the West Europeans, particularly, of course, the Germans themselves. When the Maintainers do write about the two Germanies, however, they tend to worry. Brzezinski, for example, uses the division of Germany as a major reason why policy toward Eastern Europe cannot proceed along traditional lines, but he also betrays a substantial concern with the direction of current West German policy based on that division:

> [T]he partition of Germany within the partition of Europe . . . guarantees a continuing political struggle for the future of Germany and, consequently, for the future of Europe. . . . West Germans—no longer dominated by feelings of war guilt, less mesmerized by the American ideal, and distressed by the failure of Europe to become an alternative to divisive nationalisms—are naturally drawn to a growing preoccupation with the fate of their brethren living under an alien system. The notion that the destiny of a United Germany depends on a close relationship with Russia is not a new one in German political tradition. . . . As a consequence, West Germany is already pursuing a distinctive policy of its own toward the East. It carefully avoids provoking Moscow on such neuralgic issues as Poland—the geopolitical linchpin state of Eastern Europe—and cultivates a special relationship with East Germany. . . . [This] reactionary and dangerous regime has been the beneficiary of significant West German economic assistance—and this has directly contributed to East Germany's emergence as Moscow's most important junior partner.[127]

---

[126]Johnson, 1986, p. xi.
[127]Brzezinski, 1986b, pp. 197–199.

Such fears are less typical in the United States than in France and other parts of Europe. But neither the Brzezinski expression nor those of non-German Europeans map well onto the statements of German Couplers from all parts of the political spectrum that unification is a remote ideal at best, and that the ties that *are* being created to the East must be within the compass of the Western Alliance.

ARMS CONTROL AND DISARMAMENT

The Maintainers express no peculiarly American views on arms control and disarmament; given the resonating attempts to calm European fears, particularly about Reykjavik and the zero-zero agreement, the same positions can be found as among the Couplers. But both the balance of views and the details of the way they are approached are quite different. This section, as with the corresponding discussion of the Couplers, stresses the debate over zero-zero, leaving subsequent developments for the Epilog.

The Maintainers were sharply divided over the zero-zero agreement. In 1987, for the first time in 40 years, both arms controls in Europe and arms reductions anywhere in the world suddenly looked real. Radical change is shocking; and for that reason if no other, opposition to zero-zero was more prevalent among Maintainers than support.

The opposition to zero-zero was spearheaded by General Rogers in his last days as SACEUR; that was a major reason why they were his last days. Shortly after retiring from that position and from the United States Army, he summarized his view:

Removing the land-based intermediate-range nuclear forces now would return NATO to its weak pre-1979 posture. In fact, because the Russians have continued to improve their conventional and nuclear forces, NATO would be in an even worse position now. To establish credible deterrence, two capabilities, listed in NATO's guidelines for using nuclear weapons, are vital: the ability to strike, with certainty, targets deep in the Soviet homeland . . . and a number of nuclear escalatory options between conventional forces and the use of strategic nuclear forces. The proposed I.N.F. agreement would eliminate the Pershing 2 missiles and thereby remove the first capability. It would also eliminate a crucial escalatory option.[128]

---

[128]Rogers, 1987b.

Kissinger stressed political as much as military reasons for opposing the agreement, including some major points of resonance to West European positions. He listed six flaws in the proposal: It contributed to decoupling, it reduced "the Soviet nuclear threat to Europe only slightly," it continued the abandonment of "European leaders who staked their political positions on American proposals for the nuclear defense of Europe," it gave the Soviets a veto over Western nuclear deployments, it complicated "the possible replacement of American missiles by European ones," and it created additional problems by allowing the Soviets to retain missiles in Asia.[129] The last of these objections was taken care of when the Soviets agreed to remove all intermediate-range missiles rather than retaining the 100 they had proposed to keep in Asia while we retained an equal number elsewhere than in Europe.

A few weeks later, Kissinger joined his former boss Richard Nixon in a considerably softer position, disapproving of the treaty but accepting it under two conditions, one of which was the elimination of the Asian missiles and the other a strong linkage to additional arms control agreements improving the conventional balance.[130] In the event, once the treaty was agreed to, they favored ratification, primarily on the ground that failure to ratify would be one more twist in the American erraticism that had been destroying West European confidence and threatening the Alliance itself.

How did we get to a position and a treaty seen to be so unsatisfactory? Kissinger attributes it to Washington and international bureaucracy:

As often happens in Washington, quite disparate elements combined to produce the zero option. Throughout the 1970s opponents of arms control had obscured what was an objection in principle by claiming that they wanted to go beyond freezing existing deployments to major reductions of nuclear arsenals. This had the additional advantage, from their point of view, of giving them two chances to slow down an agreement—first by urging wider reductions and then by proposing intrusive verification to check on reductions. . . . Other supporters of the zero option included neo-isolationists and military technicians who preferred U.S. missiles at sea or within the United States to reduce the automatic nature of any nuclear response. European leaders had . . . at first asked for the INF to balance the Soviet deployment of hundreds of the new SS-20 medium-range missiles. . . . But rattled by the combination of Soviet-orchestrated diplomatic pressures and growing public assaults, the European allies took refuge in an evasion—that the INF could some day be traded for the SS-20s. . . .

[129]Kissinger, 1987, p. 2.
[130]Nixon and Kissinger, 1987.

362

All this was woven together into a formal proposal by the then-dominant group in the [Reagan] White House. They knew little about strategy and less about arms control. . . .

The traditional arms controllers started out on the sidelines of this particular exercise. But committed as they were to the proposition that there is no such thing as a good new weapon, they have since joined the fray with a passion.[131]

Elizabeth Drew of the *New Yorker*, ordinarily much more friendly to arms control than Kissinger (but less friendly to the Reagan administration) presented an interpretation of the later stages of the zero-zero negotiation similar to Kissinger's story of its birth:

[F]ew people in the Administration think that an I.N.F agreement is very important—as compared, say, with a possible agreement on deep reductions in long-range nuclear weapons or an agreement on deployment of the Strategic Defense Initiative. . . . [An] I.N.F. agreement solves a number of problems for the Administration at what its officials see as little cost. Best of all it gives Reagan an arms-control agreement. . . . The situation has other benefits for arms-control opponents: some of them do not at all mind that we might reach an agreement with the Soviets that makes the Europeans unhappy. . . . One can also detect on the part of some Administration officials a certain pleasure over the fact that the potential I.N.F. agreement has split the arms control community. The subject of I.N.F. particularly lends itself to theological disputes, and the theologians have gone at it with great zest.[132]

The pro-arms control theologians were, in fact, somewhat split by the zero-zero proposal. House Armed Services Committee Chairman Les Aspin opposed it because he believed it started at the wrong end, removing the more stable nuclear weapons and leaving those least subject to central control.[133] Most, however, favored it if not because, in Kissinger's words, they thought that "there is no such thing as a good new weapon," at least because they attributed great importance to the first agreement to actually reduce nuclear weapons. In the words of Carter administration chief arms negotiatior Paul Warnke: "It is important that an intermediate-range

---

[131]Kissinger, 1987.
[132]Drew, 1987, pp. 140–141.
[133]Aspin, 1987, p. 4.

nuclear forces treaty be promptly completed so that the superpowers can get on with the more serious business of strategic-range nuclear forces."[134]

On the specific issues of zero-zero, Charles Schultze, who had been Chairman of President Carter's Council of Economic Advisors and before that President Johnson's Budget Director, questioned the anti-zero-zero view, using the same scholastic figure of speech as Drew:

[T]he Soviets would be deterred from conventional aggression by Pershing 2 missiles on the land mass of Europe but would *not* be deterred by Polaris missiles off the European coast. Only when one sets it down on paper does this argument's specious nature become clear. It implies that what counts in the Soviet mind in deciding how to retaliate against a nuclear attack is not what target was hit or what damage the missile did or even what the politico-military situation was, but only whether the delivery system was labelled "strategic" or "intermediate." This flies in the face of repeated Soviet warnings that they will make no such nice distinctions. The argument has the intellectual ring of a theological debate at the University of Paris circa AD 1250.[135]

General Rogers's response to this point of the zero-zero advocates is that:

although the Russians can discriminate between the launching of land-based ballistic missiles and the launching of submarine-based ballistic missiles, they cannot tell whether those being launched from submarines are part of the Supreme Allied Commander's limited inventory or from the American or British strategic nuclear inventory. Thus, they cannot know whether the West has began an all-out nuclear attack.[136]

To SACEUR, it is important whether it is his attack or that of the commander of the Strategic Air Command and, unlike Schultze, he believes that this will be of interest to the Soviets too.

In any case, as zero-zero moved toward the status of *fait accompli*, the tendency among Maintainers—and, indeed, Couplers as well—was to accept it and get on with the job. General Rogers's successor as SACEUR, General John Galvin, in a sense contradicted Rogers when, according to the *Baltimore Sun*, he said:

---

[134]Warnke, 1987, p. 19.
[135]Schultze, 1987, p. 3.
[136]Rogers, 1987b.

that the defense of Western Europe would be possible without U.S. medium-range nuclear missiles but that they should not be removed too rapidly. "I am talking about years, not months." ... General Galvin welcomed the planned Soviet-U.S. treaty.[137]

General Galvin was, of course, being a good soldier; had he not been willing to be a good soldier after Rogers's revolt, he would not have become SACEUR.

In fact, once it became clear that the agreement was going to be signed, Maintainers and Couplers alike fell into line. Falling into line had two implications for both schools, and one more specifically for the Couplers. It meant taking additional arms control steps seriously so that the next time the West could make proposals in its own thought-through security interests rather than playing a political game with the Soviets and its own electorates. And it meant taking steps to strengthen the Alliance in the new environment created by Gorbachev. In addition, for many of the Couplers, it meant reexamination of the concept of European security in a European context.

SUMMARY: MAINTAINER RECOMMENDATIONS

The Maintainers may constitute a tighter School of Thought than do the Couplers; at least, given the American nationality that is used here to define them, they all speak the same language, and this is not a trivial consideration. Nonetheless, they present a wide range of views in the NATO debate. It may thus be surprising that the Maintainers do reach a consensus on a set of policy recommendations, based on the three points suggested above: No Early Use, stronger conventional capabilities, and maintaining the commitment to NATO.

Further, the Maintainer consensus, for all the similarities between their debate and that of the Couplers, ends up differing from that of the Couplers, certainly in emphasis, to some degree in viewpoint. In the following list, the relevant Coupler points are summarized in italics below each Maintainer point.

The Maintainers come together not to unanimity, but to consensus, on five broad policy recommendations:

---

[137]"General urges 'years, not months' to remove missiles," *Baltimore Sun*, September 16, 1987, p. 6.

- The Alliance structure should remain as it is. European moves toward a "second pillar" are acceptable and perhaps even desirable, but not important enough to contemplate restructuring an Alliance that has maintained the peace.

  (*Europe should begin serious movement toward forming a second pillar.*)

- NATO should strive for stronger conventional capabilities even if it takes more money, and the European members of the Alliance should contribute a larger share of that money.

  (*Larger expenditures on conventional forces may have to be put up, at American insistence.*)

- Nuclear deterrence in Europe is necessary but very dangerous, and a central task of the Alliance is to raise the threshold.

  (*Nuclear deterrence remains basic to the defense of Europe. This is the most fundamental difference between the two schools.*)

- The United States has worldwide reponsibilities, including some in support of West European as well as American vital interests. If the Europeans will not participate, they should compensate, and surely they should not complain.

  (*There is danger in the United States being diverted to the rest of the world.*)

- Arms control, both nuclear and conventional, is important to security policy and world peace.

  (*The West European view continues to be suspicious of nuclear agreements between the superpowers, but in part because of the decoupling fears raised by these agreements, more and more hope is being placed on the possibilities for conventional arms control in Europe.*)

Some of these differences are marginal and some, like that over the threshold, more substantial. But what both sides of the Atlantic continue to agree on has been captured by Thomson's words that the: "solidarity of the Alliance . . . is the most vital element of deterrence." And deterrence, for Couplers and Maintainers alike, remains essential for world peace and Western civilization.

21. Epilog

(1) Western publics are becoming increasingly allergic to nuclear weapons and will become increasingly aware that NATO relies on the early use of nuclear weapons in response to nonnuclear attacks. (2) NATO has no revolutionary plan for implementing conventional force improvements or for bold innovative conventional arms control proposals which could combine to eliminate its reliance on the early first use of nuclear weapons. (3) NATO faces a Soviet leader—whatever his long run intentions may be—who appears willing, in the parlance of the American card game called poker, to "call NATO's bet and up the ante."

> —Senator Sam Nunn, Chairman,
> Armed Services Committee,
> United States Senate[1]

These developments of the defense policy of the United States and that of the Soviet Union are not new. For the first time, however, they are turning toward convergence. The denuclearization that serves the military interests of the Soviet Union responds to a yearning on the part of American public opinion and of President Reagan. It facilitates the starting up of strategic defense. The inevitable reduction for budgetary reasons of United States conventional forces may help the Soviet Union accentuate the decoupling between Europe and America. This convergence of interests provides a real impetus to the ongoing developments.

> —Deputy François Fillon, former Chairman,
> Committee on National Defense and Armed Forces,
> French National Assembly[2]

We have, without doubt, reached another "perilous moment in the history of the alliance." Although this is indeed a major turning point, it is no more than that; it is neither an end of the Alliance nor is it a radical new beginning, for example, of a separate European alliance. Nonetheless, new Soviet tactics and perhaps objectives are forcing NATO to reexamine both its internal structure and its negotiating posture, which may result in

---

[1]Nunn, 1987, p. 3.
[2]Fillon, 1987.

structural political and military changes in the Alliance—perhaps a Kissinger-like rebuilding, perhaps a new arms-control-driven conventional posture. But the restructuring is likely to end up with the same key members of the Alliance, a similar, incompletely defined flexible posture, and many of the same disagreements.

This is the most likely course, but in 1989 there does appear one perhaps major danger to the Alliance. It comes not from the outside, but like most of the perils of the last twenty years, from ourselves. NATO has not yet become obsolete; in response to radical Soviet change, however, it too must change. But if the debates over change—most of them over symbolic issues—turn harsh enough, as some have tended to, NATO could yet become the Alliance that talked itself to death. That is still unlikely, but it could happen.

This Epilog is more personal and less objective in its intent than the body of the NATO essay. It uses my own logic and interpretations rather than the quotations that have supported the major analysis. There are two reasons for this. First, it is difficult to capture a rapid change in mid-flight and predict its direction; NATO is changing rapidly, and quotations on current events that are fresh in the spring may be obsolete by the fall. Second, for the same reasons of rapid current change and examination of the future, this section depends much more than the earlier ones on unattributable conversations, although the analysis is based primarily on the research presented above.

Our Soviet opponent, who inspired the defense mechanism that became the Alliance and who has defined its existence for 35 years, has suddenly changed at least his tactics and perhaps his objectives. This has been received with worry and skepticism on both sides of the Atlantic, among both the American Maintainers and the European Couplers, as illustrated by the opening quotations from American and French legislators in corresponding positions.

Senator Nunn reflects a broad American consensus in remaining agnostic about Gorbachev "whatever his long run intentions may be" and in suggesting that we had better get our act together. Nunn concentrates on arms control negotiations, both because he foresees little in the way of unilateral improvements in Alliance posture and because he doubts that the arms control poker game will end with the double-zero agreement (nor can we or should we pick up our chips and go home). But central to the Senator's concerns is the fear that public opinion may send arms control off in its own self-propelled direction. As put by another American Maintainer, James Thomson: "The arms control challenge to the Alliance is, first and foremost, to recreate a viable security concept and rally public support around it. . . . Only when the Alliance has recreated its security consensus will our leaders be able to lead public opinion to support a sound arms control policy."[3]

Deputy Fillon is less representative of European Couplers than Senator Nunn is of American Maintainers, although Fillon's belief that threatening change comes as much from the United States as it does from the Soviet Union does represent a strong French undercurrent. This view is less than a West European consensus, but it is widespread enough that Americans and Europeans who want to preserve the Alliance will have to deal with it. Fillon's context is an argument for greater Franco-German defense cooperation. It illustrates one version of *within*-the-West adaptation to the changes of the late 1980s.

These two types of adaptation—changes in the ways in which the Alliance deals with the opponent, and changes in the political/military structure of the Alliance itself—come together into Thomson's "security concept." My belief is that his goal, "to recreate a viable" concept, is likely to be achieved by a NATO that is not too dissimilar from the one that has existed through the late 1980s.

Central to my contention is an assertion that the primary requirement for adaptation stems much more from outside the Alliance—the Soviet Union—than from American isolationist, ethnic, budgetary, or any other internal imperatives. This is, admittedly, an American view, in distinct disagreement with M. Fillon's point that we as much as the Russians are causing the upset. But even though I am not in great sympathy with the off-hand way in which President Reagan frequently made and implemented foreign policy, I believe that many of the U.S. actions that have disturbed Fillon and other West Europeans have been adaptations by existing mechanisms to new stimuli, rather than structural changes initiated by pressures from within the United States or any other part of the Alliance. True, President Reagan was erratic before Gorbachev (and so was President Carter); after Gorbachev came to power, the erraticism was reflected in Reykjavik and other responses to the Soviet Union, but they remained responses, not first causes. And the opening odds on President Bush are that he will be far less erratic than his immediate predecessors.

Most recent evidence indicates that internal Alliance structures remain stable. As a result, the Alliance is adapting nonradically to the most recent

---

[3]Thomson, 1987, p. 1. Thomson had seen INF as an important part of a "viable security concept," and he was concerned that arms control agreements, including the one removing INF as well as new proposals, have been springing up without consideration for NATO's overall security needs.

radical changes in Soviet attitudes and actions; the "subjective alliance" remains subjective. Further radical changes in Soviet behavior can be expected, however, and the variables that we can manipulate should be directed toward preserving the internal stabilities while adapting them to the new externals. The result is consistent with Nunn's and Thomson's prescriptions of a type the post-Reagan administration is likely to take seriously.

CURRENT FACTS AND INTERPRETATIONS

In understanding the external changes of the late 1980s, and NATO's ongoing and future adaptations to these changes, it is important to separate facts from their interpretations. In the following listing, the facts are italicized, my interpretations of those facts and their relevance follow.

- *The electoral situations of the major NATO nations are stable. The president of the United States at least until January 20, 1993, will be George Bush. French foreign policy maintained continuity through the 1988 elections, and the chance of electoral change through the next five to seven years is near zero. In addition, it is all but certain that current British and German governments will continue at least until elections in 1990–1992.*

The American election initially seemed destabilizing to the Alliance. Both European Couplers and many American Maintainers viewed not only President Reagan but President Carter before him as large sources of instability. The litany that began with Carter's inconstancy on the neutron bomb and continued through the "evil empire," SDI, Libya, Reykjavik, and, in some views, zero-zero, was an upsetting one; and the discomfort remained as the 1987–1988 "primary season" rolled around. Europeans knew few of the announced presidential candidates in either party, and this worried them; a few loud noises led some to believe that the campaign would spotlight the burden-sharing issue. But NATO turned out to be a nonstarter as an issue; and while Dukakis remained an unknown between the west coast of Ireland and the Adriatic Sea, he was clearly not a radical, and anyhow he was not elected. The winner fit into a familiar category that neither he nor any member of his party would admit existed any more—a Rockefeller Republican. When he filled the key foreign policy positions in his administration with professionals such as National Security Advisor Scowcroft and Secretary of State Baker, the Europeans began to feel more comfortable.

The American elections had one additional stabilizing effect: Their fixed schedule slowed down American initiatives and responses to Soviet initiatives on Europe. (Negotiations over U.S.-Soviet strategic arms controls slowed down less, but the possibility of such controls is far less upsetting to West Europeans than is the chance of further rapid changes on the continent.) For most of 1988, the American election campaign made radical changes difficult; this was reinforced by the Senate debate over ratification of zero-zero. And for 1989, President Bush made clear that he wanted to *think* about foreign policy, before enunciating it. (This process, of course, substituted charges of "foot-dragging" for those of American erraticism, but that comes within the ordinary rules of the political game.)

The French elections were even earlier than those in the United States. NATO policy was not an issue: In a two-and-a-half hour campaign debate in April of 1988, Mitterrand and Chirac devoted five minutes to all aspects of national security. Since the election, the French consensus has remained tight, although Mitterrand has edged it away from paranoia about the United States, NATO, or Germany and toward serious participation in talks on conventional arms control.

In Britain, the stable government majority and the unlikelihood of national elections before 1991 or 1992 suggest that competition for office will not be a major destabilizing factor. The rule of Mrs. Thatcher seems almost as stable as the reign of Queen Elizabeth. If Labour is to come to power in the near future, one necessary ingredient will be a substantial compromise of the party's current position favoring nuclear unilateralism; in any case, the Labour unilateralists remain staunchly in favor of NATO.

In the Federal Republic, however, the situation is more complicated. NATO policy is stable, but it is beset by many issues that could destabilize it, ranging from concern about German "singularity," through nuclear modernization and SNF negotiations, to military aircraft crashing on German villages. The current Christian Democrat/Free Democrat coalition will remain in power until the 1990 election because there is no alternative; the Free Democrats plus the Social Democrats cannot add up to a majority. Public opinion surveys, however, show the electorate to be *both* pro-NATO and anti-nuclear, which comes close, on the surface, to the position of the moderate Removers in the SPD. Nonetheless, the SPD is unlikely to govern as a majority. The most likely hope for the Social Democrats is enough of an increase to restore a coalition like that they had through 1982 with Foreign Minister Genscher's Free Democrats. For such a coalition to come into being, it would have to have a Coupler NATO policy, albeit one that deemphasized the nuclear deterrent. An SPD coalition with the Green party (the notorious "Red/Green" coalition) would be destabilizing to NATO, but it still appears unlikely. A continued Christian Democratic/Free Democratic coalition would take a more pro-deterrent Coupler position. Neither of the current coalition parties wants NATO issues to enter the election campaign; avoiding an SPD onslaught on these issues has been the major cause of Chancellor Kohl's attempt to move away from the nuclear symbolism of modernization. Nonetheless, such issues could become salient in the campaign, particularly if the United States insists on forcing the Alliance to nuclear modernization decisions the German government would like to postpone.

The American pressures illustrate one final point that should be made about national politics and NATO. Even the closest of allies have difficulties in understanding the politics of their partners. This has been most evident in Coupler misunderstandings of American politics: the tendency to confuse Kristol and Krauss's drive to get out of NATO with Kissinger and Brzezinski's desire to strengthen the Alliance through restructuring, for example. But it is also evident from the fears in France and elsewhere of a German tendency to recreate *Mitteleuropa*, a possibility quickly dismissed in all German political quarters.

- *Budgetary and other economic pressures on U.S. defense spending will remain strong.*

No *deus ex machina* is in sight to reverse the unacceptable American budget deficit. Nor, lacking the external push of an "extended period of substantially increased East-West tensions, clearly the fault of the USSR," that Thomson suggested would be needed to goad the West into financing a conventional buildup, will taxes or other devices take the pressure off the defense budget. Additionally, the need to reverse the flow of trade deficits from the Reagan years will add other economic pressures and may also sour economic relations between the United States and its NATO allies. Difficult trade problems, badly handled, may be the major threat to the Alliance in coming years.

Some of the early effects of these phenomena were reflected in Representative Schroeder's 1987 proposals to force burden-sharing. Schroeder considered running for president but ultimately chose not to; as noted, burden-sharing did not become an issue in the 1988 campaign. Neither the Bush administration nor the Democratic Congress has been pushing it since, and it seems likely that serious consideration of unilateral drawdown will at least be postponed, while negotiated NATO/Warsaw Pact decreases seem a real possibility. This is not a sure thing, however, and if conventional negotiations should fail to produce at least the promise of an agreement, budgetary considerations will renew unilateral pressures. In any case, budget-induced decreases in the number of American troops in Europe seem more possible over the longer run. Even reduced numbers will not necessarily be a first step toward complete withdrawal of the troops or of the commitment they represent.

- *European fears about the United States have calmed down.*

The combination of American electoral stability and their own, plus time as the great healer, has made Europaranoia much less of a factor than it was in the period from Reykjavik to the negotiation of the INF treaty. Reykjavik was the climax of a crescendo of Carter and Reagan administration acts perceived in Europe to be erratic at best. It led to the extremes of Jimmy Goldsmith, fear of imminent decoupling, and negative transatlantic resonance.

But by the time zero-zero was signed, most European Couplers had not only adapted to the *fait accompli*, but had adjusted emotionally. Grumbling was still to be heard on various parts of the continent, notably in the German Ministry of Defense, but it was time to move on to the next "perilous moment in the history of the alliance." The British, who had been calm, remained calm. The French, who had been tense over zero-zero adapted to the calmness of their newly reelected President, who had been for the INF treaty all along; Deputy Fillon was no longer Chairman of the Assembly Defense Committee, his party having been relegated to the opposition. Although Reagan/Gorbachev summits might have been talked down in some Coupler quarters as play-acting, they relaxed the pressure of Remover peace movements on Coupler governments. And the entry into Washington of Bush and his good old-fashioned Eastern establishment team made everything feel much better.

The potential exception was the Federal Republic of Germany. Their election was ahead of them, not behind; zero-zero had left a legacy of resentment about cavalier American handling of German vital interests, from which came many of the strong feelings about German "singularity" and sovereignty. German public opinion was more antinuclear and further out ahead in accepting Gorbachev at face value than was the leadership. NATO aircraft accidents and the brouhaha over German aid to the Libyan chemical warfare plant provided additional irritants. In this atmosphere, American pressure in the first few months of the Bush administration to decide quickly on nuclear modernization issues that most German politicians preferred to postpone until after the 1990 election, or indefinitely, added more fuel. For the May 1989 NATO "summit" in Brussels, President Bush crafted a compromise that seemed to take the pressure off the issue, but it was questionable that the immediate decompression would last through the following year and a half until the election. Nonetheless, even in the Federal Republic the fundamentals remained strong: Germans were restive, but they were a long way from questioning their need for NATO, nor was a majority pushing for a restructuring.

Radical change in the Alliance is not likely to come from within. It may come from the outside—from changes in the Soviet Union.

- *The final fact is the one with which this Epilog began: The Soviet Union is changing. The change in Soviet external policy may be tactical or strategic, malign or benign in intent, good or bad for the good guys. It may be short or long run. But change is indubitably taking place, and fast.*

The Couplers and Maintainers sections on "The Opponent" indicated the breadth of the debate over the difference Gorbachev has made. What is beyond challenge is that he has made a difference. Soviet acceptance in 1987 of the changes that led to the zero-zero agreement—intrusive inspection and extremely asymmetrical reductions, for example—were not predicted and, indeed, seemed impossible two years earlier. Nor is it likely, or even possible, that the Soviet Union will revert to the Brezhnev-Andropov-Chernenko era, any more than Brezhnev reverted to Stalin. Were Gorbachev to be overthrown by the military or by old-liners in the Communist Party, *perestroika*, restructuring, could not be re-restructured back to the 1970s. Externally, the "tough" Soviet policies that led to the SS-20s, which led (in part) to the INF, could return. But the economic failures and the political failures in Europe (the failure to prevent the installation of INF) and elsewhere (Afghanistan) would remain.

A Soviet return to overt hostility would have ironic implications for NATO. In many ways it would be comforting. The Alliance was built on Soviet hostility, and a return to such hostility might seem to facilitate a return on our side to the old familiar ways rather than the upsets of the last few years. Further, because the economic and political problems of the Soviet Union and the Warsaw Pact would remain unsolved by the means that had failed to solve them in the past, the opponent's renewed hostility would be weakened. The trouble is that Europe "can't go home again." The chief comfort for the West was that, hostile as it might have been, the pre-Gorbachev Soviet Union was clearly unwilling to go to war in Europe or, since the Berlin crises of the early 1960s, risk war. A renewed hostility, plus weakness, plus a new leadership anxious to restore Soviet positions could be a very dangerous combination. Innate Western conservatism has mourned the loss of the old pre-Gorbachev stabilities. But they *are* lost; a new conservatism should cherish the ostensibly nonhostile instabilities of the late 1980s, because hostile instabilities would be even worse.

Suppose that Gorbachev remains and continues to pursue his line of internal *perestroika* and external radical surprises. What are the implications for the West? The central theme must continue to be Becker and Horelick's caution that "The Soviet future is uncertain and we can have little confidence in our ability to shape the Soviet course," and their consequent "strategy of step-by-step engagement." Step-by-step, however, means that only the first steps can be laid out in advance; the next ones depend on responses. The overall rule must be that: *Soviet ambiguities should not allow us to accept what would otherwise be unacceptable; but Soviet activities should force us to treat seriously what was never serious before because it was never possible.* The agenda is wide open, and we should not again be caught with an arms control proposal like zero-zero, put forth in the sure knowledge that it was unacceptable to the other side.

ADAPTATIONS

NATO's adaptations to the brave new world of post-zero-zero must take place in two arenas: within the Alliance and in the relationship between the Alliance and the Warsaw Pact. Together, they will be governed by the creation or the absence of Thomson's "viable security concept."

Within the Alliance

The discussion of within-the-Alliance adaptations starts with three premises about the next several years:

- The central premise is that whatever happens in negotiations with the Pact, and indeed whatever happens with or to Gorbachev, the Soviets will not turn very much *more* hostile than they had been in the Brezhnev-Andropov-Chernenko years.
- A Soviet reversion back only as far as the hostilities and suspicions of those years would be insufficient to relax the budgetary and other constraints on substantial increases in NATO capabilities; that would take at least a return to the real military threats that apparently ended with the Berlin and Cuban crises of the early 1960s.
- The current sort of "benign" Soviet attitudes will not call forth *unilateral* within-Alliance responses greatly different from those that would have been produced by Brezhnev-style hostility; Western suspicions about the Soviets remain too great, and shifts in NATO posture will depend on the translation of Soviet attitudes into acceptable mutual arms control agreements.

Given these three premises, one major pressure and one powerful constraint will govern NATO's unilateral adaptations to zero-zero. The pressure is the fear, felt mostly in Europe but shared resonantly by many American Maintainers, that zero-zero removes part of NATO's nuclear counterbalance to the Pact's strong conventional superiority, thus leaving us dangerously exposed at the lower levels. The West Europeans further fear that the United States will strip away more of the links that couple conventional defense to the American strategic nuclear deterrent; this fear is not widely shared in the United States. The constraint on both sides of the Atlantic, however, is that neither the budgets nor the economies of the United States or the European members of the Alliance will permit substantial expenditure increases to correct the new exposures stemming from zero-zero.

The zero-zero pressure may call for two types of unilateral Alliance adaptations within the budgetary constraints: restoration to NATO of some of the nuclear capability lessened by removal of the INF missiles and reduction of the conventional imbalance by increasing the capabilities of the Alliance.

On the nuclear side, several proposals are based on reposturing of American weapons:

- "Modernizing" by replacing old missile systems, such as the Lance with a range of about 100 kilometers, with such newer systems as the "Follow-On To Lance" (FOTL), which is proposed to have a range just under the treaty limitation of 500 kilometers.
- More dependence on nuclear-capable aircraft based in Europe, perhaps by substituting standoff missile systems with ranges of several hundred kilometers for free-fall "gravity" bombs. This may raise some problems with the arms control objection to dual-capable aircraft: Controlling escalation will be difficult if an F-111 can take off in times of crisis or conventional combat without the enemy's knowing whether it is carrying a conventional or nuclear load.
- Replacing the land-based INF missiles with sea-based cruise missiles having ranges that can reach the USSR and that are dedicated to NATO and under the control of SACEUR (insofar as the INF missiles and other American nuclear weapons have been under the control of SACEUR, which means under the ultimate control of the president of the United States).[4]

Other proposals involve British and French weapons:

- Some of these are vague or symbolic. The Franco-British discussions of targeting, for example, are partly in response to the impetus of zero-zero, but how they would relate to the replacement of the INF deterrent is unclear.
- Some are more concrete but quite uncertain and long run. The French, for example, are developing an aircraft-carried missile called *Air-Sol de Moyen Portée* (Air-Ground Middle Range), and there is some talk of building into *Longue Portée*, long enough to reach the Soviet Union, possibly in collaboration with the British.
- Some are more radical, for example Jean d'Aubach's proposal for "'juxtaposition' of the French and British capabilities."[5] Their radicalism makes them unlikely except perhaps under some combination of renewed Soviet hostility and substantial U.S. withdrawal. They will become even less likely as West Europeans realize that zero-zero is not necessarily or particularly the first step down the "slippery slope" to full denuclearization of the American commitment.

One proposal not heard from European Couplers is for an independent German nuclear capability; the only debaters to suggest this are American

---

[4]See, for example, Bertram, 1987b, p. 5.
[5]See Ch. 17.

Withdrawers such as Layne. The Germans do, however, impose constraints on solutions designed to compensate for the deterrent loss of INF. For one thing, fear of "singularity" leads them to oppose missiles with ranges so short that, launched from West Germany or its allies beyond the Rhine, they can fall only on Germans of the Federal Republic or the Democratic Republic. The slogan is "The shorter the range, the deader the Germans"; FOTL would at least reach to Poland. This opposition to short-range systems has some important implications for arms control negotiations; so far as unilateral Alliance posture is concerned, it would preclude any buildup of such systems to compensate for the loss of the intermediate-range missiles. This would be unlikely in any case, however: Couplers as well as Maintainers generally agree with Congressman Aspin that the short-range weapons are the least stable; regardless of zero-zero, the Alliance has moved toward cutting back at least on nuclear artillery and mines.

In addition, German government and other Coupler fears of the peace movement make difficult *any* compensatory buildup of new or new-seeming nuclear weapons that could provide a visible symbol around which the movement could mount demonstrations. Even Germans who recognize the continued importance of nuclear deterrence to the security of the Federal Republic shy away from such weapons as FOTL, fearing that its fourfold increase in range would make it an easy symbol of newness. "Improvement" of aircraft, even by adding medium-range standoff missiles, is apparently more acceptable, because the same old airplanes are visible on the same old airstrips.

The possibilities for unilateral restoration of the conventional balance may be less constrained politically than the nuclear possibilities, but they are more constrained by economics. The importance of increased conventional capabilities has been recognized since 1952, the budgetary constraints have been recognized just as long, and this part of the debate has changed very little. The several pre- and post-zero-zero quotations from General Rogers and others advocating increases fall within a classic NATO literary genre. And unless the taxpaying electorates of the NATO nations become far more frightened of the Soviet military threat than they have been in recent years, they will continue to come to naught.

Some of the suggested budget-constrained solutions—the technological changes, the deep strategies, and the defensive ones—have been discussed. In general, no breakthroughs of strategic conceptualization seem likely, and most expert analysis treats the technological possibilities in terms of jam tomorrow, but never today. Perhaps Western science and engineering can right the conventional balance within fixed budgets, but at best the case is not proven.

Similar constrained possibilities for conventional improvements lie in the mild post-zero-zero acceleration of Franco-German cooperation. The cooperation does little to relax the budget constraints; the French had increased military budgets, but the lion's share went to improvement and modernization of their nuclear forces, and in any case, fiscal pressures are now beginning to exert major constraints on French defense expenditures. Joint Franco-German planning may lead to greater military effectiveness, but that would be marginal and could be counteracted by the failure to mesh semi-integrated Franco-German forces into the integrated NATO effort. And although sub rosa reintegration of French forces, were it possible, would surely increase the Alliance's conventional capabilities, most of the computations that still lead to unfavorable estimates of the balance have already counted French forces.

The most serious aspect of Franco-German cooperation may lie in the prospective realm of "What if American troops did leave?" The one surest effect of zero-zero on the conventional balance, however, has been the resonant delaying of any potential drawdowns of U.S. forces. After the 1984 defeat of the Nunn Amendment, the pressure became less; and in April 1987 Senator Nunn announced himself conditionally satisfied about progress to date.[6] And neither President Bush nor his advisors seemed inclined in that direction. Nonetheless, predictable budget and economic pressures will renew the drive within the United States for more European burden-sharing or American drawdowns in Europe; they are likely to strengthen substantially if arms control negotiations become stalemated, and unilateral action seems the only way to reduce expenditures on conventional forces.

The prospects for *increases* on either side of the Atlantic that could unilaterally restore the nuclear-conventional deterrent balance disturbed by zero-zero thus do not appear very promising. It might be argued that the disturbance has been trivial, that deterrence was overwhelming before zero-zero and remains overwhelming after. In fact, that argument will be made in the final and most opinionated portion of this Epilog. This does not imply that we should cease striving for better deterrence or more stability, but substantial unilateral measures seem unlikely.

---

[6]See Ch. 18.

That leaves arms control. A frequently heard view is that stated by U.S. Ambassador to the Federal Republic Richard Burt: "Arms control cannot in itself redress the imbalance of conventional forces in Europe."[7] The trouble is that arms control may not be *the* solution, but it may be the *only* solution. The prospects for unilateral solutions seem so thin that even if Burt is right, arms control may be the worst solution except for all the others, to paraphrase Churchill.

Like potential unilateral actions, post-zero-zero arms control possibilities fall into two categories, nuclear and conventional.[8]

In the nuclear realm, it is not clear what controls might come next. From the NATO viewpoint, fears of sliding down the slippery slope to denuclearization suggest that the best additional controls in the immediate post-zero-zero future would be no additional controls. This has been the position taken by the United States, Britain, and France, who want to see what progress can be made in improving the conventional balance through negotiated controls before weakening NATO's ultimate nuclear deterrent. Because of their fears of singularity, however, the Germans have wanted to accelerate nuclear negotiations; nonetheless, the wait-and-see attitude of the other allies is likely to prevail. In any case, there seems general agreement throughout the Alliance to thin out the truly short systems, the artillery; although even here, tactical and political differences make it difficult to determine whether this should be done unilaterally or should be subject to negotiations.

Some Couplers, particularly on the German left, still suggest denuclearized zones, but these proposals received no new impetus from zero-zero and current NATO governments are not seriously considering them. In addition, in his Brussels speech Senator Nunn mentioned a tradeoff of a nuclear No First Use pledge by NATO against a breaking up of major tank concentrations by the Warsaw Pact,[9] but that was apparently intended primarily rhetorically and has not been taken as seriously as the conventional arms control proposals in the same speech. In general, the view, shared by Maintainers and non-German Couplers alike, that it might be best to digest

---

[7]Burt, 1988.

[8]Controls on chemical weapons are generally considered separately, as at the Paris conference of January 1989. The issues are difficult, particularly how to verify processes that similar to peacetime processes; but chemical controls have largely stayed out of both the East/West debate and the NATO debate, although the aid given to the Libyan chemical plant by German firms has been an additional irritant between the Federal Republic and the United States.

[9]Nunn, 1987.

zero-zero before moving on to additional nuclear controls in Europe seems likely to prevail.

The feeling has been quite different on conventional controls. The stress put on the conventional imbalance by the perceived lessening of nuclear deterrence, plus the thought that in the Gorbachev era agreements to help right the balance might just be possible, have led many in NATO to treat conventional controls far more seriously than in the past. Serious negotiations have begun, for the first time ever.

For a long time, conventional arms control negotiations were tangled into a confusion of bureaucratic strings unusual even for Europe. Starting in 1973, the East and the West began the Mutual and Balanced Force Reduction (MBFR) talks in Vienna. The West, however, did not include France because France did not want to be considered part of a Western bloc; in any case, neither side was very serious in the Brezhnev era. Vienna was a nice place for Foreign Office and Ministry of Defense diplomats to do long secure tours, and the talks went on through 1988, to no conclusion. At about the same time, the multinational/no blocs Conference on Security and Cooperation in Europe (CSCE) produced the 1975 Helsinki Final Act, which led in turn to the Conference on Confidence and Security-Building Measures and Disarmament in Europe (boiled down to CDE), which in 1986 produced a series of stabilizing measures (e.g., notifications of maneuvers, observation rights), not including force reductions. After 1986, the same group carried out a review, which like the MBFR talks lasted until 1988 in Vienna. Among the other issues drawn into the bureaucratic considerations were the area to be covered (Atlantic-to-the-Urals or all of Europe, versus the Central Front, versus some other concepts) and the role of the United States in the European talks.

In 1988, a series of strong winds suddenly blew away the bureaucratic obstacles of 15 years. These were led by the desire for real negotiations on the part of both East and West and abetted by Mitterrand's interest in arms control, which quickly eliminated all the French objections (being French, they never admitted the change, they just did it). In March 1989, real conventional arms reduction negotiations (the Conventional Stability Talks or CST) began in Vienna. In the meantime, however, starting with Gorbachev's October 1988 UN speech, the Soviet Union and most of the other members of the Warsaw Pact announced a series of unilateral reductions, mostly conventional although also including some short-range tactical nuclear weapons carried by Soviet military formations. Initial analysis by Western experts indicated that the reductions, if carried out, would be important; the question of whether to respond unilaterally or only within the new Vienna talks became a subject for discussion within NATO.

Serious possibilities have produced serious debate within the Alliance, but in the initial stages it has not divided Couplers from Maintainers. Both schools include debaters who emphasize the possibilities for conventional controls, and both include debaters who emphasize the dangers and constraints; both contain Sovietologists who stress the Kremlin's real need for cutbacks, and both contain Sovietologists who stress their tactical use of negotiations. All this is as it was before zero-zero. What is new, however, is the belief that it might really happen this time; and that has provided a completely new tone to the discussion.

One of the earliest and best-known of the opening proposals was made by Senator Nunn in his Brussels speech. He suggested a 50 percent reduction in U.S. and Soviet forces deployed on the territory of their allies; because the Soviets had many more such, this would amount to an asymmetric reduction of something like two American divisions against 13 differently structured and smaller Soviet divisions. These forces were to be drawn far enough back that it would take equal time for them to redeploy back to their previous positions.[10] The speech also discussed a chemical weapons ban and the need for verification. Defense analyst Philip Karber later provided hypothetical detail to the Nunn concept (but without consulting the Senator). For someone who had previously concentrated on NATO's needed conventional improvements, Karber now waxed enthusiastic about what he saw as changed Soviet positions that "would have been hailed as a breakthrough if raised during the 13 fruitless years of the preceding Mutual and Balanced Force Reduction negotiations."[11] Karber's elaboration of the Nunn plan covered manpower, tanks, artillery and other weapons, distances of withdrawal, details of verification, and so forth. More important than the details themselves was that first-string analysts of conventional defenses had begun to analyze such details.

Another such effort, widely circulated throughout NATO, was by James Thomson and Nanette Gantz of RAND, who suggested that "substantially asymmetrical" Warsaw Pact and NATO reductions would be necessary to avoid worsening the conventional balance. Their estimated breakeven point was a 5:1 ratio of Pact to NATO reductions, based on the existing 1987 balance. Even a 4:1 or 3:1 ratio, according to their calculations, would actually turn the balance even further against the Alliance than it had been up until that time. Further, initial reductions should be large; small asymmetrical reductions would not help. All of these estimates were applied to "division equivalents," taking account of the differences in what

---

[10]Nunn, 1987, pp. 12–13.
[11]Karber, 1988.

NATO and the Pact include in a ground-forces division; Thomson and Gantz also stressed the importance of tanks and artillery.[12]

The 5:1 ratio for NATO and Pact reductions is consistent with Nunn's differently calculated 13:2 for U.S. and Soviet forces. The Thomson-Gantz report was hardly noncontroversial, however. Although asymmetry had been a feature of the zero-zero agreement, Thomson himself suggested that the Soviets were unlikely to accept such overbalanced proposals at the conventional level. This induced both a State Department response that we should try anyhow (with which Thomson would not disagree), and a comment by Jonathan Dean that Thomson was too pessimistic.[13]

The Western position going into the 1989 Vienna talks (not the NATO position, the talks were still not officially bloc-to-bloc) was consistent with these calculations. The West asked for reduction *to* 95 percent of then-current NATO levels of tanks and artillery on both sides; this was arithmetically similar to reductions *by* the asymmetrical ratios coming out of the studies. The Soviets disagreed about the starting numbers, but it was the first time they had put real numbers on the table at all; and they wanted to include air, in which they asserted that NATO had preponderance. In his May 1989 Brussels NATO "summit" proposal, President Bush agreed to negotiate on air, and on troop numbers as well, thus putting the talks on what he hoped was a fast track. Predictably the outcome would depend on the precise positions and the details; but in the first instance it depended on the willingness to agree, and for the first time in a decade and a half that seemed to exist on both sides.

CONCLUSION

Where, then, should we be going? Some of my views may be clear from the foregoing discussion, in which I have made less of an attempt at objectivity than in the analysis in the previous sections. Four central assertions summarize the viewpoint:

- The security of Western Europe is quite safe and stable after zero-zero; it was quite safe and stable before zero-zero. The Soviet military threat and even the political shadow of "Finlandization" are and have been extremely remote. Under Khrushchev, under Brezhnev, and under Gorbachev, this security has been based largely on existential deterrence—on the Soviet fear that so long as nuclear weapons existed in Western

---

[12]Thomson and Gantz, 1987, p. 13.
[13]See "Study Says Troop Pact Is Not Likely," *New York Times*, November 12, 1987, p. 3.

arsenals, the risk of escalation was too great to allow *any* military adventurism that might threaten Western Europe. In spite of the American Withdrawers, the Reagan administration never had a serious intention of denuclearizing Europe. The Bush administration is even less inclined in that direction, and existential deterrence will remain. It might well remain anyhow, based on the U.S. strategic nuclear capability, even if no American weapons were on European soil; it might remain, based on British and French weapons, even if the United States dissociated itself completely from NATO.

- West European safety and stability are safest and most stable within NATO, however; and the United States belongs within the Alliance for reasons of both national interest and national empathy. In spite of the strong statements about existentialism made in the last paragraph, European nervousness about self-preservation is understandable. The Alliance *is* subjective, and this subjectivity is important and important to understand. That "resonance" governs much of the Maintainer reaction to Europe and much of the Coupler reaction to the United States is no bad thing. If the Alliance is central to European stability, and if European stability is an American vital interest, then a lot of effort on both sides of the Atlantic should be going into preserving the Alliance.

- On the American side, this effort should include both a continued nuclear commitment manifested in ways clearly understood by our allies and our adversary and a continued substantial troop presence on the continent. It should exclude the use of drawdown threats to increase the European share of the burden; burden-sharing should be reconsidered in the light of whatever change of burdens, if any, comes out of the conventional arms control negotiations. On the European side, the effort should include an understanding that not every change in nuclear or conventional posture is a first slide down one or another slippery slope; and, unless Western Europe wants to become "Fortress Europe" in security terms, it should downplay economic "Fortress Europe" as the Common Market year of 1992 approaches. Both sides should resist the temptation to commit the other to the symbolic gesture of the year, particularly the pressure to build or deploy a specific nuclear weapon without which deterrence will surely disappear overnight.

- Gorbachev does make a difference. His seductive advances to the West may not be sincere, or his colleagues may inhibit him, or they may ultimately remove him. Even so, it would be very difficult for the Soviets to get back to where they were. Were they to try, economics might make them less of a threat than they were before. A weak, hostile, heavily armed Soviet Union, however, might be very dangerous. The only sure thing is change. "Step-by-step engagement" does not mean that we should "trust" the Soviets any more than we did before. We should not arrive at agreements that depend in any substantial measure on such trust. And we should know by now that we are far too clumsy to "help" Gorbachev by playing internal Kremlin politics; we should have learned something by trying to play internal Iranian politics. Soviet changes may mean that substantial new opportunities are opening for the kinds of agreements that we have ostensibly been trying to get for 35 years—agreements that do not depend on trust and that are based on the asymmetrical reductions we require. Such agreements can provide stronger and cheaper guarantees for West European security and American interests.

What is needed now is sober and serious Alliance consideration of what we want from negotiations with the Soviets, what we want to do by ourselves, and how we should accomplish both. The consideration and the moves should take the time necessary. What *should not* be done, however, is shouting across the Atlantic, negative resonance building into a crescendo that could make the Alliance into a victim of its own paranoia and a potential victim of Soviet exploitation. Such amplifying negative resonance seemed to be starting during the early part of the 1987 zero-zero negotiations; it seemed to die down after the *fait accompli*, some of the fights over next steps, particularly between the Anglo-Saxons and the Germans, have begun to raise it again. Although all sides recognize the need for a stronger European pillar for the Alliance, neither European rhetoric about the need for a parallel alliance because of American unreliability nor U.S. reactions that treat pillar-building as inherently anti-American are very helpful.

My own opinion is that the Soviets are very likely open to agreements to enhance the security of both sides. If so, the process could end up being exhilarating. If not, and if we exert proper care and do not talk our Alliance apart in the process, neither Western interests nor East-West stability need suffer. The North Atlantic Treaty Organization will remain a necessary keystone for many years.

PART FOUR
SUMMARIZING THE DEBATE

22. Summarizing the Debate

> In recent years many clarion calls have gone out for a "great debate" over the arms policy of the United States. But a general and coherent debate has failed to materialize. There have been books, articles, and oral discussions, sometimes based on sharp disagreements over particular policies or the views of particular individuals, but these have been so diffuse that the holders of different viewpoints sometimes have not even seemed to be talking about the same things. . . . The little debates going on have been more like the individual jousts of the Round Table knights than the final battle of Arthurian Britain (although perhaps carried out less chivalrously than either).
>
> —*The Arms Debate*[1]

This chapter takes up two tasks: It examines the relationship of the schools of thought in the current debate to those created for the arms debate of the early 1960s and it ties the separate school structures used for each of the three 1980s debate segments (Third World, strategic nuclear, NATO) into one unified set of four schools of thought, each following a different philosophy on overall arms policy. These tasks are historical and intellectual; they inform the synthesis and projection of the final chapter.

Unlike *The Arms Debate*, which stressed the overall schools of thought, the current study has saved them for the end. The major reason for this change is the vastly increased complexity of the newer debate as Vietnam evidence challenged the old verities; as West Europeans joined at least into the segment of most concern to themselves; and, most recently, as the Soviet Union has apparently veered off the track Stalin established 40 years ago. The desire to concentrate this study on the effects of the debate on *arms policy* rather than the formalities of taxonomy has dictated the structure used here.

---

[1]Levine, 1963, p. 1.

THE FIVE SCHOOLS OF THOUGHT IN THE 1960s

Figure 1 reproduces the horseshoe with which *The Arms Debate* illustrated the Schools of Thought of the early 1960s. The terms "marginal" and "systemic" in the figure are used to differentiate between those debaters who recommended incremental arms policy changes at the margin of existing policies and those more radical debaters who contended that the whole policy system needed to be changed. The reason for the horseshoe was that the systemic ends were in many ways closer to one another than they were to the middle; *The Arms Debate* illustrated this with a 1960 quotation describing the 1930s that is equally applicable to the 1980s:

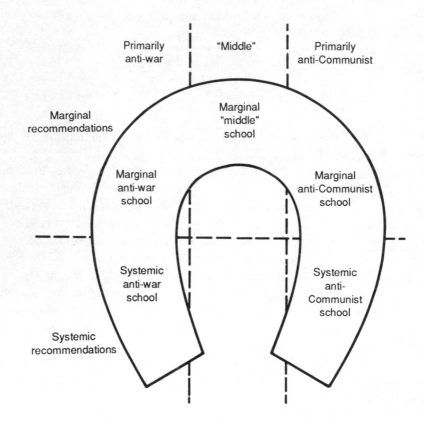

Figure 1—The horseshoe of the 1960s

Radicalism, like conservatism, thus ended in the domain of either-or. The contradictions of actuality, which so stimulated the pragmatists of Washington, only violated the proprieties and offended the illusions of the ideologists. [John] Dewey and [Harold] Laski wholly agreed with Herbert Hoover and Ogden Mills that one must have either capitalism or socialism; any combination of the two was impossible. The protagonists on each side saw themselves as hardheaded realists. But in fact they were all unconscious Platonists, considering abstractions the ultimate reality.[2]

The Arms Debate brought this to the 1960s by comparing either-or statements by unilateral disarmer Bertrand Russell and American anti-Communist politician Barry Goldwater.[3] Perhaps the best parallel from the 1980s is that the American Withdrawers, who want the United States to get out of NATO, include both strong anti-Communists who concentrate on the threat to Western values in the world outside of Europe, and strong Disarmers, who want to cut our military commitments everywhere.

The 1960s horseshoe included five Schools. Reading from left to right, they were:

- *Systemic Anti-War*, exemplified by Russell and many American Quakers, who favored unilateral disarmament and withdrawal from Vietnam.
- *Marginal Anti-War*, including such academics as Arthur Waskow and Amitai Etzioni, as well as Adlai Stevenson, Chester Bowles, and some other members of the Kennedy administration. They stressed steps toward multilateral disarmament and capture of the "hearts and minds" of the Vietnamese people. In Europe they favored NATO but wanted to move toward regional disarmament, and many of them were still suspicious of Germany.
- *Marginal Middle*, whose strategic policies were initially based on the thinking of such Cambridge dons as Thomas Schelling and Henry Kissinger, and their west coast RAND Corporation counterparts exemplified by Albert Wohlstetter and Herman Kahn. Within the Kennedy administration, Robert McNamara, McGeorge Bundy, and the President himself acted in large measure on the same premises. Their strategic philosophy encompassed controlled counterforce nuclear planning and arms controls to maintain stability, with some sorts of disarmament among the possible controls. They were pro-NATO, and although they wanted to increase conventional defenses, they understood the need for

---

[2]A. Schlesinger, 1960, p. 176.
[3]Levine, 1963, pp. 49–50.

nuclear deterrence in Europe. They thought little about the Third World, so that action in Vietnam was based on simple extension of the domino theory, the containment concept, and some of the escalation ideas derived from their strategic theories.

- *Marginal Anti-Communist*, which, like its opposite Marginal Anti-War counterparts, was largely composed of academics, in this case centered on the Foreign Policy Institute of the University of Pennsylvania, where Robert Strausz-Hupé and William Kintner had written two key studies (joined in each by other authors).[4] The title of the first of these, *Protracted Conflict*, described the focus of their strategy: We were in a protracted conflict with the Soviet Union and worldwide Communism, which one side or the other would ultimately win. In the strategic arena, they were prudent but doubtful of the Cambridge arms control concepts, and they were strongly pro-NATO; but much more than the Middle school they concentrated on the Third World, where they favored a strong "Forward Strategy" based on what they saw as military realism.

- *Systemic Anti-Communist*, from Senator Goldwater in the arena of active politics, going to the pressure-group fringes to the right. At least in words, they were willing to contemplate the nuclear threat for a variety of purposes around the globe.

THE CHANGING SCHOOLS: 1960 TO 1980

Each of the analyses of the three segments of the current debate has provided a historical trace of the roots of the schools created for that segment. This discussion shows the connections of the five overall schools of the 1960s to the segment schools of the 1980s and connects the segment schools to one another. This latter effort will provide the basis for creating overall 1980s schools.

Figure 2 provides a rather intricate roadmap. The boxes on the left represent the five 1960s schools of the horseshoe. These are then connected to the schools in the Third World segment of the 1980s debate, because the Third World schools most resemble the overall schools of the 1960s. The next two columns of boxes show the American schools collapsing into one another as the debate moves from the Third World to strategic nuclear policy to NATO. Finally, the boxes on the right bring in the European debaters, who enter as equal partners in the American debate only as it

---

[4]Strausz-Hupé et al., 1959; and and Strausz-Hupé, Kintner, and Possony, 1961.

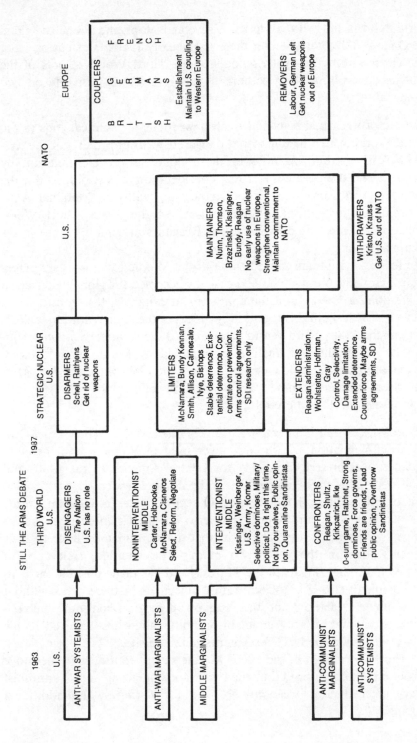

Figure 2—The Schools of Thought, from the 1960s to the 1980s

concerns NATO and who, aside from several Britons and French General Pierre Gallois, did not even enter there in the early 1960s.

The change from the 1960s schools to the Third World schools of the current debate (column 1 to column 2) has been based primarily on two phenomena:

- The use of nuclear threats and nuclear weapons for political ends in the Third World, which had appeared dangerously absurd to all but the Systemic Anti-Communists even in the 1960s, was proven irrelevant by Vietnam and disappeared as a real consideration. As it did, so did the Systemic Anti-Communist school, collapsing with the Marginal Anti-Communists into the *Confronter* school of the 1980s Third World debate, well represented by President Reagan and some of those in his administration.
- The failure in Vietnam moved some of the Middle Marginalists, notably McNamara and Bundy, who had casually accepted the global application of the domino theory and the containment principle, to reconsider and move much closer in this regard to the ideas of the Anti-War Marginalists, forming the 1980s Third World School called the *Noninterventionist Middle*. Other Middle Marginalists, exemplified by Kissinger and Nixon, remained closer to the old ideas and formed the 1980s *Interventionist Middle* school, similar in some ways to the Confronters but with their anti-Communist ideology more tempered.

The Anti-War Systemists remained largely unchanged. Their "Get-Out-Now" recommendation, which was never tried in Vietnam and therefore never failed, was prescribed equally for Central America in the 1980s and was not tried. This study renames them the *Disengagers*.

Paradoxically, although the creation of real evidence in Vietnam caused the *substance* of the Third World debate to change far more than that of the other two segments, the *schools* in that debate remained truer to their antecedents than in the other two cases. The seeming irrelevance of nuclear weapons and threats in the Third World has made possible the continued pursuit of strong anti-Communist objectives in these areas without fear of ultimate escalation; and the resultant ideological continuity necessitates less telescoping of one school into another than has occurred in the strategic nuclear and the NATO segments of the debate.

The Third World split of the 1960s Middle school continues in the move from column 2 to column 3, but the irrelevance of strong anti-Communist ideology when nuclear weapons *are* the focus causes one additional telescoping.

- McNamara, Bundy, and most of the others who moved away from Third World dominoes and containment also moved from their 1960s strategic beliefs that counterforce strategies could succeed in limiting damage and controlling escalation once nuclear war had broken out, stressing instead the need for arms control agreements. The *Limiters* school in the strategic nuclear debate is thus made up of most of the same individuals as the Third World Noninterventionist Middle.
- The strategic nuclear *Extenders* school subsumes both the Interventionist Middle and the Confronters of the Third World segment. These two divide over the vigor with which anti-Communist objectives should be pursued in the Third World, but in the strategic debate they come to general agreement on the ways that nuclear stability should be maintained: a stress on counterforce and control coupled with a suspicion of arms control. The Extenders' school included essentially all of the Reagan administration.

The 1960s Anti-War Systemists and 1980s Disengagers become the *Disarmers* in the strategic nuclear debate, with very little change of personnel, although the stress for most of them has shifted from unilateral disarmament, to hoped-for rapid movement to multilateral disarmament. The result is three schools in this debate, compared with the four on the Third World.

Moving to column 4, the American portion of the NATO debate unites the middle against the ends:

- In spite of their profound disagreement over the utility of controlled nuclear strategies, and their somewhat less profound differences on arms control, the strategic nuclear Limiters and most of the Extenders come together on the three American propositions with regard to NATO: a high threshold for nuclear threats in Europe, a strong conventional capability to make the high threshold real, and a continued U.S. commitment to the Alliance in any case. These propositions and the consequent policy recommendations define the school called the *Maintainers*, who include individuals as diverse as McNamara, Bundy, Senator Nunn, Kissinger, Brzezinski, and President Reagan.
- The extremes on the right and the left unite to propose effective U.S. withdrawal from NATO. On the right, a group consisting of some of the Third World Confronters (who had joined the other Extenders on strategic nuclear matters) believes that Western Europe is fully capable of defending itself and is diluting the required global anti-Communist focus. They are joined in their major "get-out-of-Europe" recommendation by those

Disengagers and Disarmers on the left who pay attention to Europe (most concentrate on potential nuclear holocaust and on American Third World pecadillos), who want to reduce American involvement and nuclear danger in Europe as elsewhere. The result is the *Withdrawer school*, typified by neoconservative intellectual Irving Kristol.

Like the Americans, the West Europeans, in this one portion of the American-Western arms debate which they join in full, form the two schools shown in column 5, one mainstream and the other radical.

- The radical counterparts of the primarily right-wing American With-drawers, who want to get the United States out of NATO, are the entirely left-wing European Removers, all of whom want to get American nuclear weapons out of Europe and some of whom want the United States to leave NATO and Europe completely. They include the majority of the British Labour Party, the German Greens and a portion of the Social Democrats, and substantial forces within some of the smaller NATO nations.
- The Coupler school is formed of mainstream West European officials and analysts. It is defined more by its premises and emphases than by specific common positions. The central objective, quite naturally, is the preservation of West European institutions and civilization; the central concern is that the U.S. commitment to NATO, particularly the strategic nuclear deterrent to Soviet aggression in Europe, will somehow become "uncoupled," thereby leaving West Europe vulnerable to military aggression or, more likely, to political pressure based on potential aggression. Under this common set of objectives and beliefs, Britain, France, and the Federal Republic of Germany tend to produce specific views different from one another and from the smaller members; nor are individual positions within the nations identical. Nonetheless, those in the West European mainstream tend to think of themselves as "Europeans" and frequently come together on views opposing those of the American mainstream.

THE FIVE SCHOOLS OF THOUGHT IN THE 1980s

The complex flow chart of Fig. 2 illustrates the fact that the arms debate of the 1980s is far more complex than that of the 1960s. Not only the separate entry of the West Europeans but the increasing sophistication and subtlety of the Americans and the onset of evidence from Vietnam have led to many new complications. Even so, it is possible to create meaningful schools that cut across the three segments of the current debate.

Figure 3 does this, utilizing a horseshoe similar to that of the earlier debate. Reading around the outside from left to right, and creating new names as necessary, they are:

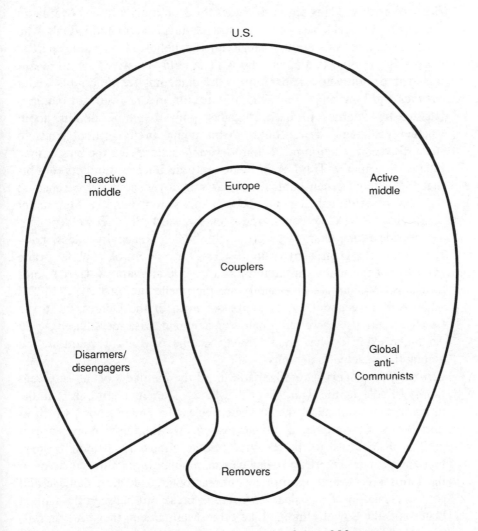

Figure 3—The horseshoe of the 1980s

- *Disarmers/Disengagers*, the group that has drawn its heritage from the anti-nuclear weapons and anti-Vietnam Disarmers of the 1960s. For the most part abandoning unilateral disarmament and many of the other simple concepts of the earlier period, this school has become more sophisticated in nuclear matters while remaining true to its earlier views on the Third World. The major European issue that engaged them in the 1960s, the fear of resurgent Nazism in Germany, has faded out, and few analysts write about Europe as such.

- *Reactive Middle.* This school includes the Noninterventionist Middle in the Third World Debate and the near-identical set of individuals who form the Limiter school on strategic nuclear policy. It subsumes part of the NATO-debate Maintainer school. The term "reactive," by no means intended pejoratively, stems from a fundamental set of doubts about whether and how much the United States (or anyone else) can manipulate events external to itself, together with matching doubts about whether we should if we could. Arms policy in this school tends to stress *necessary* reaction more than *desirable* action: e.g., the bias against intervention in the Third World, the strategic nuclear Limiters' doubts that the Extenders can control nuclear war anywhere near as much as they claim. Although the members of this school join the Maintainer consensus on NATO issues, they tend toward the "let-well-enough-alone" side rather than "let's do something!" "Reactivity" does, however, allow for great activity in fostering arms control and, for some members of the school, in attempting to moderate various Third World problems. McNamara and Bundy are the intellectual prototypes of this school. More generally, it encompasses most of the Democrats in the Congress and elsewhere, although some remain Disarmers/Disengagers. To make explicit what should have become obvious, I count myself among the Reactivists as well.

- *Active Middle.* This school is made up of the members of the Interventionist Middle in the Third World debate. The Interventionist Middle forms part but not all of the strategic nuclear Extender school, which in turn forms part but not all of the American Maintainer consensus on NATO. In contrast to the Reactive Middle, the Active Middle believes that appropriate American policy can manipulate events in our favor in the Third World, and appropriate nuclear policy can limit damage and control escalation if a nuclear war were to break out between the United States and the Soviet Union. Like other Maintainers, they are committed to NATO. The early indications are that President Bush and his key advisors fit comfortably here. At a more abstract intellectual level, some

398

Activists have proposed various schemes to cope with what they see as the erosion of NATO. Henry Kissinger and Zbigniew Brzezinski are typical of this last tendency, but the prototypical intellectual leader of the active middle, with stress upon the strategic nuclear debate, is analyst Albert Wohlstetter.

- *Global Anti-Communists.* These are the Confronters in the Third World segment, and they join others in the Extender school of the strategic nuclear debate. They divide among themselves over NATO, however; all the NATO Withdrawers of the right are Global Anti-Communists, but not all of the latter are Withdrawers. The pro-NATO Global Anti-Communists include Ronald Reagan and George Shultz; the Withdrawers are represented by Irving Kristol and his fellow NYU Professor Melvin Krauss.

Global Anti-Communists have not been conspicuous so far in the Bush administration, and if the administration is mainly Activist and the Democratic opposition (and Congressional majorities) mainly Reactivist, the debate will by no means disappear, but the chances are good that it will return to civility. U.S. foreign policy may even become bipartisan once more.

As Fig. 3 indicates, the two European schools do not fit *on* the horseshoe, but they can be conveniently located *in* it. Primarily emphasizing the NATO portion of the American debate, the Europeans may still be designated by the titles given those schools in the NATO debate:

- *Couplers*, the European Establishment, who debate with the American Maintainer Establishment (the Reactive Middle, the Active Middle, and some of the Global Anti-Communists). The European Couplers *debate with* these Maintainers, but they *worry about* the residual Global Anti-Communists, the NATO Withdrawers, to whom the Europeans assign too much importance, given their light weight in the American political and intellectual scene.
- *Removers*, the extreme European school, allied to the American Disarmers/Disengagers in anti-military philosophy, and to those who treat with NATO in their mutual desire to get nuclear weapons and perhaps American troops out of Europe. As has been noted, their recommendations for separation put them quite close to the American Withdrawers of the right as well.

The crucial question, then, is how these schools of the 1980s are likely to adapt to the potentially rapid changes in the environment of the next decade and the next century.

23. The Future

The decades ahead are likely to bring drastic changes: China, perhaps Japan and other countries, will become major military powers. Lesser powers will acquire advanced weaponry, diminishing the relative advantages of both U.S. and Soviet forces. Arms agreements may have a sizable impact on nuclear and conventional forces.

Major U.S. interests will continue to be threatened at fronts much closer to our adversaries than to the United States. Our ability to deter aggression at these distant places will be impaired by uncertainty about allies and friends granting us access to bases and overflight rights, or joining us in defense preparations to respond to ambiguous warning signals. Our difficulties of access may worsen as a result of Third World conflicts that jeopardize U.S. bases or lead to Soviet expansion in areas previously free of Soviet forces.

Military technology will change substantially in the next 20 years. We have depended on nuclear and other advanced weapons to deter attack on our allies, even as the Soviets have eliminated our nuclear advantage. If Soviet military research continues to exceed our own, it will erode the qualitative edge on which we have long relied.

—*Discriminate Deterrence*[1]

THE CHANGING DEBATE

Discriminate Deterrence

Discriminate Deterrence is the Report of the Commission on Integrated Long-Term Strategy, appointed by Reagan Secretary of Defense Weinberger, a member of the Active Middle school[2] and co-chaired by his Under Secretary Fred Iklé and Albert Wohlstetter, both of whom have been

---

[1]*Discriminate Deterrence*, 1988, p. 1.

[2]As a reminder, the Active Middle consists roughly of the Interventionist Middle in the Third World Debate, which becomes part of the Extender School in the strategic nuclear debate; the Reactive Middle is the Non-Interventionist Middle/strategic nuclear Limiters.

quoted throughout this study as seminal intellectual leaders in the various debate-segment schools that make up the Active Middle. Also on the Commission were Henry Kissinger, who has made extremely important contributions to each segment of the debate, and Zbigniew Brzezinski and Samuel Huntington, whose views have been discussed mainly in regard to the NATO debate. Not every member of the Commission can be accurately categorized into the Active Middle; some of Brzezinski's strategic nuclear views fit better among the Reactivists (the Limiters in the nuclear debate), and Iklé was quoted in Part I as being a strong member of the Confronter school in the Third World debate; biophysicist Joshua Lederberg has on occasion expressed views more akin to those of the Reactivists or even the Disengagers/Disarmers. Nonetheless, the "Integrated Long-Term Strategy" can reasonably be characterized as one designed by and for the Active Middle school.

The report is comprehensive. It is the first of what one may hope will be a series of long-overdue comprehensive strategic documents prepared by members of the various schools of thought, and it is complex enough that it can be given full justice only by being read in full. In particular, it performs a service that should be of value to all schools in the arms debate, by opening up discussion of the future, when economic and demographic trends have changed world security equations. The report's basic theme, stemming from the projections listed in the quotation opening this chapter, is that:

> We should emphasize a wider variety of contingencies than the two extreme threats that have long dominated our alliance policy and force planning: the massive Warsaw Pact attack on Central Europe and an all-out Soviet nuclear attack.[3]

The first part of this statement received substantial attention in Europe, where the downplaying of Central Europe fed standard Coupler paranoia about American abandonment.[4] Nonetheless, both halves of the statement seem generally acceptable across the American consensus including Reactivists as well as Activists; the Reactivists carry no brief stressing fear of all-out Soviet attacks, whether in Central Europe or against the American homeland.

---

[3]*Discriminate Deterrence*, 1988, p. 2.

[4]The report as a whole received more attention in Europe, where it generated immediate paranoiac reactions, than in the United States, where it tended to sink beneath the noise level of presidential-year politics, the debate over ratification of the zero-zero INF treaty, other dramatic negotiations with the Soviet Union, and, within the Defense establishment as such, the budgetary pressures imposed by the Gramm-Rudman Act and implemented stringently by then Defense Secretary Frank Carlucci.

Even so, it *is* a statement of the Active Middle. This is particularly clear in the statements on the Third World. "We will seek to contain Soviet expansion in any region of the world," and "The free world will not remain free if its options are only to stand still or retreat" embody the Activists' Third World policies, as does the recommendation for "assistance to anti-Communist insurgents who are resisting a hostile regime imposed from the outside or a regime that threatens its neighbors."[5] Similarly, on strategic nuclear policy: "Extreme versions of the doctrine of mutual vulnerability as a guarantor of 'stability' have been assailed for their contradictions ever since they first surfaced. Yet such views have, incredibly, retained an extraordinary hold over political and military elites in the West, especially Europe,"[6] evokes the Extenders' (Active Middle) accusation against the Limiters (Reactive Middle) that the latter favor the "MAD" Mutual Assured Destruction strategy, while it ignores the Limiter response that "MAD" is a probable outcome, not a preferred policy. And the recommendation for "capabilities for discriminate nuclear strikes"[7] is an Extender emphasis.

In spite of the broad opening up to new demographic and economic trends, the assumption behind *Discriminate Deterrence* is that the central conflict in which the United States will be involved over the next 20 years will continue to be with the Soviet Union. This may be, and it is a legitimate assumption. It also may not be, however, and runs the danger of leading to too narrow a focus.

To repeat, much of the report would be agreed to by both of the centrist schools in the American arms debate. And indeed, a broad band of agreement exists between the Extenders and Limiters in the strategic nuclear segment of the debate, and all American debaters other than the small number of Withdrawers can reasonably be lumped together into the Maintainer school in the NATO debate. It is only in the Third World debate that strong substantive disagreements lead to strong hostilities and incivilities among officials and analysts within the United States, and under the Bush administration, even those hostilities may be dying down. (The strong emotions invoked by the "MAD" quarrel seem to be based more on feelings of theological betrayal akin to those invoked by the Reformation than by substantive disagreements.) As fears of Soviet nuclear attack or invasion of Western Europe have faded, all the residual anti-Communist emotions of the last 40 years have been focused by the Global Anti-Communists on the

---

[5] *Discriminate Deterrence,* 1988, p. 3.
[6] Ibid., p. 35.
[7] Ibid., p. 2.

Third World. As a result, it sometimes seems that Nicaragua and Angola are more important to the United States than Europe and China.

As a Reactivist, I take the other side from *Discriminate Deterrence* on many of the issues in controversy. The value of the study, however, stems not only from its comprehensiveness and its intelligence, but also from its nonpolemic civility, even in regard to the divisive "MAD" and Third World issues. Civility is a *sine qua non* of a policy-improving arms debate, and it has eroded badly in the quarter century since *The Arms Debate*.

A New Category: Economics?

This study reflected the arms debate as it was. Traditionally, the debate was based upon a definition of national security centered on the actual and potential use of military power. Almost all the debaters have been Clausewitzian enough to understand that such power is the extension of politics by other means, so that only the strategic nuclear debate has remained almost purely military (and theological); the NATO debate has for many years been dominated by politics, particularly on the European side.

To the extent economics entered the debate, it was either as a set of budgetary constraints or occasionally as a matter of interests to which military power might be applied; in the post-1945 focusing down of "national interests" almost exclusively on anti-Communism, even economics as an interest has mostly gone by the board. Its exclusion both as an interest and as an instrument is particularly striking because some of the major debaters and participants, including Schelling, McNamara, and James Schlesinger (and me), were trained as economists.

Now economics may be coming back into its own, not merely as a national interest, but as a major influence directing national security and affecting the military components at least as much as they affect economics. In the short run this may involve East/West economics as an influence on East/West conflict, and European and transatlantic economics, particularly in the context of the 1992 Common Market "Year of Europe," as an influence on NATO. Over the longer run, it will also include the economics of the Third World, which is moving rapidly away from an identity with the "underdeveloped" world.

The debate is still over military power and politics. But a *Still the Arms Debate* of 2015 may well be dominated by economics.

A PERSONAL SYNTHESIS

Principles

The need for civility is where I start. In fact, civil debate may be upon us:

- With the end of the Reagan administration and the muting of hard ideology by President Bush and his administration.
- With the apparent changes in the Soviet Union, forcing all schools to take a serious interest in arms control, while budget stringency directs attention on cost-effectiveness as the central criterion for the choice of strategic as well as other weapons.
- With the confused and fearful West European reaction to rapid change, causing the existing U.S. consensus on NATO policy to stress even more strongly the need both for consultation with our European allies and more general resonance to their needs.

Beyond civility in debate, however, what is called for in arms *policy* over the next several years? The principal criterion I would apply is: "What *can* we do?" This is the essence of Reactivism, compared with the "What *should* we do?" of Activism. The "should" criterion is necessary, of course, for prioritization of the possible, but analysis of both the arms debate and arms policy leaves such an overwhelming sense of constraints—including but not limited to budgetary, political, and inability to manipulate our own clumsiness—that "can" must be the dominant issue. Indeed, the constraints bring with them at least one potential advantage: The expansive feeling in the first years of the Reagan administration that the budgetary and political constraints had been taken off defense spending led both to a failure to prioritize and to an overconfidence in our ability to manipulate the world. The constraints of the 1990s will force hard decisions.

Applying these criteria across the three segments of the debate:

- In the *Third World*, we can do very little with regard to indigenous internal change, no matter how distasteful (Nicaragua) or how attractive (the Philippines). Not all change need be negative from the American point of view: If our developing relations with the Soviet Union lead to a decrease of their opportunistic exploitation of Third World unrest, for example, we may be able to isolate insurgencies from direct Soviet influence. In particular, we should be able to avoid further Soviet basing and military support in the Western hemisphere outside of Cuba, and perhaps elsewhere. But manipulating internal governance is much more difficult and carries no guarantee of ending up with something "better" or more in our interest than we started out with. Nonetheless, in some cases of vital interest we may have to try; to select these cases, however, a careful definition and application of "vital interest" will be crucial. My own feeling is that global anti-Communism has little to do with it, and that outside of Europe, the Pacific rim, Mexico, and probably Israel, our vital interests in the short run probably lie in the free flow of petroleum and the control of terrorism and not much else. There is enough within this definition to keep us concerned and confused, however.

- In the *strategic nuclear* realm, we can do less than the Extenders want us to do, but we should continue to do a variety of things, with some stress on variety. To repeat the central conclusion of Part II: If deterrence is based on uncertainty rather than certainty, then the kinds of complex weapons and plans the Extenders recommend are crucial for deterrence not because they engender the kind of certainty claimed by their advocates but because they are necessary to maintain uncertainty.

What we should continue to do includes offensive weapon systems and strategies (but fewer than contemplated by *Discriminate Deterrence*) and continued movement toward defensive systems at a pace constrained by technology, budgets, and arms control agreements. The budgetary issue—the ultimate comparison of strategic nuclear demands with other arms imperatives—is discussed below, but the separate constraints imposed by arms controls may be particularly important, even in the short run. In the next several years, arms agreements may be possible that increase stability, or at least decrease weapon levels and slow down the arms race without decreasing stability. One intriguing possibility is that the combination of increasing technological complexity and the constraints on testing imposed by arms controls may cause low confidence on both sides that anything will work to design, so that nuclear options will become even less of an element in strategic planning than they are now. In an odd way, ignorance may be strength.

- In *NATO*, budgetary and political constraints will continue to preclude any substantial buildup of conventional strength, as they have for more than 35 years. Indeed, so long as arms negotiations with the Soviets and other aspects of détente continue to appear real, the political constraints in West Germany and other European nations, even on such not very costly improvements as force modernization, may preclude even modest unilateral increases of capabilities. What remains for Western policy is the attempt to negotiate a better conventional balance with the Soviets and to avoid any major erosion of the nuclear deterrent. I would argue that such erosion would in fact be difficult, even with arms controls like those discussed above: The theater deterrent is largely existential in any case; the INF treaty did it no harm, and so long as substantial numbers of nuclear weapons remain with a variety of delivery systems throughout Europe, the uncertainties necessary for deterrence will continue. All this may be insufficient to satisfy nervous European allies, however, and the "should" imperative for American policy is to try to preserve the Alliance in something like its current state by resonating to our allies. Retaining various theater nuclear weapons is necessary to this end; perhaps even more important is movement toward a conventional balance between NATO and the Warsaw Pact. Arms control negotiations show great promise of such an outcome, with future rounds leading to substantial reductions on both sides. Burden-sharing is a secondary issue. The burden-sharing issue itself, however, should be handled as part of strategy, not as a separate matter. If that strategy succeeds in arriving at negotiated arms reductions, the burden-sharing problem may also be eased. Then we can face the European and transatlantic trade issues that in the 1990s may begin to dominate more narrowly defined security issues.

Short-Run Budgets

The standard way to synthesize policies crossing many areas and considerations is through the constrained choices and priorities of budgeting.[8] Although this analysis is far too gross to present a budget even in the largest possible categories, the priority implications of the "Reactive" principles discussed above can be made explicit for the traditional five-year budget horizon. The assumption here is that the five years will see no break in the budget stringency of the late 1980s. It can also be assumed that rational Reactivists, like Activists, would subscribe to such common principles as maintaining readiness even at the cost of cutting back on new hardware, principles sometimes honored in the breach under the pressures of congressmen, contractors, and service planners.

---

[8]Although the chapter on "Managing the Defense Budget" in *Discriminate Deterrence*, 1988, p. 59 stressed that "Precisely because the years ahead are likely to be austere, we need a long-term strategy that tells us how to rank our priorities," it provided no budget or priority rankings to suggest where austerity-driven cuts might be taken.

Referring again to the three major segments that have been used for the discussion of the arms debate and arms policy:

- Short-run military budget considerations are least relevant to arms policy in the *Third World*: The issues are complex and long run enough to fall beyond the five years of budgeting; and for the sorts of Third World conflicts discussed in Part I, current expenditures are too small for major budgetary effect and likely to remain small. Lacking highly unlikely American military intervention in such situations, better contingency planning may be called for and more stress on the broad tactics of "limited" conflict; but these are cheap, and neither new weapon systems nor major new troop units seem relevant. What may be called for outside the defense budgets of direct concern here are substantial increases in foreign assistance as suggested by the Kissinger Commission on Central America, and restructuring of both assistance and economic policy as a whole regarding the Third World.
- Expenditures on *strategic nuclear* weapons provide one possible area for constraint. While maintaining the missile/aircraft/submarine "triad," we should make the hard choices among missile systems, among aircraft, and between new missiles and aircraft. Total numbers should be kept down to those necessary to combine enemy certainty that some response will be likely with uncertainty about what that response will be. Within these limits, modest spending should be continued on development of strategic defenses. None of this is inconsistent with the contention of *Discriminate Deterrence* that "heavy investment in basic research—the longest lead-time item of all—is essential."[9]
- U.S. expenditures on *NATO* should be maintained near current levels until they can be reduced through arms agreements. This involves maintenance of six-digit numbers of American troops in NATO, although not necessarily the current levels of 300,000 and above; continued serious planning for conventional war of the heavy armored type assumed for Europe, with continued stress on reinforcement; and continued efforts to fill in deficiencies, such as those in reserve supplies of ammunition and other commodities. It involves "routine" modernization of standard weapon systems, integration of new technologies, and modernization of combat strategies and tactics to match. It may involve some modernization of new capabilities types, such as new nuclear delivery systems, although these will be politically constrained. None of this is likely to bring about radical revision of the conventional balance

---

[9]Ibid., p. 60.

in our favor, but it will maintain the status quo, reducing expenditures as arms agreements make such maintenance less costly. At some point beyond the reach of current budget planning, radically new accommodations with the Soviet Union may allow for radically different Western European and transatlantic arrangements. But not yet.

The major constraints or cuts in such a budget, then, are in the strategic nuclear area and possibly, under arms agreements, in NATO. In addition, although a substantial Navy remains essential for global contingencies, it is not necessarily the Navy built up by the Reagan administration. The issues here are central to the long-run future discussed below. Their five-year budget implications are not clear, although some savings seem likely from mothballing of ships that have entered or reentered the fleet with no clear notion of their strategic use.

The Long Run: 2015

This study is based on 25 years of change since the writing of *The Arms Debate*. Symmetry thus suggests another 25 years, approximately 2015—as the horizon for a long-run examination. The world may change a lot in the next quarter-century, as issues and areas now seen as peripheral move to the center of consideration. The major issues between the United States and the Soviet Union may well continue in the new directions initiated in the last few years, but new areas of the world will add new dimensions to the arms debate, in the nuclear as well as the conventional realm. Nonetheless, within the American debate, the basic Activist and Reactivist frames of reference are likely to remain and adapt themselves appropriately.

One premise is that, although changes will occur across the board, the issues in two of the three parts of this study—NATO and the strategic nuclear debate—will retain a recognizable root similarity to those discussed here. This is not to say that the issues proceed linearly from 1965 to 2015, quite the contrary. A radical change has *already* taken place, the change in East/West relations and subsequent arms control and other steps made possible by the policies of Gorbachev. The prediction here is that the next changes, even including as a worst case as much of a Soviet reversion to pre-Gorbachev days as would be possible under economic and other pressures, will be fairly linear into the future.

- The Soviet Union is unlikely to revert to the kind of dangerous and unpredictable foe of the United States and NATO it seemed to be through the early 1960s. Substantially improved Soviet and East

European relations with the United States and Western Europe, including greatly increased trade, are more likely; but even so, the Elbe will not yet be the friendly frontier that the Rhine has become. As a result, NATO will still exist, quite possibly Kissingerized but not Krystolized. The structure may be far more European than the current one, but the United States will still belong, U.S. troops well above the token level will remain in Europe, and some variety of Flexible Response will still lead to the American strategic deterrent. The NATO debate will have changed substantially, but it will still be characterized by European concerns about self-preservation and American willingness to participate, conditioned by concerns about being drawn in too deep too soon.

- The United States and the Soviet Union will remain the only two nuclear superpowers capable of destroying one another and the world. Arms agreements will have increased stability between the two powers and reduced the numbers of weapons substantially, but nobody will have figured out how to put the genie back in the bottle. Elements of the strategic nuclear debate concerning control, assured destruction, and further agreement will remain as they are today; theology moves slowly.

It is at the periphery of the last statement that the world may change radically over the next 25 years, however. The United States and the Soviet Union may remain the only nuclear *super*powers, but they are not the only nuclear powers now. In the coming quarter-century, new (or newly revealed) nuclear powers will probably arise. They may be major in the sense that Britain and France are major because they have not only warheads but weapon systems and forces capable of delivering the warheads in a coordinated manner. And not every one of these new powers will necessarily be "responsible" in the sense that Britain and France are. In particular, if an Israel or an Iraq, an India or a Pakistan, a South Africa or a Nigeria fears an attack by its opponent, the kind of preventive or preemptive spiral feared but avoided between the United States and the Soviet Union may begin to spin. In the next 25 years, nuclear war between the United States and the Soviet Union, or involving Britain or France, is extremely unlikely. The occurrence of *some* nuclear war, however, is entirely possible.

The intricate policy questions for debate, then, will be:

- What should the United States and the Soviet Union do to prevent such a war from becoming a nuclear conflict between the two of them, and invoking the kind of worldwide holocaust they are each capable of accomplishing? This is the easiest question to answer. Technically,

409

some of the "hot-line" and other sorts of arms control measures should be able to ensure that a lesser-power nuclear explosion is not mistaken for one aimed by either superpower at the other; the desirability of such measures is not a matter of debate. In addition, minimal U.S. and Soviet ABM systems of the type suggested by Bundy, McNamara, et al., and by Senator Nunn, could help protect against escalation of a "third party" nuclear war. Politically, the United States and the Soviet Union have acted in the past to prevent nonnuclear conflict between "client" states (e.g., between Israel and Egypt in 1973) from turning to great-power confrontation; the motivations to do so for nuclear combat are much greater.

- What should the United States, with or without the Soviet Union, do to prevent such a "smaller" nuclear war from beginning in the first place? Conceptual possibilities range from doing nothing to threatening instigators of nuclear war with great power nuclear response or even using such threats to disarm lesser powers in advance. Each of these might be done unilaterally or bilaterally in cooperation with the Soviets. The most likely action is nothing until something has happened, but it is not the only possibility. For the arms debate of the future, it is not clear which side the Activists and the Reactivists might take. Wohlstetter, the Activist theorist of controlled use of nuclear weapons as a part of U.S. strategy, has been at the forefront of opponents to the spread of nuclear weapons to other countries since 1961, when he analyzed the dangers of proliferation even among America's allies.[10] How far he would go in the direction of advance control is open, particularly in conjunction with the Soviet Union, of which he retains deep suspicions. Reactivists might suppress their doubts about the possibilities for successful manipulation enough to explore options with the Soviets over the coming years.

- What should the United States, with or without the Soviet Union, do *after* a lesser power has mounted a nuclear attack on another lesser power? One answer would be "Nothing," as we have done nothing in the murderous Iran-Iraq conventional plus poison gas war of the 1980s. Nuclear attack would break a taboo much stronger than that against chemical warfare, however; and at the other extreme, U.S. or combined U.S. and Soviet measured retaliation against the attacker might not be out of the question. One issue here would be: Whose friend is the attacker, and whose the victim?

---

[10]Wohlstetter, 1961.

The point here is not to analyze the strategic nuclear debate of 2015 but to suggest that it may have a major new dimension. So long as the dimension is theoretical—what to do, if—the debate is likely to remain theological, drawing on the current repertory of prayers and incantations. The difficulty of predicting subsequent action and debate once a nuclear attack has actually taken place, however, might be likened to the difficulty of laying out a clear prediction of what would happen if the devil, with horns and brimstone, were to come up from a deep catacomb and set up shop in Rome, where they have thought about such things for almost two millenia.

The other cause for potentially important changes in U.S. arms policy and the arms debate is the changing security constellation around the world. At a minimum, as *Discriminate Deterrence* points out, the potential and perhaps the actuality of major new military power will arise in China, Japan, and possibly elsewhere. Other examples might include India, Pakistan, Indonesia, the Arab world, Nigeria, Brazil. The distribution of the economic power behind military power is likely to change radically, and some of the potential changes may involve new and very different alliances or conflicts.

Going beyond the *potential* use of military power implied by alliances, however, U.S. vital interests might be involved to the point where actual military activity of one sort or another could be called for. Geographically, the area in question is part of the Third World defined in Part I as "the less wealthy world outside of North America, Europe, Northern Asia, and part of Oceana," but some of the potential issues and actions may be very different from those analyzed there.

- The nations involved may no longer be "less wealthy" than many in the West.
- The issues may involve no confrontation with Marxism-Leninism. Indeed, in some cases, as in the potential nuclear confrontations discussed above, U.S. and Soviet interests may tend to coincide.
- Actual or potential conflict may be closer to conventional war than to the insurgencies and counterinsurgencies emphasized in Part I. The Arab-Israeli wars of 1967 and 1973 involved the most sophisticated aerial and tank combat that had ever taken place historically, or has taken place since. The Iran-Iraq war, with its use of massed troops attacking dug-in positions, and indeed with its use of poison gas, was an unfortunate throwback to 1914–18, as the casualty figures showed.

The potential threat to one U.S. vital interest, the free flow of oil, has been obvious enough since 1973 that a great deal of military thinking has gone into contingency planning. Fifteen years later, however, there is no great conviction that the United States has created any substantial capability to fight a land war in the Middle East to defend our interests, and events in the Persian Gulf in 1987 threw into some doubt our ability to mount a sea war. Another vital interest in the same area, the continued existence of Israel, may well be invoked in the future.

The Middle East is not the only area that may involve American vital interests, however defined, in the next quarter century. A dominant theme for the next 25 years is going to be *uncertainty*. And uncertainty calls for what should become a dominant response for arms policy in the same period—*flexibility*. The demands on arms policy after the next few years are highly uncertain in the world outside of Europe, perhaps even within the old continent. Where these demands will occur is uncertain, what they will consist of is equally so. In this context, flexibility means the capacity to apply military force of various types in various places around the world.

Traditionally for the U.S. military, geographical flexibility has meant Navy. Perhaps it still does. Aside from Mexico, the possible arenas for U.S. military force are all separated from our homeland by more water than land; and because transport on the surface of the ocean is far more cost-effective than transport above it, except where very short-term response is essential, the case for sea power is strong. Sea power carries firepower both from the sea itself and from sea-launched air; it can carry land power with it.

In large measure this was the rationale for the goal not quite reached by the Reagan administration, of a 600-ship Navy. The rationale, however, did not match the forces purchased. As pointed out by Komer, the "maritime strategy" was aimed directly at the Soviet land mass, for which it was peculiarly inappropriate, rather than being designed for contingencies throughout the world "less" than confrontation on the sea between the two superpowers. The nuclear-powered large-carrier task forces so dear to the admirals were designed for direct attack on the Soviet Union and are far too clumsy to be optimal for the multi-contingency flexibility needed for the future. Their substitution for classical minesweeping capabilities proved rather embarrassing for the Navy in the Persian Gulf in 1987, as did the necessity to mount firepower against small boats by flying Army helicopters off Navy vessels.

Although large nuclear carriers may not be the ideal instruments for global flexibility, they are more cost-effective for the mission than starting all over again with small carriers. The same is true for B-52s. Unlike the carriers, they were appropriately designed for a certain mission, but they are being superseded by newer weapons for that mission; now they are being retreaded as global carriers of conventional weapons, a mission they first undertook in the Vietnam war. They may not be optimal, but their use is more cost-effective than building new aircraft for the same purpose.

For the future, flexibility for both the Navy and the Air Force should mean the design of weapons and weapon carriers that can bring their own integral firepower or transported firepower to bear across a range of situations and places. In a lot of these places, however, the ultimate combat is likely to be on the ground. This is the mission of the Marine Corps and the Army. In the past, the Marines' central mission has been the rapid-response "light" mission; bemused by their naval parent's entrancement with war against the Soviet Union, they have begun to drift toward heavy warfare against heavily armed enemies, a direction one may hope can be reversed.

As for the Army, its central mission for the last 40 years has been in Europe; the Vietnam war was an aberration and was fought like one. It was suggested above that Europe is still the central mission, but it does seem to be phasing down, although by no means out. In its own interest and that of the nation, the Army should begin to examine the future in terms of transportable forces not required to be heavy or sophisticated enough to face the Russians on an electronic battlefield and should begin to fight to obtain the necessary transport from the Navy and the Air Force.

Flexibility may have small influence on the immediate budget. But if thinking and planning do not turn in that direction, depending on muscle-bound military forces optimized for a declining threat while the nation's vital interests are at risk elsewhere has disturbing implications.

CONCLUSION

With regard to strategic nuclear policy and NATO, the arms debate has already turned a corner from the line drawn from the early 1960s to the mid-1980s. The Soviet constant, which indeed was constant long before the 1960s, has become a variable, and the Western debate has turned with it. The contention here is not that there will be no more changes in the strategic nuclear and NATO debates in the next 25 years—the Soviet variable may continue to vary, but within the constraints of economic and military reality. Rather, the changes will proceed more directly from recent ones, turning no more corners.

The Third World debate turned a corner in the 1960s because of Vietnam. *The Arms Debate* captured the beginning, and Part I of this study analyzed the turn. Now, another turn may be beginning, not in the Third World debate over insurgency and counterinsurgency discussed here and in *The Arms Debate*, but in the emergence of a new kind of Third World, armed in part with nuclear weapons, economically powerful in part, invoking U.S. interests outside of the East/West conflict. Perhaps this will be a Fourth World or a fourth segment of the debate; the taxonomy is not important.

What is certain is uncertainty; what is necessary for policy is flexibility. And what is necessary for the debate is civility. With the waning of strong anti-Communist ideology at the center of Washington, and with the change in the nature of some of the issues, such civility may be upon us. This does not mean that the Active Middle and the Reactive Middle will no longer disagree. Lacking the post-nuclear nirvana (or the post-holocaust hell) of the Disarmers, different implicit estimates of the ability of one nation—superpower or not—to manipulate the events of the world and consequent different concepts of the use and meaning of force in world affairs will cause debates over the new issues that will be traceable back to the debates over the old ones.

But the civil debates of the next century may finally and for all shake off the "Red or Dead" dichotomy that shaped the modern arms debate as it began in the late 1950s and has been a major ingredient ever since.

Bibliography

Abshire, David M., in *Managing Entry into the 21st Century*, Atlantic Institute for International Affairs, Paris, 1986.

Abshire, David, speech to the Southern Center for International Affairs, reprinted in the *Congressional Record, Senate*, June 20, 1984.

Acheson, Dean G., "The Premises of American Policy," *Orbis*, Fall 1959.

Ackland, Len, and Steven McGuire (eds.), *Assessing the Nuclear Age*, Educational Foundation for Nuclear Science, Chicago, 1986.

Adomeit, Hannes, "The Political Rationale of Soviet Military Capabilities and Doctrine," in *Strengthening Conventional Deterrence in Europe: Proposals for the 1980s*, the European Study Report of the Special Panel, Westview Press, Boulder, 1985.

Alford, Jonathan, "Perspectives on Strategy," in Steinbruner and Sigal, 1983.

Allison, Graham T., *Essence of Decision: Explaining the Cuban Missile Crisis*, Little, Brown and Company, Boston, 1971.

Allison, Graham T., Albert Carnesale, and Joseph S. Nye, Jr., *Hawks, Doves, and Owls*, W. W. Norton, New York, 1985.

Altenburg, Wolfgang, "Adapting Security Partnerships to Contemporary Requirements," in *Managing Entry into the 21st Century*, Atlantic Institute for International Affairs, Paris, 1986.

Alternative Defence Commission, *Defence Without the Bomb*, Taylor and Francis, London, 1983.

415

"America Betrayed by its Friends," *Chicago Sun-Times*, August 4, 1987.

American Friends Service Committee, *Speak Truth to Power*, Philadelphia, 1955.

Arbuckle, Tammy, "A Vietnam Lesson Unlearned? Same Hardware, Same Tactics, Same Conclusion in El Salvador," *Armed Forces Journal International*, December 1985.

Asmus, Ronald D., "West Germany Faces Nuclear Modernization," *Survival*, November/December 1988.

Aspin, Les, "But Battlefield Nuclear Weapons Should Go First," *International Herald Tribune*, April 28, 1987 (reprinted from the *Washington Post*).

Ball, Desmond, *Can Nuclear War Be Controlled?* Adelphi Paper No. 169, International Institute for Strategic Studies, London, 1981.

Barnet, Richard J., "Reflections: The Four Pillars," *New Yorker*, March 9, 1987.

Barre, Raymond, "Foundations for European Security and Cooperation," *Survival*, July/August 1987.

Beaumont, Roger A., "Military Elite Forces: Surrogate War, Terrorism, and the New Battlefield," *Parameters*, March 1979.

Becker, Abraham, and Arnold Horelick, *Managing U.S.-Soviet Relations in the 1990s*, The RAND Corporation, R-3747-RC, February 1989.

Berger, Markus, "La Force de Dissuasion Française et la Sécurité de la République Fédérale d'Allemagne," in Kaiser and Lellouche, 1986.

Berlin Green Party, *Thesen für eine gruene Deutschlandpolitik*, January 1984, in *Reader zum deutschlandpolitischen Kongress der GRUENEN*, March 1984.

Berman, Larry, *Planning a Tragedy: The Americanization of the War in Vietnam*, W. W. Norton, New York and London, 1982.

Bertram, Christoph, "Europe and America in 1983," *Foreign Affairs*, Winter-Spring 1984.

Bertram, Christoph, "Europe's Security Dilemmas," *Foreign Affairs*, Summer 1987a.

Bertram, Christoph, "Trade Europe's Land Missiles for Seaborne," *Los Angeles Times*, May 11, 1987b, Section II.

Bingham, Joan, "The Resurgence of Europe," *Nashville Tennessean*, Outlook Section, July 19, 1987.

Blaufarb, Douglas F., *The Counterinsurgency Era: U.S. Doctrine and Performance, 1950 to the Present*, The Free Press, New York, 1977.

Blechman, Barry M. (ed.), *Rethinking the U.S. Strategic Posture*, Ballinger Publishing Co., Cambridge, Mass., 1982.

Bonnart, Frederick, "Dangers of Divorce," *NATO's Sixteen Nations*, February-March 1987a.

Bonnart, Frederick, "NATO Is an Alliance that Should Not Be Disbanded," *International Herald Tribune*, September 24, 1986.

Bonnart, Frederick, "West Europe Ponders Soviet Aims," *International Herald Tribune*, May 6, 1987b.

Bounds, Gary L., and Scott R. McMichael, "Counting Costs of Elite Forces," *Army*, November 1985.

Bowles, Chester, *Agenda 1961*, The Rosenfeld Lectures at Grinell College, Grinell, Iowa, April 1960.

Bowles, Chester, *Ideas, People, and Peace*, Harper, New York, 1968.

Boyer, Yves, "The Development of the Strategic Rationale for United States Forces in Europe," paper presented to the Conference on Conventional Forces, jointly sponsored by The RAND Corporation, IFRI, and the Royal Institute of International Affairs, at Wiston House, England, March 1987.

Bramall, Lord, *House of Lords Official Report*, Parliamentary Debates (Hansard), Her Majesty's Stationery Office, London, 25 March 1987, Columns 194–195.

Brennan, Donald G. (ed.), *Arms Control, Disarmament, and National Security*, George Braziller, New York, 1961.

Brown, Harold, and Lynn E. Davis, "Nuclear Arms Control: Where Do We Stand?" *Foreign Affairs*, Summer 1984.

Brown, Harrison, "Introduction" to Ackland and McGuire, 1986.

Brumberg, Abraham, "Moscow, Seen Clearly," *New York Times*, September 2, 1987.

Brzezinski, Zbigniew, "To Climb Out of the Foreign Policy Pit," *New York Times* (National Edition), December 16, 1986a.

Brzezinski, Zbigniew, "The Future of Yalta," *Foreign Affairs*, Winter 1984/1985.

Brzezinski, Zbigniew, *Game Plan*, The Atlantic Monthly Press, Boston and New York, 1986b.

Brzezinski, Zbigniew, "Peaceful Change in a Divided Europe," in Thomson and Nerlich, 1988.

Brzezinski, Zbigniew, and William Griffith, "Peaceful Engagement in Eastern Europe," *Foreign Affairs*, July 1961.

Buckley, William F. Jr., "Generals Can Be Right," *National Review*, July 31, 1987.

Bull, Hedley, "European Self-Reliance and the Reform of NATO," *Foreign Affairs*, Spring 1983.

Bundy, McGeorge, *Danger and Survival: Choices About the Bomb in the First Fifty Years*, Random House, New York, 1988.

Bundy, McGeorge, "The Bishops and the Bomb," *New York Review*, June 16, 1983.

Bundy, McGeorge, "Nuclear Weapons Policy: Where Are We Now?" speech at the University of Maryland Law School, January 10, 1986.

Bundy, McGeorge, Morton H. Halperin, William W. Kaufmann, George F. Kennan, Robert S. McNamara, Madalene O'Donnell, Leon V. Sigal, Gerard C. Smith, Richard H. Ullman, and Paul C. Warnke, "Back from the Brink," *Atlantic Monthly*, August 1986a.

Bundy, McGeorge, George F. Kennan, Robert S. McNamara, and Gerard Smith, "Nuclear Weapons and the Atlantic Alliance," *Foreign Affairs*, Spring 1982.

Bundy, McGeorge, George F. Kennan, Robert S. McNamara, and Gerard Smith, "The President's Choice: Star Wars or Arms Control," *Foreign Affairs*, Winter 1984.

Bundy, McGeorge, George F. Kennan, Robert S. McNamara, and Gerard Smith, "Reykjavik's Grounds for Hope," *New York Times*, National Edition, October 19, 1986b.

Burt, Richard A., "An Increased Emphasis on Conventional Forces: Problems and Possibilities," in Thomson and Nerlich, 1988.

Burt, Richard, "The Relevance of Arms Control in the 1980s," *Daedalus*, Winter 1981.

Burt, Richard, "Why American Forces Should Remain in Europe," *International Herald Tribune*, March 25, 1987 (reprinted from the *Washington Post*).

Canby, Steven L., "High-Tech, High-Fail Defense," *Los Angeles Times*, September 16, 1985a, Part II.

Canby, Steven L., "New Conventional Force Technology and the NATO-Warsaw Pact Balance: Part I," in International Institute for Strategic Studies, *New Technology and Western Security Policy: Part II*, Adelphi Paper 198, London, Spring, 1985b.

Carrington, Lord, "Picturing Soviets as Sirens over European Landscape," *Los Angeles Times*, September 27, 1987, Part V.

Carrington, Lord, "Requirements for Stable Security Relationships," in *Managing Entry into the 21st Century*, Atlantic Institute for International Affairs, Paris, 1986.

Carter, Ashton B., John D. Steinbruner, and Charles A. Zraket (eds.), *Managing Nuclear Operations*, The Brookings Institution, Washington, D.C., 1987.

Carter, Jimmy, *Keeping Faith: Memoirs of a President*, Bantam Books, Toronto, New York, London, Sydney, 1982.

Chace, James, "Deeper Into the Mire," *The New York Review of Books*, March 1, 1984.

Chaliand, Gérard, *Revolution in the Third World*, Penguin Books, Harmondsworth, England, 1978.

Chaliand, Gérard, *Terrorismes et Guérillas*, Flammarion, Paris, 1985.

"Che Lives," *Los Angeles Times*, July 20, 1986, Part V.

Chirac, Jacques, "Allocution du Premier Ministre devant l'Assemblée de l'U.E.O," Paris, December 2, 1986, in Ministère des Affaires Étrangères, Direction des Affaires Politiques, *Questions Politico-Militaires*, 2ième Semestre 1985, Année 1986a.

Chirac, Jacques, "Discours devant l'Assemblée Nationale—Développements Touchant la Défense," in Ministère des Affaires Étrangères, Direction des Affaires Politiques, *Questions Politico-Militaires*, 2ième Semestre 1985, Année 1986b.

Chirac, Jacques, *Discours du Premier Ministre devant l'Institut des Hautes Études de Défense Nationale*, September 12, 1986c.

Chomsky, Noam, *American Power and the New Mandarins*, Vintage Books, New York, 1969.

Chomsky, Noam, *Turning the Tide: U.S. Intervention in Central America and the Struggle for Peace*, South End Press, Boston, 1985.

Cirincione, Joseph, and Leslie C. Hunter, "Military Threats, Actual and Potential," in Leiken, 1984.

Cisneros, Henry G., in National Bipartisan Commission on Central America, 1984.

Clark, Grenville, and Louis B. Sohn, *World Peace Through World Law*, Harvard University Press, Cambridge, Mass., 1960.

Cockburn, Alexander, "Beat the Devil," *The Nation*, December 18, 1985, January 4, 1986, and March 15, 1986.

Cohen, Stephen F., "Gorbachev Is Ripe for a Deal," *Los Angeles Times*, November 3, 1985, Part IV.

Cohen, William S., "Fix for an SOF Capability That Is Most Assuredly Broken," *Armed Forces Journal*, January 1986.

Colby, William E., and David Riley, "Respect the ABM Treaty," *New York Times*, National Edition, October 24, 1986.

Cole, Jeffrey U., "Those El Salvador Tactics Work," *Armed Forces Journal International*, May 1986.

"Commitment in Saigon," *The New Republic*, May 22, 1961.

Conine, Ernest, "Europe May Find It Can Go It Alone," *Los Angeles Times*, July 13, 1987, Part II.

Cordesman, Anthony H., "Alliance Requirements and the Need for Conventional Force Improvements," in Thomson and Nerlich, 1988.

Cox, Arthur Macy, "Revising U.S. Perceptions of Gorbachev's New Thinking," *Los Angeles Times*, March 8, 1987, Part V.

D'Aboville, Benoît, "La France, la RFA et le Contrôle des Armements: des Malentendus à la Cooperation," in Kaiser and Lellouche, 1986.

D'Aubach, Jean, "To Gather Europe for Its Defense," *Commentaire*, Spring 1987 (trans. Michel Klem).

"Dare We Negotiate?" *The New Republic*, November 6, 1965.

De Montbrial, Thierry, "Sur la Politique de Sécurité de la France," *Commentaire*, Winter, 1987–1988.

De Rose, François, "NATO's Perils—and Opportunities," *Strategic Review*, Fall 1983.

Dean, Jonathan, "Military Security in Europe," *Foreign Affairs*, Autumn 1987a.

Dean, Jonathan, *Watershed in Europe: Dismantling the East-West Military Confrontation*, D.C. Heath, Lexington, Mass., 1987b.

DeLauer, Richard D., "Emerging Technologies and Their Impact on the Conventional Deterrent," in Pierre, 1986.

Department of the Army, *Low Intensity Conflict*, Field Manual 100–20, 16 January 1981.

Depuy, William E., "Vietnam: What We Might Have Done and Why We Didn't Do It," *Army*, February 1986.

Destler, I. M., "The Elusive Consensus: Congress and Central America," in Leiken, 1984.

Destler, I. M., Leslie H. Gelb, and Anthony Lake, *Our Own Worst Enemy: The Unmaking of American Foreign Policy*, Simon & Schuster, New York, 1984.

Dickey, Christopher, "'Obedezco Pero No Cumplo' ('I Obey But Do Not Comply')," in Leiken, 1984.

Discriminate Deterrence: Report of the Commission on Integrated Long-Term Strategy, Department of Defense, Washington, D.C., January 1988.

Diskin, Martin (ed.), *Trouble in Our Backyard: Central America and the United States in the Eighties*, Pantheon Books, New York, 1983.

Dominguez, Jorge I., *U.S. Interests and Policies in the Caribbean and Central America*, American Enterprise Institute, Washington, D.C., May 1982.

Drell, Sidney D., *Facing the Threat of Nuclear Weapons*, University of Washington Press, Seattle and London, 1983.

Drell, Sidney D., Philip J. Farley, and David Holloway, *The Reagan Strategic Defense Initiative: A Technical, Political, and Arms Control Assessment*, Stanford University Press, 1984.

Drew, Elizabeth, "Letter from Washington," *New Yorker*, May 4, 1987.

Dumoulin, Jerome, "Paris-Bonn: Ce Que Demandent les Allemands," *L'Express*, February 17-March 5, 1987.

Dunn, Keith A., and William O. Staudenmaier (eds.), *Military Strategy in Transition*, U.S. Army War College, Carlisle Barracks, Pa., 1983.

Dunn, Keith A., and William O. Staudenmaier, "The Retaliatory Offensive and Operational Realities in NATO," *Survival*, May/June 1985.

Etzioni, Amitai, *The Hard Way to Peace: A New Strategy*, Collier, New York, 1962.

"Euromissiles: le Oui Resigné des Européens," *Le Monde*, May 28, 1987.

Farer, Tom J., "At Sea in Central America: Can We Negotiate Our Way to Shore?" in Leiken, 1984a.

Farer, Tom J., "Breaking the Deadlock in Central America," *The Washington Quarterly*, Spring 1984b.

Federal Republic of Germany, Ministry of Defense, *Weissbuch*, 1985.

Fillon, François, *1988–1992: Les Relations Franco-Allemandes en Matière de Défense*, Journées Parlementaires du R.P.R.—Bordeaux, September 1987 (mimeo.).

Finer, S. E., "The Military and Politics in the Third World," in W. Scott Thompson (ed.), *The Third World: Premises of U.S. Policy*, ICS Press, San Francisco, 1983.

Flynn, Gregory, and Hans Rattinger (eds.), *The Public and Atlantic Defense*, Rowman and Allenheld, Totowa, N.J., 1985.

Forsberg, Randall, "A Bilateral Nuclear Weapons Freeze," *Scientific American*, November 1982.

Freedman, Lawrence, *The Evolution of Nuclear Strategy*, St. Martin's Press, New York, 1981.

Freedman, Lawrence D., *The Price of Peace: Living with the Nuclear Dilemma*, Firethorn Press, London, 1986.

Freedman, Lawrence D., "U.S. Nuclear Weapons in Europe: Symbols, Strategy and Force Structure," in Pierre, 1984.

Fromm, Erich, *May Man Prevail?* Doubleday, Garden City, 1961.

Frye, Alton, "Strategic Build-Down: A Context for Restraint," *Foreign Affairs*, Winter 1983/84.

Fryklund, Richard, *100 Million Lives*, Macmillan, New York, 1962.

Gabriel, Richard A., "No Light in the Tunnel: Can U.S. Unconventional Forces Meet the Future?" *Conflict Quarterly*, Fall 1981.

421

Gallois, Pierre, *The Balance of Terror*, Houghton Mifflin, Boston, 1961.

Garber, Larry, and Robert Leiken, "The Nicaraguan Elections: An Exchange," *The New York Review of Books*, January 30, 1986.

Gates, David, "Area Defense Concepts," *Survival*, July/August 1987.

Gelman, Harry, *Gorbachev's Policies Toward Western Europe: A Balance Sheet*, The RAND Corporation, R-3588-AF, October 1987.

Gelman, Harry, "Soviet-American Mutual Perceptions in the 1980s—How Far Have We Come, and How Far Are We Going?" The RAND Corporation, P-7508, November 1988.

Genscher, Hans-Dietrich, "Toward an Overall Western Strategy for Peace, Freedom and Progress," *Foreign Affairs*, Fall 1982.

Gladwyn, Lord, *House of Lords Official Report*, Parliamentary Debates (Hansard), Her Majesty's Stationery Office, London, 25 March 1987, cols. 190–191.

Gnessoto, Nicole, "Le Dialogue Franco-Allemand depuis 1954: Patience et Longeur de Temps," in Kaiser and Lellouche, 1986.

"Going But Not Gone," *The New Republic*, November 6, 1961.

Goldsmith, Jimmy, "Le Levier de la Défense," *L'Express*, February 27–March 5, 1987.

Gonzalez, Edward, "Central America: U.S. Policy and Its Critics," The RAND Corporation, P-7216, April 1986.

Gonzalez, Edward, Brian Michael Jenkins, David Ronfeldt, and Caesar Sereseres, *U.S. Policy for Central America*, The RAND Corporation, R-3150-RC, March 1984.

Goodpaster, Andrew J., General Franz-Joseph Schulze, Air Chief Marshall Sir Alasdair Steedman, and Dr. William J. Perry, *Strengthening Conventional Deterrence in Europe: A Program for the 1980s*, The European Security Study Report of the Special Panel, Westview Press, Boulder, 1985.

Gorman, Paul F., Statement before the Senate Armed Services Committee, *Hearings on Department of Defense Authorization for FY 85*, Part 2, February 2–23, 1984.

Gorman, Paul F., Statement before the Senate Armed Services Committee, *Hearings on Department of Defense Authorization for Appropriations for FY 86*, February 27, 1985a.

Gorman, Paul, talk to the National Defense University, December 28, 1985b, mimeo.

Gray, Colin S., "Nuclear Strategy: The Case for a Theory of Victory," *International Security*, Summer 1979.

Gray, Colin S., *Nuclear Strategy and Strategic Planning*, Foreign Policy Research Institute, Philadelphia, 1984.

Gropman, Alan L., *The Air War in Vietnam, 1971–1973*, n.d., mimeo.

Halperin, Morton, *Limited War for the Nuclear Age*, Wiley, New York, 1963.

Halperin, Morton, *Nuclear Fallacy: Dispelling the Myth of Nuclear Strategy*, Ballinger Publishing Co., Cambridge, Mass., 1987.

Haltzell, Michael H., "Germany Has Its Own Priorities," *Los Angeles Times*, August 31, 1986, Part V.

Hamilton, Andrew, "Redressing the Conventional Balance: NATO's Reserve Military Manpower," *International Security*, Summer 1985.

Harris, W. H., "Morality, Moralism, and Vietnam," *Christian Century*, September 22, 1965.

Hassner, Pierre, "La Coopération Franco-Allemande: Achille Immobile Grand Pas?" in Kaiser and Lellouche, 1986a.

Hassner, Pierre, "L'Europe entre les États-Unis et l'Union Soviétique," *Commentaire*, Spring 1986b.

Hassner, Pierre, Letter to the Editor, "Morality and Deterrence," *Commentary*, December 1983.

Hayden, Tom, "Image and Reality: The Vietnam Years," *Los Angeles Times*, June 22, 1986, Part V, p. 2.

Healey, Denis, "A Labour Britain, NATO and the Bomb," *Foreign Affairs*, Spring 1987.

Heisbourg, François, "Conventional Defense: Europe's Constraints and Opportunities," in Pierre 1986a.

Heisbourg, François, "Coopération en Matière d'Armements: Rien est Jamais Aquis," in Kaiser and Lellouche, 1986b.

Heisbourg, François, "Europe at the Turn of the Millenium: Decline or Rebirth?" *Washington Quarterly*, Winter 1987a.

Heisbourg, François, "Europe, USA et Option 'Double Zéro,'" interview in *Libération*, April 17, 1987b.

Heisbourg, François, "Realités et Illusions," *Le Monde*, 1985.

Herzog, Arthur, *The War-Peace Establishment*, Harper and Row, New York, 1965.

Hoagland, Jim, "A Horse Race in France," *Washington Post*, April 3, 1987.

Hoffman, Fred S., *Ballistic Missile Defenses and U.S. National Security: Summary Report*, U.S. Department of Defense, Washington, D.C., October 1983.

Hoffman, Fred S., "The 'Star Wars' Debate: The Western Alliance and Strategic Defense, Part I," in *New Technology and Western Security Policy, Part II*, Adelphi Paper No. 199, International Institute for Strategic Studies, London, 1985.

Hoffman, Stanley, "The U.S. and Western Europe: Wait and Worry," *Foreign Affairs*, Spring 1984.

Hoffman, Wilfried, "Is NATO's Defence Policy Facing a Crisis?" *NATO Review*, August 1984.

Holbrooke, Richard, "East Asia: The Next Challenge," *Foreign Affairs*, Spring 1986.

Holloway, David, "Lessons of the Arms Race," in Ackland and McGuire, 1986.

Holst, Johan Jorgen, "Denial and Punishment: Straddling the Horns of NATO's Dilemma," in International Institute for Strategic Studies, *Power and Policy: Doctrine, the Alliance and Arms Control: Part II*, Adelphi Paper 206, London, Spring 1986c.

Holst, Johan Jorgen, "Flexible Options in Alliance Strategy," in Holst and Nerlich, 1977.

Holst, Johan Jorgen, "Moving Toward No First Use in Practice" in Steinbruner and Sigal, 1983.

Holst, Johan Jorgen, "NATO and Northern Security," address at the opening session of the Oslo International Symposium, "Perspectives on NATO and the Northern Flank," Akershus Castle, August 10, 1986a.

Holst, Johan Jorgen, "Nordic Security Perspectives," address to Oxford University Strategic Studies Group, All Souls College, March 10, 1987.

Holst, Johan Jorgen, "Security and Low Tension in the Northern Regions," lecture at a seminar arranged by the Advisory Council on Arms Control and Disarmament of the Norwegian Government, Bodo, 12 June 1986b.

Holst, Johan Jorgen, and Uwe Nerlich (eds.), *Beyond Nuclear Deterrence*, Crane, Russak and Co., New York, 1977.

Hook, Sidney, "Escape from Reality," *The New Leader*, May 29, 1961.

Hosmer, Stephen T., and Thomas W. Wolfe, *Soviet Policy and Practice toward Third World Conflicts*, Lexington Books, Lexington, Mass., 1983.

Hough, Jerry F., "New Deal in Moscow," *New York Times*, February 13, 1987.

Howard, Michael, "On Fighting a Nuclear War," *International Security*, Spring 1981.

Howard, Michael, "Reassurance and Deterrence: Western Defense in the 1980s," *Foreign Affairs*, Winter 1982–1983.

Howe, Sir Geoffrey, "The European Pillar," *Foreign Affairs*, Winter 1984–1985.

Huntington, Samuel P. (ed.), *The Strategic Imperative*, Ballinger, Cambridge, Mass., 1982.

Hyland, William G., "Reagan-Gorbachev III," *Foreign Affairs*, Fall 1987.

Iklé, Fred Charles, "Can Nuclear Deterrence Last Out the Century?" *Foreign Affairs*, January 1973.

Iklé, Fred Charles, "Nuclear Strategy: Can There Be a Happy Ending?" *Foreign Affairs*, Spring 1985.

Iklé, Fred Charles, *U.S. Policy for Central America—Can We Succeed?* remarks to the Baltimore Council on Foreign Affairs, September 12, 1983.

Intriligator, Michael D., "Why Not a 'Star Wars' Partnership?" *Los Angeles Times*, October 20, 1985, Part IV.

Intriligator, Michael D. and Dagobert L. Brito, *Non-Armageddon Solutions to the Arms Race*, CISA Reprint No. 1, Center for International and Strategic Affairs, University of California, Los Angeles, 1984.

Joffe, Joseph, "Cruisin' for a Bruisin': The INF fallout," *New Republic*, October 5, 1987.

Joffe, Joseph, "Stability and Its Discontent: Should NATO Go Conventional," *Washington Quarterly*, Fall 1984.

Johnson, A. Ross, *The Impact of Eastern Europe on Soviet Policy Toward Western Europe*, The RAND Corporation, R-3332-AF, March 1986.

Kahn, Herman, "The Arms Race and Some of Its Hazards," in Brennan, 1961.

Kahn, Herman, *Thinking About the Unthinkable*, Horizon Press, New York, 1962.

Kaiser, Karl, Georg Leber, Alois Mertes, Franz-Joseph Schulze, "Nuclear Weapons and the Preservation of Peace," *Foreign Affairs*, Summer 1982.

Kaiser, Karl, and Pierre Lellouche (eds.), *Le Couple Franco-Allemand et la Défense de l'Europe*, IFRI, Paris, 1986.

Kaplan, Fred, "Analysts: Soviet Force in Europe Exaggerated," *Boston Globe*, April 26, 1987.

Kaplan, Fred, *Wizards of Armageddon*, Simon and Schuster, New York, 1983.

Karber, Philip A., "Conventional Arms Control Options," in Thomson and Nerlich, 1988.

Karber, Philip A., "NATO Doctrine and NATO Operational Priorities: The Central Front and the Flanks: Part I," in International Institute for Strategic Studies, *Power and Policy: Doctrine, the Alliance and Arms Control: Part III*, Adelphi Paper 207, London, Spring 1986.

Kaufmann, William W., *The McNamara Strategy*, Harper and Row, New York, 1964.

Kaufmann, William W., "Nonnuclear Deterrence," in Steinbruner and Sigal, 1983a.

Kaufmann, William W., "Nuclear Deterrence in Central Europe," in Steinbruner and Sigal, 1983b.

Kennan, George F., "Containment Then and Now," *Foreign Affairs*, Spring 1987.

Kennedy, Robert F., *To Seek a Newer World*, Bantam Books, New York, 1968.

Kent, Glenn A., with Randall J. DeValk and Edward L. Warner III, *A New Approach to Arms Control*, The RAND Corporation, R-3140-FF/RC, June 1984.

Kiep, Walther Leisler, "The New Deutschlandpolitik," *Foreign Affairs*, Winter 1984/85.

Kinnock, Neil, address to the National Press Club, Washington, D.C., December 4, 1986.

Kinnock, Neil, "How Labor Would Defend Britain," *New York Times*, March 27, 1987.

Kirkpatrick, Jeane J., *Dictatorships and Double Standards—Rationalism and Reason in Politics*, Simon & Schuster, New York, 1982.

Kissinger Commission, *see* National Bipartisan Commission on Central America, 1984.

Kissinger, Henry A., "Defining Defense by U.S. Purpose," *Los Angeles Times*, July 27, 1986a, Part V.

Kissinger, Henry A., "A Formula from Reykjavik: Arms Proposals Full of Peril," *Los Angeles Times*, November 16, 1986b, Part V.

Kissinger, Henry A., "Missiles: A Zero Option Is No Choice," *Los Angeles Times*, April 5, 1987, Part V.

Kissinger, Henry A., *Necessity for Choice*, Harper and Row, New York, 1960.

Kissinger, Henry A., "Nicaragua: Pressure Sensitive," *Los Angeles Times*, Part V, April 13, 1986c.

Kissinger, Henry A., *Nuclear Weapons and Foreign Policy*, Harper and Row, New York, 1957.

Kissinger, Henry A., "A Plan to Reshape NATO," *Time*, March 5, 1984, pp. 20–23.

Kissinger, Henry A., "The President's Men: Too Weak for the Job," *Los Angeles Times*, December 21, 1986d. Section V.

Kissinger, Henry A., "Reagan Was Right to Shun Accords That Were Traps," *Los Angeles Times*, October 19, 1986e, Part V.

Kissinger, Henry A., "Redo NATO to Restore the Alliance," *Los Angeles Times*, May 11, 1986f, Part V.

Kissinger, Henry A., "Talking Down Arms," *Los Angeles Times*, September 8, 1985, Part V.

Kissinger, Henry A., "What Next When U.S. Intervenes?" *Los Angeles Times*, Part V, March 9, 1986g.

Kissinger, Henry A., *White House Years*, Little, Brown and Company, Boston and Toronto, 1979.

Kissinger, Henry A., *Years of Upheaval*, Little, Brown and Company, Boston and Toronto, 1982.

Kissinger, Henry A., and Brent Scowcroft, "Old Wine in New Bottles," *Wall Street Journal*, November 12, 1984.

Klare, Michael T., "The New U.S. Strategic Doctrine," *The Nation*, January 4, 1986.

Koefoed, Ole, "Aspects of 'Defensive' Military System Discussed," *Berlingske Tidende*, December 23, 1985.

Komer, Robert W., *Bureaucracy at War: U.S. Performance in the Vietnam Conflict*, Westview Press, Boulder and London, 1986a.

Komer, Robert W., *Maritime Strategy or Coalition Defense?* University Press of America, Lanham, Maryland, 1984.

Komer, Robert W., "Problems of Overextension: Reconciling NATO Defence and Out-of-Area Contingencies: Part II," in International Institute for Strategic Studies, *Power and Policy: Doctrine, The Alliance and Arms Control: Part III*, Adelphi Paper 207b, London, 1986.

Kondracke, Morton M., "Make 'em Pay," *New Republic*, October 12, 1987.

Krauss, Melvin, *How NATO Weakens the West*, Simon and Schuster, New York, 1986a.

Krauss, Melvin, "It's Time to Change the Atlantic Alliance," *Wall Street Journal*, March 3, 1983.

Krauss, Melvin, "Let Europe Negotiate with Gorbachev," *Wall Street Journal*, March 6, 1987.

Krauss, Melvin, "Why Has Reagan Yielded to Europe?" *New York Times*, January 6, 1986b.

Krell, Gert, *INF, SDI, and Conventionalization: West German Approaches to Defense and Detente*, paper for the PRIF-University of California, Santa Barbara Conference on "Arms Control in U.S.-West German Relations," Bad Homburg, December 1–3, 1986a.

Krell, Gert, *Ostpolitik Dimensions of West German Security Policy*, Peace Research Institute, Frankfurt, December 1986b (mimeo.).

Krell, Gert, "Reykjavik and After," Peace Research Institute, Frankfurt, April 1987, mimeo.

Kristol, Irving, "Foreign Policy in an Age of Ideology," *National Interest*, Fall 1985.

Kristol, Irving, "'Global Unilateralism' and 'Entangling Alliances,'" *Wall Street Journal*, February 3, 1986.

Kristol, Irving, "Nuclear NATO: Moment of Truth," *Wall Street Journal*, July 9, 1987.

Layne, Christopher, "Atlanticism Without NATO," *Foreign Policy*, Summer 1987a.

Layne, Christopher, "Deutschland Über Allies," *New Republic*, September 28, 1987b.

Leiken, Robert S. (ed.), *Central America: Anatomy of a Conflict*, Pergamon Press, New York, 1984.

Leiken, Robert, "Reform the Contras," *The New Republic*, March 31, 1986.

Leites, Nathan, and Charles Wolf, Jr., *Rebellion and Authority: An Analytical Essay on Insurgent Conflicts*, Markham, Chicago, 1970.

Lellouche, Pierre, *L'Avenir de la Guerre*, Mazarine, Paris, 1985.

LeoGrande, William M., "Slouching Toward the Quagmire," *The Nation*, January 28, 1984.

Levin, Carl, speech in *Congressional Record, Senate*, June 20, 1984, pp. S7768–S7770.

Levine, Robert A., *The Arms Debate*, Harvard University Press, Cambridge, Mass., 1963.

Levine, Robert A., *The Arms Debate and the Third World: Have We Learned from Vietnam?* The RAND Corporation, R-3523-FF/CC/RC, May 1987a.

Levine, Robert A., "Facts and Morals in the Arms Debate," *World Politics*, January 1962.

Levine, Robert A., *NATO, the Subjective Alliance: The Debate Over the Future*, The RAND Corporation, R-3607-FF/CC/RC, April 1988.

Levine, Robert A., *Public Planning: Failure and Redirection*, Basic Books, New York, 1972.

Levine, Robert A., "The SDI Debate as a Continuation of History," CISA Working Paper No. 55, Center for Strategic and International Affairs, University of California, Los Angeles, March 1986.

Levine, Robert A., *The Strategic Nuclear Debate*, The RAND Corporation, R-3565-FF/CC/RC, November 1987b.

Lewis, Flora, "The Doldrums at NATO," *New York Times*, July 27, 1987a.

Lewis, Flora, "Rating 'Double-Zero'," *New York Times*, September 27, 1987b.

Lewis, Leslie, with the assistance of Holly Korbonski, *U.S. Policies toward Latin America and Their Implications for U.S. Army Long-Range Planning*, Arroyo Center, Jet Propulsion Laboratory, JPL D-2552, Pasadena, June 1985.

Lifton, Robert Jay, "Toward a Nuclear-Age Ethos," in Ackland and McGuire, 1986.

Lippman, Walter, *The Communist World and Ourselves*, Little, Brown and Company, Boston, 1959.

Livingstone, Neil C., "Fighting Terrorism and 'Dirty Little Wars'," *Air University Review*, March-April 1984.

Lowenthal, Abraham F., "Threat and Opportunity in the Americas," *Foreign Affairs*, Winter 1986.

Lowenthal, Richard, "The German Question Transformed," *Foreign Affairs*, Winter 1984/85.

Luttwak, Edward N., "Notes on Low-Intensity Warfare," *Parameters*, December 1983.

MacMillan, Whitney, and Richard H. Ullman, "America's Self-Interest in Helping Gorbachev," *New York Times*, October 7, 1987.

Maechling, Charles Jr., "Insurgency and Counterinsurgency: The Role of Strategic Theory," *Parameters*, Autumn 1984.

Mailer, Norman, "Statement on Vietnam," *Partisan Review*, Fall 1965.

Marshall, S. L. A., "The Big River," *The New Leader*, May 28, 1962.

May, Michael, "A START Proposal," Research Note No. 14, Center for International and Strategic Affairs, University of California, Los Angeles, July 1983.

McNamara, Robert S., *Blundering into Disaster*, Pantheon Books, New York, 1986.

McNamara, Robert S., "Defense Arrangements of the North Atlantic Community," *Department of State Bulletin*, July 9, 1962.

McNamara, Robert S., "The Dynamics of Nuclear Strategy," *Department of State Bulletin*, October 9, 1967.

McNamara, Robert S., "The Military Role of Nuclear Weapons: Perceptions and Misperceptions," *Foreign Affairs*, Fall 1983.

Meyer, Deborah G., and Benjamin F. Schemmer, "An Exclusive Interview with Noel C. Koch," *Armed Forces Journal*, March 1985.

Middleton, Drew, "U.S. Is Too Eager for Missile Pact with Soviets," *Air Force Times*, July 6, 1987.

Mills, C. Wright, *The Causes of World War Three*, Simon & Schuster, New York, 1958.

Mitterrand, François, *Allocution Prononcée par Monsieur François Mitterrand, Président de la République Française sur la Défense de la France*, Paris, 1988.

Mitterrand, François, interview in *Le Monde*, July 31, 1980, quoted in Lellouche, 1985b.

Moisi, Dominique, "As the Pillars of Postwar Stability Shake, Europe Looks for Shelter," *International Herald Tribune*, April 4, 1987a.

Moisi, Dominique, "U.S. and Soviet Images Shift in France," *Los Angeles Times*, February 4, 1987b, Part II.

Montgomery, Tommie Sue, "Liberation and Revolution: Christianity as a Subversive Activity in Latin America," in Diskin, 1983.

Morgenthau, Hans J., "Russia, the U.S. and Vietnam," *The New Republic*, May 1, 1965.

Murphy, Charles J. V., "Cuba: The Record Set Straight," *Fortune*, September 1961.

The Nation, January 28, 1984.

National Bipartisan Commission on Central America, Report, Washington, D.C., January 1984 (also known as the Kissinger Commission).

National Conference of Catholic Bishops, *The Challenge of Peace: God's Promise and Our Response*, Washington, D.C., 1983.

"NATO's Central Front," *The Economist*, August 30-September 5, 1986.

Neal, Fred Warner, "A Ray of Hope for Agreement on Nuclear Arms," *New York Times*, November 19, 1986.

Nerlich, Uwe, "Change in Europe: A Secular Trend?" *Daedelus*, Winter 1981.

Nerlich, Uwe, "Conventional Arms Control in Europe: The Objectives," in Thomson and Nerlich, 1988.

Nerlich, Uwe, "La force de dissuasion nucléaire française et la sécurité de la RFA," in Kaiser and Lellouche, 1986.

Netherlands Institute of International Relations, Clingendael, *Conventional Balance in Europe: Problems, Strategies and Technologies*, Zoetermeer, The Netherlands, May 11–13, 1984.

Nitze, Paul H., "The Objectives of Arms Control," *Current Policy*, No. 677, Department of State, Bureau of Public Affairs, Washington, D.C., March 28, 1985a.

Nitze, Paul H., "SDI: Its Nature and Rationale," *Department of State Bulletin*, December 1985b.

Nixon, Richard M., *No More Vietnams*, Avon Books, New York, 1985.

Nixon, Richard M., and Henry A. Kissinger, "To Withdraw Missiles We Must Add Conditions," *Los Angeles Times*, April 26, 1987, Part V.

Nunn Amendment, *Congressional Record, Senate*, June 20, 1984, p. S7721.

Nunn, Sam, Speech to the DMS Symposium on Industrial Cooperation within NATO, Brussels, April 13, 1987.

Nye, Joseph S., Jr., "Farewell to Arms Control?" *Foreign Affairs*, Fall 1986a.

Nye, Joseph S., Jr., "Motives, Means and Consequences," in "Kirkpatrick and Her Critics," *Society*, March/April 1985.

Nye, Joseph F., Jr., *Nuclear Ethics*, The Free Press, New York, 1986b.

O'Neill, Robert, "Conclusion," in International Institute for Strategic Studies, *Prospects for Security in the Mediterranean, Part III*, Adelphi Paper 231, London, 1988.

Osgood, Charles E., "Reciprocal Initiatives," in Roosevelt, 1962.

Osgood, Robert, "Summation," in Netherlands Institute of International Relations, 1984.

Palmer, Bruce, Jr., *The Twenty-Five Year War*, The University Press of Kentucky, Lexington, 1984.

Paschall, Rod, "Low-Intensity Conflict Doctrine: Who Needs It?" *Parameters*, Autumn 1985.

The Pentagon Papers, as published by The New York Times, Bantam Books, Toronto, New York, London, 1971.

Petersen, Nicolaj, "The Scandilux Experiment: Towards a Transnational Social Democratic Security Perspective," *Cooperation and Conflict: Nordic Journal of International Politics*, March 1985.

Petras, James F., and Robert LaPorte, Jr., "Can We Do Business with Radical Nationalists: Chile, No," *Foreign Policy*, Summer 1972.

Pfaff, William, "Europe: Toward Independent Defense?" *International Herald Tribune*, April 19, 1987.

Pierre, Andrew (ed.), *Nuclear Weapons in Europe*, Council on Foreign Relations, New York, 1984.

Pierre, Andrew (ed.), *The Conventional Defense of Europe: New Technologies and New Strategies*, Council on Foreign Relations, New York, 1986.

Pipes, Richard, "Call Iceland What It Was—a Trap," *Los Angeles Times*, October 21, 1986a, Part II.

Pipes, Richard, "Why Hurry into a Weapons Accord?" *New York Times*, October 10, 1986b.

Platt, Alan, *Soviet-West European Relations: Recent Trends and Near-Term Prospects*, The RAND Corporation, R-3316-AF, March 1986.

Raskin, Marcus, "The Megadeath Intellectuals," *New York Review of Books*, November 14, 1963.

Rathjens, George, "First Thoughts About Problems Facing EXPRO," January 25, 1985 (mimeo.).

Rathjens, George W., Steven Weinberg, and Jerome B. Wiesner, Letter to T. E. Caywood of ORSA, reproduced in U.S. Senate Subcommittee on National Security and International Operations, Senate Committee on

Government Operations, *Planning-Programming-Budgeting—Defense Analysis: Two Examples*, Washington, D.C., 1969.

"Reagan: 'We Have a Right to Help'," *Time*, March 31, 1986.

Record, Jeffrey, "Beyond NATO: New Military Directions for the United States," in Jeffrey Record and Robert J. Hanks, *U.S. Strategy at the Crossroads: Two Views*, Institute for Foreign Policy Analysis, Inc., Cambridge and Washington, July 1982.

Revel, Jean-François, *How Democracies Perish*, Doubleday, Garden City, N.Y., 1983.

Reynolds, Clark W., "Guns and Butter Still Don't Mix," *Los Angeles Times*, Part II, January 30, 1984.

Risse-Kappen, Thomas, "'Final Respite' or 'Unconditional No'? The Church and Questions of Peace in the Federal Republic of Germany," *Bulletin of Peace Proposals*, Vol. 15, No. 3, 1984.

Rogers, Bernard W., "The Atlantic Alliance: Prescriptions for a Difficult Decade," *Foreign Affairs*, Summer 1982.

Rogers, General Bernard, in conversation with Ian Davidson, transcript of a recorded documentary, British Broadcasting Corporation, London, May 13, 1987a.

Rogers, Bernard, "NATO's Strategy: an Undervalued Currency," in International Institute for Strategic Studies, *Power and Policy: Doctrine, the Alliance and Arms Control: Part I*, Adelphi Paper 205, London, 1986.

Rogers, Bernard W., "Why Compromise Our Deterrent Strength in Europe," *New York Times*, June 28, 1987b.

Roosevelt, James (ed.), *The Liberal Papers*, Doubleday, Garden City, N.Y., 1962.

Rosenfeld, Stephen S., "The Guns of July," *Foreign Affairs*, Spring 1986.

Roth, Senator William, *Congressional Record, Senate*, June 20, 1984, p. S7728.

Rowen, Henry S., "The Old SALT Gang Returns," *Wall Street Journal*, November 2, 1984.

Ruehl, Lothar, "1982: La Relance de la Coopération Franco-Allemande," in Kaiser and Lellouche, 1986.

Ruehl, Lothar, *Mittelstreckenwaffen in Europa: Ihre Bedeutung in Strategie, Rustungkontrolle und Bündnispolitik*, Nomos Verlagsgesselschaft, Baden-Baden, 1987.

Safire, William, "Europe After NATO," *New York Times*, June 22, 1987.

Schell, Jonathan, *The Abolition*, Avon, New York, 1984.

Schell, Jonathan, *The Fate of the Earth*, Avon, New York, 1982.

Schelling, Thomas C., *The Strategy of Conflict*, Harvard University Press, Cambridge, 1960.

Schelling, Thomas C., "What Went Wrong with Arms Control," *Foreign Affairs*, Winter 1985/86.

Schelling, Thomas C., and Morton H. Halperin, *Strategy and Arms Control*, Pergamon Press, Elmsford, N.Y., 1985.

Schelling, Thomas C., and Morton H. Halperin, *Strategy and Arms Control*, Twentieth Century Fund, New York, 1961.

Schlesinger, Arthur M., Jr., *The Bitter Heritage*, Fawcett Publications, New York, 1967.

Schlesinger, Arthur M., Jr., *A Thousand Days: John F. Kennedy in the White House*, Houghton Mifflin, Boston, 1965.

Schlesinger, James R., "An American Perspective," speech reprinted in *Congressional Record*, June 20, 1984, p. S7748.

Schlesinger, James, testimony before the House of Representatives Committee on Armed Services, *Military Posture and Procurement of Aircraft, Missiles, Tracked Combat Vehicles, Torpedoes and Other Weapons—Title I, H.R. 12564, Part 1 of "Hearings on Military Posture, Department of Defense Authorization for Appropriations for Fiscal Year 1975," Washington, D.C., 1974.

Schlesinger, James R., testimony before the Senate Foreign Relations Committee, February 6, 1985, quoted in *The Wall Street Journal*, July 30, 1985.

Schmaehling, Elmar, "Nuclear Weapons Out of Our Country," *Stern*, December 29, 1988.

Schmidt, Helmut, *A Grand Strategy for the West*, Yale University Press, New Haven, 1985.

Schmidt, Helmut, "Saving the Western Alliance," *New York Review of Books*, May 31, 1984.

Schmidt, Peter, "Europeanization of Defense: Prospects of Consensus?" The RAND Corporation, P-7042, December 7, 1984.

Schroeder, Patricia, "Burt's Right on One Thing: Allies Must Pay More," *International Herald Tribune*, October 14, 1987 (reprinted from the *Washington Post*).

Schultze, Charles L., "Decoupling Dubious Arguments Against Arms-Control Agreement," *Los Angeles Times*, May 9, 1987, Part V.

Schulze, Franz-Joseph, "La Nécessité d'une Reaction de Défense Immédiate et Commune," in Kaiser and Lellouche, 1986.

Schweigler, Gebhard, "Anti-Americanism in Germany," *Washington Quarterly*, Winter 1986.

Schweigler, Gebhard, *Normalcy in Germany*, paper prepared for Wilson Center European Alumni Association conference, Dubrovnik, May 20–27, 1988.

"SDP Successor Generation Less Sympathetic to U.S., E.C. Goals," *Berlingske Tidende*, April 28, 1986.

Sewell, John W., Richard Feinberg, and Valeriana Kallab (eds.), "Overview," *U.S. Foreign Policy in the Third World: Agenda 1985–86*, Overseas Development Council, New Brunswick and Oxford, 1985.

Shulman, Marshall D., "U.S.-Soviet Relations and the Control of Nuclear Weapons," in Blechman, 1982.

Shultz, George, "America and the Struggle for Freedom," address before the Commonwealth Club of San Francisco, February 22, 1985, in *Department of State Bulletin*, April 1985a.

Shultz, George, "The Ethics of Power," address at the convocation of Yeshiva University in New York, December 9, 1984, *Department of State Bulletin*, February 1985b.

Siccama, Jan-Geert, "Rejoinder," in Netherlands Institute of International Relations, 1984.

Slocombe, Walter, "An Immediate Agenda for Arms Control," *Survival*, September/October 1985.

Sloss, Leon, "The Roles of Strategic and Theatre Nuclear Forces in NATO Strategy: Part II," International Institute for Strategic Studies, *Power and Policy: Doctrine, the Alliance and Arms Control: Part I*, Adelphi Paper 205, London, Spring 1986.

Snow, C. P., "The Moral Unneutrality of Science," address to the American Association for the Advancement of Science, New York, December 27, 1960, reported in the *New York Times*, December 28, 1960.

Social Democratic Party of Germany, *Peace and Security*, Resolutions adopted by the Party Conference, Nuremberg, 25–29 August 1986.

Solarz, Stephen J., "It's Time for the Democrats To Be Tough-Minded," *New York Times*, June 20, 1985.

Steinbruner, John, "Arms Control: Crisis or Compromise," *Foreign Affairs*, Summer 1985.

Steinbruner, John D., "Introduction," in Steinbruner and Sigal, 1983.

Steinbruner, John, "U.S. and Soviet Security Perspectives," in Ackland and McGuire, 1986.

Steinbruner, John D., and Leon V. Sigal (eds.), *Alliance Security: NATO and the No-First-Use Question*, Brookings Institution, Washington, D.C., 1983.

Stratmann, K-Peter, "The Conventional Balance of Forces in Central Europe," Netherlands Institute of International Relations, 1984.

Stratmann, K-Peter, "NATO Doctrine and National Operational Priorities: The Central Front and the Flanks: Part II," in International Institute for Strategic Studies, *Power and Policy: Doctrine, the Alliance and Arms Control: Part III*, Adelphi Paper 207, London, Spring 1986.

Strausz-Hupé, Robert, William R. Kintner, James E. Dougherty, and Alvin J. Cottrell, *Protracted Conflict*, Harper, New York, 1959.

Strausz-Hupé, Robert, William R. Kintner, and Stefan Possony, *A Forward Strategy for America*, Harper, New York, 1961.

Strengthening Conventional Deterrence in Europe: Proposals for the 1980s, European Study Report of the Special Panel, Westview Press, Boulder, 1985.

Sutton, Boyd, John R. Landry, Malcolm B. Armstrong, Howell M. Estes, and Wesley K. Clark, "Strategic and Doctrinal Implications of Deep Attack Concepts for the Defense of Central Europe," in Dunn and Staudenmaier, 1983.

Svec, Milan, "Let's Warm Up Relations with Eastern Europe," *New York Times*, January 23, 1987.

Tarr, David W., "Political Constraints on U.S. Intervention in Low-Intensity Conflicts," *Parameters*, September 1980.

Thomas, Norman, "Let the President Call for a Cease Fire," *New Politics*, Winter 1965.

Thomson, James A., "The Arms Control Challenge to the Alliance," Address to the North Atlantic Assembly in Plenary Session, Oslo, September 25, 1987.

Thomson, James A., "Strategic Choices: Their Roles in NATO's Defence Planning and Force Modernization, Part I," in International Institute for Strategic Studies, *Power and Policy: Doctrine, the Alliance and Arms Control: Part I*, Adelphi Paper 205, London, Spring 1986.

Thomson, James A., and Nanette C. Gantz, *Conventional Arms Control Revisited: Objectives in the New Phase*, The RAND Corporation, N-2697-AF, December 1987.

Thomson, James, and Uwe Nerlich (eds.), *Conventional Arms Control and the Future of Europe*, Westview Press, Boulder, 1988.

Tonelson, Alan, "The Real National Interest," *Foreign Policy*, Winter 1985/1986.

U.S. Senate Subcommittee on Conventional Forces and Alliance Defense, *Beyond the Bean Count: Realistically Assessing the Conventional Balance in Europe*, January 20, 1988.

"Une Interview du Chef d'État: Mitterrand Fait le Tour du Monde," *Libération*, November 23, 1988.

Vaky, Viron, "Reagan's Central American Policy: an Isthmus Restored," in Leiken, 1984.

Valladao, Alfredo, "Priorité au Désarmement Conventionel," *Libération*, November 23, 1988.

Van Oudenaren, John, *Deterrence, War-fighting and Soviet Military Doctrine*, Adelphi Paper 210, International Institute for Strategic Studies, London, 1986.

Varas, Augusto, *The Militarization and International Arms Race in Latin America*, Foreign Relations of the Third World Series, No. 4, Westview Press, Boulder, 1985.

Voigt, Karsten D., "Nuclear Weapons in Europe: A German Social Democrat's Perspective," in Pierre, 1984.

Voigt, Karsten D., "Strategic Policy Options and the Implications for Arms Control, Stability and East-West Relations," in International Institute for Strategic Studies, *Power and Policy: Doctrine, the Alliance and Arms Control: Part II*, Adelphi Paper 206, London, Spring 1986.

Von Bulow, Andreas, "Defensive Entanglement: An Alternative Strategy for NATO," in Pierre, 1986.

Warnke, Paul C., "An Abiding Love Affair with the Bomb," *New York Times*, August 13, 1987.

Waskow, Arthur I., *The Limits of Defense*, Doubleday, Garden City, New York, 1962.

Watt, David, "As a European Saw It," *Foreign Affairs*, Fall 1983.

Weinberger, Caspar W., "Facing Reality on NATO Security," *Los Angeles Times*, September 13, 1987, Part V.

Weinberger, Caspar W., "The Rationale for Strategic Defense," excerpts from a speech to the Foreign Press Center quoted in the *Wall Street Journal*, January 2, 1988.

Weinberger, Caspar W., "The Uses of Military Power," based on remarks to the National Press Club, Washington, D.C., November 18, 1984, *Defense 85*, January 1985.

Westmoreland, W. C., *Report on the War in Vietnam*, Department of Defense, Washington, D.C., 1968.

Wiesner, Jerome B., "Comprehensive Arms Limitation Systems," in Roosevelt, 1962.

Willetts, Harry T., "Disarmament and Soviet Foreign Policy," in The American Assembly, *Arms Control: Issues for the Public*, Prentice Hall, New York, 1961.

Williams, Phil, "West European Security After Reykjavik," *Washington Quarterly*, Spring 1987.

Wohlstetter, Albert, "Au delà de la strategie du pire," *Commentaire*, Winter 1985–1986.

Wohlstetter, Albert, "Between an Unfree World and None: Increasing Our Choices," *Foreign Affairs*, Summer 1985.

Wohlstetter, Albert, "Bishops, Statesmen, and Other Strategists on the Bombing of Innocents," *Commentary*, June 1983.

Wohlstetter, Albert, "The Delicate Balance of Terror," *Foreign Affairs*, January 1959.

Wohlstetter, Albert, letter, *New York Review of Books*, December 26, 1963.

Wohlstetter, Albert, "Nuclear Sharing: NATO and the N+1 Country," *Foreign Affairs*, April 1961.

Wohlstetter, Albert, "Swords Without Shields," *National Interest*, Summer 1987.

Wohlstetter, Albert, and Richard Brody, "Continuing Control as a Requirement for Deterring," in Carter, Steinbruner, and Zraket, 1987.

Wohlstetter, Albert, and Brian Chow, "Arms Control That Could Work," *Wall Street Journal*, July 17, 1985.

Wrage, Stephen D., "U.S. Finds Itself Dealt Out of European Debate," *Los Angeles Times*, August 26, 1987, Part II.

X, "The Sources of Soviet Conduct," *Foreign Affairs*, July 1947, reprinted in *Foreign Affairs*, Spring 1987.

"Z," "The War in Vietnam: We Have Not Been Told the Whole Story," *The New Republic*, March 20, 1962.

Zinn, Howard, *The Logic of Withdrawal*, Beacon Press, Boston, 1967.

Index

Duke University, 354
Dulles, John Foster, 37, 229, 231
　on Massive Retaliation policy, 124–125
　on nuclear weapons use, 11
Dumoulin, Jérome, 258
Dunn, Keith, 332

East Bloc, economic ties to West, 21
Eastern Europe (*see also* specific country)
　Couplers' views on NATO and, 287–290
　Maintainers on, 357–361
　NATO's role in, 222, 238
Economic issues, 403 (*see also* Burden-
　sharing in NATO; European
　Economic Community)
　cooperation with Soviet Union, 283–284
　NATO debate and, 239
　political/military alliance and, 20–22
Eisenhower, Dwight D., 170*n*33, 229
Elbe River, importance of, 221, 253
Ellsberg, Daniel, 127
El Salvador, 52, 95, 100, 103–104
　counterinsurgency in, 73–75
　Kissinger Commission on, 76–77
　military priority for, 100
　Noninterventionist Middle on, 105–107
　Reagan administration and, 42
"Emerging Technologies," 276
Enthoven, Alain, 127
*Essence of Decision: Explaining the Cuban
　Missile Crisis*, 1*n*2
Estes, Howell M., 330, 331, 435
Etzioni, Amitai, 195
Eurocommunism, 16, 233
Europe
　American nuclear deterrence of Soviets in,
　　146–150
　commitment to NATO, 221, 251–260
European Defense Community (EDC), 228
European Economic Community (EEC), 219,
　229, 283–284
European Security Study, 327, 329
"Evil Empire" speech, 234, 281
"Existential" deterrence, 12, 13, 155–157,
　167, 171, 201–202
　Limiters on success in Europe of, 169
Extenders, 400*n*
　analytical premises of, 137–143
　on arms race, 143
　on damage limitation, 144, 145–146, 201
　policy recommendations, 146–153

in Reagan administration, 134–135
on SDI, 150
on Soviet nuclear strategy, 140–141
value judgments, 143–146
views of, 118–123, 152–153

F-111 aircraft, 318, 377
Farer, Tom, 105–106, 108
Farley, Philip, 321
Federal Republic of Germany (FRG), 230
　elections and NATO policy, 371–372
　and France cooperation, 221, 252–260,
　　379
　and importance of American nuclear
　　commitment, 247–248
Feinberg, Richard, 92*n*10
Fillon, François, 367, 369
Finer, S. E., 41
"Finlandization," 210, 280, 301
"Firebreak" concept, 169–170, 322
Flank states, importance in defense, 278–279,
　311, 334
Flexible Response doctrine, 14, 211, 230,
　264–265, 278, 316–318
　and *Riposte Graduée,* 265*n*60
Follow-On Forces Attack (FOFA), 223, 276,
　276*n*89, 277, 327, 330, 331, 332
Follow-On To Lance (FOTL), 377, 378
Force de Frappe, 230
Ford, Gerald, 232
Forrestal, James, 234
Forsberg, Randall
　counterforce strategy, 182
　nuclear freeze movement, 189–191
A Forward Strategy for America, 36, 39
Fossedal, Gregory, 309
France, 346
　American commitment in Europe, 218
　Communist parties in, 229
　concern about U.S. commitment,
　　241–244
　doubts about U.S., 14
　elections and NATO policy, 371
　and England cooperation, 377
　and Germany, 221, 252–260, 271–272,
　　342–344, 379
　nuclear weapons, 271
　revisionism, 308
　withdrawal from NATO, 228, 230
　zero-zero proposal, 290–291
Franco, Francisco, 90

Iran, 46
Iran-Contra affair, 286, 337
Isolationism, 305–306
Italy, 229, 233

Japan, 21, 223, 339, 399n73
Jenkins, Brian Michael, 65
Joffe, Joseph
  on conventional defense, 278
  on zero-zero proposal, 291
Johnson, Lyndon, 57–58, 104, 230
Johnson, Ross, 359
Jorgensen, Anker, 303, 304

Kahn, Herman, 118n4, 134
Kaiser, Karl, 240, 248, 265, 267
Kallab, Valeriana, 92n10
Kaplan, Fred, 125n1, 324, 334
Karber, Philip, 327, 383
Kaufman, William, 127, 128n11, 157–158
  on conventional weapons balance, 324,
    325
  on use of American nuclear forces,
    316–317
Kennan, George, 125n2, 157–158, 234, 248
  on ABM Treaty, 174
  on no-first-use, 169–170, 315, 322, 323
  on SDI and arms control, 177–178
  "The Sources of Soviet Conduct,"
    234–235
Kennedy, John F., 58, 230
  on intervention, 43
Kennedy, Robert, 9
  on domino theory, 90
  program for Vietnam, 99
Kennedy administration
  new Defense Department members,
    126–127
  Third World debate and, 9–10
Kent, Glenn, 174, 177
Khomeini, Ayatollah, 19
Krushchev, Nikita, 229
Kiep, Walther, 288
Kinnock, Neil, 295, 298–299
Kintner, William, 36, 39
Kirkpatrick, Jeane J., 91, 105
  on U.S. role in democratization, 45–46
Kissinger, Henry, 30, 64, 78, 105, 125,
    132n17, n18, n19, 233, 307

on anti-Communism, 57
on arms control and verification, 149–150
on arms reduction, 143
on conventional defense, 236
on goals in Vietnam, 59–60
on imbalance in Alliance, 341–342
on Nicaragua, 84–85
on political view of nuclear issues,
  132–133
on SDI, 152
on U.S. forces in Europe, 346–347
on Vietnam, 51, 69
on zero option, 362–363
Kissinger Commission report on Central
  America, 30, 64–65, 96, 102
  military recommendations on El Salvador,
    76
  military vs. economic recommendations,
    103
  needs of Central America, 77
  Noninterventionist Middle attack on, 96
  recommendations on Nicaragua, 84
Klare, Michael T., 52, 53, 55–56, 73
Koch, Noel, 81
Kohl, Helmut, 234
  on SRINF, 250
Komer, Robert, 268n71, 347, 348–349
  on "overmilitarization" of Vietnam War,
    69–70
  on U.S. intervention, 79
Kondracke, Morton, 339
Krauss, Melvin, 216, 306, 307–309, 311
Krell, Gert
  on counteroffensive proposal, 277
  on reunification of Germany, 287, 288
  on zero-zero proposal, 251
Kristol, Irving, 216, 305, 307, 310–311
Kubrick, Stanley, 127

Laird, Melvin, 76
Lake, Anthony, 107
  on American foreign policy consensus,
    113
Landry, John R., 330, 331, 435
Laos, 66
LaPorte, Robert, 51
Latin America, 102–103 (*see also* Central
  America; specific country)
  business interests and foreign policy in,
    51–52, 63
  Catholic Church on intervention in, 53

Van Oudenaren, John, 140
Varas, Augusto, 54n16
Verification, 150, 176
  Extenders on, 140
Vietnam, 5, 11, 55, 58–59, 89–90
  air war in, 68
  and changes in American views, 25–28
  Confronters on, 39–42
  Disengagers on, 49–51
  effect of, 33–34, 50–51
  goals in, 60
  importance of, 58
  military emphasis in, 66–70
  NATO and, 230–231, 232
  "overmilitarization" in, 69–70
  U.S. goals in, 59–62
  U.S. intervention in, 50–51
Vietnamization, 76
Voight, Karsten, 264
  on Flexible Response, 265
  on nuclear free zone, 292–293
von Bulow, Andreas, 302

Wallerstein, Immanuel, 71n29
Warnke, Paul C., 363–364
  on preemption and failure of control,
    157–158
Warsaw Pact, 229
The Washington Post, 92
Waskow, Arthur, 195
Watergate, 232
Watt, David, 246–247
Weapons (*see also* specific weapon;
    Conventional weapons; Nuclear
    weapons)
  conventional vs. nuclear, 223–224, 228
  modernizing, 377–378
Weinberg, Steven, 130
Weinberger, Caspar, 2, 246, 327, 400
  on MAD concept, 145
  on public opinion and use of power, 83
  on using military to oppose Communism,
    63–64
Western Europe
  "Alliance within Alliance," 252
  cooperation, 343–345
  security of, 383–384

Western European Union, 243
West Germany, 346
  desire for detente, 308
  and GDR, 287–291
  peace movement in, 297–298
  rearming of, 13
  Removers in, 303
  on U.S. commitment to NATO, 219
Westmoreland, William, 40
White, Robert, 100
Wiesner, Jerome, 130. 195
Willets, Harry, 198–199
Williams, Phil, 292, 320
Wilson, Harold, 233
Withdrawers (*see* American Withdrawers)
Wizards of Armageddon, 125n1
Woerner, Manfred, on offensive defense, 277
Wohlstetter, Albert, 127, 198, 201, 400
  on Acheson Commission report, 315
  on arms agreements, 148–149
  on arms control, 12
  on *The Arms Debate*, 2
  on conventional weapons, 236
  on dangers of nuclear deterrence, 125–126
  on deterrence, 136
  on MAD, 145
  on military targeting, 138
  on SDI, 319–320
  on Soviet nuclear strategy, 141–142
  on Soviet objectives, 140
  on Soviet value system, 144
  on use/misuse of DOD data, 130
Wolf, Charles, 40–41
Wolfe, Thomas, 62
World Federalists, 186–187
World Peace Through World Law, 187
Wrage, Stephen, 336–337

Yom Kippur War, 201
Yugoslavia, 222

Zero-sum game, 36–37, 38
Zero-zero proposal, 290–292, 309, 320,
    361–364, 376
Zinn, Howard, 55

Selected List of RAND Books

Alexiev, Alexander R., and S. Enders Wimbush (eds.). *Ethnic Minorities in the Red Army: Asset or Liability?* Boulder, Colo.: Westview Press, 1988.

Builder, Carl H. *The Masks of War: American Military Styles in Strategy and Analysis.* Baltimore, Md.: The Johns Hopkins University Press, 1989.

Dorfman, Robert, Paul A. Samuelson, and Robert M. Solow. *Linear Programming and Economic Analysis.* New York: McGraw-Hill Book Company, 1958. Reprinted New York: Dover Publications, 1987.

Fainsod, Merle. *Smolensk under Soviet Rule.* Cambridge, Mass.: Harvard University Press, 1958. Reprinted Boston, Mass.: Unwin Hyman, 1989.

Horelick, Arnold L. (ed.). *U.S.-Soviet Relations: The Next Phase.* Ithaca, N.Y.: Cornell University Press, 1986

Hosmer, Stephen T. *Constraints on U.S. Strategy in Third World Conflicts.* New York: Taylor & Francis, 1987.

Hosmer, Stephen T., and Thomas W. Wolfe. *Soviet Policy and Practice toward Third World Conflicts.* Lexington, Mass.: Lexington Books, 1983.

Johnson, A. Ross, Robert W. Dean, and Alexander Alexiev. *East European Military Establishments: The Warsaw Pact Northern Tier.* New York: Crane, Russak & Company, 1982.

Korbonski, Andrzej, and Francis Fukuyama (eds.). *The Soviet Union and the Third World: The Last Three Decades.* Ithaca, N.Y.: Cornell University Press, 1987.

Leites, Nathan. *Soviet Style in Management.* New York: Crane, Russak & Company, 1985.

Leites, Nathan. *Soviet Style in War*. New York: Crane, Russak & Company, 1982.

Nerlich, Uwe, and James A. Thomson (eds.). *Conventional Arms Control and the Security of Europe*. Boulder, Colo.: Westview Press, 1988.

Nerlich, Uwe, and James A. Thomson (eds.), *The Soviet Problem in American-German Relations*. New York: Crane, Russak & Company, 1985.

Quade, Edward S., revised by Grace M. Carter. *Analysis for Public Decisions* (Third Edition). New York: Elsevier Science Publishing Company, 1989.

Ross, Randy L. *Government and the Private Sector: Who Should Do What?* New York: Taylor & Francis, 1988.

Williams, J. D. *The Compleat Strategyst: Being a Primer on the Theory of Games of Strategy*. New York: McGraw-Hill Book Company, 1954. Revised 1966 edition reprinted. New York: Dover Publications, 1986.

Wolf, Charles, Jr. *Markets or Governments: Choosing between Imperfect Alternatives*. Cambridge, Mass.: The MIT Press, 1988.

Wolf, Charles, Jr., and Katharine Watkins Webb, (eds.). *Developing Cooperative Forces in the Third World*. Lexington, Mass.: Lexington Books, 1987.